In *Mastering Formative Assessment Moves*, Brent Duckor and Carrie Holmberg elaborate specific instructional moves to help both novice and seasoned teachers deepen their formative assessment practices. Their vision is not to be added on top of other reform initiatives but fits perfectly within equity-focused, ambitious teaching practices aimed at deeper learning. I like that the authors push back against quantitative indicators as the best means for tracking learning progress and offer ways, instead, for triangulating and building upon qualitative windows into student thinking.

—*Lorrie Shepard*
Distinguished Professor and Dean Emerita
University of Colorado–Boulder

For two full decades, formative assessment's prevalence in our schools has fallen far short of its proponents' predictions—particularly given the research evidence supporting its effectiveness. Drawing on their own experiences as practitioner-researchers, Duckor and Holmberg have come up with a marvelous set of implementable guidelines, for both prospective and seasoned teachers, showing how the formative assessment process can sparkle.

—*Jim Popham*
Emeritus Professor, University of California–Los Angeles
Graduate School of Education

An insightful, wise, and highly usable guide to formative assessment that draws from research and is inspired by the wisdom of practice. Emphasizes how assessment as an integral feature of high-quality teaching draws upon deep content knowledge and goes well beyond mere technical skill. The book is the enlightened collaboration of a practice-enriched teacher educator with deep roots in secondary school reform and a superb board-certified (and renewed!) teacher and teacher educator from a newly minted doctoral program.

—*Lee Shulman*
President Emeritus, The Carnegie Foundation for the Advancement of Teaching
Charles E. Ducommun
Professor of Education Emeritus, Stanford University

Mastering Formative Assessment Moves offers educators a rich, new conception of practices that can help bring the process of formative assessment to life in the classroom. Rich with guidance, research rationale, examples, and "do now" activities, the book makes the invisible visible in seven high power moves that can fuel educators' journey to being expert formative assessment guides, guides who open up "new worlds of classroom learning and communication (p. 4)" for teachers and students alike. Kudos for a very thoughtful approach!

—*Joan Herman,*
Co-Director, Emerita
National Center for Research on Evaluation, Standards and Student Testing, UCLA

Whether you call it assessment for learning or formative instruction geared towards deeper learning, Duckor and Holmberg have given us a great resource—with their new model and their inviting terminology for making pedagogical life for students in today's classrooms more meaningful, relevant, and effective. Teachers who didn't "get it" in previous encounters with formative assessment will with this innovative approach. My advice to teachers and professional learning coaches in language arts and literacy is to implement this new, sensible framework without hesitation.

—*P. David Pearson, Professor, Language & Literacy & Human Development*
Dean Emeritus, Graduate School of Education, UC–Berkeley

The compelling research of formative assessment and its significant effectiveness on student learning has been well documented for over twenty years by Black, Wiliam, Thompson, and many others. Yet, there still exists a large implementation gap between the educational research and typical classroom practices. Duckor and Holmberg have contributed an additional resource to teachers to make sense of their "moves" by offering a framework to unpack and examine instructional and assessment practices—minute by minute, day to day in their classrooms.

—*David Foster, Executive Director, Silicon Valley Mathematics Initiative*

By reframing how we understand and discuss formative assessment, and illuminating the nuances and interconnectedness of high leverage instructional and assessment moves, Duckor and Holmberg have invited our field to reenvision formative assessment as critical to equitable teaching practice. Collaborating and weaving a new narrative around assessment brings us closer to authentic student learning and teacher efficacy.

—*Annamarie Francois, Executive Director, UCLA–Center X*

Years of research and practice has yielded insights into the power of formative assessment to transform educational outcomes. In this innovative and highly readable book, Duckor and Holmberg use rigorous academic standards—rooted in the Habits of Mind—with a deeper focus on instructional effectiveness by offering practitioners intuitive strategies to engage in real-time formative assessment moves. Program researchers, content experts, and policymakers can build on the capacities and skills these scholar-practitioners have suggested to further support assessment for learning.

—*Deb Sigman, Director, Center on Standards and Assessment Implementation, WestEd*

Teacher educators know formative assessment makes a difference. We have worked to embed it in our university coursework, professional standards, teacher performance assessments, and licensure frameworks—now we have a book that guides our candidates, cooperating teachers, and university faculty in how to make formative assessment happen for beginners!

—*Helene Mandel*
Director of Field Experiences and Coordinator of Teacher Credentialing Programs in the
School of Leadership and Education Sciences, University of San Diego

The authors have performed a rare feat—they explain the "why" of formative assessment at a high level, but Duckor and Holmberg also get into the nitty gritty of actual classroom level practice. Educators, both new and experienced, will find much they can use here.

—Ben Daley, Chief Academic Officer, High Tech High

No teaching skill has ever had a greater amount of supportive research and laudatory testimony than formative assessment. It absolutely must become part of every teacher's repertoire of skills, and this admirable book tells how to accomplish that. It may be a game changer for the field.

—David C. Berliner, Regents' Professor Emeritus,
Mary Lou Fulton Teachers College, Arizona State University

Any effort that takes assessment of instruction out of the hands of distant corporations and politicians and places it in the hands of teachers is to be applauded. So, give it up for Duckor and Holmberg!

—Gene V. Glass, Research Professor, Educational Foundations, Policy & Practice
University of Colorado–Boulder

Quick fix assessment technologies have increased our appetite for easy solutions to complex learning problems. In *Mastering Formative Assessment Moves*, Duckor and Holmberg provide a necessary and helpful mix of instructional insights, practical tips, and research on assessment for learning. The chapters highlight a critical insight for teachers and teachers of teachers: in order to help move students along their domain-specific learning progressions, teachers must recognize that they, too, are on a formative assessment learning trajectory.

—Arthur Camins, Former Director
Center for Innovation in Engineering and Science Education
Stevens Institute of Technology

Duckor and Holmberg have written a remarkable book, one that connects specific classroom practices of high quality formative assessment with broader democratic goals of public education. Immensely helpful to teachers and students, the book links vital questions of critical pedagogy to the ways that formative assessment promotes skills of critical inquiry for *all* students. It will, I believe, influence our current discourse about assessment, educational opportunity, and equity in learning.

—Douglas S. Reed, Director, Program in Educational Transformation
Georgetown University

Rarely do we see the advances in nationally recognized assessment design and the principles of classroom evaluation woven together in a handbook for teachers, counselors, principals, and district leaders who seek agreement on what matters most—deeper learning, better assessment strategies, and more effective ways to improve student achievement. Duckor and Holmberg have given us a glimpse of how to get stakeholders on the same page, moving the field a little closer to consensus on why formative assessment is essential to any school improvement plan.

—*Carolyn Huie Hofstetter, Vice Chair & Associate Teaching Professor*
Education Studies, UC–San Diego

This book it is an important contribution to both teachers in the field and to research on teaching and teacher development. Duckor and Holmberg's "7 Moves" framework contributes to defining "good teaching" from a teacher development perspective, thus helping shape the emerging concept of a "teacher learning progression," particularly for those seeking to better understand teachers' work in primary and secondary schools. Teachers and researchers in the United States and abroad will benefit from a close reading of what it may take to better capture indicators of professional growth in high leverage practices related to formative assessment.

—*María Veronica Santelices, Associate Professor, Faculty of Education*
Pontificia Universidad Católica de Chile

Brent Duckor and Carrie Holmberg show the importance of formative assessment to effective teaching and bring to life how teachers can learn to do it well. Clearly grounded in research, this book is full of practical examples and concrete strategies that will stimulate teachers to think hard about formative assessment and, no matter where they are in their professional career, to develop their formative assessment skills for the benefit of all students.

—*Margaret Heritage, Senior Scientist, WestEd*

Mastering Formative Assessment Moves is a theoretically sound and pragmatically well-crafted vision of learning and assessment as a mutually constituted, continually evolving dialogue. The crafts of teaching and assessment are powerfully intertwined and grounded so that the promise of a progressive education is renewed and revitalized. Perhaps most important, the interplay between learning and assessment featured and consistently exemplified throughout this volume describes a new accountability, oriented toward thick descriptions of student learning that can help practitioners envision productive pathways for instruction.

—*Rich Lehrer, Frank Mayborn Professor*
Department of Teaching & Learning, Peabody College, Vanderbilt University

Mastering Formative Assessment Moves

Mastering
Formative
Assessment
Moves

7 High-Leverage Practices
to Advance Student Learning

Brent Duckor
Carrie Holmberg

Foreword by John Hattie

Alexandria, Virginia USA

1703 N. Beauregard St. • Alexandria, VA 22311-1714 USA
Phone: 800-933-2723 or 703-578-9600 • Fax: 703-575-5400
Website: www.ascd.org • E-mail: member@ascd.org
Author guidelines: www.ascd.org/write

Deborah S. Delisle, *Executive Director;* Robert D. Clouse, *Managing Director, Digital Content & Publications;* Stefani Roth, *Publisher;* Genny Ostertag, *Director, Content Acquisitions;* Julie Houtz, *Director, Book Editing & Production;* Darcie Russell, *Editor;* Reece Quiñones, *Senior Graphic Designer;* Mike Kalyan, *Director, Production Services;* Valerie Younkin, *Production Designer;* Kyle Steichen, *Senior Production Specialist*

All web links in this book are correct as of the publication date below but may have become inactive or otherwise modified since that time. If you notice a deactivated or changed link, please send an e-mail message to books@ascd.org with the words "Link Update" in the subject line. In your message, please specify the web link, the book title, and the page number on which the link appears.

PAPERBACK ISBN: 978-1-4166-2262-8   ASCD product #116011 n6/17

PDF E-BOOK ISBN: 978-1-4166-2477-6; see Books in Print for other formats.

Quantity discounts are available: e-mail programteam@ascd.org or call 800-933-2723, ext. 5773, or 703-575-5773. For desk copies, go to www.ascd.org/deskcopy.

Library of Congress Cataloging-in-Publication Data
Names: Duckor, Brent, author. | Holmberg, Carrie, author.
Title: Mastering formative assessment moves : 7 high-leverage practices to advance student learning / Brent Duckor, Carrie Holmberg.
Description: Alexandria, Virginia : ASCD, [2017] | Includes bibliographical references and index.
Identifiers: LCCN 2017008275 | ISBN 9781416622628 (pbk.)
Subjects: LCSH: Educational tests and measurements—United States. | Academic achievement—United States. | Educational evaluation—United States.
Classification: LCC LB3051 .D667 2017 | DDC 371.260973—dc23 LC record available at https://lccn.loc.gov/2017008275

26 25 24 23 22 21 20 19 18 17   1 2 3 4 5 6 7 8 9 10 11 12

To Bob, Bettina, and Tim at UCSC for never letting
me forget the true purpose of a public education:
to push beyond the convenient truths and to seek the
foundations of an education worth fighting for.

—Brent Duckor

To Joan Owen, model of continuous growth,
professionalism, service, humor,
and compassion for so many of us.

—Carrie Holmberg

Mastering Formative Assessment Moves

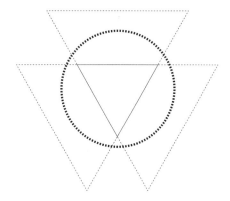

Acknowledgments

Every book is the culmination of years of struggle to broaden the horizon of a topic. The topic of formative assessment is a shared collective passion for many of us, part of a larger conversation that has taken place in many settings, with different participants, over many years.

First, we would like to thank the teacher candidates and graduates from the College of Education at San Jose State University for whom this book began to take shape in EDSC 182 Classroom Evaluation and Assessment as part of their preservice coursework. With their authentic engagement, sharp criticism, intellectual curiosity, and continued patience, we worked out the broad strokes of the argument for *Mastering Formative Assessment Moves: 7 High-Leverage Practices to Advance Student Learning*. To those 182ers who took up the challenge and extended our own thinking on the topic of formative assessment—integrating novice and expert practices in a set of teacher learning progressions which ultimately became their own—we owe a deep debt of gratitude. These former students are now teachers, department chairs, vice principals, and instructional coaches. We are especially thankful to Courtney Arndt, Natalia Babella, Sarah Bass, Andrew Christian, Tim Ciardella, Marco della Maggiore, Paul Durdle, Ally Finch, Kaila Glassburner, Mary Gustafson, Jon Hinthorne, Nick Honda, Chris Johnson, Chelsea Kavanaugh, Erica King, Emily La, Corey Liggins, Sylvia Liu, Maria Mesa, Sarah Michelet, Onette Morales, Carl Ponzio, Russ Ramos, Manny Vasquez, Brett Vickers, Roy Walton, Wen Xi, and Julia Yeager for helping us to think through different aspects and important turning points in the development of the framework.

We are also grateful to our in-service colleagues in mathematics and science who have allowed us to conduct research in their middle and high school classrooms. Among these are Marie Pink, Mikaela McKenna, Steven Shirley, James Sperry, and Diana Wilmot. Each participated in the public dissemination of the "FA [Formative Assessment] Moves" story in district professional development workshops, state and national conferences, and other public forums.

As we shared our findings and discoveries about formative assessment moves with new audiences, we owe a special thanks to folks in the Pacific Northwest. In Oregon, we were welcomed by several district leaders, including Reta Doland (La Grande Unified) and Melissa Linder (Astoria), and a group of dedicated, tireless teacher-advocates for formative assessment. A special thanks to Cristen McClean and Derek Brown at the Oregon Department of Education for offering us the opportunity to share new tools, approaches, and materials to professional development in their districts and school communities.

In California, we found fellow FA travelers in urban, suburban, and rural school districts. Professional associations and multidistrict consortia, including the East Side Alliance, invited us to join them in a deeper commitment to assessment for learning. A special thanks to Robert Linquanti and Neil Finkelstein at West Ed; Margaret Heritage and her group at the Council of Chief State School Officers-FAST SCASS; Manny Barbara at Silicon Valley Education Foundation; Angelica Ramsey, Cecilio Dimas, and Bernadette Salagrino at the Santa Clara County Office of Education; and David Plank at Policy Analysis for California Education, for offering us the opportunity to tell our story from the vantage point of a large, diverse public teacher education program. At a time when state university systems struggle for resources, visibility, and support, these educational leaders invited us to tell our story.

Of course, we cannot forget how this story began and the people who made it possible at ASCD. The publication of "Formative Assessment in Seven Good Moves" in spring 2014 in *Educational Leadership* was the basis for this book. Thank you to Marge Scherer, who was *EL*'s editor in chief, for putting our FA Moves framework in the issue dedicated to "Using Assessments Thoughtfully" and with august company. With this stepping stone, we sought out and began a tremendously important relationship with our editors at ASCD, Genny Ostertag and Darcie Russell, who also believed in us as newcomers. Genny's broad experience, inspiring analytic skills, and compassion for our vision, combined with Darcie's hard eye for what really matters and how to best express it, has made us better writers. Any errors and omissions, of course, remain our own, but we learned from the ASCD team and we thank them for their patience with and concern for us as emerging writers in this genre.

Family, friends, and colleagues are ultimately the unsung heroes of any long-term project. We are blessed to have partners to live through the promise and ultimate joy of producing this book. Without the sustaining love and commitment of our spouses, Barbara Nakakihara and Bob Holmberg, we cannot imagine standing here today with our book in hand. Our children—Sydney, Vivian, and Hazel—have also inspired, cajoled, and pushed us to think more deeply about the promise of formative assessment in the middle and high school years. Many morning car rides, dinner table discussions, and banter along the hiking trails have been spent in dialogue about formative assessment. We are grateful to our children in particular for sharing their passion for formative feedback, and reasons why formative assessment matters to them as learners.

We remain grateful for the ongoing support from Misa Sugiura and Lorri Capizzi, who read versions of the manuscript and provided hope when deadlines loomed and we were overwhelmed by the competing demands of family, school, and work. They reminded us that there are no shortcuts to working in your own voice, and that limited time and resources must never be the enemy of professional integrity and personal truth.

Other friends and colleagues from the university and educational research community kept an open ear as we bounced ideas off them over the years. We are grateful to professors Mark Wilson and Richard Shavelson for their unwavering support for the ideas and principles that animate this book. We have also gathered many insights about teachers and teaching from colleagues over the years including Roberta Alqhuist, Paul Ammon, Carlos Ayala, Wendy Baron, David Berliner, Tim Boerst, Karen Draney, Mark Felton, Bruce Fuller, Maryl Gearhart, Margaret Heritage, Joan Herman, Carolyn Huie-Hofstetter, Jonathan Lovell, Deborah Lowenberg Ball, Diane Mayer, Pamela Moss, Dan Perlstein, Jim Popham, Joanne Rossi Becker, María Verónica Santelices, Lee Shulman, Deb Sigman, Kip Téllez, Mike Timms, and Mary Warner.

We owe a special debt of gratitude to John Hattie, whose professional generosity and intellectual clarity remind us of the importance of this work and how much more there is to be done. These scholars and education leaders have written about what is best in public education and what works; none has lost sight of the power of formative assessment to shape outcomes and achievement for all students.

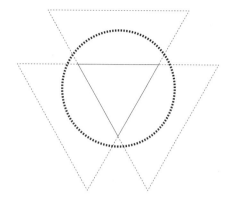

Foreword

This book does something new for its reader. It brings to life—with real world examples drawn from rich engagement with new and seasoned teachers—how to think of one's self on a trajectory of powerful practices that unite instruction and assessment. The idea of developmental approaches to student learning is not new, but the authors have seized on something with their new framing of the literature, what they provisionally call *teacher learning progressions* in formative assessment practice. This is not the place to explore the merits of such an approach. Instead, we need to make room for new voices and a new vision that the next generation of scholar-practitioners has brought to the table. This work invites us into a fresh conversation.

For those of us with long memories and the willingness to look across our respective ponds, the debates about the true meaning of assessment have raged for decades in the United States, Australia, and, of course, England. We all have had different ways to communicate what assessment means—to different audiences, in different times and settings. Bob Stake (1976) has said that when a cook tastes the soup to make just-in-time improvements, it is formative. But, when a guest sits down to taste the soup and evaluate the "final product," it is summative. Formative evaluation occurs during the learning, summative at the end of the marking period. Both are important to schools, teachers, and students.

Surely the point of tasting the soup, while the cook and staff are gathering feedback about its progress, is to maximize the chances that when the guests taste the dish, it will be an excellent result—from multiple perspectives. Viewed

xviii   Mastering Formative Assessment Moves

this way, the process of formative feedback leads us to optimal summative achievements. Both purposes of assessment matter, but in different ways.

Today's evaluation theorists make the distinction between formative and summative very clear, as did Michael Scriven (1967) when he invented the terms 50 years ago. He claimed the difference between formative and summative was related to the *purposes, goals, timing,* and how *information is used* in a system or organization. Formative was more to improve and guide stakeholders; summative to provide a set of claims about what has happened, that is, what value we can attach to the target performance or outcome.

Soon after Scriven wrote his work, Bloom "borrowed" several ideas about the role of evaluation in educational settings. The term formative and summative assessments (Bloom et al., 1971) were coined. This move was unfortunate in that it set up a language game we now play, labeling some test instruments formative, others interim, and still others summative. The ostensible type of the instrument—not the purpose, use, timing, and information uses of *any* instrument—became the decisive factor in our evaluation and assessment discourse. Educational assessment experts never gave Scriven sufficient credit for the invention of the terms and his specific approach to making judgments. Instead, we were left with boxes, categories, and labels for tests—with many unfounded claims about the power of the "summative" test instrument and little evidence for the efficacy of the uses of any particular tool.

For too many students in primary and secondary schools today, assessment has become synonymous with numbers and grades. The principals, school districts, or government officials make a set of summative claims about what students know and can do. They put up charts, color codes, and mark the students' work as done. Summative assessment has become a powerful signal: learning is over; the grade or number is your "feedback" and it's now time to see how you stack up against another.

Duckor and Holmberg reverse these claims about "formative" versus "summative" assessment by providing a lens that relies much more on the nature, timing, and use of assessment information during the lessons; much more on the interpretations by students and teachers of so-called "soft data" generated with attention to speaking and listening; much more reliance on understanding the staccato and cycle of learning, where the students are right now and the possibilities for moving them forward.

But the authors do something more: no longer are we stuck in debates about the meaning of the objects—the tests, the quizzes, the homework—in assessment and evaluation. Rather, we can move toward the challenges and opportunities of using all sources of data. In this book, classroom data are generated by subjects (persons) for subjects (other persons) to learn from and interact with during instruction. Rather than focus on *assessment*, which signals a stand-alone event or an alpha-numeric ranking, the authors rightly emphasize the process of *assessing*. Their new language of moves and tangible practices refocus the field toward pedagogical action in the classroom.

In the Introduction, Duckor and Holmberg ask: So, why another book on formative assessment and evaluation—and why now? Hasn't it all been said before? Everyone knows that formative assessment and evaluation in the classroom make a difference in students' lives and produce better outcomes, right? My provisional reply: Yeah right, so why is there still an overemphasis on summative testing; an overemphasis on providing scores and numbers; an overemphasis on commercial companies pouring out "mile-wide, inch-deep" tests used for accountability purposes to see if teachers are doing their jobs? Why have teachers not been provided with tests aligned with the curricula and their immediate teaching needs that measure growth?

For decades, the research community has known that formative evaluation and assessment stand at the center of effective instruction. My own work (Hattie, 2012), as well as many others' work, reminds us that assessing during learning makes a real difference in student outcomes. Powerful, tangible results come from teachers who are assessing and reassessing student learning—minute by minute, hour by hour, day by day. But it is the quality of information from this assessing "for learning" that is the focus of this book.

We need to move away from defending the use of formative evaluation in terms of it being better than summative, and, instead, ask how to implement formative thinking to thence maximize the summative impact on students. This means, as this book ably demonstrates, striving for a deeper understanding of instructional decision making, ways of thinking and reflecting before the whole class, and powers of listening well and demonstrating to students that you have listened before offering feedback. The authors further remind us: formative thinking means developing an expansive and flexible repertoire of speaking, listening—and therefore, thinking—skills on behalf of teachers for students.

During my years working in New Zealand I led a team to develop the national assessment scheme for elementary and high schools (e-asTTle). It was based on providing teachers, students, parents, and school leaders with up-to-date information and interpretations about *where students were going, how they were going,* and *where they were going next.* The emphasis was on providing assessment information back to teachers about their impact (especially over time)—who had they impacted? About what? And to what magnitude? Our approach to assessment was as much about generating feedback to teachers about their impact as it was for students to gauge growth. Our goal in these systems was to allow formative evaluation and assessment information to provide feedback to teachers about their progress with their students' and their own development.

The primary function of classroom assessment must be to support learning by generating feedback that students can act upon in terms of where they are going, how they are going, and where they might go next. This involves, necessarily, that students participate in the assessment of their own learning—and that they learn to recognize and understand main ideas and to apply new learning in different ways and situations. The core notion is that students who have developed their *assessment capabilities* are able and motivated to access, interpret, and use information from quality assessments in ways that affirm or further their learning.

One of the central questions addressed by this book is how to support teachers who are developing classroom assessment approaches that reveal rather than obscure these feedback loops (Sadler, 1989). By reframing the formative assessment and evaluation literature as high-leverage, interlocking, and real-time instructional moves that yield assessment information for teachers and students, Duckor and Holmberg have reminded us of the interconnection between good teaching and good assessment practice. Rather than merely expect that teachers transmit knowledge to students about their status or standing, the authors invite us to see how various classroom-based assessment moves can, in fact, maximize information exchange and flow. Like cooking or dancing or orchestrating "live action," theirs is a lively, enriching, and optimizing approach to the formative purposes and practices in classroom assessment.

The theme throughout this book is on the depth and use of pedagogical knowledge by teachers; the shift from spotlighting their talking to honing their skills in active and informed listening; the focus on ensuring students understand their feedback; and the critical nature of the moment-by-moment decision making about the learning. Developing this depth and these capacities—and using them well to advance student learning—is, as they testify, not easily done. Teacher progression in these areas takes commitment, effort, time, and support.

Duckor and Holmberg's work has implications for teacher development. That is clear. Their work, however, could also influence changes needed in how observations of teachers could help them progress in their practices. Observations of teachers have tended to lead to recommendations about how to change how they teach or what teachers should do. It is much harder to "see" the decision making, the judgments that teachers are making unless we focus on observing the impact of the teacher on the students. Quite a mind shift. Duckor and Holmberg offer language and ideas—a conceptual framework, the seven moves—for classroom practice that can help make what's hard to see more "seeable" and more discussable. Groups of teachers being able to discuss their practices together through the lens of the moves may be the most powerful impact this book will have.

These formative assessment (FA) moves highlight the importance of teacher listening, seeing learning through the eyes of students, and checking to see whether their feedback has been understood by the students. It is not sufficient to merely give formative feedback, but to check whether the feedback has been understood, and is therefore usable by the student. These are strong messages for teachers who wish to pose questions more strategically, to reduce their talk time, and to use visible pausing and listening procedures, while inviting students to "think aloud" about their current understanding.

The authors also remind us that we must first create high levels of trust so that students can say "I do not know" and seek formative feedback from one another and their teachers. In this moves-based framework, there is a relentless checking for understanding—minute by minute—by probing to see what the student understands and does not yet understand. There is focus on interpreting, categorizing, and evaluating the students' learning experience (they call this "binning") so that valid and reliable instructional decisions are more likely. Duckor and Holmberg remind themselves as teacher educators on this journey as much as us the readers: the power of formative is very much in the "not yet." We all have a role to play to make this happen.

The message that also weaves through this book is on the depth of pedagogical knowledge by the teachers, the move from the talker to the listener, the focus on ensuring students understand the teacher's feedback, and the critical nature of the moment-by-moment decision making about the learning. Working for over a decade with novice teachers, Duckor and Holmberg have earned their knowledge of formative evaluation and assessment "in the lab," so to speak, of preservice credential programs. They find teachers are individuals, working within the norms and code of particular subject disciplines, each struggling to make a move in the mathematics, art, physical education, world language, history, science, English, or the music classroom. As they share the stories of teacher candidates, we see how much harder it is to prime, pose, pause, probe, bounce, tag, and bin than we first thought. It turns out these seven high-leverage practices require a deep respect for the student teacher, what they bring to the university class and clinical placement, how they think and react, their motivations and how to enhance these, and their understanding of what it means to learn to become a formative assessor.

The FA moves framework requires building trust not only between the teacher and the students but among students for them to seek help, expose their misunderstanding, and explore together how to improve. These moves invite teachers to move beyond surface content knowledge to enabling students to make connections and explore the joy and creativity of forming new relations between seemingly unrelated ideas. These moves require the development of so-called expert teachers who are reflective, enthusiastic, passionate, and knowledgeable about the content and understanding of the lesson. These seasoned teachers and those they mentor into the profession need to care to make the difference, preferably caring about their subject matter, and caring about all their students' achievements.

For those who study and advise teachers, classrooms, and schools, the seven moves are powerful reminders of the expertise required to invoke formative evaluation during the lesson. It is so much easier for educators to keep talking, to pathologize the students as having problems (because of their post-code, their lack of prior knowledge, their deficit motivation, their lack of attention), and to say "I taught but they did not learn." It is so much easier to announce "Wait, in eight weeks I will give you a test and you can see if you learned anything from this course!" It is so much easier to talk in generalities and "do nows" about formative assessment as if one could separate practice from theory. Duckor and Holmberg ask us to pause, giving us a new grammar of practice and robust theoretical framework, connecting instruction with real-time, embedded assessment.

Years ago, Dylan Wiliam and Paul Black (1996) advised us not to use the terms formative and summative assessment, as their experience in the United Kingdom was that these terms were too easily misused. Governments started adopting these labels for almost everything they do in hope of providing a cloak of respectability to any measure they advanced! Educational systems and policy makers were also apt to misuse both terms, and justify their "data driven" policies without careful consideration of either the formative or summative claims advanced on behalf of their "metrics."

In an age obsessed with "big data" and quick solutions, Duckor and Holmberg have given us a rare treat by placing the assessment emphasis back on the work of teachers and students, who are teaching and learning together in a community, and making sense of the assessment information that may be formative or summative depending on its use. More exciting, they have moved the field forward with their focus on the seven ways of thinking and doing FA and they have presented a rich tapestry of ideas and strategies to maximize the power of formative evaluation in today's classroom. Enjoy.

—John Hattie
Laureate Professor, Director of the Melbourne Education Research Institute
Melbourne Graduate School of Education

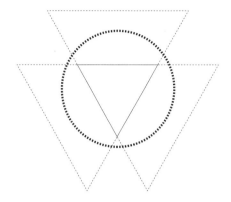

Introduction

Why a book on formative assessment—now? Hasn't it all been said before? Everyone knows that formative assessment (FA) in the classroom makes a difference in students' lives and produces better outcomes, right?

For decades the research community has known that formative assessment or formative evaluation (as it is called in the United Kingdom, New Zealand, and Australia), stands at the center of effective instruction. Hattie (2012) and others remind us that assessing for learning makes a real difference in student outcomes. Powerful, tangible results come from teachers who are assessing and reassessing student learning—minute by minute, hour by hour, day by day.

If Rick Stiggins (2002) and other educational researchers know it works, and teachers acknowledge its practical uses in classroom assessment, why are we still talking about "assessment for learning" all these years later?

The Challenge

The paradox is that most of the "hard" data we have on the powerful effects of formative assessment on student achievement is built around the unglamorous work and sustained understanding and use of "soft" data in the classroom. We know that exit slips, word webs, gallery walks, peer feedback, quick writes, pair-shares, and a host of other techniques generate the soft, difficult to quantify data needed to make instructional decisions on the fly. Only by carefully attending to this classroom-level data can we hope to provide better feedback to our students.

We wrote this book to raise and address these essential questions: What if the "formative" aspect of classroom assessment isn't that visible or easy to do after all? What if "assessment for learning" looks a lot like what everyone else calls "good" teaching? What if FA is just another fancy way to talk about "checking for understanding"?

It is true. Deep formative assessment practices blur the line between instruction and assessment. Most people associate assessment with quizzes, homework, and test events: the "stuff" of classroom assessment and evaluation. But assessment for learning occurs *during* our lessons. FA practices are interwoven into teaching segments and each invites an exchange of information between teachers and students. To those who are unfamiliar with the complexity and intricacies of the dance, it can be hard to know what we are observing in the formative assessment-rich classroom. Moves are invisible; dynamics are undetected. Hence the familiar reply to this literature: "Aren't we just talking about good teaching?"

Formative assessment—the moves, strategies, and daily tactical adjustments used to check for understanding—seem obvious to those who are effective teachers. The careful, sustained observation of FA "moves" can seem like a black box (Black & Wiliam, 1998) to those who are interested in traditional classroom assessment. It takes a trained eye to know what to look for and how to evaluate and coach formative assessment-driven instructional practices.

In our roles as educators—teaching at the university, supervising clinical placements, and working in professional development contexts—we have discovered through trial and error that the formative assessment story is hard to tell. The basic narrative is that it works, try it, it couldn't hurt. Although by now extensive research shows that assessment for learning has benefits that accrue to a diverse group of learners, the fact remains: we don't always know *which* practices are most effective, *when* to enact them, and *why* a particular combination of moves actually worked for a particular student in a particular classroom.

Take the example of feedback, a hallmark of the formative assessment lexicon. We know that best formative feedback practices must be specific, addressable, timely, ongoing, and content-rich (Wiggins, 2012). But many teachers, school counselors, paraprofessional staff, and administrators don't have a clear idea of what these terms mean or how to best observe them, let alone coach others to improve. Moreover, grading and accountability policies often place competing demands on teachers' time, energy, and available resources for enacting best practices in classroom assessment and evaluation.

Part of the challenge with the formative assessment story goes beyond finding mutual agreement of terms and definitions or the adoption of a particular expert's framework. We venture a more provocative explanation regarding the many barriers to becoming a formative assessor. This book takes a look at those challenges and opportunities by breaking down "high leverage" practices, as we dive deeper and explore how different moves are connected.

We hope you will agree: the biggest challenge to assessing formatively during instruction is to recognize a new stance—toward oneself and one's students. We are all learning to become formative assessors. We each have a stake in moving the work of assessment for learning forward. There is no single correct path on this journey but there is a complex continuum of development and growth—for teachers, by teachers, and with teachers building their professional knowledge and skill base.

Teachers as Learners

Our book puts the focus on the development, growth, and journey of those who are learning to become formative assessors, whether new to the profession or not. We honor the prior knowledge of all teachers, that they are struggling to assimilate and accommodate new concepts and information, and that the gap between where they are with classroom assessment routines and where they want to be with formative assessment best practices is real. Of course, beliefs about grading, standards, and testing are also a part of the teachers' prior knowledge; each conditions how we build new and replace old mental models of classroom assessment. We speculate, after working for nearly a decade with preservice teachers, that what we call "teacher learning progressions" are just as important as student ones (Shavelson et al., 2010).

We have written this book to help you walk the walk and not to merely talk the talk of formative assessment. The formative assessor is not solely a teacher who transmits knowledge to students and this book is not written in the spirit of a sit-and-get session or a step-by-step program to immediate success. Rather, we wrote it to guide you toward the professional vision of being a lifelong learner, thus the emphasis on the journey and becoming (rather than on being) a formative assessor. We want you to feel that sense of aspiration and promise that comes from discovering new skills, powers, and capacities to learn about FA moves.

As you read ahead, we also want you to imagine yourself more and more as a formative assessment "guide on the side" for your students. You are becoming, with a little coaching chapter by chapter, a formative assessment guide who is opening up new worlds of classroom learning and communication, where people exchange ideas, give one another feedback, solve problems, and face difficult subjects with intentionality and care.

We predict that you and your students will feel frustrated, get stuck, and wonder why you can't just get back to normal routines in classroom assessment (what we call "doing school"). After all, we all know there are times when "doing formative assessment" is a lot harder than handing out a quiz, collecting homework, or administering the unit test. Posing questions is messy. Probing for deeper responses is time-consuming. Tagging student ideas can be risky. Pausing for "think time" may become awkward and counter-productive.

The difficulty of making formative assessment moves can be compounded by concerns, especially when well-regarded strategies and practices fail to bring about an immediate, positive, or visible change in classroom dynamics. Beginning teachers sometimes get uncomfortable and nervous. Mentor teachers and university supervisors are not always convinced about the power of formative assessment. Principals and administrative staff may continue to wonder: *Why are you asking* why *so much? The kids are shouting out and are still too noisy. No one seems to be listening. The room looks and feels chaotic when everyone goes to the whiteboard. Too many want to speak at the same time. Do you really have time to make that word web and call all students to the board to add their ideas with sticky notes?*

Part of the challenge is agreeing upon a new frame. In this book, we argue that it's time to see ourselves—all teachers, school counselors, administrators, and staff—on a continuum of growth in understanding and practicing formative assessment moves. It's time to address, support, and coach one another—as we make progress—with this highly complex, nuanced set of instructional practices that are also assessment practices. We must move beyond the expert–novice divide that reinforces a deficit approach where some teachers are more literate about classroom assessment than others. Rather, we propose that there are trajectories of moves and progressions of practice in the world of formative assessment. Some known, others not as much. The key is to uncover and discover where one is.

Becoming a formative assessor means finding one's own zone of proximal development—with students and with colleagues—and embracing the journey.

Toward a New Formative Assessment Frame: One Move at a Time

If formative assessment is a process (not merely an event or tool) that occurs during instruction, then we should be able to map the "FA moves" that bring it to life in our classrooms.

We maintain that how teachers, new and experienced, can grow in their formative assessment practice will depend in part on the coaching, feedback, and adjustments available to guide the teaching and learning experience. As you read along with us, imagine these FA moves are major units of instruction on how to master formative assessment; inside each chapter we've offered some lessons, examples, and "do now" activities to support your learning. But you will inevitably discover, along with us, how unique and particular practices fit best into your own classroom and school.

Our teacher-driven learning progressions framework consists of a set of seven interrelated instructional moves, each with its own distinct trajectory, bottlenecks, and occasional pitfalls.

Let's take a moment and revisit the essential question that drives our story: what makes assessment formative and how do we know when we witness it? Is assessing formatively an impossible ideal in a world of standardized testing? Is assessment for learning an over discussed, passing fad that obscures the real work of mastering the subject and making the grade? Does *doing formative assessment* well mean we should stop assigning points to quizzes or spend more time collecting exit slips rather than uploading grades each night? Hardly.

Doing formative assessment in today's culturally, linguistically, and economically diverse classrooms depends greatly on teachers' and students' use of academic language—producing language, taking in language, and sharpening language skills (Hakuta, 2013). Some conceptualizations of formative assessment are more explicit than others in their focus on language use. Ours puts a premium back on verbal and non-verbal feedback—real-time exchanges—among teachers and students.

Our concept of formative assessment is based on the notion of teacher learning progressions that are enacted during instruction—a set of *FA moves* we call *priming, posing, pausing, probing, bouncing, tagging,* and *binning.* See Figure 1 for the FA moves a teacher can orchestrate in myriad combinations.

Each FA move lends itself to sustaining a deeper focus on the development of academic language for all students, which is critical to fostering equity in, for example, STEM learning and teaching. *Doing FA* means teachers initiating and

Figure 1   Formative Assessment Moves for Teachers

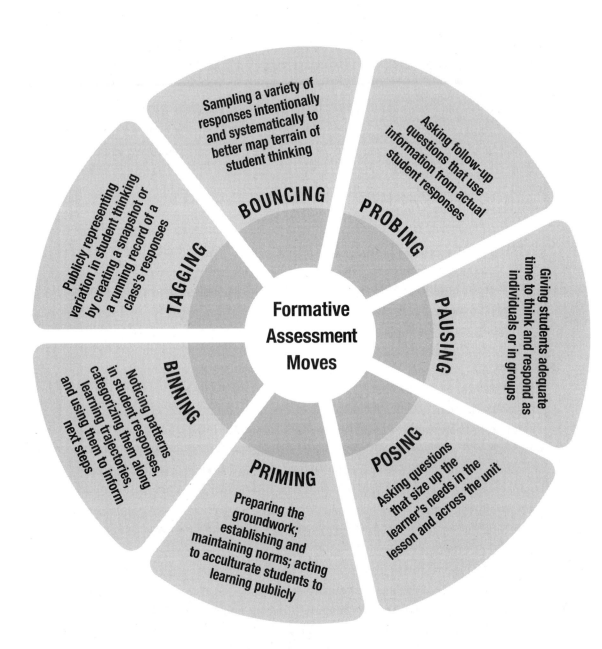

orchestrating openings for scientific and mathematical reasoning and investigations (CCSSI, 2010). A primary goal during these FA-driven lessons is to keep the dialogue among the teacher and students flowing, with just-in-time *moves* that promote conscious, strategic uptake of student thinking that can be used to make instructional decisions during the lesson (Duckor, Holmberg, Rossi Becker, 2017).

Whether teaching elementary, middle, or high school, FA is more than "checking for understanding." Formative assessment as we conceptualize it helps teachers to learn more about students' understandings and to productively respond to those understandings (not merely "misconceptions" or "wrong" answers) during class. We think of FA as a dynamic pedagogical process among students and teachers. It requires acts of planning, instructing, and reflecting on soft data to make better decisions.

It will be clear as you make progress through each chapter that our conceptualization of FA moves, like Sadler's (1989), places a premium on feedback loops in classroom talk, the building up of repertoires of auditory and verbal skills, and providing instructional space for students to use academic language and register as they work together in real-time. Like Shepard (2009), our definition contrasts with those who orient formative assessment toward high-tech products, data mining, and interim testing events. We also agree with Linquanti (2014) and his colleagues that assessing formatively should emphasize real-time instructional processes and the uses of actionable feedback.

For those of you who've been at this work for a while, it is worth noting that our moves-based conceptualization of classroom formative assessment relates to Dylan Wiliam's framework, in particular, how teachers can engineer effective classroom discussions and present tasks that elicit evidence of learning (Wiliam, 2007). We recognize the significance of classroom discourse in laying groundwork for effective feedback, especially how teachers can consciously pose questions that serve various purposes and provide a "window into thinking" (p. 1,069).

These seven FA moves, as we call them, create opportunities for *all* students to interact productively and persistently with higher-order thinking. In combination with the teacher's subject preparation and content knowledge, the FA moves can help teachers make sense of what students know, make connections among ideas, and facilitate the process of learning in more transparent, visible ways (Heritage, 2007, 2010).

The Art and the Science of FA

Teaching is the art of balancing lesson planning with improvising, move by move, with your students during instruction. Sometimes it is hard to see that improvising FA moves can yield insight into student thinking about the lesson topic. We forget that re-posing a question, scaffolding a probe with a sentence frame, or reintroducing a think-time procedure in response to students' verbal and nonverbal action—or inaction!—are assessment strategies that have as much or more power than traditional classroom assessment tools such as worksheets or quizzes.

Although it's tempting, especially for beginning teachers, to gravitate toward the "test event," we strongly suggest staying the course with assessment for learning strategies. A sustained focus on posing and re-posing questions, scaffolding probes with visual aids and cues, priming wait-time and sampling procedures, and tagging all student responses publicly will pay off. But it takes time, practice, and a willingness to learn, re-think, and re-adjust one's "first draft" moves (Lovell, Duckor, & Holmberg, 2015). We've noticed a few things working with beginning teachers: they tend to focus on the test or quiz event, the concrete assessment task, the "thing" they can collect, evaluate, and grade.

This should not surprise us. We are drawn to what appears to be hard data, not soft. We like to believe that one type of assessment data is objective, the other subjective. We privilege the numeric score or letter grade over the informal student response or idea shared on the dry erase board. Is it time to flip the model and get better at using all the available (soft, informal, fleeting) data in the classroom? In a word: yes.

Formative assessment for the next generation of classroom teachers will look different from the last. An FA moves framework will necessarily emphasize the role of developmental trajectories and learning progressions—for students and for teachers—on the path to 21st century learning and skills development (see, e.g., Masters & Wilson, 1997; Black, Wilson, & Yao, 2011). It will emphasize trajectories of growth and feedback for teachers. The new FA moves framework will go beyond technique—it will evoke a new mindset.

Bottom line: FA is more than parroting a guided inquiry pedagogical technique or calling more frequently for "thumbs up, thumbs down" during a lesson. The FA moves-based framework requires pedagogical, affective, and cognitive strategies for re-engaging students who say, "I don't know," or "Huh, what is a function?" or just shrug their shoulders and stare when they inevitably get stuck.

"Stuckness" is, as we now know, part of the learning process. When we struggle to learn something new, we have to assimilate and accommodate, encode and retrieve, call up old and work with new information. Formative assessors embrace how kids learn, and they prepare lessons to make it happen.

The vision of FA explored in this book asks us to open the flow of communication—in all aspects of our teaching—and to take up the challenge of making moves that make a difference with and for our students. We invite you to join us. Now.

Our Journeys in Teaching and Learning

Brent Duckor

I began my high school teaching career in Hungary in 1989 and continued in New York City in the 1990s. Both U.S. and international educational contexts have shaped my deep appreciation for the role of school systems, public policy, and community values in what is considered possible for students and teachers striving to become active, engaged learners in democratic societies.

At Central Park East Secondary School's Senior Institute in East Harlem, I taught government, economics, world history, and (later) social entrepreneurship as part of a federally funded school-to-college program from 1996 to 2000. I am forever grateful to the students, teachers, staff, and parents at Central Park East Secondary School who taught me the meaning of assessment for learning (before I'd ever heard the term), while encouraging diversity of thought and academic excellence for all students.

With the pending passage of No Child Left Behind in 2001, it was time to return to graduate school to obtain a PhD in Quantitative Methods and Evaluation at the University of California–Berkeley, to better understand the critical role of standardized testing on alternative assessment systems developed by New American and Urban High School projects that had flourished at the close of the 20th century. The Big Picture Company, High Tech High, and the Coalition of Essential Schools had all supported new approaches to assessment—eventually my perspectives broadened to the historical, public policy, corporate, and technical "purposes" of educational testing and evaluation.

The faculty at UC–Berkeley's Graduate School of Education intensified and invigorated my commitment to the study of educational assessment—as a lever for classroom change and not merely an accountability tool for policy makers.

Following in the footsteps of my mentors, professors Mark Wilson and Richard Shavelson, the potential link between formative and summative assessment systems continues to fascinate me, though my research has taken a deeper dive into the former practice to explore new ways of conceptualizing teachers' growth.

Since 2008, I have taught preservice teachers in the Single Subject Credential program at San José State University's College of Education. In one of the most diverse public teacher preparation programs in the California state university system, we have pioneered a course called Classroom Assessment and Evaluation, devoted to deeper study of research-based assessment practices, and have graduated a new generation of teachers ready to take up the call of assessment for learning. Working closely with language arts, mathematics, physical education, science, art, music, social science/history, and world languages teachers in both preservice and inservice contexts over the years has humbled and deepened my appreciation of the nuance and complexity of becoming a formative assessor.

Looking back on the 20th century innovations in portfolio-based assessments, exhibitions, rubrics, oral examinations, and graduation committees assembled to review student work and to check on standards of excellence—all these educational reforms seem like a distant dream now. What remains for me, in writing this book, is the promise of formative assessment for all. I now see hope in the drive toward a deeper commitment to teaching students to use their minds well, and to create spaces in classrooms and schools for deeper engagement with our students, in part by speaking with and listening to them more than we imagined necessary or possible. At this moment in the history of schooling, the call could not be clearer.

Carrie Holmberg

I taught 9th grade English, Intermediate English Language Development, Advancement Via Individual Determination (AVID), and journalism at a racially, ethnically, linguistically, and economically diverse Title I comprehensive high school of nearly 2,000 students in a K–12 unified school district in Silicon Valley for several years. At Wilcox High School, I learned to work as a member of a highly collaborative, reform-oriented, creative, ambitious English department. Prior to the implementation of No Child Left Behind, I thrived with my students and colleagues as we focused on writing as a process, one-on-one conferencing, reading for pleasure, portfolio assessment, and project-based learning. We may not have called it formative assessment back then, but we certainly lived assessment for learning with our students.

After having transitioned to work mentoring and inducting new teachers at middle and high schools partnered with Stanford University, I renewed my National Board Certification by "borrowing" a class of junior English Language Arts students at a small charter high school in San José. Nearly all became the first in their families to attend college and that invigorated my commitment to the power of assessment to change lives. Engaging in research projects with the Stanford Partner School Induction Program and the Silicon Valley New Teacher Project, as well as working as a teacher consultant with the Bay Area Writing Project, helped me hone my clinical work with teachers.

I joined the College of Education at San José State University as adjunct faculty in 2011. I've been fortunate to work closely with preservice teachers in the Single Subject Credential Program and to teach courses in Phase I student teaching, English methods, and classroom assessment. In June 2014, I enrolled in the doctoral program at SJSU. Under the guidance and advisement of Dr. Brent Duckor, Dr. Joanne Rossi Becker, and Dr. Diana Wilmot, I pursued my dissertation research, which explores teacher learning progressions in formative assessment. My work focuses on posing, pausing, and probing progressions in the context of middle school mathematics classrooms for the purpose of improving "lesson study" feedback to teachers. I will obtain my EdD in educational leadership in 2017 from SJSU.

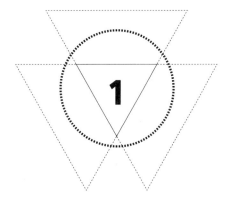

Priming

Letting students in on what's *coming*, what *is* taking place, and *why* the class is doing what it's doing goes a long way to supporting the trust and safety students need to take intellectual risks. How can they learn without regularly taking risks to reveal to others where their understandings, especially their confusions and questions, are?

Janey, economics and civics teacher

I start off well with priming for equity of participation. We create equity cards, talk about how they help, and I use the cards. But after that first day, I don't remind us all why equity of participation and their staying engaged is so important. I assume they remember. Worse, I forget to use the cards!

Alicia, English teacher

I could have students use their journals as a way of priming them for elaborating and explaining. I haven't yet, even though I have no reason to *not* change how students are using their journals. So I suppose my main priming challenge is mine.

Alex, science teacher

What Is Priming?

Priming is everywhere. We hear it when the teacher says: *Let's hear from everyone* or *There are no right or wrong answers to this question* or *I bet someone could build on this—who wants to try*?

We prime the lesson every day when we say: *Okay, everyone, take out your notebooks and let's review those hypotheses from yesterday's lab* or *It's time to put our listening ears on.* When we say *Let's review what we accomplished yesterday,* we're priming.

Priming is what's done to prepare the groundwork. We use it to establish and maintain norms. We do it to support and acculturate students to learning publicly with one another. Priming always remembers that learners are in the classroom learning space together.

Priming moves, as we describe them, aim to support students through the new learning situations. Formative assessors value priming because it honors the confusion, uncertainty, and bottlenecks that come from new procedures and practices when orchestrating "live action" in the classroom. Every lesson can benefit from priming students as they move through the formative assessment-rich classroom.

Inevitably, the situations described in this book will feel strange and uncomfortable at first. For many teachers and students it will never be easy to be asked to listen to a question posed, to pause and wait before offering an answer, or to respond to our probing, especially with open-ended questions. Formative assessment puts high demands on children and asks a lot of ourselves. It asks students to interact and be present with adults and their peers. It asks us to raise the bar on classroom assessment practices, the just-in-time interactions, and the "goodwill" that underpins assessment for learning.

We know from both experience and research that priming for a formative assessment-rich learning environment will ask us all to place equity of voice over rush to judgment. Priming moves emphasize the role of setting up everyone for success rather than rolling the dice and hoping a few students are engaged.

Teachers who are learning to become formative assessors can expect their students to engage in posing, pausing, probing, bouncing, tagging, and binning moves, but only if everyone is primed for action first. Priming moves function preventatively, responsively, and reflectively. They help our students and ourselves to set the tone, understand norms, and take up the risky work of using new academic language, or being challenged to deepen an initial response or see patterns in others' thinking on the whiteboard.

Why Prime? For Whose Good? For What Good?

The learning space is constructed by our expectations, what we think our roles are, and how we enact routines that satisfy our values. If we believe that all voices should be heard, we will remind our students every minute, every period, every day: *Has everyone had the opportunity to ask their burning question yet?* If we hope for more engagement from students who are typically the least verbal (in our classrooms or others'), then we will set up visible scaffolds to support their use of new academic language and expand the range of voices heard in a call and response routine. Bottom line: If we value every child's right to learn, then our classroom will be primed for reflection and inquiry—with a relentless focus on how kids think.

We prime because if we don't, many of our kids in our classrooms will be left behind. Bringing these students along requires discovering their thinking, making it visible, and responding wisely to it. To make student thinking more visible, however, we need new strategies for listening and speaking in the classroom learning space. Priming moves will figure prominently. They must.

Why prime? Because priming can help make not only *learning* visible, priming can go a long way toward making *students* visible. Priming can help teachers and students work together to influence how school is done (Garmston & Wellman, 1999).

Let's remember that teachers who are developing their skills in priming for formative assessment are trying to understand and practice a new way of school life—for themselves and for their students. Many students in the building have become accustomed to "doing school" (Pope, 2001). Lemke (1990) calls it "playing the classroom game." Others refer to it as "doing the lesson" (Jimenez-Alexiandre, Rodriguez, & Duschl, 2000). After years in the graded classroom, our students (and their teachers) have been acculturated to the habits, scripts, and routines of assessment *of* learning—summative assessment.

Students have learned that most questions are rhetorical. Answers will be supplied by a few. In the higher grades, students who sit quietly (and in back rows) are accustomed to being left alone. Unfortunately, the notion of what it means to be a good student has been largely synonymous with being invisible (Powell, Farrar, Cohen, 1985; Sizer, 1984, 1996; Cuban, 1993).

It's not uncommon for students who have suddenly been immersed in a classroom culture that does school differently to wonder:

- Why is the teacher asking *Why?* so much?
- Why is the teacher using equity sticks (popsicle sticks with a student's name on each) to call on us?
- Why is the teacher waiting a bit before taking answers, instead of just calling on Carly and Josh, who have their hands up?
- Why is the teacher putting all answers on the whiteboard, even the wrong ones?
- Why is the teacher always answering a question with another question?
- Why can't the teacher just solve the problem and write the correct answer on the board so we can move on?

Our students need to know satisfactory answers to these questions as much as we do. Priming takes this into account and works to help students understand not just the *what* and the *how* of classroom activities, procedures, and structures, but also the *why*.

 FORMATIVE ASSESSMENT TIPS

Questioning the Roles We Play

Sage on the Stage, Commander in Chief, Classroom Management Expert—however appealing these roles and moves may be, none of the traditional modalities of teaching capture the challenges of becoming a formative assessor.

The formative assessor, we contend, is not merely a teacher who transmits knowledge: *she is also a guide connected to the values, beliefs, and aspirations of her students as they discover new skills, proficiencies, and capacities to learn.*

As you read on, we invite you to imagine yourself more and more as a formative assessment (FA) Guide on the Side. The FA Guide takes her students into a new world of classroom communication, where people exchange ideas, give one another feedback, solve problems, and face difficult subjects with intentionality and care. The FA Guide studies how the roles she plays and the moves she makes influence classroom culture and student learning.

What the Research Says

For almost two decades, we've known that formative assessment practices rank among the top interventions that improve educational outcomes. We also know that students benefit from teaching approaches that emphasize learning intentions, success criteria, and metacognitive strategies in the classroom. Hattie (2012) found that, "when teaching and learning are visible, there is a greater likelihood of students reaching higher levels of achievement" (p. 21).

Yet making teaching and learning visible requires an accomplished teacher as evaluator and activator of students' prior knowledge and experience. Research tells us that visible learning strategies are, in fact, visible. They require a formative assessor to play a critical role in her classroom: the role of leading and orchestrating such that every child can indeed engage in a classroom culture that is rich in formative assessment to support their progress toward achieving meaningful learning targets. Every child can participate if first the child knows the scripts, roles, and routines associated with it. Visible learning means laying out, or priming, what we are doing. The moves-based approach to classroom formative assessment we offer can play an important role in the work of supporting visible learning.

Our work adds to the existing knowledge base on the use of elementary teachers' reflective practices to advance the skills required to bring about more powerful classroom mathematics and language arts discussions and to make teaching and learning more visible to students (Ball & Cohen, 1999; Lampert, 2003; Grossman, 2005; Sleep & Boerst, 2012). Fortunately, we also have video and case study examples in middle and high schools of teachers and students who are familiar with priming moves that support a formative assessment-rich classroom culture (Gold & Lanzoni, 1993; Lieberman, 1995; Darling-Hammond, Ancess, & Falk, 1995; Duckor & Perlstein, 2014).

Some literature on adolescent development in general can help inform teachers as they plan their priming. Deci and Ryan (2000) and more recently Elias (2004) and Cervone and Cushman (2014) have spoken to the universal needs students have for autonomy and self-determination, connectedness and belonging, and competency and control in classrooms. Jacquelynne Eccles and Carol Midgley's seminal studies in the 1980s explored how developmental changes in adolescent cognition and social behavior interacted with classroom environments and teacher practices. Damon and associates (2008) have also uncovered the need for purpose and meaning in young people's educational experiences and lives.

These experts help explain why many students decline in their school-oriented effort in the middle school years. Their work can also help us better understand the real need for better, more developmentally appropriate priming for formative assessment practices with our students.

Unfortunately, the literature on building, nurturing, and sustaining—what we call *priming*—a formative assessment culture in today's classrooms is thin. Not much attention is given to how different students experience the cognitive, affective, and cultural demands of formative assessment. Personal and cultural identities certainly play a role (Perrenoud, 1991). We need more conversations and sharing among teachers about FA moves—what is working? For whom and why? How can we ramp up classroom discussions that are inclusive of "unorthodox" thinking or "naive" beliefs? And how can we circle back to students who are not yet ready to join others at the table—perhaps because of a perceived (and potentially real) lack of voice in our schools today?

Although there has been a renewed policy interest in the United States with embedding the core skills of speaking and listening in public school classrooms, we still need more insight into what works and how to set up—how to prime—favorable conditions for educational interventions that will make positive differences each and every day.

Going Deeper with Priming

Priming sets the stage for all other formative assessment moves. Priming is both the glue that holds members of the learning community together and the structural framing that supports what a class can build together. Priming is the careful, intentional, and rewarding process of establishing norms, protocols, and frameworks of inquiry that all stakeholders can contribute to in your classroom.

Although, generally speaking, the benefits of priming in the classroom learning space *are* universal, can we really expect that priming is also one size fits all? Rather, shouldn't we expect priming to look different in each of the subject areas? And perhaps more important, won't the flavors and directions of priming look different depending on students' ages, maturity, and grade levels?

In this chapter, we, too, lean on studies from Boaler and Humphreys (2005) that have highlighted the importance of social norms in the creation of effective classroom environments. Paul Cobb (e.g., McClain & Cobb, 2001) has identified the importance of subject-specific norms in determining the quality of student-teacher interaction. Along with formative assessment pioneers Black and Wiliam (2009), we agree in principle that "what counts as a good explanation in the mathematics classroom would be different from what counts as a good explanation in the history classroom, although they would also share certain commonalities" (p. 27).

Although priming moves are *not* one size fits all, priming in different subject areas does share certain commonalities. We assert this based on empirical observations carried out in our preservice teacher credential program that works in more than 30 schools across eight different subject areas in a culturally, linguistically, and economically diverse region of California.

We have found these three basic truths about priming across all contexts:

- Priming involves students. (It is not just "done" to them, without their input.)
- Priming is more than just prepping for and warming up students for a lesson.
- Priming addresses more than students' feelings about learning.

Priming, like preparing lessons, is familiar to all teachers. But priming involves the students directly in "the work." They must, in effect, help prepare pathways to formative assessment-driven lessons. Students must feel empowered to speak to, listen for, and engage big ideas and rich tasks. We downplay the role of students in formative assessment-driven classroom cultures at our peril.

Priming is a process. It requires sizing up challenges that students will have with formative assessment moves. It is not easy or natural for students to know what to do when they are expected to elaborate on an answer to a question.

Priming well takes work behind the scenes—before and after each lesson. It is about preparing students for the process of delving into content, content that will—no matter how carefully chosen, introduced, and thoughtfully spiraled—frustrate, flummox, inspire, irritate, and bore some students.

Planning your priming moves means taking a moment to think: *Who will respond to my questions today? Who will come to the board and share an answer on the word wall this morning? Who will feel safe to answer in the group when I ask, "Can someone explain or elaborate or say more?" Who may not? Why might that be? What can I do, or set into motion, that might help?*

Priming, however, is *not just* about preparing students for a test or an assessment activity. Priming is also about supporting them—and supporting them to support each other—*through* the struggles for visible classroom learning. We are priming our students for lifelong learning, as they journey through school and eventually into the worlds of college and work.

 IN THE CLASSROOM

Priming Is What You Already Do

When you smile and shake hands with your students as they enter your classroom, you're priming.

When, as a physical education teacher, you tell students, "We'll be debriefing your team's performance today. Notice something a teammate does to help. It might be an encouraging word, a pass, or a look. Take note," you're priming.

When you tell your choral students, "As we sing this next phrase, and you try the new breathing technique, I don't expect we'll get it perfect," you're priming.

When you tell one of your quieter, shyer students as you circulate during group work, "The class would really benefit from knowing how you approached this. Perhaps we could hear from you during the whole class share out. What do you think?" you're priming.

When you ask the class, "Before you begin your small group discussions, remind me, what's the most important agreement your group came up with for safe, productive interactions?" you're priming.

When you pay attention to signals that suggest students feel uncomfortable, unsafe, or disengaged, and you take action to restore safety and invite engagement, you're priming.

When you invite your students to prepare for homework challenges by setting aside class time to tell them, "Take a few moments to name a roadblock you're likely to come up against as you take the next step with your history project tonight. See if you can write down two ways you could meet, overcome, or perhaps even prevent this roadblock," you're priming.

When you encourage your students, "Congratulate your group members on working your way through your very first high school chemistry lab—we are doing science!" you're priming.

When you bring empathy and curiosity to your students, a commitment to meet them where they are—to *see* them as best you can—and the willingness *to learn new ways of working or being* in order to do so, you have done the most essential priming move possible: you have primed yourself to become publicly vulnerable as the leader of your learning community. Your journey in becoming a formative assessor is about to get exponentially more rewarding, scary, challenging, and satisfying.

Priming Well Takes Knowing and Supporting FA-Friendly Values and Beliefs

As we've said, priming aims to support the culture of the classroom such that it becomes a place where all can work together to bridge learning goals with trust and respect for each student's ideas. It's true, we're asking a lot of priming moves. Yet we've witnessed—as we know you have too—the magic that happens when learners begin to trust, risk, and work together in ways that bring them toward deeper engagement with conceptually difficult material.

Why do things sink and float? Who was responsible for the Cold War? How does a thesis differ from a hypothesis? Do all functions have a limit? What difference does it make that no one uses the formal *you* in the United States? What is a ratio? Can measuring heart rate really make me a better athlete?

Such essential questions can set up challenging learning targets. We need to remind our students—prime our students—that getting stuck, being confused, asking for clarification, and having breakthroughs is the way we all learn. Good questions cause us to stretch, feel a little pain, and scratch our heads. Skillfully practiced, priming for formative assessment moves (such as posing and probing) can make breakthroughs for more of your students much more likely.

Everyone in the learning community needs to know the learning expectations and the classroom norms. Better yet, everyone needs to play a role in making class agreements. We have found that it is best to make time for establishing these agreements right away.

The responsibilities of the teacher as formative assessor are great. She must model the behavior she wants to see when she is all-too-human, pressed for time, and juggling lots at once. She must also artfully face and improve situations when classroom values and agreements are not being upheld (an eager student interrupting a slower-to-share student as she is responding or a student making fun of another student's idea).

Fortunately, "Safe havens have many allies." When students enjoy the benefits of a well-functioning FA culture, and when they witness classroom norms being respected and maintained, they will do their share to help the learning community thrive.

It helps, of course, if we stack the deck, so to speak, toward an optimal learning community, one that can sustain our best intentions. Setting up our K–12 classrooms such that our students can satisfy their universal needs for autonomy and empowerment, connectedness and belonging, meaning and purpose also boosts bringing about the kinds of well-functioning learning communities we, as teachers becoming formative assessors, desire.

Priming moves should serve and bolster classroom procedures and practices that embody the values and beliefs necessary for formative assessment to flourish. Here are some examples that can serve as agreements and examples going forward. We encourage you to create and explore your own examples with your particular students:

- Each and every student is important and needs to be heard.
- Our actions have a purpose.
- Your voice, what you have to say, matters.
- We can listen with our hearts as well as our ears.
- We respect vulnerability—it's necessary for growth and learning.
- We are here to learn together.
- It's okay to make mistakes, to be wrong.
- You don't know that *yet*.
- We each learn differently, and it takes time.
- Outside your comfort zone is still a safe place in this classroom.
- Exercising patience—with yourself and others—is a wise choice.
- There are multiple points of view and each will be heard.
- We value inquiry.
- We practice kindness and curiosity.

 FORMATIVE ASSESSMENT TIPS

Priming by the Numbers:
Aligning Classroom Conditions with Developmental Outcomes

Structuring classrooms, units, and lessons so students can meet their universal needs for autonomy, relatedness, and competency is important. But the question is: how old is old enough to cultivate and meet these needs?

Research led by Jacquelynn Eccles and Carol Midgley (Eccles, Midgley, & Adler, 1984; Eccles, Lord, & Midgley, 1991) reminds us that a "mismatch" tends to occur between the developmental needs of adolescents and the learning conditions of classrooms and schools in many middle grade settings. In early adolescence, when

💡 *Continued*

developmentally students are becoming ready to assert increasing personal autonomy and assume greater responsibility for their learning, middle grade classrooms are often found to be more (not less) restrictive, placing greater emphasis on teacher control and diminishing opportunities for choice and autonomy. Conditions aligned to students' developmental stage would do the opposite.

Formative assessment moves will function better in learning spaces where conditions are intentionally aligned to students' developmental needs. The inverse holds too. For instance, no amount of priming a preschooler—no matter how well done—will be able to get said preschooler to sit still for longer than is reasonable to expect of learners who are three years old. And just try "priming for success" on a day when she needs a nap but hasn't had one!

Making Key Elements of Classroom Formative Assessment Culture Visible

Priming can be viewed as actions taken to make and keep agreements amongst members of a learning community. Here are four agreements essential to living out a formative assessment-rich experience in the classroom learning space. We need to prime in order to make them visible—and real.

1. We will be activating prior knowledge and sharing ideas.
2. We will be asking questions.
3. We will be listening for responses.
4. We will be inviting fairness, trust, and respect for others' voices.

We Will Be Activating Prior Knowledge and Sharing Ideas

Students and teachers have important roles to play in ensuring that activation of prior knowledge gets its due. Students need to get in the habit of sharing what they think—no matter what they think. Getting around fear, anxiety, and one's *affective filter* is no small challenge. (The term *affective filter* describes a set of complex psychological factors that can inhibit or facilitate student learning.)

Most students have been conditioned to avoid sharing in class. Sometimes the signal is strong: if you don't have the right answer, loads of confidence, or the proper training in "doing school," then be quiet. Avoid exchange of ideas as much as possible. Just play along.

Teachers know this. We may even play along as if we plan to break the cycle (and codes) of silence. Our lesson plans may say "check for prior knowledge." Yet we also know that meaningfully activating the prior knowledge of each member in a learning community is difficult. It's messy. And time-consuming. In addition, our students are not used to doing so, except in haphazard, cursory ways.

Deeper learning requires more. Piagetians, Vygotskians, and constructivist learning theorists know this. New knowledge is constructed; it requires scaffolds. The language of priming is a mental tool to support learning. It signals to our students that we are "in the zone" and getting ready to acquire more powerful understandings and ways of doing things.

Let's agree now that the best-designed lessons cannot come to life unless we know our students, what they bring to the learning situation, and how their experiences connect to the material we are asking them to engage with on a particular day. Priming for formative assessment in general requires us to let our students know that we will ask questions, listen for responses, probe deeper on those responses, and make connections to the lesson every day. Priming each lesson means setting up reminders, visual cues, posters, even warm-up exercises to break the ice again and again. It requires dialogue (Easton, 2009; Graybill & Easton, 2015).

We Will Be Asking Questions

We will be asking a lot more questions. Questioning is a core value in the room. It is okay to question—the teacher, other students, oneself. No one has a monopoly on the truth. Yes, there are correct answers. But that is not the point of every lesson. Sometimes we want everyone to contribute an idea about the topic. Everyone's opinion counts in the formative assessment-driven classroom. And to prove it, the teacher needs to ask questions of herself: *Did this work today? Why did José get stuck and put his head down? How can I coach you all out of the habit of interrupting one another?*

Questions are clues to thinking. They reveal orientations. They can reveal priorities. They can be like shining a flashlight where we want to learn more. Questions can also be wielded like bludgeons. Just about every student has experienced being "bludgeoned" by a question before—whether in school, at home, or on the playground. We need to be keenly aware of this as we lead our classroom culture in a new direction.

Additionally, as we prime our classrooms to become spaces where questions proliferate, we will need to process moments where our own—and our students'—questioning is so clumsy as to be painful. Teachers need to prime for these inevitable moments.

Learning theory reminds us that effective cognitive processing is more likely when we reduce extraneous load. Our students' working memory is limited by duration and capacity to chunk information. Attention and memory are affected by too many questions, thrown too fast, at our students. It will help the learning process if we have scaffolds and tools to slow down and be more deliberate. Assessing for learning will go better if there has been a classroom conversation prior to launching a question/prompt. We must trust that we have time to say: *Remember when we talked about how questioning takes practice? Who can tell us what helps everyone to share an answer? Why are we interested in all voices? Good. Let's take 2 minutes of silence to write our responses. Then I'll ask you to share aloud.*

The "we" in *We will be asking questions* means that our classrooms become places where *students* compose, ponder, ask, celebrate, revisit, revise, critique, and explore questions. This is not to downplay teachers' roles as leaders and models of intellectual curiosity. Nor is it to downplay teachers' roles as skillful and purposeful formative assessors whose questions get students engaging, speaking, rethinking, and elaborating. It is to emphasize that an important aspect of priming is priming for students to become the ones who get better and better at forming, asking, categorizing, revising, and even postponing questions.

Priming a learning community for the experience of asking and responding to *one another's* questions differs from priming students for teacher questions. What will it take for your students to ask and respond productively to *their own questions* in the classroom learning space? If we want a classroom culture rich in formative assessment, we need to make this inquiry. The "we" in *We will be asking questions* means everyone. We prime for meaningful engagement from all.

We Will Be Listening for Responses

As we've said, priming is work the teacher and students do, individually and together, to help make their classroom a place where "safe talk, safe listening" occurs. A set of classroom mottos created by your class is best. Posters with visual reminders can help with mottos such as *Safety first—Careful listening means listening carefully; Who has the talking stick?; Be kind and pass the monkey; Listening well to others takes energy and focus.* Formative assessors can set the tone and set up procedures to serve as reminders. An important part of our responsibility as intentional cultivators of a formative assessment-rich classroom culture is to lead students into listening carefully to their classmates' responses. Unfortunately, in today's public discussions and arenas, these habits are exceedingly rare. It seems our technology has accelerated the need to be heard rather than to hear. We cannot be tempted to believe that learning occurs best when those who talk the most or the loudest dominate.

 FORMATIVE ASSESSMENT TIPS

Careful Classroom Listeners Are Made, Not Born

Careful listening in the classroom learning space does not come naturally. It's a skill. As adults, we may already be adept listeners in other areas of our lives. However, listening actively to students as they work to make sense of new content and new concepts in terms of their present schema is not akin to the kinds of listening we do in other areas of our lives. It's much more specialized.

Teachers have different purposes when we listen carefully to student responses. We listen for strengths, nascent understandings, misconceptions, presumptions, and probe-worthy areas. We listen for unasked questions and barely noticeable body language amidst student responses. Our purposeful listening often relates to the academic content and subject matter, such as physics or physical fitness, which can be highly specialized. Careful listening is cognitively demanding work for all involved in the formative assessment exchange.

Getting better at such listening takes practice. The good news is we do get better. Reflection and analyses, with support from caring and skillful colleagues and instructional coaches, can accelerate our development.

We Invite Fairness, Trust, and Respect for All Voices

These days we talk a lot about the role of classroom learning environment and school climate in sustaining and promoting academic success. What if we could prime for core values—trust, respect, fairness, community—in our own lessons by simply putting more attention on these questions, in the company of our students:

- What makes classroom speaking and listening different from our everyday conversation? What does this mean for us as a learning community?
- How does fairness or respect in a classroom conversation about the causes of war differ from a conversation with a good friend?
- Are some conversations harder to follow than others? Is it easier to listen in a pair-share, in a small group, or with the whole class? Why?
- Who gets to break agreements? How and why?
- How do we handle incidences when breakages of our shared agreements and classroom norms occur?
- What are our tools for repairing with others and resetting the terms of trust when breakages occur?
- We each deal with verbal conflict and differences of opinion differently. What do we need to know about one another *right now* to make this work?

Running classroom meetings where such questions are considered and discussed is challenging work. Coming up with a list of class agreements is not easy. Making them explicit and public is critical. But even harder, as every teacher knows, is working to live by those agreements as a community once they are explicit.

Here is the deal: some students will experience this new, formative assessment classroom culture as strange. They will feel embarrassed. Some will experience questions as harassment and become defensive or angry. We must remember that many of our students have been conditioned to remain silent. We must remember, too, that fairness, trust, and respect for *all* voices includes not only respect for others' voices but for their own voices as worthy contributors to the classroom learning space.

We must admit that too many of our students have not experienced respect for their beliefs, ideas, and experiences. There is room for checking understanding and uncovering prior knowledge. The FA moves-based framework can change the dynamics of chalk and talk. But first, we must reset the clock on outmoded attempts at classroom management and control. Priming for classroom fairness, trust, and respect for all voices has a significant role to play in helping students learn to use their minds and voices well and become contributing citizens in our democracy. It will take time. But it's worth the effort to deepen your classroom assessment practice.

Principles, Procedures, and Practices

Try Priming Differently for Different Within-Class Configurations and Contexts. We know that context matters. Teacher candidates in the very beginning of their student teaching notice it. Reyna, having just begun teaching English to 9th graders, noted:

> My students have proven they can have heated and critical discussions in small groups, but not with the entire class. I would like to broaden the small group discussions to larger, whole class discussions. But that seems harder.

Reyna is not sure how to go about priming her students through a transition she'd like to see her students make. More experienced teachers, of course, have scaffolded their students through such transitions before and they realize "setting up" is as important as "cleaning up."

Reyna's learning curve reminds us that teachers' priming moves will differ according to context and configuration. Teachers will work differently as they prime the whole class, a small group of students, or individuals. Try to prime in ways that take advantage of the circumstances of each configuration. For example, priming with small groups of students is especially suited to teachers who are helping students increase their thresholds for (safely and respectfully) challenging one another's academic assertions. Commit to becoming a master of the "on the fly" verbal nudge. Encourage and model. Celebrate successes.

Advice for Improving Your Priming Practices. Priming helps make new ways for students to engage in the classroom learning space more likely. Priming helps make learning visible and supports deeper learning. Priming aims to give everyone access to new skills, new learning, and new ways of being together. Being able to intentionally prime with your students is a prerequisite for becoming a formative assessor.

Perhaps the most demanding aspect of priming is that it is ongoing. It's never done. Influencing students' usual ways of "doing school" calls for lots of teacher-initiated priming moves and lots of repetition. You need to believe that if you work at priming, you can make positive differences in how your students interact with one another and with you. And you need to be relentless.

How and what you prime will change day by day, week by week, and month by month as you adjust your moves to meet your class's changing needs over time. Your students need to trust that in your class you will never give up on them, as individuals and as a learning community.

Here are the most important things to support your developing priming practice:

1. **Prioritize your priming moves.** Focus, focus, focus. Choose one or two priming moves to work on first, as major priming themes. For example, put your energy and attention to *priming for equitable participation* before trying to prime for other "things" in your class.

2. **Introduce new priming methods to your students gradually,** instead of all at once, to prevent overwhelming them. Let them pick a "Procedure of the Week." Use a stuffed monkey as an alternative to a talking stick. A fuzzy bear. The school mascot. "*This week, we will bounce the dolphin to hear everyone.*"

3. **Invite students into the meaning and use of the priming moves.** Make connections to the worlds of work, college, and life. Why is priming relevant as a life skill? Ask students to reflect on specific priming practices (e.g., pair-shares for pausing or sticky notes for tagging) after they have used it. Use their feedback to decide if and how to revise the practice.

4. **Set up the learning environment** to support the ongoing, iterative nature of priming; change things up if necessary. Hang posters that name and support class values and beliefs. Have a student committee present a five-minute report on the "state of priming" (what and how we primed and how it went) in the class at the end of each unit.

5. **Prime to inspire and move "the work" forward.** Let your students know that you know they are working toward mastering new knowledge, skills, and habits. Progress is key. The secret words: "Not yet."

Misconceptions and Challenges

Priming beyond *what, how,* and w*hy*: priming to inspire. A misconception about priming is that it's solely about preparing students for the *what* (content acquisition and specific learning objectives of the day) and the *how* (processes and procedures) of learning. Most people see priming as another way to set expectations and they are represented in contracts or lists of rules on a wall.

Priming the "what" and the "how" of how we engage in pausing or tagging, for example, is essential. But so is the *why* behind our priming moves. "We prime because…" is a sentence starter every student and teacher should be able to answer in the formative assessment-rich classroom.

When teachers who are learning to become formative assessors work with students to prime the *why* behind their classroom procedures, routines, and ways of managing the classroom, they are modeling the relevance of "what we do" and "why we do it." Not all students feel they need wait time, for example, and others do not see the purpose behind pausing for thinking time in a pair-share. But when the teacher takes the time to explore "why we pause" with students and gives examples outside the school setting, students have a better chance of seeing the purpose for pausing moves.

Students need to know the relevance of any particular classroom instructional or assessment practice to buy into learning efforts more deeply. We owe them an answer to the questions: Why are we pausing? For whose good? For what good?

Thinking about priming in terms of everyone in the room being clear on the *what*, *how*, and *why* of lesson content and processes is useful, yet priming encompasses still more. Priming includes supporting how a learning community can forge new territory together. Priming readies a group for the unknown. We call it "priming that inspires."

Priming that inspires involves helping students, individually and collectively, envision an outcome they feel is possible. Leading your class into the unknown with confidence and in ways that inspire may be the most important purpose of priming. Students get inspired when they can envision an outcome and feel the worth in working toward it. As David Smith, one of our favorite administrators in New York's public schools, was fond of saying: "Every so often a student will tell me, 'I don't know how to do that.' And my reply is, 'You don't know how to do that—yet.' That's an empowering word: yet. Our purpose, you see, is not to provide them with the answers but with the tools they'll need to find the answers for themselves" (Wulf, 1997).

Your confidence to prime into the unknown comes from your faith in your skills as a group temperature-taker, boundary-keeper, and facilitator. You've taken classes' temperatures so many times that you know when more time needs to be given to a pair-share, or when a small-group work session has maxed out. You keep boundaries by calmly reminding students of agreements you've set together: *Let's pause here. We agreed that in today's discussion we would only bring up people in the reading or public figures. Not others.* You know how to facilitate repairs, especially when some way you have acted has possibly negatively affected a student: *Hold on. That didn't come out how I meant. I may have run over your idea. I want to hear it better. Are you game?*

Priming into the unknown will have you and your students working at the edges of traditional ways of doing school. You know what that entails from your most vulnerable students—lots of attitude and expressions of frustration. Our advice: for now, ignore much of the "negative" attitude and "unprofessional" demeanor of your "difficult" students as they struggle with the new rules and boundaries. That they feel safe enough to express their frustrations is positive. Let them push and pull. Keep your eyes on the prize! Working at your edges together also brings deep, meaningful engagement and learning. Prime to inspire that. It never grows old.

 IN THE CLASSROOM

Priming That Inspires

• Stay with it. Writer's block is part of the game. When you get this draft to me, your accomplishment will feel all the sweeter for the hard work you're putting in. I can coach you to the next level.

• I can hardly wait to see the different ways you'll tackle this challenge. I've seen you do it on the field. Let's see what can be done in the lab this afternoon.

• Let's hear you talk this through. Think of your favorite younger cousin. How old is she? How would you describe to her what you're doing? Tell me as you'd tell her.

• We're not sure exactly how this will go. That's okay! We can count on our deadlines, benchmarks, and protocols to keep us moving forward productively. I will always be clear about what's negotiable and what's not negotiable, so you will have choices, individually and as a class.

• I was telling my neighbor about this class, how so many of you have embarked on STEM projects that demand time commitments he couldn't even imagine. He said: "It's so much harder now for the kids. We just had to do homework and take tests. Now teachers make it so much more real world. Are they really ready to work that hard at this age?"

I told him what I tell you all: "My students are doing it because it involves creativity. They want to see what they can come up with and how to communicate it to others. Yes, it's hard. But so is being a professional at work and going for an advanced degree."

So let's check in: how much progress have you made on your robot and what are your group's next steps?

⚠ Misconception Alert: "I already prime my class with a contract at the beginning of the school year."

Priming is ongoing. Priming moves do more than just put students into gear. Priming should occur more often than just at the beginning of lessons, units, and school years. Priming is ongoing. Some degree of priming usually needs to happen at nearly every transition in a lesson. For example: *Now that each group has presented their poster, let's get ready to use some of that information in the argument we're constructing.* But priming happens not just at transitions between activities and critical lesson junctures. If teachers need to remind a class about an agreement, and they need to "interrupt" a lesson to do so, they do. That's also priming.

Priming is also ongoing because it's not always successful at first try. Why would it be? Learning new skills—especially as a group—takes time. Learning is messy. When one cognitive skill is being challenged, another will temporarily fall away. It looks like backsliding.

Early cognitive scientists such as Piaget understood this phenomenon in children. If we apply Piaget's theory to priming, we should expect that the new classroom culture of formative assessment will create a state of disequilibrium, or an imbalance between what is understood (a student is used to thinking *My answer is my answer*) and what is encountered (this student meets a teacher who asks after his first response: *Can you elaborate or say more?*).

Students naturally try to reduce such imbalances by using the stimuli (the teacher's questioning strategies that require uptake and interaction) that cause the disequilibrium and developing new schemes ("Okay, I can trust this situation and try to explain"), or adapting old ones ("I'll just say, 'Because' and see if that works") until equilibrium is restored.

This process of restoring balance in the learning environment is called equilibration. Learning depends on this back and forth process. Teachers can orchestrate priming, in combination with all the other formative assessment moves, to support this back and forth. When equilibrium—or in this case, classroom talk dynamics—are upset, teachers can make formative moves that make a difference. They can help everyone in the classroom learning space capitalize on opportunities to grow and develop.

⚠ Misconception Alert: "I tried priming the other day. I told the students they would have to give complete answers. They still just ignore my instructions."

Priming is persistent. Teachers have told us: "It seems like no matter how much I've primed the class, many students are still surprised when I say, *Tell me more*, or ask, *Can you expand on that*? It's like they're being punished, or being told they're wrong."

We must remember that our "friendly requests" are actually probes, which require wait time, or pausing. (We'll go deeper into pausing in Chapter 3 and deeper into probing in Chapter 4.) As we've said, the formative assessment moves interrelate and must be woven together in a sensible and coherent way. Although all teachers know that pausing is important, fewer teachers speak about *priming for pausing*. They just do it, and hope for the best.

We maintain that priming for pausing is necessary but not sufficient to widen the sample of student responses in your classroom. Don't be surprised if some students still slink into their seats when you ask, *Can you expand on that?* But priming for pausing—in thoughtful combination with other formative assessment moves—can be a routine that helps protect student think time, improves the quality of students' (initial *and* follow up) responses, and increases equity of participation.

Priming for pausing might sound like this: *Let's dig deeper. But before I ask for elaboration, we're going to pause a full 30 seconds. Then you'll pair and share with your elbow partner, and then we'll hear more about your thinking.*

💬 TEACHER VOICE

I model for the students how to respond to invitations for elaboration and exploration. I pick a student to put in the position of the teacher. This student will ask me a given question, to which I give the right answer. Afterwards, that student will say, "Please elaborate," to which I will respond in a way that shows my thinking: "Because we know *A*, want to find *C*, so we have to use *B* to get to the answer." A specific answer helps to prime the students to understand what I mean when I ask for elaboration and exploration after they have given a correct answer. Priming this way begins to address the 'I'm being punished' feeling that many, many students feel when asked to elaborate and explain.

—Regina, high school English teacher

Take the Challenge: Priming for Equity of Participation

Novice teachers we've had the privilege of working with struggle with priming for equity of participation in their classes. Whether it's balancing participation norms amongst 80 students in symphonic band or on the track field, or priming for Spanish III so that nonnative speakers don't hang back thinking the 'native' speakers will always get the correct answer—priming takes lots of work and patience. Beginning teachers may value equity of participation but quite naturally they, too, face challenges. The question for us all: how can we make priming for FA moves an everyday habit?

Let's take an example: priming for bouncing throughout the lesson. First, a quick word: *bouncing* encompasses how we manage opportunities for *all* students to speak in class. Bouncing is not solely about equity of participation and maximizing student voices as we shall see in Chapter 5, but this move does require us to prime participation.

Bouncing student participation through the room intentionally and systematically is key to orchestrating a class that lives equity of participation. So priming different bouncing routines used in a class is crucial to priming equity of participation. Before they've bounced to anyone, we advise our novice teachers to prime for equity of participation by

- *Communicating* the method of participation you will use that day. Strategies include methods for randomizing such as equity cards, sticks, and apps;
- *Mixing up* the methods by "snaking" through the room, holding and passing the stuffed dolphin, or using the "popcorn" approach while explaining what you are doing and why;
- *Talking* about how you will let students know when you want them to respond freely or in a structured way;
- *Reminding* students of scaffolds and supports (e.g., graphic organizer, wait time, pair-share) available to underpin their responses *before* each lesson segment; and
- *Defining* at each transition to an activity the amount of time you're going to give them to think about a response.

As one novice teacher told us, "Priming student participation provides lucidity in what I am expecting and sets students up to provide in-depth responses. When I do this consistently, there are no surprises or gimmicks in what I want from them."

The Challenge of Staying with Priming and Adjusting Priming to the Needs of the Class

Students need teachers both to stay with their priming moves and to adjust strategies and tactics to keep the priming fresh. To help teachers with this dual set of challenges, we prime by communicating to the teachers with whom we work: *Your journey in becoming formative assessors has just begun. You will try out different FA moves. Some will take off and others will fall flat. You will get frustrated, even bored. Go back to your notes. Try again. Use your self-assessment matrix, your FA lesson plan, your question maps to guide you. But don't forget: old habits die hard. Prepare to stretch yourself and your students like never before.*

There will always be ways for those learning to become formative assessors to go deeper and get better with any move or new combinations of them. The kids, the curriculum, and the daily contexts for learning inevitably shape and mold our work as formative assessors. Modeling a positive attitude toward striving for improvement and following through—again and again—is key.

All teachers are capable of trying on new hats and improving on their efforts to reach as many students as possible. There is no perfect execution of a move; no one is a natural-born formative assessor. Priming novice teachers for the reality of the challenge ahead is one of the most powerful "things" we teach and we want them to teach to their students!

This is not to give the teachers we work with a pass on being accountable for their students' learning of content or mastery of skills. Not at all. Procedural fluency and conceptual understanding in mathematics, for example, is hard won. But so is the art of compassion for the learner. After all, both teachers and students are engaged in challenging and extremely important work in their classrooms. We want to honor priming-for-posing tough questions and honor everyone in the quest to unpack the skills and dispositions necessary to demonstrate understanding. This may be one of the most powerful "big ideas" we teach our students all year.

Priming Repeatedly and Consistently and Responsively

One aspect of "ongoingness" of priming—for posing, pausing, probing, bouncing, tagging, and binning—is negotiating the tension between priming repeatedly and consistently, and priming responsively in order to adjust to students' changing needs. Students and teachers both need routines, cues, and repetition. They need consistency. Yet this need for consistency is at odds with students and teachers' cravings for novelty and the need to prime responsively.

Priming responsively means adjusting how you prime to meet the changing needs of individual students and whole classes. It requires, as Vygotsky reminds us, both the intentional removing of scaffolds by the teacher and the improvisation required to replace supports when students falter.

For example, students in science labs typically need priming regarding safety procedures. As time passes and students demonstrate that they can work safely without as much priming, the priming changes. Although priming never goes away, the safety-oriented priming of March looks and sounds different from that in September. Yet priming in science classes is about much more than using chemicals and Bunsen burners safely.

This same science teacher's priming to support his students to elaborate and explain will look and sound different in April than it did in October. In October the teacher primed his students with the tightly structured direction, "Write an explanation of which of your predictions were accurate or inaccurate. Use these two sentence frames: A) My prediction that… was *accurate* because… and B) My prediction that…was *inaccurate* because…" In April this same teacher might be able to prime by saying, "We're going to discuss the accuracy of your predictions in 10 minutes. Jot some notes about this if you haven't already. Then talk with your table partner. Be ready to contribute at 10:20."

Priming Restarts and "Do-Overs"

What do we mean by priming restarts and do-overs? When a teacher sees a change in the learning community is necessary, decides action must be taken, and primes for the action, this is priming a restart. Restarting the lesson, the activity, the procedure—it is okay to publicly acknowledge the need for a "do-over."

Formative assessors give themselves and their students permission to address the feelings of failure that accompany an instructional plan gone awry, a whole class conversation fumbled, even a quiz or exit slip that led to particularly poor results.

Calling a "do-over" out loud gives everyone a fresh start. Like a "time-out," it sends the signal, "Hey folks, it's time to revisit one or more classroom agreements."

Javier, a middle school Spanish teacher, told us about the power of the restart when the first round of priming falters:

> I simply need to bite the bullet and reflect on how, why, and what we do to build relationships, deepen understanding, and reflect in our learning community. My challenge is how to do a restart midway through the year so that a new stage is set and our learning community moves to develop deeper reflection and relationships amongst *all*. I want it to be more of a mutual shift in our learning process and community, however, as opposed to a change imposed only from the top down.

We applaud Javier's courage and commitment. He planned to follow through on priming the restart by involving his students: "I want to brainstorm with my students some question strategies and question examples that we can all use." Smart move!

He also told us, "We'll revisit our classroom agreements, the ones we created together at the start of the year. I bet students can identify areas to add to or change so that our classroom is primed to be a better landscape for formative assessment."

Priming restarts is not easy. We were encouraged by Javier, who was in his fifth year of teaching:

> I am not a person stuck in my ways. I am willing and eager to tweak, reflect on, and move forward in my understanding and practices in the classroom. I want to better understand who my students are, what they are thinking, and what, how, and why they are learning.

> Although I worked hard at the start of the year and I feel that we have a good learning environment, I also feel I can, we can, always work to improve it. We still have about 15 students who freeze when I ask them a question. We can do better.

We *can* do better as formative assessors. Above all, priming for each and every FA move presumes we can. Every instructional transition needs to be primed for success. Priming inspires us to circle back. We all need gentle reminders about how to proceed and to live up to our agreements. Priming moves help to orchestrate concrete support for students who are struggling to keep on topic and to experience school as a place to learn.

Learning to Look Back: Reflections on the Just-Taught Lesson

What if all our lessons were just like first drafts? What if beginning to improve your formative assessment practice, required us—teacher educators, school administrators, educational policy makers—to acknowledge your ongoing development toward becoming professional educators in your school community? What if we started seeing all teachers—"expert and novice" and "experienced and newbie"—as potential formative assessors who could directly benefit from positive, specific, timely, and content-related feedback on "next steps" for revising their lessons? What if we could just admit—without guilt or shame—that priming is a difficult move? Period.

Here is what Kevin, a veteran of the Iraq war with a passion for teaching social studies in the California classroom, found as he unpacked the "priming challenges" in his just-taught lessons:

> I have two consistent priming challenges. The first is engaging all my students. I always like lively discussions in class, but I understand that my energy and demeanor can seem intimidating to young students struggling with their command of language and subject matter. I have been building in more think-pair-share opportunities so that students can address the subject with each other before I call on them to share with me and the entire class. I have also tried small group discussions. I should be able to work in some gallery walks where students can share ideas anonymously. We do interactive notebooks and quick writes or exit tickets to provide better insight into student understanding and frustrations, and I engage students while patrolling during our class work activities. I will incorporate more think-pair-share opportunities because I have a good community and they work well with each other and seem to respond to ideas brought up in class, but few students want to discuss those ideas with me. This technique matters because the more voices we have contributing in class, the better the group as a whole will function. Students invited into contributing their knowledge and expertise will be less likely to want to disrupt a class where they are likely to contribute.
>
> The second priming challenge is my timing for students to pause for understanding. I talk fast. Back east, we all talk fast. When I am trying to cover as much history as I can in a tight 45-minute class, I want to move through material quickly. Pausing for 20 seconds to wait for a response seems like an

eternity of dead air. There are several things that I can try to build in a routine to wait for students to respond. One routine is to take a sip of coffee or water, or walk across the room to get something or move something. I have a watch, but looking at my watch might convey a sense that I am impatient and want to move on (which I am, and I do, but I don't want the students to see that). I am trying to develop the courage to stay calm. This technique is important because if I appear comfortable and relaxed as we engage the material, more students will try to emulate that behavior. If I pause just long enough to let every student think through their ideas, then they will be less frustrated with the material and themselves.

In sharing this reflection, our goal is simple. We invite you to consider how you would coach teachers (yourself included) who are struggling to become formative assessors. Labeling teachers "novice" or "preservice" or "ineffective" or "needs improvement" is unlikely to produce much insight or improvement in the practices we've outlined in this chapter. There is no evaluation tool or data management system on the horizon that will provide formative feedback to teachers learning how to become formative assessors. It's up to us. We need to prime expectations and provide supports (including "do-overs") for a new growth mindset to take hold in our profession.

We are sure that Kevin would not benefit much from receiving a score, a letter grade, or a ranking based on whether we "somewhat agree" he primes his class on a regular basis. Rather than pretend our summative teacher evaluation tools have formative purposes, it is better to engage in the kinds of deep, sustained formative assessment practices that allow Kevin and others like him to grow and develop along a learning progression with clear criteria, exemplar documents, and (fallible, foible-filled) human coaching.

If, as Margaret Heritage reminds us, formative assessment is a systematic process to continuously gather evidence about learning and Sadler's (1989) insight that the true purpose of formative assessment for teachers is to narrow the gap between where they are with practicing a particular move, where they can go with coaching and support, and how to narrow the spread between what is actual and what is possible "at the next level," then our work has only just begun.

Kevin, like so many other novice formative assessors, will need our guidance. As his mentors, we will have to do the heavy lifting by providing him with formative feedback—on his instructional moves, his lesson plans, even the video we use to debrief "what was working well" and "what can be improved."

Throughout this book, we will invite all teachers into the practice of thinking through their ongoing, evolving project—to make more assessment moves that address the tremendous yet rewarding struggle of teaching and "re-teaching" the imperfect lesson. Perhaps by seeing the lesson-as-text—as well as seeing the teacher-as-author struggling to convey meaning to an audience—we can reset the clock on teacher evaluation and accountability together (Lovell, Duckor, & Holmberg, 2015).

Putting It All Together

In classroom learning communities, priming—in all its myriad forms—readies learners, eases transitions, supports risk-taking, and involves students directly in "the work." Like priming a surface so that it's ready for a new coat of paint, we prime in classrooms to set up and support our communities for new learning. As Radhika, one of our student teachers, wrote: "Priming is like painting; if you want the top coat to shine, you should definitely prime. The same holds for students: if you want your students to shine, you should prime them for what's ahead."

As teachers, however, it is not our goal to "paint over" what is in the minds and hearts of our learners. We don't just add a coat of new learning. As professionals we know this is not how students learn. It's not how learning communities function.

High school English teacher Tyson observed, "I think of priming as unraveling the first thread in a knot, the knot being the affective filter." We think Tyson's metaphor offers important insights worth reflecting on for those becoming formative assessors, and for those supporting them. What would it take to unravel the knot of cognitive, affective, and cultural demands of formative assessment—with your students, in your classes, in your school, in your community?

Throughout this book, we are simply learning to think about student thinking and learning more reflectively. But to do so, we need to first think about what we say and hear every day in the classroom. To be an effective formative assessor who captures a wide range of student experience with the curriculum, we need to practice our speaking and listening skills and set up (prime) routines and habits that invite richer engagement. We also need a few new frames for thinking about the give-and-take experiences in the classroom among students and teachers. Priming is a move that gets everyone involved in habits of mind, heart, and work that help make learning visible.

Using the Assessment Triangle and What the Experts Know to Guide Us

As we move forward in the next several chapters mapping out our moves, let's take a moment to review the logic behind formative assessment from the assessment experts' perspective. In *Knowing What Students Know: The Science and Design of Educational Assessment,* a panel of experts made an argument that we should take seriously as teachers: "Every assessment [should be] based on three interconnected elements: a theory of what students know and how they develop competence in a subject domain (*cognition*); tasks or situations used to collect evidence about student performance (*observation*); and a method for drawing inferences from those observations (*interpretation*) (National Research Council, 2001, p. 36).

Visually, the elements and connections among the three vertices are represented in Figure 1.1.

Key to the logic of assessment is the notion that everything rests on how students learn and master a subject. We must carefully attend to cognition; that is, our assessment strategies and tools should be appropriate to a well-defined set

Figure 1.1   The Assessment Triangle

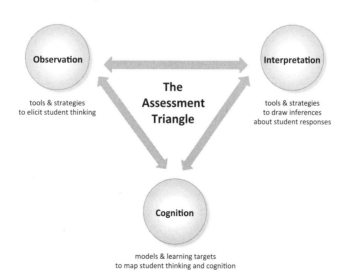

Source: National Research Council (2001).

of learning targets. In this book, we refer to these learning targets as Habits of Mind, higher-order thinking skills, and a host of other taxonomical reference points that guide the curriculum (e.g., Bloom's and Structure of Observed Learning Outcomes (SOLO) taxonomy, Webb's Depth of Knowledge levels). Choosing meaningful learning targets is half the battle—meaning that we need to carefully assess students to discover what they know and can do.

Moreover, the NRC report also emphasizes that it is "crucial" that "each of the three elements… not only must make sense on its own, but also must connect to each of the other elements in a meaningful way to lead to an effective assessment and sound inferences" (p. 49). Formative assessors who embrace the journey in this book will want to think more and more about the quality of their inferences, the evidence trail provided by each move, and the "soft data" supporting their decisions to reteach or skip ahead in a lesson or unit.

Let us be clear: these first principles of good assessment design apply not only to traditional summative test instruments, but also to classroom assessment done well. The challenges of aligning classroom-based practices of formative assessment—the moves—with these principles may seem daunting. Our goal in this book is to help. We want you to live out these first principles of the science and design of formative assessment with your students. We want to help you become a formative assessor by making moves that make a difference. The assessment triangle guides our journey because it represents what matters for the valid and reliable use of assessment data to better instruction and learning. See Figure 1.2, p. 42.

CASE STUDY

Priming: Nathan's Case

When I began thinking about how priming moves differ from explaining directions, my priming grew by leaps and bounds. Just about all direction-giving is a kind of priming. When we tell students, for example, *Take a minute to think about this, and the way I want you to respond is [fill in the blank]*, we're giving directions and priming.

But not all priming is direction-giving. Priming can, and should, communicate more than what actions need to happen in class. These aspects of priming play an essential role in supporting the development of a classroom culture that is rich with formative assessment. For example, when we make moves to normalize our students not knowing something—yet!—this is priming that isn't about giving directions. In my high school physics class this might sound like: *Now, at this point, I know none of you knows how to get the answer to this question, unless for some reason you studied ahead. But by the end of today we are going to learn, and we are actually going to calculate how much energy in joules (J) we need to completely transform a 1-kilogram block of ice at 0-degree Celsius ice into 100-degree steam.*

I think of this as *context-giving priming.* In my classroom this kind of priming often sounds like: *We are doing this because* x; or *Lots of students experience this as* y; or *Be on the lookout for* z; or *Don't be discouraged if* q *happens, since often that's a sign that* r, *which is* s.

There's a strong sense of reassurance with such priming. There's probably science behind how reassuring students through cognitively oriented statements (e.g., *These are the reasons why*) or affectively oriented ones (e.g., *I know you'll be able to do this eventually; I believe in your capabilities*) helps them shift into states of mind more conducive to problem-solving and metacognition. Sometimes, this reassurance is as simple as getting students' beliefs out where we can all (potentially) see them, making their beliefs visible to themselves, me, and their classmates, and then I can tell the class, *Okay, these are reasonable things to think about and to believe. We've not come to the answer yet. We're going to think about all this.* Deep, genuine respect gets conveyed through such priming. Every learner merits this respect.

I love rules of thumb for teaching (e.g., If a student can do it, a student should). My mentor teacher was fond of saying: *If you're reading every word students write for your lab assignments or if you need to explain every detail again and again, your students aren't working hard enough to evaluate their own progress and see if they are on the right path.*

I'm not sure there's a rule of thumb about or an optimal ratio regarding priming-that-is-strictly-direction-giving to priming that is much more than direction-giving. Such a ratio would probably depend on what students are used to and what you're trying to do with them. I bet it's safe to say, though, that boosting your present ratio more toward "context-giving priming" is likely to noticeably influence classroom culture. My students need to know why we are doing things and how that matters to being a scientist—not just that they need to do "the work."

It took me a while to realize just how much what other teachers did with students before and after my class affected how students functioned in my class. This jumped out at me the year we got a new economics teacher. My physics students derived benefits from this teacher's class, where they were debating claims and presenting evidence. Students from his classes seemed more comfortable defining preconceived notions, challenging presumptions, and interrogating evidence than other years and groups of

(continued)

students. I realize this is an oversimplification. But there's something to it. That's part of why sharing a common language with colleagues around what you're trying to do with formative assessment helps. In areas where other teachers, coaches, and family members are especially strong in supporting students, I seem to need to prime less.

I also realized that my priming could get better if I checked in with students more often about what was going on in class and in their lives. Sounds so basic, but it's true. Although I want to anticipate how students are going to react—what will puzzle them, what misconceptions they'll likely hold—I can't always. I have to come back to what students are telling me about their experiences and their thinking, and check that information with the story I'm telling myself about how class might unfold, should unfold, *is* unfolding.

So I have to prime myself for the unexpected. If I'm not open to what is actually happening with my students, which includes what I can't expect, how can I formatively assess well? I'll miss much. I probably do. It's inevitable, I suppose. There are, after all, limits to what a teacher can process, compute, integrate, and act on during class. Yet I'm convinced that skillfully using formative assessment moves can help me notice more that's critical to my students and make better decisions based on the evidence—and that priming plays a pivotal role.

Figure 1.2   Using FA Moves with the Assessment Triangle Supports Better Instructional Decision Making

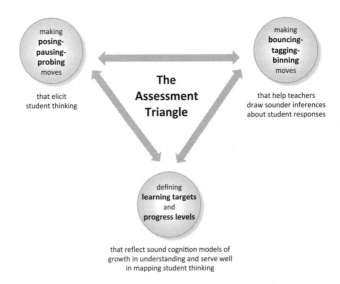

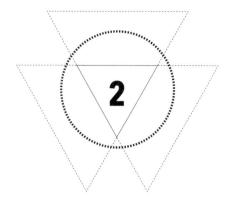

Posing

Pose questions that empower. Students learn by engaging meaningful questions and asking questions themselves. The sound of learning comes when students are comfortable giving responses, all kinds of responses. It is important to refrain from asking only questions that yield absolute answers.

Bill, beginning middle school teacher

When you pose open-ended questions, feel free to rule with an iron fist.

Ian, beginning high school teacher

Bill's and Ian's advice to other beginning formative assessors reveals important reasons *to pose* and some of the challenges *of posing*. Like many of his much more experienced teacher-colleagues, Bill is convinced that the art and science of posing questions is essential to learning, related to power, tied to student voice, and inextricably woven into the fabric of classroom community.

We agree and so would Ian (now). We highlight Ian's advice because it reveals an aspect of posing critical to consider—discomfort in using open-ended questions alongside the real needs for order, control, and tidy boxes to capture student answers efficiently. Beginners feel this acutely.

We think it's fair to push back on posing. We can and should ask: how *do* teachers balance students' need to speak in order to learn—and the time, risks, and messiness that speaking-to-learn entails—with moving through the "material"? How can we stay on track and keep focused on the day's learning objective when we must make more time for language demands and language learners than ever before? How can we formatively assess and make the grade each night, so to speak?

Such are the tensions, challenges, and vulnerabilities inherent in mastering formative assessment moves. The journey requires asking: *Why* pose? For *what* purposes? For *whose* good?

The journey in this book invites us to live out our answers in our classrooms, with our students. A focus on *posing*'s role—and *why* posing functions as it does—will put the kinds of tensions, challenges, and vulnerabilities Ian's advice raises front and center. With him, we will feel the need to resist questioning. We, too, share the anxiety of needing the "right question" for the right time and place.

Becoming a formative assessor asks us to engage our students in a world filled with questions. It asks us to stop hiding behind canned questions and to invent a few on the fly. Meanwhile, posing moves also aim to support those students who struggle with asking and answering questions in real time—without the comfort of technology or having memorized the correct answer.

As we promote learning, community, and our own professional growth and satisfaction in this journey, we begin with a question mark.

What Is Posing?

Posing. What comes to mind?

Standing still. Prom photos. "Quiet on the set!"

The definition of "to pose" is "to present or constitute (a problem, danger, or difficulty)" or "to assume a particular attitude or position in order to be photographed, painted, or drawn." Considering the definition can help us conceptualize the potential of posing moves in classroom learning communities. Posing can cut to the core of content, introduce a big idea, highlight the essentials, invite deeper concentration, and involve students directly in the work of engaging their Habits of Mind (Meier, 1995).

As these definitions suggest, posing powerful questions can cause, produce, and create the conditions for learning. But posing is also fraught with problems, dangers, and difficulty. Posing can get you in trouble. Recall Socrates and Galileo: One was put to death; the other put on trial. Luckily today, things are not so risky for those who raise questions and eyebrows at the same time.

As with posing for a portrait that has already been primed, we want formative assessors "to assume a particular attitude and disposition" toward the practice of questioning. We wish to see flexibility and commitment. Take a risk, relax that iron fist.

Using "good questions" is critical. Yet rather than encourage beginning formative assessors to find, create, and stick with "the right" question, we encourage teachers to be flexible in the range and types of questions they use. Some questions will invite openings into students' thought processes. Others, inevitably, will cloud up thoughts more than they clarify. We can learn from both. As formative assessors, we take responsibility for getting better at making strategic decisions about posing: when, how often, to whom, on which occasions, and why. We mix it up. We adjust.

Formative assessors along with Vygotsky and other educational psychologists use questions to gauge the zone of proximal development for each learner. Questions help to size up where students are, where they might be, and how far they can go with more support (Shepard, 2005). Formative assessors adjust questions for particular kids, contexts, and content, and they flexibly access and skillfully use both higher-order questions ("Why do you say that?" "When does that hold?" "Where is this most likely to occur?") and lower-order questions ("Who said that?" "Can you define it?" "How does this process work?").

Working one-on-one or whole class, formative assessors strive to avoid "Posing Overload." Asking too many challenging—or rhetorical—questions in rapid succession, without providing spaces or scaffolds for students to engage, induces Posing Overload. But as beginning formative assessors focus attention on their posing practices—and how students react to them—they often don't stay with such amateur moves for long.

Above all, when it comes to the practice of posing, formative assessors demonstrate in their dispositions a commitment to developing strategic and conscious decision making regarding posing. This commitment rests on caring and compassion for what students think, say, and do. Curiosity also counts, doesn't it?

Posing Is What You Already Do

"Did you get your homework done, Ms. Sanchez?" "Mr. Pham, I noticed you didn't have a chance to complete your exit slip yesterday, can you take a minute before class starts to do it?" "Does everyone have the notes from yesterday's lab? Who can summarize for us?"

Day in and day out we pose questions—sometimes for the purpose of review, other times to get on the same page as our students, most of the time to direct the class's attention. Posing questions is so routine that we forget to notice it.

Consider the following examples:

As a PBS documentary finishes with 10 minutes left in class, the teacher goes to the computer and types an exit question: "What were *causes* of the Cold War?" She asks students to write three or four sentences and collects their answers as they file out.

A bowling ball is positioned next to a fish tank. The teacher asks her students, "Will this bowling ball sink or float? Consult your table partners and use your Predict-Observe-Explain graphic organizer." As the students work, she reminds them, "Remember, state your explanation for your prediction!" After a few minutes, the teacher follows up, "Before we drop the ball into the tank, can anyone share a prediction and say why your table thinks the bowling ball will sink?" Following that discussion, the teacher asks, "Is there another prediction—can someone say why your table partner thinks the bowling ball will float?"

After working for two weeks on the Civil Rights movement, the teacher asks his students to prepare for an essay question. He hands out a paper with the question at the top: "Should the integration of public facilities extend beyond the ruling on education addressed by the *Brown v. Board of Education* decision?" The teacher reminds students that there are many questions couched within this one big question. "Let's go on 'Pose Patrol' and break this question down a bit," he says. "Can anyone help me with the meaning of *integration, public facilities, ruling*, and *decision*? Underline the terms, then turn to your table partner and explain them in your own words."

The art teacher asks her students, "After looking at these cubist paintings and the graffiti from New York subway cars, can you see a connection between the two? How are they similar and how are they different?"

The biology teacher asks, "What is the structure and function of the cardiovascular system? Can anyone help us represent the parts of the system?"

The math teacher asks, "What if we solved this problem algebraically rather than arithmetically? Why do we need to define variables before solving a word problem?"

The music teacher asks, "Does anyone have perfect pitch? Who? How would we know? What's our evidence?"

When we bring a spirit of inquiry—a commitment to asking about the world—to our classrooms, we are modeling the work of teaching and learning. Posing is the alpha move, the way forward in creating a classroom learning environment built on the first principles of pedagogical science. Aristotle, Plato, and Socrates knew the value of posing. Socrates, in particular, knew a teacher must teach by constantly assessing understanding through questioning. Your journey in mastering formative assessment moves begins when you embrace the art of posing as fundamental—for you, for your students, for the wider community that relies on your lessons to build and nurture a democratic society.

How to Approach Posing

But how best to face the challenges of posing "good" questions that advance students' understanding?

We maintain that posing "powerful," "good," and "effective" questions is best approached with a focus on learning goals and targets (Brookhart & Nitko, 2006). Deciding on clear goals for lessons and units isn't easy, but it's essential to posing questions that matter.

We need to acknowledge, too, that as teachers we lead students to more than just lesson and unit goals. Every classroom has other explicit and implicit learning goals. Some are part of the so-called "hidden curriculum" (Dewey, 1916; Jackson, 1968; Snyder, 1970; Apple, 1979; Anyon, 1980); others are spelled out on posters and newsletters: "We strive for academic excellence." "Read now, read forever." "Students will demonstrate skills in resolving conflicts through positive, nonviolent actions." "Everyone has a stake in understanding science!" Through these goals and aspirations, we work to embed meaningful experiences and purpose in the curriculum. We also hope to support and encourage our students' academic, vocational, and social and emotional development, as they prepare for college and work.

The challenges of agreeing on what is worth posing to students gets complicated: by subject matter specializations, by competing policy interests, by how schooling is delivered and organized (Siskin & Little, 1995). In middle and high schools, in particular, we tend to think of ourselves as math teachers, English teachers, or music teachers first. This has implications for what we want to see posed, to whom, and when. It makes deciding—or agreeing—on a set of questions for the student body incredibly challenging.

Using the Assessment Triangle for Making Better Moves

We suggest approaching the challenges—and rewards—of posing from a different angle: by setting out a framework for posing moves we can all agree makes sense. Rather than try to provide readers with a collection of golden, foolproof questions, this chapter—and our framework—leans into the logic behind posing.

Why? Because understanding the logic behind posing—*from a formative assessor's point of view*—empowers us to create, curate, and use a constellation of questions that have the strongest chances of working well with our own students in our own teaching and learning contexts. See Figure 2.1.

Figure 2.1   Using the Assessment Triangle for Making Better Posing Moves

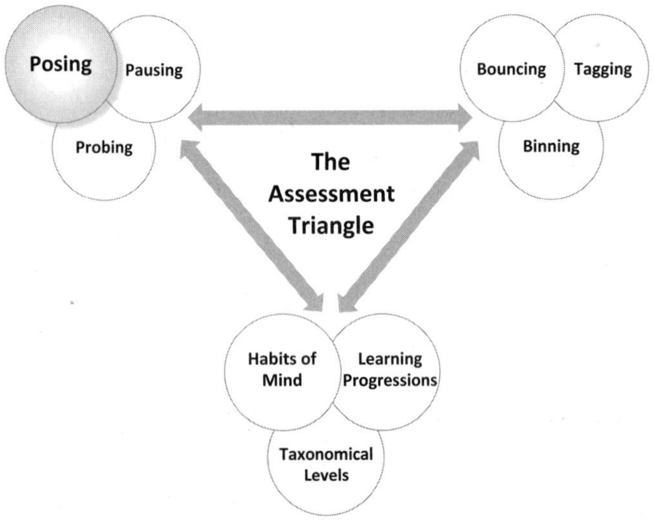

Following the NRC Council's advice, in this chapter we will remind ourselves of the centrality of connecting questions (oral or written, prompts or tasks, on the fly or planned) to each of the other elements in the assessment triangle. The goal is to develop a repertoire of posing-pausing-probing routines in the observation vertex that allow teachers to formatively assess in a meaningful way, leading to sound inferences.

We have noted that these first principles of assessment apply not only to traditional summative assessments, but also to the in-class practices, strategies, and tools of formative assessment. The experts' logic applies to FA moves and summative tests: we must know why particular learning targets matter and how students are expected to demonstrate what they know and can do as learners. Moreover, this pillar that we call "posing for a purpose," honors the NRC's finding that student cognition is the foundation of the assessment triangle.

The challenges of aligning in-class practices of formative assessment—the moves—with these principles may seem daunting or downright annoying. Our goal is to help ease the pain. We want you living out these first principles of good assessment design with your students. We want to help you become a formative assessor by making moves that make a difference. The assessment triangle guides our journey because it represents the first principles of all assessment design whether we are interested in the diagnostic, formative, or summative uses of our data.

In this chapter, the assessment triangle as both a metaphor and mental model reminds us that if you pose *any question* in your classroom, it is crucial that the questions have a close relationship to a learning target defined in advance. Knowing the demands and difficulty of questions you plan to pose will also help you make sounder, more valid inferences about the meaning of student responses.

 TEACHER VOICE

I find posing questions difficult. What if my questions are too simple or too difficult? How do I match them to the needs of the class as a whole? I've come to realize that posing a good question isn't about finding the correct answer, it's about the process of coming to that answer. Even "wrong" answers can be used to help further the class's learning.

—*Tony, physical education teacher*

Posing Across the Content Areas

Formatively assessing through posing moves that support making sound inferences about student responses should not be a solo endeavor. To give ourselves chances at meeting students—children—where they are, we need to work together, regardless of our content specialties. Subject matter competence matters to the extent you believe you are teaching a subject—not growing and developing *children*. Put another way, subject matter competence is necessary but not sufficient for good teaching (Shulman, 1987).

Powerful questioning, particularly posing moves infused with an interdisciplinary lens, can unite us around the work of teaching our K–12 students. Our commitment to children, to people, should inspire us to help our students make connections across disciplines. Let's highlight that in a global economy that requires citizens to guide public policy and to participate in democratic institutions, posing questions beyond familiar boundaries is fundamental. Today more than ever, the mission of schooling must be to teach our children to use their minds well. Learning to answer essential, enduring, and vexing questions is the key to the success of that mission in democratic societies.

The content and form of our posing naturally varies—by discipline and disposition. Math and music teachers helping students handle symbolic representations on the calculator and across the music sheet will have a bank of questions that differ from science and physical education teachers helping students study biological and physiological systems. Art and history teachers helping students examine social and cultural movements in particular civilizations and time periods will pose questions that differ from world languages and language arts teachers helping students learn writing conventions and the rules for engaging the audience or reader. But most teachers will agree: seeing the big picture with the help of a few good questions can make all the difference.

The key to good posing (of any question, in any format) is taking up the challenge to get individuals, small groups, and your whole class ready for formative assessment in action. Questioning lies at the heart of the FA moves framework and those actions. You might get your students warmed up by asking: *Are you all ready to answer a big question? To share a response whether you think it's right or wrong? To present a point of view today to help us get started? Okay, here we go!*

What the Research Says

Why pose? Posing helps students develop the speaking and listening skills necessary for academic, social, and workplace success. Plato reminds us that learning to ask and answer questions makes us fully human. Posing puts us all on the path to the examined life.

As Alexander (2006) notes, "Children, we now know, need to talk, and to experience a rich diet of spoken language, in order to think and to learn. Reading, writing and number may be acknowledged curriculum 'basics,' but talk is arguably the true foundation of learning." (p. 9). According to Levin and Long (1981), approximately 300 questions are posed in a single school day, most of them by teachers and falling into two broad categories: (1) closed or open, and (2) higher- or lower-order.

Some studies have tried to account for differences among subject matters in the quantity and quality of questions posed by individual teachers (e.g., Erdogan & Campbell, 2008; Kaya, Kablan, & Rice, 2014; Oliveira, 2010), but it is important to take into account the roles of context, curriculum, and the kids themselves in these observational studies. Why is it, for example, that science teachers appear to ask more higher-order questions than other teachers? Or that higher percentages of lower-order questions seem to be asked by teachers with poor subject matter knowledge? Without a deep sense of the variations in posing practices, it is hard to assess the validity of such findings.

Much of the literature also fails to consider how students' socioeconomic, linguistic, and ethnic backgrounds affect their reactions to posing, or why students from traditionally underserved communities should conform to the norms and values of an inquiry-based education. Is it possible that some teachers are afraid to pose particular kinds of questions, to particular "types" of students? Or that some school systems and cultures frown upon too much student participation? If so, we might rightly worry about why that is and seek to learn more.

Research on questioning addresses wait time, or *pausing*, which we take up in Chapter 3. Usually, teachers do not wait long enough after posing questions (Rowe, 1974; Kaya et al., 2014). When they do, research tells us the most common discourse pattern in classrooms is still I-R-E, for a teacher's Inquiry, followed by one student's Response, followed by the teacher's Evaluation of that response (Mehan, 1979; Kaya et al., 2014). In Chapter 3 we'll explore challenges and opportunities of pausing. For now, let's keep the focus on posing for a purpose.

On one point the research *is* clear: posing can make a difference for student outcomes. Learning how to think more powerfully about any subject requires asking and answering questions, and students cannot follow our lead unless we provide them with on-ramps to join the conversation. Nor can we expect students to voice their nascent understandings if their contributions are ignored.

Successful teachers recognize the promise and possibilities of creating safe talking and listening spaces (Palincsar & Brown, 1984). According to Chin and Osborne (2010), the use of effective posing moves is associated with teachers who provide lots of scaffolds and entry points for classroom discussion.

Christenbury and Kelly (1983) also found that scaffolding encourages students to engage more with teachers' questions.

Henning and colleagues note that effective posing is often absent from mathematics instruction in U.S. schools:

> In comparison with their international counterparts in Germany and Japan, mathematics teachers within the United States spend a majority of their instructional time illustrating symbolic manipulation of isolated procedures for students, breaking down complex tasks into manageable chunks for ease of student comprehension, and providing assistance and direction to students at the first tangible sign of struggle or confusion. In contrast, German and Japanese mathematics teachers present integrated and more challenging mathematical concepts to students through the use of problematic and realistic contexts, structure classroom discussions that lead to the construction of relationships between mathematical concepts and procedures, and facilitate the interactive and productive struggle of students through reasoning and communication. (Stigler and Hiebert, 1999)
>
> Thus, US school mathematics is often dominated by contrived, textbook-generated examples of symbolic manipulations that students have been trained to copy verbatim and without question. (Henning, McKeny, Foley, & Balong, 2012, p. 454)

A lack of effective posing isn't limited to the mathematics instructional practices observed in this report—we all can pose better. Posing questions is an equal opportunity provider. With support and coaching and feedback, our questioning strategies will get better.

Going Deeper with Posing

It is often said we learn by doing. Let's add that we also learn by asking. Consider children learning to make sense of the world: at some point in their development they start rattling everyone with a barrage of nonstop questions. "Why, Daddy?" "Why, Nana?" "Why, Tio?" "Why?"

Little children feel the power of questioning—questions get attention. Yet somewhere along the course of child development, those playful, bold verbalizations of curiosity recede. The young child learns that becoming an adult means not asking so many questions.

Questioning, however, is essential. In a democratic society, we want people to question authority. We demand answers to pressing questions—about taxes, healthcare, and the environment. To solve our complex problems we need to ask powerful questions. One of the most fundamental learning goals in public education is the aim that every student can ask and answer questions (Dewey, 1990). Our children must have the habits, capacities, and skills to think freely and use their Habits of Mind (Meier, 1995). Posing questions is fundamental to developing these Habits.

Whether you teach algebra, fine arts, physics, or French, the challenge is to foreground questioning in daily classroom routines (Walsh & Sattes, 2015, 2016). We all have the power to write a question on the board. Every class can highlight powerful disciplinary queries posed to all.

Perhaps most significantly, teachers can—and ought to—do this work together as formative assessors. If schools are to build *connections* across departments, posing can play a role to facilitate new dialogues. Teachers and students together can and should explore cross-cutting skills and concepts in the curriculum. The "essential" questions they commit to engaging in a community can lead their explorations and discoveries. We say it's time to pose: but what questions might unite us in this cross-curricular vision of teaching and learning?

First let's consider how we already connect around learning goals for K–12 students.

 FORMATIVE ASSESSMENT TIPS

Finding Common Ground

Let's zoom out a bit. We believe that learning goals should drive the work of formative assessment. Although teachers will disagree on what counts as progress and which content is worth learning, we can probably all agree on the following basic goals for our students. We want evidence that our students

- Understand the material
- Are ready for the next class in the subject area
- Are prepared for college or the workplace
- Know how to work smarter with new tools
- Are able to pick themselves up and try again when they fall short

No matter where we are in the K–12 system, surely these are goals that we all can embrace.

Planning for Posing: Guiding Questions

Developing lessons and unit plans that emphasize the art of posing is no small task. Neither is generating *questions that matter* for your students. Whether you are planning by yourself, as a department, or as a school faculty, the following questions can guide you. Think of these three questions as an "unskippable warm-up phase" of lesson development and unit planning.

1. Why is this lesson important?

Review your unit plan or two to three of the lessons you have planned for the week. Humbly and honestly ask yourself: why would any of my students actually care to learn this material, do these activities, or take my quizzes and tests? You must be able to identify the *relevance* of each lesson for your students. If you can't describe why the lesson is important or how it connects to the real world, then it's no surprise if students don't pay attention. No amount of classroom management can disguise a lack of curricular purpose or a paucity of learning targets.

And it's not just students who ask, "So what? Why study this? Why is it important?" Administrators, parents, and policymakers—from their differing perspectives and viewpoints—will ask about lessons: How do these questions fit into a larger curriculum and preparation for college and work? Do they connect to a big idea that animates the field and informs professionals and practitioners? How do these questions engage students in higher-order thinking? Will these queries help students move toward greater depths of understanding, making connections between subjects more visible? To what extent are our questions—in writing prompts or call-and-response mode—aligned with current standards and standardized tests that require students to explain and justify their responses?

All stakeholders have a right to know why our lessons matter, and we have a responsibility to provide answers. As professionals, we can and should provide insight to others into what makes our work with our students powerful: it's not just the responses students provide, it's also *the questions they wrestle with as lifelong learners,* moving toward career and college goals (Dewey, 1900, 1920).

2. How will these particular questions yield insight into the discipline and student thinking more generally?

Recall the assessment triangle. Before we can start writing good questions to pose in our classes, we have to wrap our minds around the larger learning goals and targets of our curriculum. These learning targets—which may be big ideas, essential questions, or higher-order thinking skills—form the first vertex of the NRC's Assessment Triangle.

Knowing what the learning target is and why it's important for your students is a critical first step in deciding which questions can and should anchor the learning enterprise. Consider the following example.

> At the beginning of a 6th grade math class, students are individually working on a complex do-now problem about building and painting a fence that requires them to distinguish area from perimeter. After several minutes, the teacher gets her students' attention and asks, "So, how did you know how much paint to buy for this project?"
>
> Dawn looks down at her shoes. Victor sighs. Rana starts chewing on her pencil. Trevor looks the teacher in the eye and shoots up his hand. Tina, Cassandra, and Ricardo also raise their hands. "I didn't finish," blurts Vanessa. "2 gallons!" shouts Devi.
>
> "As I walked around, I saw you tackling this problem in many different ways," says the teacher. "Now, take two minutes to compare your approach to the problem with that of your elbow partner. It's okay if you didn't finish solving it."
>
> The students pair up and the room starts to buzz. The teacher works her way through the entire classroom, making out snatches of dialogue: "drew the fence," "wrote down what I know," "I'm stuck," "added up the sides," "multiplied," "this is stupid," "try the area," "is that the perimeter?" As the teacher circulates, she looks at the students' worksheets to see who approached the problem arithmetically, who approached it algebraically, and who didn't finish solving it. In this way, she can calibrate how best to proceed with the lesson.

The teacher chose a simple but challenging prompt, the crux of which is embedded in the essential question, "How do you know?" Her query yielded a gold mine of cognitive and affective responses from the students. The treasure trove of student responses is the raw material we need to decide where we are and which next steps to take *during* the lesson. The various moves the teacher employed—the do-now assignment, the pair-share exercise, the walk around— invited students to provide *evidence* of their reasoning. It also allowed her to see patterns in typical responses: some of which were on task, others which were mired in procedural errors, and still others that seemed to lack the degree of conceptual understanding she was aiming for in the lesson.

Yes, more probing on students' initial responses is both warranted and necessary. We know that student responses (just like test scores) vary by mood, energy, even time of day. So we need to probe further to uncover the meaning and dependability of these preliminary student responses. We'll explore mastering probing moves in Chapter 4. For now, let's agree that though the students need more opportunities to elaborate on their answers, the question-prompt has purchase. It provided the formative assessor with soft data as a basis for making sound instructional decisions while meeting the needs of the students for more support and practice.

Part of the power of posing questions is knowing which questions are actionable. Questions, prompts, or requests that hit the mark allow the teacher to begin learning from her students' responses. To size up. To make sense. To figure out the feedback needed to move learning forward. But not all questions work equally well in helping set up such moments and opportunities. That's what makes posing so scary and risky. Assessment experts know this. They spend years assembling, fine-tuning, and eventually deploying their foolproof items for high-stakes tests. Formative assessors in the classroom can do the same. But we will need one another to share ideas, pool resources, and figure out what's working and what can be improved in our posing practices.

3. At each turn of this lesson, which kinds of student responses ("correct," "misconceptions," "unorthodox") are anticipated by your questions and prompts?

With practice, formative assessors can get better at formulating questions that meet their learning goals and instructional purposes. For example, to elicit a wide variety of student responses—that might later be categorized into many different bins—we ask *open* questions. Open-ended questions with appropriate scaffolding also can serve to activate students' prior knowledge and prime their cognitive motors for action (Harmin, 1998).

Asking the most open questions possible works well to start class brainstorming sessions at the beginning of any new unit. We've also seen open Prime-Pose-Prime combos used as anticipatory sets and lesson hooks to good effect: "Today we are going to share our ideas with a word web [Prime]. I am going to ask: 'What comes to mind when you hear the word *function*?' [Pose] Remember, there are no right or wrong answers [Prime]."

To help uncover students' misconceptions, posing thoughtfully constructed *closed* questions can serve other purposes just as admirably. For example,

Nathan, a physics teacher who student-taught at a local high school, posed the following multiple choice question to discover which of his students shared a common misconception about transfer of energy (a common misconception is to think that heating something always results in increasing its temperature).

By constructing an assessment task that formatively diagnosed which students would choose (incorrectly) either answer choice B or C, Nathan committed himself to checking for prior knowledge before he began a lab demonstration that day. He posed the following query:

A cup of 0°C ice water stands in the sun on a hot day. Predict what will happen during the first minute:

    A) the ice will begin to melt,

    B) the water will increase in temperature, or

    C) both of the above.

Nathan read the prompt twice, asked students to choose a group that best represented their point of view, and then circulated around the classroom to check for understanding of the task and prompt. In addition to these priming moves, his posing with higher-order "analysis" and "prediction" level questions was also accompanied by other moves such as pausing, bouncing, and tagging to make student thinking visible—in fewer than seven minutes.

Each learning situation will call for its own mix of questions. We predict that formative assessors, given the right circumstances and conditions, will begin to develop and catalogue their own "item banks" to be drawn upon unit by unit, lesson by lesson, minute by minute. Remember that it is okay to differentiate your questioning strategies with multiple "item bank" accounts: *Who, what, when, how,* and *why* questions can all be valuable when used strategically. Eventually you will find better ways to parse and employ your questions. For now, the goal is to get started.

Remember there is no perfect question or magical prompt! We do not ascribe to the cult of the "deep" versus "surface" question debates. *Why* questions, lauded by many educators because they purportedly elicit higher-order thinking can, in fact, fall flat in the classroom. Academic language load, affective filters, and extraneous cognitive demands can interfere with students' best responses to so-called higher-order questions. There is a benefit to asking these sorts of questions as they can sometimes give teachers rich student responses. But these open-ended "deeper" questions can also trigger defensive reactions, throwing us off the evidence trail, especially if we ask on the fly without appropriate wait time or proper scaffolding.

Why not try constructing questions that get at *why* without using the word *why* in the stem? *What might explain X? What do you attribute that to? What are some reasons for X we can think of?* could yield a different, less anxiety-provoked response from your students.

To construct questions that require—and anticipate—higher-order thinking, we must become reacquainted with the action verbs from, for example, Bloom's taxonomy. Bloom's and other taxonomies (e.g., Biggs & Collis, 1982) can serve as scaffolds for building question shells and maps. However, we recommend for the emerging formative assessor at first using softer, more inviting wording than *predict*, *justify*, or *evaluate* in your lesson. Instead try to pose a more inviting question: *What might happen under these conditions? Can you share your prediction with your partner and then share with us your reasons for the conclusion? If you were ranking these predictions from "very likely" to "not very likely," what would your group base its decision on?*

Principles for Posing: Posing Is More Than Learning to Question

Context is critical and teachers play the most important role in helping create contexts that support deep posing. Teachers do so by having an aim, a goal, and a set of guiding principles to assist their work in supporting a culture that encourages deeper questioning. We offer the case of Central Park East Secondary School (CPESS) to illustrate and inspire about what's behind the real work of posing for a larger purpose.

At CPESS, a small school in East Harlem, New York, a group of teachers were guided by Habits of Mind, or what assessment experts who use the NRC's Assessment Triangle call a theory of *cognition*. The Habits of Mind formed the cornerstone of the curriculum and essential schoolwide learning goals at both the middle and high school. Through this cognitive lens, the teachers sought to develop interdisciplinary courses to better foster their students' curiosity, intellectual engagement, and academic mastery in preparation for college. The teachers also embedded cross-cutting skills and concepts into the curriculum to promote healthy skepticism and deeper empathy, which they saw as the core of democratic thinking and global citizenship (Duckor & Perlstein, 2014).

In keeping with the school's focus on active inquiry, the schoolwide learning goals were cast as first-order questions in every subject discipline. In grades 7–12, these questions appeared in every classroom:

- How do you know what you know? (Evidence)
- From whose point of view is this being presented? (Perspective)
- How is this event or work connected to others? What causes what? (Connection)
- What if things were different? (Supposition)
- Who cares? Why is this important? (Relevance)

These middle and high school educators believed that the Habits of Mind simultaneously reflected the essential questions of intellectuals and scholars working across the range of academic disciplines and industries. Teachers used these Habits of Mind to better focus lessons on genuine, higher-order learning. Moreover, the strategic use of concepts related to *Connections*, *Perspective*, *Evidence*, *Supposition*, and *Relevance* added weight to their claims to preparing students to use their minds well, in a variety of settings and circumstances. These Habits promoted the critical thinking skills and problem-solving capacities necessary for life in a complex, ever-changing world.

The shared, authentic, and public commitment to the Habits of Mind allowed students and parents to know what was expected of them and allowed teachers to know what they could expect of one another. In the words of the school founder Deborah Meier, "to agree not only on what to teach, but also on how their teaching and their kids' learning would be assessed" (1995, pp. 49–50).

The NRC's Assessment Triangle and the CPESS example remind us that questions need to be tied to clear, explicit learning targets. For the teachers and students, the Habits of Mind were both the theory of cognition ("how and why we learn the way we do") and the learning targets ("what we know and can do") on which an authentic school-based assessment system was constructed. The careful, deliberate synthesis of schoolwide learning targets and classroom assessment practices was the foundation of what experts call assessment *for* and *of* learning (Stiggins, 2002).

We know that for formative assessment practices to be effective, we must set goals and communicate them to our students (Hattie, 2012). The Habits of Mind brought the school community together—teachers, counselors, coaches, paraprofessionals, staff, and parents. Questions tied to the Habits of Mind permeated academic and nonacademic life, including lessons, labs, and assignments; school plays and convocations; conflict mediation sessions, internship debriefings, and staff meetings. Taken together, the Habits of Mind constituted a deeply constructivist theory of student cognition that drove teaching, learning, and assessment at the school.

CPESS was a special public school and produced visible and meaningful outcomes for its students and teachers (Darling-Hammond, Ancess, & Falk, 1995; Newmann, 1996; Darling-Hammond, Ancess, & Ort, 2002; Bensman, 2000). We highlight this school, and the many others like it today, to remind ourselves that such outcomes are not only for the best of the best or the well-connected. Learning environments that are guided by Habits of Mind and animated with questions (aligned with clear, visible learning targets) are possible for every teacher and student.

Every school that has the time, energy, and resources to make changes shows its respect for teachers. Yes, teachers who are learning to become formative assessors need structural support, planning time, and a place to work out and share ideas, tools, and techniques. Teachers also need space to lead to create the kind of authentic formative assessment-rich culture that they want for their students. We think a focus on posing moves is the place to start.

🗩 TEACHER VOICE

It is up to us as teachers to make posing questions part of our classroom routine and to work at becoming better at guiding the ensuing discussion. We can always reflect on and modify our practice later. I am often hesitant to ask questions unless I have successfully mapped out every aspect of a lesson from beginning to end. Injecting more open, unpredictable questions into my practice would blow up a big chunk of my Question map, but I think that's the point—that's where some really good stuff is hidden, in the space where the students can create.

—*Roberto, 7th grade math teacher*

The teachers at CPESS and other schools in the Coalition of Essential Schools (Sizer, 1996) dared to ask a lot of public schools. They tackled tough, seemingly intractable questions: What is power and who has it? Is biology destiny? Do all functions have a limit? How does a thesis differ from a hypothesis? What difference does it make that no one uses the formal *you* in the United States? Who is responsible for war? For the students and teachers at CPESS, the deep posing that these questions supported made a difference.

Now, to help you in carrying out more intentional, more focused efforts to support deep posing in your classroom and school, we offer a few reminders.

Developing Essential Questions Aligned to Standards and Learning Targets

A good place to start building your posing repertoire is by developing a few essential questions (EQs):

- EQs have no one obvious right answer.
- EQs raise additional important questions, often across subject areas.
- EQs address the philosophical or conceptual foundations of a subject.
- EQs naturally recur.
- EQs are deliberately framed to provoke and sustain student interest.

Essential questions can set up challenging learning targets for a class (Wiggins & McTighe, 2005). Whether we refer to questions with such characteristics as *essential*, *important*, *higher-order*, or *big idea* questions, good questions will cause students to stretch, to feel a little pain, to scratch their heads, to struggle. Therefore we must always prime for the posing of questions tied to class learning targets. It can help to prime—and periodically reprime—by reminding our students that getting stuck, being confused, asking for clarification, and having breakthroughs are the ways we *all* learn.

 FORMATIVE ASSESSMENT TIPS

Priming for Posing: Connecting the Dots

Posing goes to the crux of the challenges of becoming a formative assessor: you have to want learners to trust, risk, and work together in ways that bring them toward deeper engagement with conceptually difficult material. You have to want them to use their habits of mind, heart, and work. Then you have to help make it happen, which necessitates priming. As we said in the previous chapter, priming aims to support the "FA culture" of the classroom. By priming lessons that open with a question, you are saying to your students: "This is a place where all can work together to reach learning goals" and "I trust and respect your ideas."

We offer three guiding principles to help generate better posing strategies that are based in learning theory and anchored in the first vertex of the assessment triangle.

Guiding Principle #1: Student Thinking and Academic Language Use Matter

When sitting down to write a few questions, or develop prompts for your formative assessment tool kit, start by mapping out the easy and harder ones first. Maybe you need to consult the standards for your course of study this year or semester. Or maybe it's time to review the objectives for a set of lessons in a unit. It might even help to put a copy of Webb's Depth of Knowledge or Bloom's Taxonomy on your desktop to help you map out the higher- and lower-order questions.

No doubt, the questions you pose are important. How many, how they are worded, how much space or time you provide to answer—all these considerations affect posing. Yet posing is about more than just the questions, most of which today can be easily copied from the Internet or bought from a testing company. Posing is also about the exchange between "poser" and "posee," if you will, and most importantly what this exchange of ideas implies for both participants.

Learning theory needs to inform our posing practices. Therefore, we ought to consider how insights from Piaget and Vygotsky can help us become better formative assessors, in part, by learning how both frame the relationship between the learner and the learning environment (Rogoff, 1998). At the core of the constructivist approach to teaching and learning is the notion that students will experience our questions in cultural, developmental, and linguistic terms.

In this light, we can take a few tips from those who work closely on academic language and understand the demands posing places on particular students (Hakuta, 2013). Our students need opportunities to see language (its meanings, functions, and operations) as a piece of the learning puzzle. They need explicit, visible, public representations of language in their study of science, mathematics, social studies, art, music, and physical education.

Our students need powerful experiences with the interplay between academic language and the subject content knowledge of a discipline. There are specific language conventions, turns of phrase, ways of setting up a problem, and ways of seeing an issue, even forms of communication that pervade our adult world.

We are so used to language, we forget its special power to shape and transform our thinking (Bodrova & Leong, 2007). To illustrate, consider the word *function*.

When economists talk about "functions" it is different than when scientists do. Physicians see functions differently than professional athletes or mathematicians. The word function has general and specialized meanings; it can appear in a textbook, on a product label, or as English teachers note, "in the wild." For children to acquire these habits of speech and thinking, they need models, mental tools, and scaffolds to help them make connections. Posing questions that cut across disciplines and professions can help them learn more about how adults talk, write, read, and query to make meaning.

When you pose questions in these different contexts, we suggest you unpack the academic language demands embedded in each prompt. Teach toward the new knowledge or schema your questions imply. Highlight terms and concepts such as *direct, indirect, explicit,* and *implicit,* which probably aren't going to be easy for students no matter the subject. Even seemingly easier academic language, such as *weigh*—as in "weigh the evidence" or "weigh the liquid"—will need unpacking and support.

As we've mentioned, students need your support in learning to use language in ways that are particular to a discipline or subject. You can do this by highlighting, unpacking, and providing multiple opportunities for students to use academic language in a variety of modalities. There is no separating this critical need your students have to practice—speaking, listening, responding, and answering—from your posing practices. When formative assessors prime their questions (with scaffolds, graphic organizers, and wait-time routines) their students grow more adept at using academic language across different registers (Zwiers, 2013).

Teachers who are learning to become formative assessors will appreciate the Question Map as a planning tool. Maps can be sketched on the back of a napkin or laminated for a classroom poster. Either way, question maps are a way to get control over defining learning targets and operationalizing them with questions you can, in fact, ask in a 55- or 90-minute classroom period. See Figure 2.2 (p. 67) as an example of a question map aligned with standards.

Guiding Principle #2: Define Learning Targets Carefully Based on Mental Models

Now it's time to focus on formative assessment-rich lessons that aim for developing, supporting, and promoting student learning. To get there, we need to add more texture and layers to the *student cognition/learning targets* vertex of the assessment triangle. By getting more specific about learning targets, we can uncover and unpack "the information" that drives the pursuit of classroom-based evidence that learning is "on track." Good questions point the way, but they are not the destination. If we are working with students in real-time on mastery of a challenging concept such as ratio, or acquisition of a powerful skill such as expository writing, everyone needs to know where we are headed and where we just came from.

The question for formative assessors is: how can we map these learning targets for ourselves and for our students?

We've established that there is no substitute for well-chosen, overarching learning targets. We may need and use lists of questions aligned with lesson objectives to guide the first drafts, but such lists cannot serve the crucial function of systematically defining learning targets based on, for example, Habits of Mind.

Above all, we need ways—not merely tools and tactics—that help us *characterize student responses* in relation both to our smaller, grain-sized lesson objectives and our larger-grain-sized learning targets. The point is to make question maps that help us *hone in on appropriate learning targets* for our students. (We show how later in the chapter.)

Experts in educational psychology offer us some mental models for mapping different learning targets. Organized in different ways, these taxonomies offer provisional maps for formative assessors interested in principled posing. Some mental models/maps are categorized by *levels of knowledge* such as Bloom's taxonomy or Webb's Depth of Knowledge system; others are organized by *levels of student responses* such as the Structure of Observed Learning Outcome (SOLO) taxonomy developed by Biggs and Collis (1982).

Still other sets of learning targets are sorted by *knowledge type*, for example, into declarative, procedural, schematic, and strategic knowledge. Similar to the five Habits of Mind and multiple intelligences theories of student cognition, such sets of learning targets organized by knowledge type do not necessarily imply a hierarchy, such as "of less to more." Learning targets organized around knowledge types do not imply that possessing declarative knowledge is "less valuable" than possessing procedural or strategic knowledge.

Since knowledge depends on it uses, according to this approach, there is no need to rank or scale it. All types of knowledge are needed to form good questions and probe on student understanding. Many cognitive theorists argue that skillful teachers know how and when to draw out—and scaffold—different types

Figure 2.2   Question Map

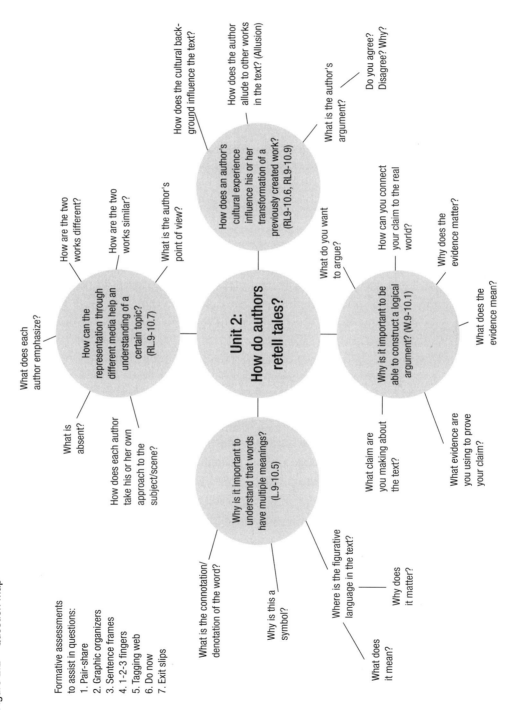

Formative assessments
to assist in questions:
1. Pair-share
2. Graphic organizers
3. Sentence frames
4. 1-2-3 fingers
5. Tagging web
6. Do now
7. Exit slips

of knowledge. These experts focus on knowledge-type use in their students at different places and times in their lessons (Shavelson, Ruiz-Primo, & Wiley, 2005).

These days many reformers want to get "back to basics" or feel the need for a "teacher-proof" curriculum to advance learning. But we know there are no shortcuts or excuses for an unthinking curriculum that chops up knowledge into neat boxes, which are disconnected from how kids think about a topic. Assessment experts (NRC, 2001) have made it clear: every good assessment begins with a theory of what students know and how they develop competence in a subject domain (*cognition*). It is the same for teachers developing a repertoire of questions to use for their posing routines, day in and day out.

Guiding Principle #3: *Use Multiple Questioning Strategies to Gain Insight into Student Learning*

We often hear that questions can be placed on continua—from lower to higher order, simple to complex, prestructural to extended abstract, surface-level to deep—the implication in all cases being that questions will vary in difficulty, and that we can anticipate their difficulty based on their category. The complaint most often lodged against teachers is that they favor lower-order questions (e.g., *who*, *what*, *when*, *where*, even *how*) over higher-order ones (e.g., *why*, *what if*). Whether true or not, we can begin to peel back the assumptions behind our question designs and rationale for their use.

Those who favor nonhierarchical question typologies add that we don't really need a continuum from easier to harder questions. The advocates for declarative, procedural, schematic, and strategic types of questions see our students' knowledge and skills falling into distinct buckets. Each bucket has its place in the classroom lesson. Classroom teachers can ask procedural and conceptual questions—they need not be related, with one ranked higher than the other. Similar to the perspective on learning advanced by the fans of multiple intelligences, the argument about which questions are best will depend largely on your learning targets.

Our stance towards learning targets and taxonomies for the formative assessor is an agnostic one. We prefer to dig into the sorts of questions, issues, and practical problems that beginners typically have with posing moves and questioning strategies. Here is what they typically tell us or say:

- How do I know what I know about effective questioning strategies in my classroom? Is there any research to back up which types of questions to use, when or with whom?

- I could pose the best questions in the world, but if I can't capture the results, look at patterns, and draw valid conclusions about what my students know and can do, it doesn't matter. Asking questions without recording answers leaves me hanging.
- I try to ask a range of questions, but I can't keep track of who got which type/level of question. Is there a way to tally who is getting which sorts of questions "correct" and who is not?
- How can I be sure that I am really understanding the meaning of Jacintha's explanation? Maybe she had a bad day, didn't eat breakfast, got in a fight with her best friend, is feeling overwhelmed. Some days kids give better, more reliable responses than others.
- Standardized tests may be difficult to take. And I can appreciate that lots of students struggle with them. But these assessments seem a whole lot more valid and reliable than me asking a bunch of "airy fairy" questions in my classes. For one thing, when I assess, everyone gets the same set of test questions, on the same piece of paper—that seems more fair. Plus when I am doing a call and response I rarely spread the same question around to everyone, adding to the sample bias.
- How do I know, on the fly, that my questions themselves are not confusing students? Poorly worded questions can lead to an unreliable picture of my students' thinking skills and abilities—just like standardized tests. It gets even more complicated: what I think is a good response another teacher might think is not. There seems to be bias in how I or another individual teacher might interpret things.

We applaud this push back. These are tough, engaging questions and observations from teachers who are learning to become formative assessors. Yes, let's use our own Habits of Mind throughout this book. We encourage great questions without easy answers! Formative assessment experts and novices need to expose the complexity, depth, and nuance of posing practices—not cover them up with buzzwords and quick tips. We need to listen better and harder to these essential questions within our community rather than look for fixes from curriculum providers or testing companies. We need to challenge one another and ourselves about the efficacy and meaning of formative assessment if we are to mount credible responses to these concerns.

Right now we invite you to post your own notes, including ahas and objections, in this chapter. Take out a sheet of paper. Write in the margins of this book.

Annotate. Underline. Throw down question marks and exclamation points. Disagree with us. Push back on what you read. But most important, start using your Habits of Mind to engage the problems of posing practice. What questions do you have for us? We are in this together.

Principles, Procedures, and Practices

Scaffolding Your Posing: Creating a Question Map

CASE STUDY

Posing: Jenny's Case

The broadness and flexibility of teaching English attracted me. I loved the infinite possibilities. I was fortunate to join a department that encouraged curricular innovation. The most valued overarching goal in the department, no matter the prep, was: *Help students become better critical thinkers and more altruistic human beings*. Awesome.

Then I would sit down to plan a unit. Suddenly "infinite possibility" made my palms sweat. Perhaps out of stubbornness, ignorance—maybe something else—I never considered using off the shelf curriculum. Nor did my department expect me to. Borrow from colleagues and create with them, yes. Download off the Internet, no. Even as my views on "others' curriculum" have evolved, I remain committed to the benefits of DIY.

Sweaty palms struck only when planning units, not individual lessons. It was an odd anxiety. It felt, momentarily, as if I had forgotten everything I'd ever learned about unit planning and the topic at hand.

I craved a sure-fire method to gain purchase and be reassured that the unit I would create and teach would be a coherent, meaningful experience for my students. Looking over state standards and district scope and sequence agreements only helped so much. I experienced a big shift when I began approaching both sets of documents through a specific lens—the Habits of Mind—and using a Question Map.

The Habits of Mind help me make sense of the verbiage, bullet points, and subheadings of the standards in ways that work for me and my students. My previous experiences with unit planning and question posing were like handling a gushing fire hydrant. The never-ending flow of standards, learning targets, and lesson objectives left me feeling knocked down and overwhelmed. I knew I was responsible for doing something useful with all of it with my students, but I didn't know how until I acquired some thought-tools (the Habits of Mind), some real tool-tools (the Question Map), and some experience at interacting with everything in play purposefully and strategically.

Of the five Habits of Mind (Connection, Perspective, Evidence, Speculation, and Relevance), I started with Evidence. The need to weigh and consider evidence cuts across many professions and much college coursework. Helping my students learn more ways to consider evidence will help them become better critical thinkers. I'm convinced of this. It's a value judgment worth making and acting on.

This gave me a starting point. Next I ask, *What are the challenges particular to English Language Arts regarding evidence?* Challenges included students not knowing how to access evidence (e.g., students who haven't done the reading, or students who have done the reading but need guidance about what to look for in terms of evidence). And challenges included students who were unsure how to analyze quotes they've chosen or how to incorporate excerpts into their arguments. These are challenges nearly all English teachers—and teachers of other subjects—face with their students.

With my challenges articulated, I then ask, *Where can I pose questions about evidence in this unit?* This order—challenges first, questions second—puts my mind to how to scaffold students for the questions I generate. As I'm brainstorming questions, I map them. I've experimented with organizing my unit question maps several ways: by "big ideas," by essential knowledge and skills I want students to acquire, and by the Habits of Mind themselves. Using the Habits of Mind as an organizing principle ensures that "So what? Why is this academic content important? Which skills must I focus on in my questioning strategies?" never gets glossed over.

Mapping my questions helps me analyze my questions while I'm planning. Is there balance? How much academic language do they feature? Which questions are deceptively complex? Which seem too easy? Or trite? What patterns do I notice? Colleagues are in a better position to help me plan when we can examine questions together. Questions are possibilities—a good space to be in with colleagues—and remind me why I want to teach!

As I teach a unit, I refer to my question map to guide checks for understanding during discussions and group work. I use my map when I'm creating prompts for quick writes and exit slips and when I'm making quizzes.

I also annotate my question map while I reflect on lessons. Which questions fell flatter than I'd expected? What priming might help? Which questions generated buzz? What differences did I notice when a question was revisited a third time? A fourth?

A question map keeps me honest and oriented through a unit. Perhaps most important, a map says that questions are important, worth honing, revisiting, and exploring together.

Lately I've been wondering about a transition I feel is important to make: how can I get students generating the questions we'll ask next?

Five Steps to Creating a Question Map

Posing questions is cognitively demanding work. Having a "posing routine" can help you put your focus where it needs to be—in the moment with your students. A question map helps too. Part of the challenge with your posing routine is related to planning. Of all the possible questions you have access to—you need to decide in advance which to actually pose, at a particular turn in the lesson or day in the unit.

Here are five important things to do as you develop and carry out a "conscious posing routine" with intention, with care, and with appropriate adjustments for your particular students.

1. Visualize the question space and a potential universe of items.

The results of these visualizations will become a road map, of sorts—not to control your journey with your students, but to refer to as you improvise during the lesson segment. Consider the following parameters as you design a posing routine/strategy that is aligned with learning targets:

- Boundaries: What will be the "outer" limits of your question space? How deep into the territory of "deeper" questions are you prepared to go? Are some questions "off limits"? Which ones? Why?
- Content: Will all the questions be your own? From a published curriculum or guide book? What percentage of questions can be generated from students? Colleagues? Parents?
- Style/format: Will the question space be presented like a mind map? An outline? A matrix/graphic organizer?
- Anchor: At the center of your Question Map, will you include an essential question? For the unit? Semester? Or discipline more broadly, cutting across grade levels?

After reviewing these parameters, commit to drawing or writing out the first draft of your visualization of posing for a purpose that is tied to your classroom learning targets.

2. Introduce questions around specific nodes, such as Habits of Mind (HoM).

We recommend starting with one of the five Habits of Mind: Relevance, Connection, Perspective, Evidence, and Speculation. You can even borrow a few of the questions that align with the HoM, such as "How do we know?" or "What's the available evidence?" presented in this chapter. "Evidence" is a good "cross-cutting" node that you can branch with specific content-related questions. The Habits of Mind at Central Park East Secondary School have a proven track record. However, you might choose another organizing principle for your question nodes and you might use colors to indicate Taxonomical Levels or Types of Knowledge with subheadings.

3. Connect nodes around a common theme.

For your content and your particular students, what connects these nodes? Draft questions worthy of considering again and again over the course of the unit. Take advantage of your students' interests and life stages to choose a theme that will capture and sustain their interests.

4. Revise the visualization of the question space, the "map."

Less is more. Now that the Question Space is more sketched out, do you need to change its boundaries before you use it with your students? Prioritize. Align your priorities with goals for your students. Think about the modality for posing: verbal questions, quick write responses, short answer quiz or test prompts, even visual cues to invite action.

5. Mark up/annotate the map as you use it.

What question nodes are getting lots of play? What new nodes are needed? Jot down after a lesson or observation of your colleague's lesson, which questions and modalities seemed effective, and which ones, not so much. We encourage you to formatively assess *your own* posing practices after a lesson and rethink what works and what can be improved upon. The Map is just a provisional guide. Take notes.

Preloading and Priming for Posing

We have noticed that "preloading" the questions we pose is paramount. Formative assessors have to think through their questions before they toss them into the arena. This became abundantly clear in a session with one of our student teachers, James, who struggled earnestly with teaching physics in his middle school placement. He made several good moves to try to warm-up the unit with an opening question: "What's the first thing that comes to mind when you see or hear the word 'vector'?" With chalk in hand, he wrote the "big idea" on the board, explained that all ideas were welcome, waited a few seconds, and... waited a few more. (James reported crickets could be heard, not his students.)

Upon hearing James's story, we stopped class and asked him to demonstrate for us: "Show us what you did and we will give you some warm and cool feedback." James was game. He did a good job with the brainstorm/warm-up, and luckily, got a few responses from his math and science colleagues. Very few.

Someone asked: "What do you do when the question you pose falls flat?" Another spoke up: "Yeah, this happens to me all the time." Soon enough the whole class was wondering about the value of posing questions that fly over the kids' heads. Precisely.

So we put the problem a different way in the form of a quick write: how could James have preloaded the word "vector" before putting it on the board?

Sometimes we need to unpack the big idea before we present the big idea. We gave 10 minutes for everyone to respond and then share out strategies and tactics to prime "the alternatives" to posing with a purpose.

Here is what James's colleagues in our preservice program came up with on index cards:

- Choose the big idea carefully. ("Vector" as a big idea is problematic—instead of "vector" try "arrow.")
- Consider how many different entry points your question about the big idea has.
- Try to anticipate responses: "What is my kids' schema for this big idea?" before posing.
- Show a drawing/picture/photo—lead students through a "gallery walk" and have them make observations about pictures of vectors in the real world.
- Tell a story or anecdote about lines that became vectors.
- Discuss what the concept means in one subject, discipline, or area of life, what it means in another, then compare and contrast with a t-chart.
- Show a YouTube clip about vectors and ask: what were some examples?
- Assign pairs of students to play with slips of paper and to post responses to the prompt: "Draw a *vector* on the 'vectors-for-beginners' wall." Get them moving around.
- Give all students a short reading, and pair-share, then ask them to highlight the formal definition and one real-life example.
- Find a similar word/concept that the students do know about from media, film, cartoons. Show how the "new" big idea isn't that new.

Together, working with James, our student teachers generated feedback he could use. Customized. Caring. Positive and specific.

Misconceptions and Challenges
Posing to Manage Versus to Think

"Is everyone done yet?" "Are you paying attention?" "Did you copy the information?" "Does anyone need more time?" "Who needs a pencil?" Beginning teachers tend to use questions to assert control over the classroom. Their questioning strategies are aimed at behavior, not learning targets; for the most part, they use questions to grab, direct, and maintain attention. As teachers who are moving along a teacher learning progression for posing, however, we can expect them eventually to release this posing-to-manage practice and replace it with a more sophisticated one.

Often next in their progression of posing moves, teachers will sense that questions can be aimed at other learning targets; their questioning will focus on reviewing skills related to academic learning objectives. We see rapid-fire questioning of students' academic skills emerging from their former "command and control" mode. Because the academic skills they are focused on are procedural in nature, we see lots and lots of lower-order, close-ended questions. Such beginning teachers are still more comfortable monitoring students' use of conventions and discrete tasks related to "information download" than to exploring and expanding students' conceptual understanding.

We do see beginning teachers making the connection between their reflexive proto-posing moves and their expanding notion of the question universe. "You mean that *all* my questions are just verbal prompts that elicit evidence? I can pick and choose them just as I do for quizzes, tests, and other formal assessments?" In a word: yes.

Anxiety often accompanies their new conception of questioning. "What if I can't come up with good questions? How do I choose which questions to use when? How can I tell if a question bank is appropriate for my subject or grade level? Will the 'items' be useful to this particular lesson?"

As teachers' posing repertoire grows and their freedom to choose becomes more apparent, so does the sense that they cannot stay stagnant—even if they are not sure how to make the next leap. Colleagues, coaches, and principals who recognize this phase can help these emerging formative assessors discover how to proceed.

For example, beginning teachers often need to practice handling what comes back at them when they venture to pose a question: name a function. Such a move could bring about a barrage of shouting: "Conjunction-junction!" "Erector sets!" "Diapers!" But it could be worse. Asking open-ended questions can make the entire classroom community vulnerable to an "intriguing response" that might be inappropriate because it's sexually explicit or an inside joke that most of the class doesn't understand but an individual student or group of students finds hurtful and another finds humorous. What does the formative assessor do then?

We encourage beginning teachers to use their poker faces as they handle such surprising, intriguing, and unorthodox answers. Seasoned formative assessors know that everything, we mean everything, goes on the board (which we discuss in Chapter 6 on Tagging). Because in the end, only by scribing without censorship can we hold everyone in the room accountable to our agreements. Does this mean we joyously validate every student response? Put simply, no. Or that we have no standards of decency and decorum? Hardly.

But when we pose a powerful question, we have to remind ourselves that we are not serving as judge, jury, and executioner in the response gallery. Our questions can be redirected, we can restate them, and we can reinforce the rules of engagement by priming with a vengeance. Formative assessors are not leaders of an encounter or self-help group. Eventually, we will—we must—impose order on answers as we bin them for instructional decision making (Chapter 7).

It's easy for teachers to fall into cheerleading and gush with praise (its own form of judgment) for every student contribution. Of course we are happy that more than two students said something today in response to our preplanned questions! But there can be sound reasons to refrain from lapsing into effusive positive judgment on an initial brainstorm.

We respect the teacher learning to become a formative assessor when she says using open-ended questions (Why do things sink and float? Who benefits from taxes? Are graffiti artists cubists? What is the best measure of health and fitness? Did Chuck Berry rip off Beethoven?) can be scary. One beginning teacher admitted that his fear of posing open-ended questions is that student responses may be unacceptable and the classroom reaction gets out of control. We applaud this honesty. So much about the tensions, challenges, and dilemmas inherent in becoming a formative assessor are revealed by our beginning teachers' reflections about posing each semester.

We believe formative assessors can distinguish between the desire to impose order from the top down and the need to generate rules of engagement from the bottom up when it comes to asking and answering questions. In the last chapter, we noted how students and teachers together can set the rules, norms, and procedures for learning in a culture—of respect, trust, and tolerance. Sound posing technique can and must be the subject of these initial joint discussions about the classroom learning environment that promote safe talk and safe listening. Again, we prime-pose-prime to see what works.

When a question is posed and there is no apparent correct answer, this can cause confusion and disequilibrium in the group. The fact that some questions hang in the air, unanswered, is perplexing and discomforting at times. Managing our anxiety about losing control of responses to questions is also part of the FA moves challenge.

Reflections on a Just-Taught Lesson

Some beginning teachers are ready to become formative assessors. They sense that the typical triumvirate in classroom assessment of quiz-test-homework doesn't find much purchase with their students. In too many schools, our students fail to study the night before the quiz, they regularly fail to turn in homework, they even fail to care much about the consequences of the test. The barrage of warnings, threats, and not so subtle hints to "get it done" do not persuade these students. These students know the teacher is managing paperwork, uploading grades onto a website, and minimizing the level of interaction between what the subject demands and what anyone actually thinks or feels about those demands.

Max teaches history in a low-income urban high school as part of his Phase II teaching placement. Last semester we asked him to reflect on the power of posing questions in his discipline. We sensed early on that Max was looking for an alternative to his mentor's grading practices. We asked him to reflect on his own lesson plans. With this invitation, he set out to characterize what posing means, in his opinion, for history teachers:

> My subject area is history and asking a question in this discipline means to encourage our students, either directly or indirectly, to question not only themselves, but their culture as a whole. I think that students sometimes fear learning about the past because they fear invalidating some part of who they are or who they think they are. In a history course, looking into an ancient civilization by putting it "under the microscope," means that we are capable of scrutinizing our own culture and this, I think, is what students dread;

having to look into their lives and maybe realizing that not all of what they think they know is as they were told.

Max was not satisfied with the questions and learning culture that pervaded his placement. He was ready to ask higher-order, strategic, and essential questions to his 2nd period students. To prove it, he made a list of questions to pose over the week:

> How did the Great Depression change the government in relation to social welfare? During the Great Depression, why do you think that the farmers who had a surplus of goods decided to let it rot rather than use it to feed those who were harshly affected? Was the New Deal a success? Why or why not? How do you think Roosevelt would react to Obama's Affordable Care Act? If you were alive in 1932, an election year, would you be more likely to reelect Hoover or do you think you would vote for Roosevelt? Explain your answer. How do you think our government would react to a depression were it to occur in the present day?

In asking Max to share his reflections on posing and its possibilities, we ignited something. How he enacted those questions, scaffolded them, or monitored their uptake we do not know from our position in the university. Only Max, his mentor, and the students know which questions landed, which fell flat, which overshot the current level of understanding, and which were pitched way below the week's learning targets.

We share Max's example for several reasons. He is emerging as a formative assessor. He knows what higher-order questions are and how to formulate them based on a well-established taxonomy. He also has a keen sense of the need to make connections, establish relevance, and form conjectures about major historical events and tie them to contemporary social and political issues. Max was a lively contributor throughout the semester, and he brought a healthy skepticism to our course on the FA moves ("Why 7 and not 17?" he posed again and again to his classmates).

A week rarely went by without a challenge from Max. He felt caught in the middle—languishing between formative and summative assessment paradigms. He knew from experience that asking questions was best pedagogical practice, especially in a history and social science department that teaches underserved kids. He had a duty to model the work of the historian to his students: question sources, authority, and opinions he believed wholeheartedly. Max was the first in his family to graduate from university and he learned to effectively argue for his positions on, among other things, the value of posing. But as a new teacher without a license (or tenure) he also had a responsibility to play the game—to hand out homework, to give tests, to assign letter grades, and of course to upload results ("hard data") for the school administration and parents to see each night.

Max reminds us that there are powerful forces at play in our schools today. Not everyone wants to see teachers become formative assessors. Too much of the work of formative assessment is invisible to outsiders. Numbers, points, and scores are tangible indicators. Society needs these symbols to function. Summative assessment will always win the day. Scores and grades count as currency, so to speak, to college and employers. "Rich," "thoughtful," and "unorthodox" student responses to difficult questions on the fly... not so much.

We admit that it is neither natural nor obvious to ask teachers to step up to the plate, take command of their professional knowledge, and articulate why posing questions is more important than writing a good test or quiz item, which allows them to write a letter grade or score on students' work. People in the educational policy world want data, not more questions, questioning strategies, or posing moves in the classroom. They want answers—did the student "know it or not."

Formative assessors who align their posing strategies with Bloom's taxonomy will not be rewarded if these instructional methods do not lead to higher test scores. Consequently we are stuck between a rock and a hard place: we either encourage Max to become a formative assessor, build a question-mapping procedure into his planning routines and step up our game as teacher educators to support him, or we discourage him by telling him to focus on grading, getting to know how to efficiently upload results each night, which is necessary to get a job. Either way, Max is learning to play the assessment game.

Putting It All Together

If this book has one central message, it is this: the only way to more powerful formative feedback is through posing questions that matter. Formative feedback has been shown to produce high levels of student achievement (Hattie & Timperley; 2007; Hattie, 2012). We see posing moves as an essential part of what makes a formative assessor because it's the one high-leverage, feedback-generating practice at our disposal as teachers. We can learn, along with our students, to use our minds well by asking the tough, smart, and productive questions. The responses to these questions give us clues about what has been learned, where we are stuck, and what to do next.

The foundation for posing good questions (oral or written) in your classroom rests on the grounds of caring and compassion for what our students think, say, and do. We remind ourselves daily that our students are children. Yes, they are becoming adults. But they remain in fundamental ways a "work-in-progress" throughout the teenage years. And we must not forget: it's their work, not ours, that leads to true maturity and growth into adulthood. We are at best shepherds, coaches, and guides for the children we teach.

Posing forms the foundation of formative assessment. It is a move that brings us as educators to the real work—of appreciating the habits of mind, heart, and work in our students. There must always be room for asking hard questions—we owe it to generations past and those to come. Questions count. They put us closer to the aims of a truly public education—by all, for all.

Checks for Understanding

Let's think about posing to check if we are ready to move on. These questions, prompts, and tasks are designed to help you take the ideas and thoughts in this chapter a few more steps forward. You can use the Warm-Up Prompts as self-checks and the ideas in Try-Now Tasks as conversation starters and exercises for independent study or group work.

Warm-Up Prompts:
- Why pose questions?
- Which scaffolds and procedures will help your posing moves?
- What key roles do students and teachers play in posing?
- How are other FA moves (priming, pausing, probing, bouncing, tagging, and binning) related to posing? How can they support it more fully?

Try-Now Tasks:
1. Let's brainstorm some strategies for posing for a purpose with our students. Take out a blank sheet of paper. Write the word RELEVANCE in the middle of the sheet. Start with the "big picture." Who cares about this subject? What is the significance of this unit to the field? Does anyone actually use this knowledge or these skills in the real world? Write down everything and everyone who comes to mind around the word RELEVANCE.

Challenge task: Open tomorrow's lesson with this brainstorm exercise (don't forget to prime it!) and compare the results across several class periods. Or meet with peers in a PLC and repeat for each Habit of Mind. Next up is Evidence or "How do we know?"

2. Finding questions that motivate a unit is difficult. Use a Habits of Mind graphic organizer as scaffold (see Figure 2.3). There are 5 nodes: Connections, Perspectives, Evidence, Speculation, and Relevance. For each node, write out one or two questions that can be organized under each node.

Figure 2.3   Habits of Mind Graphic Organizer

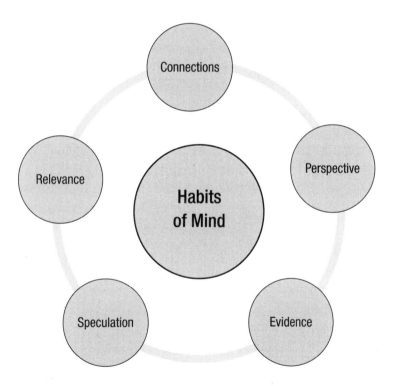

Challenge task: Cross-reference your nodes or questions with a district or state standards document. Or meet with peers in a PLC and repeat for each learning target by interdisciplinary team. Check for alignment and which standards naturally support questions targeted on, for example, Evidence or Viewpoint.

3. Think of a time you experienced a really difficult or challenging question. How—and when—did priming help or hinder you? Is it possible to reduce extraneous cognitive load or reduce affective filters when posing in your classroom?

Challenge task: Create a scaffold to prepare your students for question mapping. Have the students help you decide the best procedures to support how they will create questions. Make a list of three agreements (e.g., we will use pair-shares, table talk, and sticky notes for share-outs this week) to abide by as a class.

4. As you read back over this chapter, review the section on Principles, Procedures, and Practices. Imagine you are setting expectations for the learning environment in the first week of school. To build the foundation for your formative assessment-driven classroom culture, you need your community of participants to help define the tone, values, and supports to make it come to life. The students can and must set expectations with you, but they must also envision ways to repair and mend agreements when things fall down. Plan a lesson that includes a Four Corners exercise on Priming-the-Pump-for-Posing. Write on the board the following text:

Corner 1: Warm-ups and icebreakers to support posing

Corner 2: Tools, scaffolds, and technologies to use when posing

Corner 3: Statements and sentence starters helpful for posing

Corner 4: Values and beliefs about posing

Create groups in four corners of your classroom. Assign roles to a team leader, a recorder, and a scribe. Have each team list all the ways that we can support or prime (on materials provided). Tag all lists and combine into a whole class visual. Discuss what to do when we get stuck, or fall down, or forget our agreements.

Challenge task: Have one person in each group explain why a particular procedure may support more effective priming in the classroom for a particular student or group (e.g., designated ELLs, students with special needs, or visual and kinesthetic learners). Allow another person to push back and say why these moves may not work—for whom, which group, and why?

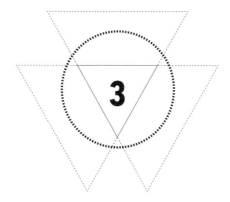

Pausing

Pausing communicates caring—that what students say and do is worth slowing down for.

Deidre, 6th grade art teacher

Pausing is hard. It takes time to learn how to do it.

Oscar, high school intern

Teachers often have to work hard to coax students through pausing routines. Growing up in a world with online search programs at their fingertips, today's students have been conditioned to react fast, find shortcuts, and get questions answered immediately. Performing a search online or "Googling it" has always been an option for them.

Engaging with questions in other ways—ways teachers who are becoming formative assessors will expect them to—can feel strange. Pausing to let questions sink in, pausing to give themselves and others time to use their own inner search programs, so to speak, can jar, frustrate, and challenge students.

Orchestrating pausing moves with individual, groups, and whole classes of students challenges teachers, too. We are citizens in a world that values efficiency, productivity, and getting things done. We feel pressure to push the pace. Protecting the pausing our students—and we ourselves—need for processing and learning isn't easy. Internal and external factors affect our classroom pausing practices. Agreements on curricular goals and scope and sequence of our curriculum—that we may have worked hard to reach and may be established by the department, school, or district—can influence our pausing routines, too.

Stopping, even temporarily, can seem a luxury that we can't afford. If it's deeper learning we're after, however, we can't afford *not* to pause. It seems fair to ask: why pause for think time?

We pause because *everyone*—students and teachers—needs to pause to process the information and because pausing encourages more optimal engagement with subject content and conceptually difficult material. One thing we know from studying the human brain and the science of how people learn is that pausing matters (NRC, 1999; Gardner, 1985). It doesn't matter if you are a teacher or a student. All learners require think- and wait-time to process and make sense of information.

We know that all students, even quick-acting eager beavers, benefit from pausing that supports cognitive processing and deeper reflection. Every learning community, as an entity, needs a repertoire of pausing moves to support more equitable and better participation in the classroom. And because participation usually goes hand-in-hand with student growth, development, and achievement, pausing to support equity matters a great deal. Teachers also need pausing to do what they do—better. Pausing improves teachers' decision making and instructional adjustments.

When we commit to pausing in the lesson, it can become a ritual that students and teachers alike grow to love for its gifts: chances to slow down, recenter, go deeper, and to engage and connect with the questions, individually, with others, and in the moment. Pausing renews and refreshes.

What Is Pausing?

- *"Before you turn and talk to your partner, think about how you would finish the sentence on the board. Take 20 silent seconds."*
- *Students huddle around their posters, getting ready to present the day's project challenge. You notice that several of them are stuck on how to represent the central focus of their projects, seemingly confusing the theme with the thesis. A pattern seems to be emerging, but you need to hear from more tables. Before making an announcement to the class, you wait a few minutes.*
- *Students shuffle in to class. Some take their seats straight away, others need some nudging-by-eye-contact before they sit. Everyone is waiting. What will*

today's class be like? The clock turns to 9:05; conversations fade, the room grows quieter.

- *A few students pull out their notebooks and start copying the word problem on the board. Others are pausing; they still have headphones on and a few are texting under the table. Without saying a word, you walk nearby. Students put their phones away. You smile and point up at the board. "Oh, right!" you can almost read students' thoughts, "I need to copy the problem now."*

Google defines *pausing* as the "brief interruption of action or speech" and provides us with an instructive example: "She paused, at a loss for words." And pausing does suggest *loss*—a loss for words, of confidence, of footing. It is a temporary state that, more often than not, we hope will quickly pass.

One of the important tasks on our journey to becoming formative assessors is to help our students understand that, on the contrary, we *gain* when we pause. Pausing is key to acquiring a deeper understanding of the content. It allows us to pull "files" from long-term memory, fully engage in our cognitive processing capacities, and build the confidence we need to successfully move forward in a lesson activity.

Pausing is known by other names: wait time, think time, and transition time. Pausing routines may use a clock, a bell, or even background music to signal transitions in and out of "silent time." Whether we are in school or out in the world, we all need time to take note, to quietly reflect, to think to ourselves. When we catch a student daydreaming or seemingly adrift, let's recognize the inherent humanness of this act. Attention is an issue, but so is seeing how to make pausing a part of your teaching practice so that students *actually* have time to move "files" around.

We invite you to become aware of how much pausing is needed to support deeper—and more equitable—learning in your classroom. We encourage you to recognize, seize, and create opportunities to make pausing moves more deliberate and more visible to your students. Your journey in becoming a formative assessor is tied to how you use wait time, think time, and all available transition time to facilitate learning. You can learn how to make silence and quiet a friend, an ally—another coach in the classroom to bring more students into the evolving, often fast-paced lesson.

Where and How Pausing Resides Within the Assessment Triangle

By understanding the logic and flow of the assessment triangle, and where and how each FA move fits within it, we can build a conceptual framework for formative assessment practice. Supported by research and informed by experts, we will be in a better position to anchor our classroom practices and know why we proceed as we do. As formative assessors we are entrusted with improving learning outcomes for all students.

Pausing supports both the *observation* and *interpretation* vertices of the assessment triangle (see Figure 3.1). This is because pausing helps teachers *observe* more representative student responses. All else being equal, more wait time equals more relevant or at least better formed responses. By helping us collect better evidence ("soft data" from student answers), pausing moves help us make better, more valid *interpretations* about students' thinking. Most importantly, pausing sits between posing and probing moves to help us make better instructional decisions about "what to do next" based on "where students are now" in the lesson.

Figure 3.1   Pausing and the Assessment Triangle

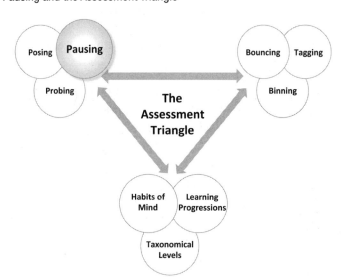

From a formative assessor's point of view, pausing moves work best once the learning target/cognition vertex of the assessment triangle has been established. These agreed upon outcomes anchor students and teachers; both know where the learning is headed, and which questions are being posed, and how each is aligned with specific learning targets. Under these conditions, the work of pausing moves can serve the *observational strategies/tools* vertex. As we recall from Chapter 2, this vertex deals with question prompts, tasks, or situations that are used to collect evidence about the current level of student performance. For formative assessors, the task that students are responding to most often is a question posed in class. Whether written on the board or spoken on the fly, pausing moves help elicit better evidence about student thinking, including misconceptions they may hold or places they seem stuck.

We also recall from the Posing chapter and the NRC's principles of assessment design that the quality of classroom evidence influences the validity of the *interpretations* you can make from that evidence. Higher quality evidence about what students know and can do in a lesson must be based on adequate wait-time to support the formation of those initial responses and provisional answers.

Put another way: without effective pausing practices (e.g., think-time, wait-time, transition-time routines) in our classrooms, the inferences we make from evidence using student responses to our rapid-fire questions is compromised. In classrooms—at least in classrooms taught by beginning teachers—this often looks like a teacher trying to make inferences about an entire class solely from the evidence provided by three or four quick-thinking, precocious, and verbally confident eager beavers. You see the problems in that. Most kids never get on deck to take a swing at the fast moving, rapid-fire questions. Pausing moves can help.

- *What's your name?* It takes us all less than a second to answer that question.
- *How do I get from here to there?* Depending on your location and how complicated the route, we pause longer—it's more complex.
- *Can you please explain the structure and function of the cardiovascular system?* Now hold on a minute, this is going to take some time. *Can you repeat the question?*

How long should pauses last? How much time do our students need to answer questions? The answer, of course, is that it varies; it depends on the difficulty of the question and the unique filter each student brings to the question-and-answer process. We do know that the more time we provide students to think through their responses, the deeper a picture we get of their *current level* of content knowledge and cognitive skills. For this reason, pausing is enormously important to the formative assessment journey of every teacher.

To lead effective pausing routines, teachers need an accurate sense of how challenging the questions posed in the lesson are likely to be for their students. Question taxonomies—Bloom's, Structure of Observed Learning Outcomes (SOLO), Webb's Depth of Knowledge—can help. From a content mastery perspective, good questions are aligned with well-defined learning targets and taxonomies, essential questions, and standards that can serve as scaffolds for developing sets of questions for the formative assessor to pose in class (refer back to Chapter 2 on Posing).

Whether our sets of questions are represented by well-defined Question Maps or by simple graphic organizers, we should use them to help us tie our pausing practices to our posing moves. Tougher questions get more pausing, more structured pausing routines, and more integrated support for different learners' needs. Easier questions still need pausing, but the supports teachers orchestrate around the pausing for questions they *know* will be easier for their students will look different.

For better, more intentional pausing, besides knowing the *type* of question (e.g., a factual recall question such as *what? when?* or a procedural question such as *how?*) and the *level of difficulty* of a question, formative assessors should also have a sense of the *range of typical responses* students can be expected to give to a question. This includes anticipating the nonresponses.

Becoming a formative assessor asks us to respond productively to *I don't know*, shrugs, and silent, blank stares. All responses—including these—can be the beginning of deep learning experiences, especially when we use pausing moves well. As challenging as that may be, we know from experience that questions are more powerful when they are nested in safe learning environments. We also know pausing has a critical role to play in promoting feelings of connectedness and well-being in the classroom.

Let's dig into the research on why pausing is so necessary for classroom learning to occur and what that research means for those learning to become formative assessors.

What the Research Says

There are reasons why some questions are harder than others. Cognitive scientists have begun to discover that both *content* and *process* affect student response time. We also know from research studies that working memory is limited in both capacity and duration when we are confronted with new information (Artino, 2008). Some researchers have found that humans are probably only able to manage two or three items of new information at a time (Kirschner, Sweller, & Clark, 2006).

Becoming a formative assessor means acknowledging, understanding, and working with these limitations and what they suggest for classroom learning. Let's explore how cognitive load plays a role in thinking through pausing moves.

Cognitive Load Theory

According to what's known as "cognitive load theory," there are at least three potential sources of cognitive load: *intrinsic, extraneous,* and *germane.*

Intrinsic cognitive load refers to the number of elements that the brain processes simultaneously in working memory for schema construction. Questions with too many prior-knowledge elements can bog students down and increase processing time needed. Question frames, sentence starters, "scribing" responses, and other scaffolds can reduce intrinsic cognitive load but not eliminate it.

Extraneous cognitive load refers to questioning techniques and situations that require learners to engage in working memory activities that are *not directly related* to students constructing schema or automating learning tied to the learning targets; therefore, this kind of cognitive load is unnecessary (see, e.g., Sweller, 1994). For example, we may see students spend their cognitive resources to process information that is not related to the learning target but that has been unintentionally mixed in with a question or prompt. Illegible writing on dry erase board, small font on a presentation slide, even the delivery of a question can adversely overload students.

Germane cognitive load refers to cognitive processes that prime responses to questions. Metaphors, analogies, symbols—visual and auditory representations and elaborations—that help students build schema and conceptual understanding tied to the learning targets make up germane cognitive load. A challenge is knowing our students well enough to decide which analogies, for example, will guide them, rather than distract or confuse them, in cognitive processes directly related to achieving learning targets.

Becoming a formative assessor requires us to get to know our students and their contexts (cultural, social, generational) to better anticipate and address these types of cognitive load.

 FORMATIVE ASSESSMENT TIPS

Pruning Extraneous Cognitive Load in Question Prompts

Formative assessors should work to reduce and eliminate extraneous cognitive load when possible. Often, less really is more.

Questions posed using overly complex vocabulary *when simpler words would serve your purposes better* increase the extraneous cognitive load of questions. The challenge is how to get the particular *less* that really is *more* for our students?

How we decide and proceed depends upon the purposes we are prioritizing. For example, teachers almost always have a priority of fostering their students' academic language development, so they model using academic language in their speech. This is especially important for students who may not be supportively exposed to academic language outside class. As teachers model academic language, they naturally pose questions in this register. The key is doing so intentionally, with awareness.

Reducing extraneous cognitive load in your questions takes knowing your students well. It also depends upon establishing clear learning targets; knowing your priorities and how your work reflects them; having a keen awareness of your language use; knowing which analogies and representations are likely to work for your students; dialing in just the right amount of "stretch language"; and being able to adjust skillfully when your language under- or overshoots their "stretch zone."

It also takes incredible intentionality and discipline. Similar to meditation, it's a practice. One tip: share your questions/prompts with a family member, a friend, or a student who is in a grade level a few levels below your current assignment. Ask: Does this make sense? How could I improve it to make it clearer?

Wait Time Affects Cognition

Formative assessors will want to look over their question banks, maps, and other scaffolds and begin to think about the implications of research on wait time and cognition for their students. Although most researchers expert in cognitive load theory do not address differences among student groups (e.g., second language learners, kinesthetic learners, students with differing special needs), their findings on cognitive demands for "typical" learners do allow us to draw a few conclusions for practice in heterogeneous classrooms. Chief among them is that increasing the *frequency* and *length* of wait time pauses in classrooms is important. For emerging formative assessors, it will take planning, experimenting, and adjusting to what is learned—day by day, hour by hour in the classroom to get our pausing strategies in line with learners' needs.

Mary Budd Rowe is generally acknowledged as having first introduced the concept of "wait-time" as an instructional variable. In a landmark study, she discovered that wait times of three or more seconds have positive effects on students' and teachers' behaviors and attitudes. According to subsequent research, the practice of providing adequate wait time is associated with an increase in correct answers, volunteered responses, and high test scores for students, as well as with more varied and flexible learning strategies that address higher-level thinking (Casteel & Stahl, 1973; Rowe, 1974a, 1974b, 1974c; Stahl, 1990; Tobin, 1987). Tobin (1980, 1986) found that the use of extended wait time across science, math, and language arts classrooms helps students to think more carefully about teacher directions, explanations, or questions before responding.

Black and colleagues (2004) note that many teachers wait less than one second for a response after asking a question. The key to changing this dynamic is "to allow longer wait time. But many teachers find it hard to do this, for it requires them to break their established habits. Once [these habits] change, the expectation of their students are challenged" (p. 11). As one teacher, Derek, told researchers in the United Kingdom after reflecting on his wait-time practices:

> Increasing waiting time after asking questions proved difficult to start with due to my habitual desire to "add" something almost immediately after asking the original question. The pause after asking the question was sometimes "painful." It felt unnatural to have such a seemingly "dead" period, but I persevered. Given more thinking time, students seemed to realize that a more thoughtful answer was required. Now, after many months of changing my style of questioning, I have noticed that most students will give an answer and an explanation (where necessary) without prompting (Black, Harrison, Lee, Marshall, & Wiliam, 2004, pp. 11–12).

Derek is no different than the rest of us. He is in the habit of avoiding awkward silences and does not want to appear ineffective or out of control. Derek is acutely aware of the demands of pacing and covering the day's material. He is in the habit of going through the call-and-response motions and trying to get kids to participate.

Unfortunately, we do not know much about Derek's priming for pausing procedures and routines. To what degree did his classroom culture encourage safe talk, safe listening, and a safe waiting period before sharing? Was Derek "minding the gap" between rapid-fire answers and slow-to-emerge answers? What sorts of scaffolds (e.g., agreements were in place prior to whole class sharing) or hand-holds (e.g., sentence-starters and pair-shares), if any, did Derek employ as his students struggled to share more elaborate thoughts to more complex questions?

Derek, like us all, is learning to hone his craft as a formative assessor. We honor his development as he learns to make moves that can make a difference.

Going Deeper with Pausing

When we watch students without speaking, when we use proximity to manage their behavior, when we notice a pattern or draw a connection in our minds on a "walkabout" in the classroom—we are pausing. When we pay attention to signals that students feel uncomfortable, unsafe, or disengaged and then take action to make things better, we are using wait time and think time to figure out next steps. When we encourage our students to step back, wait a second, or slow down before they dive in, we are modeling and coaching the development of pausing moves.

Pausing happens all the time. It's like breathing: we all do it, but we rarely give it much thought. We have to pause all the time—between breaths, between words, between thoughts. And being mindful about the role of pausing is more important than ever today, when processing speeds are measured in nanoseconds and we exchange information with the stroke of a key. Let's be realistic: it can be hard to focus on the nuances of classroom wait time in a world that doesn't have much time for waiting.

Still, we are optimistic—particularly if teachers who are learning to use formative assessment moves adopt a reflective stance toward pausing moves. *Who will need extra time to respond to my hinge questions? How can I set up space in my lesson for extra cognitive processing? Is there a natural break in class for a pair-share and team response to my prompts? Whom should I ask to remind the class why we use pausing moves? Is there a visual aid I might use to reduce extraneous cognitive load and increase germane load?*

Pausing is not just about getting ready to listen to our students; it's also about supporting them—and ourselves—through the awkward silences. We all need to learn to think of pausing as an opportunity to go deeper into our best thinking. Having a plan and being reflective can help.

Making Our Moves Deliberate and Visible to Students

As teachers on a formative assessment journey, we need to make our pausing moves deliberate and visible to students. We said in the Posing chapter that good questions will cause your students to stretch, feel a little pain, and scratch their heads. Students may feel stranded, want a lifeline, and look to end the stage fright that comes with being in the class spotlight.

Your students are watching your moves. Setting up your collective pausing agreements with students is a great way to strengthen the use of pausing moves in class. Make the process fun—ask students to discuss moments in their lives when silence was particularly golden (or cricket-laden).

Send the message loud and clear: as eager beavers, brash bears, silent Sallies, and silent Bobs, we are all in this together. Remind students that pausing is a sign of respect, showing that we recognize differences and share a common cause. Review core values related to pausing:

- We believe every voice matters.
- We can listen with our hearts as well as our ears.
- We respect vulnerability, which we know is necessary for growth and learning.
- We know it is okay to stop-wait-think-share.
- We learn in different ways, at different rates.
- We remember it takes time to figure things out.
- We are all here to learn together—being speedy isn't the goal.

Four Goals for Deeper Pausing

Keeping the following four goals in mind when we enact pausing moves helps us to get the most out of wait time and think time in the heterogeneous classroom.

Goal 1: Constantly check for students' prior knowledge. Formative assessors need to activate students' prior knowledge, and pausing moves ensure that students have the time necessary to access their storage files in long-term memory. A smart way to work toward this goal is to review your lesson plan and count how many "thinking breaks" you've included for students. How much time will you provide so that students can carefully think about and communicate more reliably their prior knowledge and understanding of the material?

Priming to activate prior knowledge means setting up routines and procedures for pausing. Students can help you by supplying reminders, visual cues, and posters, and leading warm-up exercises to ensure sufficient wait time. One idea is to select certain students to serve as "wait-time monitors"—maybe even with their own stopwatches!

Goal 2: Ask a range of questions to deepen academic engagement. If questioning is a core value in the classroom, then we ought to try to develop questions that are suitable for every student's level of knowledge or skill—and different levels of questions will require different amounts of wait time with different kinds of "Wait Time Supports" built into them. For example, consider the following questions, each tuned to a different level of thinking:

- Describe three causes of World War II. (Requires simple recall)
- Describe the most important causes of World War II. (Requires longer periods of cognitive processing/think time to distinguish between causes and rank them)
- Describe a model (e.g., poster or chart) that you might use to represent the cause/effect relationships in World War II. (Requires a deep understanding of the political, economic, and social factors of the war and consideration of how best to represent them in a diagram)

At best, a good set of questions will reveal students' thought patterns, orientations, associations, and what Piaget and other constructivists call schema. When figuring out how much wait-time you should allot to different types of questions, it's a good idea to write the questions down and note the pausing moves (e.g., turn and talk, then share on board) that you intend to use with each one.

Goal 3: Capture as many responses as possible. Let's not forget that the main purpose of pausing is to increase the sample of responses for any given question (we discuss this more in Chapters 5 and 6 on Bouncing and Tagging). If we don't systematically allow for wait time in our lessons, we will only be able to glean informative responses from a small fraction of our students, leaving us as teachers unclear on the overall level of understanding in the class. We should always strive to gather enough data to be able to make a thoughtful generalization about where most of our students are with the material.

Goal 4: Promote equity in the classroom. Public schools are charged with upholding the promise of democratic education, in part, by giving everyone access to a quality learning environment regardless of race, creed, gender, sexual identification, and disability. To this end, it is vital that we as teachers prime our classrooms for equity and access to powerful ideas and disciplinary thinking. We also need to promote and protect *opportunities for all* students to share answers to essential questions.

From a formative assessment standpoint, doing so has the added benefit of increasing our sample size, making our instructional decisions based on a wider range of responses more effective. Formative assessors send the signal daily that *all* voices count—and that all will be counted upon to make progress in the lesson/unit. As Sevan, a middle school mathematics teacher put it: through the FA moves framework, we learn from listening and listening harder (Duckor, Holmberg, & Rossi Becker, 2017).

Some Words of Experience

Let's pause to consider the words of a teacher who has taught English and Japanese at a diverse Title I high school for nearly a decade. We asked Misa, "How did you get to be a teacher who intentionally uses pausing to good effect in your classes?" Here's how she responded:

> You need trust. I suppose you could pause a class without feeling that trust—you could just stand there and count the seconds. But it's not the same.
>
> You need to believe that the students need the pause, that they're going to use it, and that their pausing will yield something worthwhile—that it will be fruitful.
>
> You also need to have faith that the pausing is going to work—that a classroom management issue you don't know how to handle isn't going to pop up because of a pause in the class action. That's a real fear. It's amazing how much I felt it when I began teaching.

We share Misa's insight, "So much about teaching is about control, isn't it?" When we're pausing, we don't have that feeling of control that we're used to.

When students are speaking, we believe that we are getting a window into their thinking, and that feels good to us. But when our students are silent, we have no idea what to think. We are afraid to pause or to process. Some of us are great at filling-in-the-blanks ourselves: These kids must be thinking "What a dope!" "Get me out of here." "This sucks." Body language can give us some hints, but we really don't know what students are thinking when they're pausing (yes, even daydreaming or "spacing out") and it can be uncomfortable for us, especially beginning teachers.

Patience with pausing, and the myriad micro-moves that surround it, is required. We have to wait and think before we act to shut it down. Have a little faith, you'll get better over time.

Principles, Procedures, and Practices

We like the idea of generating procedures and practices for pausing from the ground up—with your colleagues and your students. When teachers have open conversations and are trusted to develop best practices themselves, they are better able to bridge the gap between what researchers want and what teachers need.

Mozart famously said, "The music is not in the notes, but in the silence between." When priming for pausing moves, we ought to bear in mind that the silence of pausing is inextricably linked to the music of other FA moves. (Of course, pausing doesn't always require literal silence—in fact, playing music during think time is an effective pausing move that we recommend considering for *some situations and students*.)

Prior to priming for pausing, it's important to find out how your students define it. This information will be invaluable for developing customized moves. It's also important to have a good idea of your *purpose* for initiating pausing moves. For example, if your purpose is to give students enough time to prepare a response, you might say, "We'll have no hands waving around so that we all can concentrate on what we want to say." By contrast, if your purpose is to give students a chance to check their work before turning it in, you might say, "Use the time remaining to check over your work with a partner."

We recommend priming students by asking them to reflect on specific pausing practices and by drawing connections to the worlds of work, college, and life. Remind them that the benefits of pausing are irrefutable and incorporate their feedback into your own moves. Make agreements. Put them on the walls. Point to "Pausing" signposts and reminders in life to keep it real—use a road sign to help students remember.

Above all, be deliberate and wise about how you prime your students for pausing. If things don't go as well as you had envisioned, don't give up—try again, but this time with fewer words. (You might also consider placing students who love the spotlight and throwing out rapid-fire responses in charge of priming the class for pauses. Replace the student of the month award with "Best Timekeeper" of the week).

Changing Your Pausing Habits

Here are some guidelines for changing your pausing habits as you move forward on your journey. Begin by taking an inquiry stance on your current pausing habits. Why might what is currently happening be happening? No time to wait—ask yourself "Why don't I typically 'wait'?" "What is the rush?" Is it the kids? The curriculum? The time of day? The period right before lunch?

In *The Power of Habit* (2012), Charles Duhigg explains a research-supported framework for reshaping habits. In our world as educators, Duhigg's insights apply to identifying the pausing "routine" you want to change. At first you may not have awareness of what your routine is, such as waiting for less than a second before calling on a student. You pounce on the first hand up. You rush through the hour trying to cram as much material as possible into the lesson to beat the bell.

Next inquire *why* you might be doing what you habitually do. Is it tied to enjoying the energy of quick exchanges with the most eager students? Is it because you forgot to use the equity sticks or don't feel comfortable with technology and avoid downloading randomizer apps for choosing whom to call on? Perhaps your habitual pausing routines (or nonpausing ones as is the case with most teachers) are related to the discomfort many of us—students and teachers alike—feel during even brief moments of silence or awkward transitions? Might you believe—as many beginning teachers—that all wait-time does is frustrate students, and leave you open to more classroom management challenges that you don't want or don't feel ready to handle?

After examining your *whys*, come up with several different new things to try. Why not invite a student to be "The Think-Time Superhero" or "Pause Master Flash" for a class? Ask a high-energy student to help with timekeeping responsibilities—for developing responses to questions, prompts, and other queries in a lesson segment—be it with a low-tech sand timer or a clock on a smartphone. Whatever you think to try out tomorrow, know you'll need to prime your students, and win their active support.

Right now we invite you to make a plan for trying the new routine in your next lesson. Think about how you'll prime for it. Systematically try out different routines. Self-monitor. Revise until you come up with several go-to routines that you can rely on. Add them to your FA toolkit and commit to using them with intention and care.

This way of tackling both the concept and practice of pausing is consistent with research on how people learn and change their habits of work. It is no different for teachers than for our students. We all need scaffolds, footholds, and fixed rope for when we inevitably fall down and forget to use wait-time.

We are also suggesting we honestly confront our conceptions of teaching and learning in this book. Teachers and students often crave being—or at a minimum looking—competent, in control, and efficient. It is not surprising that we enact routines that give us these feelings. If "wait time," "think time," or any other pedagogical routine related to cognitive processing does not satisfy these needs, we will not use them.

Duhigg's work suggests that infusing strategic, reflective cognitive effort into your pausing routines can help you figure out new rituals that will provide you and your students the time you need for improved cognitive and affective functioning to advance educational outcomes. Always remember: you aren't alone on your journey to becoming a formative assessor. We are all learning to become better at our FA moves one lesson at a time, over time. The clock starts now.

Values and Beliefs

Enacting pausing moves in the classroom can be especially challenging for teachers who feel they are always working against the clock. Posters can remind everyone of the importance of honoring wait time, but what's most important is that we actually abide by our agreed-upon values. Here are some value statements to consider:

- We respect every student's need to take time to answer a question.
- We encourage everyone to use wait time—it's there to help.
- We make pausing visible in our classroom. Look at the stop sign and the stopwatch.

- Take a second and think "What do I know?" and "How can I best share it?" Then wait to share.
- Everyone deserves a chance to respond and share an idea today.

Pausing: Mark's Case

When I first began teaching, it's amazing how much fear I associated with pausing. The fear, I became aware, was about control, or more specifically, fear of losing control of the class. So much about teaching is about control. The teacher controls how the class should operate: what choices students can make, what choices are *not* for them to make, which norms to reinforce and how often, when to cut students—and ourselves—slack, and when *not* to.

When pausing, there isn't the feeling of control that I'm used to. When a student is speaking, I feel I have a decent window into his or her thinking. As a teacher, that feels good. I want evidence of where a student's thinking is, because then I can do something productive with it. That's my job, my responsibility—to make productive choices regarding a student's thinking.

But when a student is silent, I have no idea what he or she is thinking. On top of that, the student may be exhibiting body language that suggests frustration, impatience, and boredom. Teenagers are famous for expressing boredom regarding class content that teachers think will be interesting to them, or, at the least, important for them to consider.

Some of us, and I was one of these teachers in the beginning, are great at making up and filling in what a student could be thinking. When you magnify that by several students—imagine a classroom of kids thinking during a pause: *This class is awful. This teacher doesn't know what he's doing. Can we leave now?* No wonder whole-class pauses are uncomfortable! They can feel downright dangerous, especially in the beginning when we're not used to them, when we don't yet truly understand how needed pauses are and why they're so important.

During whole-class pauses especially—pauses of even seconds—I feared a classroom management issue that I wouldn't be able to handle would pop up. Better to keep going. Just keep the class going and not allow that possibility. If I couldn't handle what popped up, that would mean I was incompetent. More than anything, I wanted to be a competent teacher.

I had to learn to be patient with not *immediately* knowing what students were thinking. To give them chances to think. Because that's what pausing is, really, opportunities for students to process. How can they learn well without those opportunities? And how can I get the best, most complete responses if I am constantly rushing?

I found that patience with not knowing what students are thinking during pauses comes more easily with trust. Trust on my part that pausing is worth it—yes, I read about it in grad school, but I wasn't sure it would work for me. When I began to believe that students needed the pause, that they were going to use it, and that the pause was going to yield something worth happening (and not result in a classroom management nightmare!), my discomfort with pausing got bearable. It takes time, I learned. I am learning to relax into this move.

The silences in my lessons shifted from unintentional ones that terrified me— *What do I do now? No one is answering my question. All eyes are on me. This is scary*— to expected ones. Yes, I get crickets still. But now I just reset things. I'll step back, breathe, and re-pose from another angle.

Another thing really helped me with my pausing. I began to trust that I could handle what might come *after* the pause. When I was first teaching, I had a hard time anticipating students' responses. Students can say some bizarre things that you just don't know what to do with. This can be disconcerting, and—as odd as it may sound— discourage a beginner teacher from allowing *any* pausing to occur during class time. Less pausing means fewer opportunities to get embarrassed by unexpected comments or impossible-to-answer questions from students.

But when I added stock phrases such as *Interesting; I love that—I never thought about that… You are making me think about this in new ways* to my teaching toolkit, and to use pauses to help me circulate around the room, things opened up. As I wondered about a student's response, "Do I pursue this right now? Is this where the class needs to go?," I also began to grow more confident that I would know what to do with even the student responses that surprised and puzzled me. Using those stock phrases was a way to give *myself* more think-time while adding to theirs.

Now I relish the silent surprises, the chances to quietly probe, the sense of holding all students accountable for sharing ideas because now we have the time to share! When I found confidence and trust in listening to student ideas, and a good lesson plan template that highlights pausing, it really helped me. I suppose you could use pausing moves without feeling that sense of trust and curiosity in what students are really thinking—you could just stand there in front of the class and count the seconds. But it's not the same.

Pausing Combos

Combining some of the moves in this book into "FA combos" is an excellent way to optimize your teaching. Here are two effective combos that one of our preservice teachers, Kari, used in a middle school music class:

Prime-pause. *Prime:* "One last thing before we start. Can we add a two-measure decrescendo in measures 15 and 16? Please take a second to write that in your music." *Pause:* The teacher steps off the podium and waits as students write, then returns once everyone is done.

Prime-pause-bounce. *Prime:* "Just a reminder about the dynamic changes on the repeats. Before we start, take a quiet moment to remind yourself of what those are for your instrument. Then I'll check with a half-dozen of you." *Pause:* The teacher waits five to ten seconds calmly with her right hand in the air. *Bounce:* Drops her hand to her side, "Franklin, start us off, please."

Phrases and Sentence Starters

When it comes to pausing, "talking the talk" can help classroom communities "walk the walk." You can use phrases and sentence starters to remind everyone that pausing is about to happen. Those students who need to shift gears, stop-look-listen, and rev down can do so with your support. Those who need extra time *to process*, *to verbalize*, and *to share out* in small groups can with carefully constructed scaffolding embedded in a lesson. We've identified a few sentence scaffolds and starters to support pausing practices in Figure 3.2.

Figure 3.2   How to Signal Pausing

The following phrases and sentence starters serve to signal pausing moves.
- "Take a few moments to..."
- "Put your thinking caps on and..."
- "Transport yourself to another time and..."
- "Reminder that while we are thinking..."
- "I know you may have an answer now, but I want you to..."
- "You have [X seconds] to think before sharing with the class."
- "Before sharing with the whole class, talk it over with your partner."
- "No hands, no voices, please. It's time to think before sharing with the class."
- "Take some time to write down your thoughts before sharing with the class."
- "Take [X minutes] to develop your first draft responses."

As part of their metacognitive development, the following prompts can help students reflect on their pausing moves and how to use them fruitfully.
- "How did having some extra time help you respond?"
- "What happened when you jotted down your answer during the 'think time session'?"
- "Whose responses changed—when they had more time than usual? How so?"
- "What's something you gained from the last pause-pair-share? What's something you think we might have gained using this pausing procedure—as a whole class?"

Misconceptions and Challenges

⚠ Misconception Alert: "I Have No Time To Pause, I Have a Pacing Schedule"

There is a common misconception about pausing that we've encountered in our work with preservice teachers. Many beginning teachers believe that pausing is a threat to their best laid lesson plans, others see it as a luxury for teachers who don't work off a pacing guide or have to cover difficult, rigorous content before sending students to the next grade level. People in our profession tend to think that math teachers hold this misconception in larger numbers than, say, humanities and language arts teachers do. Not so. We've observed a wide range of subject teachers over the years and many, across disciplines, seem to struggle with this misconception.

Take for example one of our credential candidates who teaches music and has struggled with the tension between pausing and pacing. Sometimes the fear of falling behind or the anxiety of being under the watchful eye of a mentor teacher or administrator exacerbates her struggle with pausing moves. Erin shared with us how things play out in her mind:

> I find that with my high school students it is really important and almost always necessary to keep them moving at a fast pace. Because of this, I sometimes forget to use pausing or wait time because I'm so focused on moving quickly. I've come to realize that there is a difference between pacing and pausing. Just because my pacing is moving quickly doesn't mean that I need to speak quickly or ignore wait time. As long as the time spent pausing isn't excessive, it can be very useful to my students.
>
> It's funny because I've noticed lately that when I pose questions without allowing for wait time, the same students raise their hands first. In an attempt to diversify the students who are answering questions, I try tactics such as "can someone from the soprano section answer this question?" or "can someone from the back riser answer this question?" Although these are useful ways to give other students opportunities to speak, pausing can be used to solve this problem more effectively. It is helpful to say "take a few seconds to think about this question and then I'll take some responses," before asking the question. This acknowledges that there will be wait time and that it is okay to collect their thoughts and form their opinions.
>
> Note to self: don't be afraid to pause. Pausing does not mean that you will lose the students' attention or control of the class. Everything in moderation."

What is interesting about formative assessors who are learning about pausing moves is how much they concentrate on their own experience with wait time or how they perceive it may look to others in their building. Perhaps the idea that there is a contradiction or impossible tension between pacing demands and pausing moves is rooted in larger cultural and social values. There is no doubt that efficiency, productivity, and competition have put a premium on pacing, getting things done, and moving faster and faster. Technology is a major driver of the rush to press play—and to avoid the pause button. Our students have been conditioned to react fast, to find shortcuts, and to expect everything to be at their fingertips.

No wonder our beginning teachers (many are Millennials) hold onto these preconceptions and notions about the perils of pausing. Despite the advice of educational researchers and university professors (many are aging Baby Boomers), the next generation of teachers will rightly feel torn about pausing. Pausing, for these tech-savvy, super busy, quick-moving student teachers is not totally in-sync with the rhythms of today. Tech solutions that promote pausing can help the formative assessor. But only if we know how and why to use them in a lesson.

⚠ Misconception Alert: Pausing Is Like Beating a Dead Horse

There is another common misconception about pausing that we've encountered in our work with preservice teachers who are career changers. Many of these beginning teachers come from industry, where they worked as engineers, managers, and business people at large companies. Intellectually, they understand the purpose and use of pausing. They can write a persuasive rationale for the use of wait time based on research. They have, so to speak, done their homework and know how to pass our teacher educator "tests for understanding." One such seasoned, middle-aged teacher candidate who worked in engineering for three decades wrote in response to a quick write in our assessment class:

> Giving students more question response time is desirable for the reasons described in the Quick Write assignment. For questions posed to the class at large, wait time allows for thoughtful answers. The amount of extra time provided should vary by type of question. I would not provide too much wait time for a question requiring the knowledge of routine for function calculations. I would certainly allow ample time to reconstruct a process required for a complex question. Also, I would provide extra "low pressure" time for

students to resurrect prior knowledge, especially if it wasn't relatively current. Identifying the correct amount of wait time before applying scaffolding requires a trade-off between accommodating individual student needs and using class time wisely. Waiting a little for a profound insight is certainly desirable. Beating a dead horse, however, is counterproductive. I hope these judgment calls will become easier for me with experience."

We wanted to ask our would-be formative assessor: Who are these "dead horses"? What do they look like? Which races have they already lost? Is there any hope for using more wait-time and on the fly feedback to help achieve a win with a word problem? Can pausing along the racetrack help to train them better? Is slowing down the action, or breaking things down with adequate think time during class, likely to make a difference? Or is it better to judge them as winners and losers with quizzes and tests? To advance those who are talented and to handicap the odds occasionally for those who mostly struggle with math?

Our hope is that by asking more questions (as opposed to giving "incorrect" answers low marks on this quick write) we might coax this candidate and others like him into the realization that how we frame learning for students will play a role in how we teach them.

But we shouldn't be too hard on this new teacher. He is in good company with Aristotle, who was also fond of competitive races and wondered when an "academic" education might be counterproductive to the needs of society (Barnes, 1982).

Learning to Look Back: Reflections on a Just-Taught Lesson

Brian is a former small-business owner with significant experience in the biotech industry and desires to start a new career in teaching. We asked him to reflect on a just-taught lesson at his school where he serves as an intern.

> Wait time is a bit like walking on an old fence that's wobbly and shaky. A sense of precariousness permeates the room as students anxiously try to think through their answers. But what matters is that a fair amount of learning is taking place. Even the one-word or short-phrase answers that emerge during pauses can help you get a feel for the direction of the class. If students are migrating toward an answer that is inconsistent with academic goals, you can make real-time corrections to your practice. These detours can function

as legitimate teaching moments as we model correcting our mistakes and rerouting our thoughts for students.

   I'll sometimes ask students to come up with answers for which they don't have the appropriate background knowledge. For example, I once asked students in a DNA extraction lab how they might visualize DNA with the naked eye. I expected them to come up with two or three possibilities, one of which was likely to do with a visualization technique that is used in industry. Although we'll ultimately cover the technique, we hadn't progressed that far into the unit. I realize now that I was asking a probing question that would have better served students later in the semester. Although there was significant processing during the probing exercise, I think I fell off the fence.

As Brian's self-reflection shows, some questions will crash and burn no matter how much wait time we provide to students. Questions that overshoot your students' zone of proximal development will fail. Brian is making progress on the continuum of professional growth that is his formative assessment journey. He is recognizing the degree to which his learning environment is in constant flux; learning that students and teachers, like bobbers caught up in tidal forces, can at any moment diverge from their intended courses. Sometimes, our teaching strategies and materials in the lesson plan predict where the useful currents of (mis)understanding are; other times, they simply have us floating in circles.

This self-reflection is exemplary in so many ways. The teacher who is struggling to become a formative assessor must surrender to the facts on the ground. Brian says it all when he acknowledges, "I'll sometimes ask students to come up with answers for which they don't have the appropriate background knowledge." On rare occasions, we get lucky and a few volunteers try to rescue the teacher. But that is not the point. Being humbled by the complexity and nuance of formative assessment practice is.

In this example, Brian (or "Mr. Bucholz" as his students in a high-needs school know him) appears to need a lifeline. But does he really *at this stage* of his pedagogical development? If we believe in a continuum of professional growth by and for teachers, it may be that Brian is actually making good progress as he leaps toward new levels of formative assessment practice.

We argue that Brian has made a discovery on his apprentice's journey into a new career; he talked about making detours that can function as legitimate teaching moments *"if* we model correcting our mistakes" and rerouting our thoughts for students. That sense of "if" is worth a thousand PD hours and teacher evaluation reports. We see it as half the battle with becoming a formative assessor—in an age that seeks to take the wonder, developmental demands, and contingency out of our profession. We contend (with you) there is no substitute for self-reflection in the company of colleagues and peers who share the same goals in a profession.

 FORMATIVE ASSESSMENT TIPS

Insight Corner: Why Pausing Is So Challenging for Beginning Teachers and What Is to Be Done

Pausing challenges beginning teachers because pausing sits at a nexus of unquestioned habits, untested skills, and uncomfortable feelings.

Questioning classroom habits can benefit all teachers. Beginning teachers, however, usually haven't questioned the habit of their digital-induced, tech-driven fast pace of living, nor what it implies for their teaching. Student learning requires a slower, more deliberate pace.

The skills teachers need to carry out effective pausing are not easily acquired in other areas of teachers' lives. As a result, our pausing skills are untested, until the moment we need to pause our students. This differs from posing skills we bring to our beginning teaching.

We've spent a lifetime asking questions. But who among us novice teachers has had any experience in getting 36 energetic—or half-asleep—teenagers to pause and reflect on The Gettysburg Address, transformational geometry, or *The House on Mango Street*? "Not yet" is the answer most beginners in this profession will select.

Pausing makes beginning teachers uncomfortable. They use the words *painful*, *weird*, *unnatural*, *awful*, and *precarious* to describe how they feel orchestrating classroom pausing.

The good news? The uncomfortable feelings diminish as skills grow through guided experience.

What does this mean for coaches of those becoming formative assessors? Expect beginning teachers to feel incompetent with pausing. Support them in questioning habits of "moving on" acquired through years and years of the apprenticeship of K–12 observation (Lortie, 1975). Recognize that teacher *beliefs*, *misconceptions*, and *habits* need to be addressed.

Continued

Get teacher candidates to express reasons why pausing matters so much—to them, to others. Review the cognitive psychological research in this chapter or other sources from their coursework. Digest the meaning of "cognitive overload" for particular groups of students.

Help these mentees to create a plan for developing their wait-time and think-time skills. Help them to follow through with concrete procedures embedded in a lesson plan. Take time to debrief what's working today, and what can be tried out tomorrow. Chip away at the "doing school" and the "Is everyone done yet, can we move on?" mentality, one lesson at a time.

Putting It All Together

Waiting—for discoveries, for insights, for the gears to start turning—matters. We must now make more space in the classroom for contingency, which means opening up to what students say and do as they respond to our questions through speech and writing. Pausing routines, signs, and supports allow complex student thinking to emerge no matter how awkward those moments of silence may be—for them or for us.

Current standards call for embedding the core skills of speaking and listening in our public school classrooms. We are told that teachers must become more adept at facilitating classroom talk and that students must become more fluent and articulate in expressing academic language and discipline-specific ideas. Globalization and market forces demand more 21st century skills related to problem solving, collaboration, and distributed communication within and across STEM fields.

Policymakers have all sorts of recommendations, but we pause to ask: Are *they* also committed to pausing? To reducing the curriculum and testing load to make room for speaking and listening? To supporting schools and teachers, rather than emphasizing the time it actually takes to promote conceptual understanding and procedural fluency in a subject such as mathematics or art? Will politicians interested in education reform pause long enough to allow communication skills to fluorish in our K–12 classrooms?

Only time will tell. In the meantime, we'll follow what the research says. Every student needs think time to process information, to learn well. It's our job to protect and serve these goals.

Checks for Understanding

Pausing takes practice. The following checks for understanding are designed to guide your journey forward. Pausing well takes planning, care, and reflection. These questions, prompts, and tasks are designed to help you take the ideas and thoughts in this chapter a few more steps forward. You can use the prompts in Warm-Up Prompts as self-checks and ideas in Try-Now Tasks as conversation starters and exercises for independent study or group work.

Warm-Up Prompts:

- Why pause? For whose good?
- What are consequences of *not* pausing in a lesson?
- What makes for *effective* pausing routines? How do you know? Got evidence?
- Is priming for pausing *necessary*? For which students?
- What are some ways pausing can *influence* teacher decision making on the fly?

Try-Now Tasks:

Day 1. Explain to students that it's time to create a word web. Remind them that word webs are warm-ups that help us to start thinking about a topic. Write the word *pausing* on the board and ask students what the word brings to mind for them. Add their responses to the board. (30 seconds or less)

Day 2. Same as above, but the students write their responses on sticky notes and place them on the board. (2 minutes or less)

Day 3. Same as above, but students discuss their responses in pairs before writing them on sticky notes and placing them on the board. (5 minutes or less)

Day 4 & 5. After enacting these tasks earlier in the week, reflect on your use of wait time. Note whether patterns of participation changed depending on the scaffolds you provided.

Review the Principles, Procedures, and Practices section in this chapter. Now imagine you are setting expectations for your classroom in the first week of school. You will need your community of participants to help define the tone, values, and supports to bring a formative assessment-rich classroom to life. The students can and must set expectations with you, but they must also envision ways to repair and mend agreements when things fall down. Plan a 10-minute lesson that primes the pump for pausing and supports this class discussion.

Challenge task: Have one person in a PLC or lesson study group explain why a particular procedure may support more effective pausing in the classroom. Allow another person to push back and say why these moves may not work—for whom and why that matters? Will students designated with a particular language level or IEP support plan related to attention benefit from this procedure? Be honest and respectful as you deliberate these different points of view. Then pull up your sleeves to solve the challenge with three possible strategies for everyone to try next before reporting back on the results.

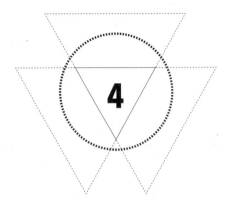

Probing

If students aren't interested in the subject matter, probing will be an irritation, a nuisance.

Diego, 8th grade science teacher

Of all the moves, probing seems easiest to mess up in ways that can really jeopardize a teacher-student relationship.

Lucia, music teacher

Probing can be dicey work. It calls for careful attention to verbal and nonverbal cues. Of teachers, probing demands a stance—the belief that every child has important contributions to make. Probing well requires agreements, tools, and routine procedures to help bring students' contributions to light. Of students, probing asks cooperation and openness. Probing says: Can you go a little deeper, say a little more, explain your reasoning? Students feel vulnerable when their statements, thinking, and performances are probed, especially publicly. Probing takes trust that all involved are going to benefit from the risks they are taking together. Probing, like all other FA moves, takes patience and practice.

What Is Probing?

Most often, probing is the act of asking follow-up questions. Sometimes probing includes invitational statements, such as, "I'm not quite getting your point," or "I'd like to hear more." Probing aims to make thinking visible to students and teachers alike. Probing also strives to spur thinking in our students. Teachers probe. But students probe, too. Push back is a form of counter-probing and it happens all too often. *You want me to write all that down? What do I have to do next? Why are we doing this?*

Probing can be a form of formative feedback, such as questions written by the teacher on first drafts of a science lab or essay. It can accompany verbal comments made on an art project or during a musical performance.

Probing supports the act of revision—it asks us to rethink our first answers. Probing moves, in particular, ask an individual student or an entire learning community to revisit a thought, an artifact, a performance, or an action they might not be completely aware of. A probe such as "I noticed each group took longest with the third task. I'm wondering about that," can go a long way toward supporting individual students' metacognition or raising awareness of group dynamics and the social processes of learning.

As formative assessors by now know, for probing to be aligned with learning targets in the assessment triangle, teachers need to be keen observers, listeners, and recorders. Our probes are intended to elicit student thinking and to explore misconceptions or even preconceptions related to the student cognition. Using the logic of the assessment triangle to our advantage, we situate probing moves in the observational strategies/tools vertex: it's how and why we collect "soft" data to gauge the current level of classroom understanding.

Why Probe? For Whose Good? For What Good?

Why probe? To help make student thinking visible. To get a more complete picture of individual cognitive processes, learning styles, and thinking. To explore the often-surprising explanations that underpin students' seemingly correct answers. Misconceptions abound below the surface of seemingly correct answers, incorrect answers, and unorthodox responses. Research has shown that all mental models or "p-prims" students bring to a subject merit deeper exploration (DiSessa, 1983).

Probing done well, because it requires deep listening, can be a graceful expression of professional care. Probing models curiosity. It is an exemplar of scientific inquiry. Probing also sends a strong signal to our students: deeper academic thinking and problem solving require us to use noncognitive skills and dispositions such as perseverance, self-regulation, and care for others. Probing embraces revision—of thinking, of working, of living "an examined life."

Ultimately, though, as formative assessors, we probe so we can make informed decisions about how to press onward with learners. *Do they understand yet? How can I be sure? Is there more they are not telling me?* Probing honors the provisional nature of working closely with students trying to use newly emerging academic skills and exercising emerging noncognitive and affective capacities.

Why have students probe? Because beyond helping them become critical thinkers and problem-solvers, we know the world outside school values probing as part of professional life. Journalists, doctors, nurses, lawyers, counselors, psychotherapists, and many other professionals have established practices and routines for probing. Asking follow-up questions is the most obvious example. Teaching students how to probe—into a controversial historical topic, a medical study, a public policy issue—may be a prerequisite to their becoming full citizens and college-ready learners. Professionals at the top of their game have probing moves at their disposal. Learning to probe may help our students get good jobs and live more productive, engaged lives in society.

Public Probing: For the Common Good

Elaborate. Explain. Say more. I am not sure I understand, can you say it in your own words?

These generic prompts ask students to go deeper, to use higher-order thinking processes, to produce responses that satisfy educational standards and workplace readiness in the professions. They probe for more than surface knowledge and recitation of facts. They demand a degree of expertise from our students. They set the bar higher—for students and teachers alike.

But today's educational standards aren't really new, nor is the practice of probing for deeper knowledge. Teachers and students who have sought deep, authentic learning together have always engaged in earnest dialogue and have always probed one another's thinking. As we learned in previous chapters, the Habits of Mind are invitations to probe deeper into information introduced in class (Meier, 1995). You might consider the Habits of Mind one of the pioneer approaches to *inquiry-based standards*. Centered on questions, the Habits of Mind ask for—even require—engagement with a subject and the world around it. These Habits invite probing rather than resist it.

The learning targets centered on Evidence, an essential Habit of Mind, ask us: "How do we know what we know?" This Habit sets the pace and tone for teaching students to use their minds well. It says: we are in a community of learners that probes its present understanding of a subject, the world, and the authorities who claim expertise. Probing for deeper understanding is clear: Evidence counts. Claims matter. Be prepared to back up what you say. We are all accountable to facts on the ground. Fake news is fake. Not all explanations are equally valid.

Probing tackles the "why" of things, events, and ideas head on. Setting learning targets with students that invite probing moves will signal permission to participate, to venture into a land beyond opinion, to risk using higher-order thinking skills in the curriculum. Probing moves "green light" the project of looking for support in an argument or explanation. They invite a healthy skepticism toward a topic without allowing us to backslide into cynicism or complacency. Now, perhaps more than ever, our students face seemingly intractable social, economic, political, and environmental problems. It's our job to provide them with the mental tools and educational experiences to address their future.

Not only are these cognitive Habits—of making connections, seeing different perspectives, analyzing evidence, making conjectures, and exploring relevance—not new, these learning targets may be as old as schools and educational institutions themselves. As long as teachers have had students, the challenge of probing students' thinking in order to take them to the next level of thinking has been a central focus of a good education.

We know, for example, that probing moves are at least as old as Greek civilization. When Socrates was not satisfied with the responses of his young interlocutors, he probed for more satisfying explanations. In Plato's *Dialogues*, the pedagogical movement of posing and probing is an elaborate, intricate exchange of ideas. Socrates poses questions, the students provide "answers," and Socrates probes again and again. Through Plato's eyes we see how student understanding grows through a relationship, a conversation, held in public. Centuries later we still admire this illustration of students making sense of their thoughts and opinions through Socrates's skillful probing.

Yet Socrates never wrote out his formative assessment-rich lesson plans nor did he explain the rationale for his teaching moves in the context of state and federal accountability. We rightly doubt Socrates taught 37 students of diverse cultural and linguistic backgrounds five times a day for 55 minutes each period. Socrates didn't have to navigate grading technologies, nor the demands from parents and colleges for "hard data" on student achievement. We have it on fairly good authority that Socrates, like many other of the world's great teachers, was not accountable to high-stakes test results nor to educational policymakers' demands for "value added" outcomes.

Our times are different. We are public educators living in a democracy situated in a highly competitive global economy. Nonetheless, by law and custom, we have a duty to educate all children in a fair and equitable manner. Dewey's injunction (1900) that "what the best and wisest parent wants for his own child; that must the community want for all its children" (p. 7) inspires us. U.S. citizens who pay taxes for public good expect a common good in public education. As teachers we help deliver on the promise of a truly democratic education.

We are not arguing that public schools are consistently realizing this democratic injunction to teach all children well. Nor do we contend that most students are getting what they deserve from our schools. Others have asserted that the right to learn in the United States is deeply interwoven with the quest for equity, social justice, and excellence in education (Darling-Hammond, 1997). We see something more at stake: every child deserves an opportunity to experience a rigorous public education that aims to deepen understanding, but that goal can only be obtained when teachers are free to pursue new moves and modalities in the classroom. Posing, pausing, and probing—the daily work of formative assessment—cannot be sacrificed for new "smarter," "balanced," "21st-century" forms of standardized assessment. Our community and schools must hold the line. The promise of assessment of learning is not the same as the real challenge of preparing teachers for assessment for learning. To move forward, K–12 teachers will have to demand forms of preparation and support that bring resources back to classrooms—not consortia and companies.

Formative assessors need to learn to probe their students' thinking skillfully in the lesson and they need support in bettering their practices in today's classrooms. Before moving to probing strategies and examples, let's better situate probing within the logic of the assessment triangle.

Along with Posing and Pausing, Probing Resides Within the Observation Vertex of the Assessment Triangle

We probe to elicit, to coax, and to make visible student understanding. For formative assessors, probing moves are rooted in the learning target/cognition vertex of the assessment triangle and are based on a range of questions/prompts aligned with specific instructional and curricular goals. If we are teaching a middle school mathematics or a high school physics course, we know that learning progressions can guide what to probe, when, and why.

Teachers working to master formative assessment moves need to be keen observers of students and their learning. To better observe the current level of understanding, we have to ask targeted questions, gather responses, and then probe a little deeper to test the "firmness" of student explanations. Teachers seeking evidence of where students are—in the lesson activity, the unit, or scope and sequence of the curriculum—will inevitably need to probe.

Looking at the NRC's Assessment Triangle we can see how probing (along with posing and pausing) moves serve the *observational strategies/tools* vertex by expanding our lexicon. Whether written on the board; handed out on a sheet of paper; or communicated on the fly as you circulate the classroom, table by table; probing moves help elicit better evidence about student thinking. To bring misconceptions to the surface, we must first see, hear, and observe them. Just as with the Posing and Pausing chapters, the quality of classroom evidence or "soft data" directly influences the validity of the *interpretations* you can make about what your students know and can do, and therefore what your next steps are.

Probes, like questions posed, must be aligned with the *cognition/learning targets* vertex in a logic similar to the one outlined in the National Research Council (2001) Assessment Triangle. If the teacher asks "Can you say more?," the request for elaboration is meant to explore the learning targets in the classroom. If evidence is that target, then probing on students' claims, data analysis, and supports for a conclusion will guide the teacher's lesson planning. But we will also need a repertoire of instructional strategies to observe the students' use and understanding of evidence during instruction.

Probing moves, as shown in Figure 4.1, allow the formative assessor to modify initial questions, prompts, and tasks intended to elicit student learning. Being purposeful, intentional, and aware of the paths we expect our probing to take us can go a long way toward helping the formative assessor learn from the learner. The key is learning how to observe and collect data on that learning.

Probing Is What You Already Do

- When you ask students how they're doing, they reply, *Fine, Good,* or *Okay,* and you follow up with, *I saw you on the field yesterday with Mr. Certa. Are you ready for the track meet today?* you are probing.

- When you ask your Spanish I students a question in Spanish, a reply comes in English, and you request a response in Spanish, you are probing.
- When you invite students to look at a *Predict-Observe-Explain* graphic organizer and ask, *Can someone remind us why we* make predictions *in the first place? What other words about* predicting *and* predictions *do we know? What connection can we make to the language of science and how scientists talk (remember Mr. Spock)?* you are probing.
- When you notice nonverbal cues that suggest a student feels anxious, distracted, or upset, and you ask, *Are you okay? What can I do to help? What do you need to feel safe and successful today?* you are probing.
- When you invite students to debrief a homework problem after school and you say, *How do you feel about this unit? Logarithms are not easy. Where do you think I can help? Who else can help today?* you are probing.

When you bring an open mind to your students' responses and a commitment to meeting their initial thoughts and opinions with respect and curiosity, you are on the path to probing. The leader of a formative assessment-driven learning community commits to asking more—of herself, of her students, and of other adults in the building. She knows that probing helps us get a grip on what we know and how we know it.

Figure 4.1   Probing and the Logic of the Assessment Triangle

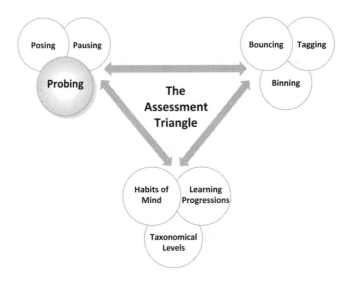

What the Research Says

Knowing that probing has been an enduring feature of teaching and learning does not make probing easy—for children or adults. To complicate matters, some theorists (Kohlberg, 1970) have argued that children's stages of moral, cognitive, and socio-emotional development may place constraints on the depth of knowledge that any single child can demonstrate, regardless of our probing skills.

Recent research on teenagers' cognitive development raises serious questions about when and in which cases adolescents' evaluative capacities are fully developed (perhaps not until 25 years of age). It may be that adolescents do really struggle to make sense of the world in ways that adults expect (Dobbs, 2011).

Not surprising to formative assessors, most research on teacher questioning supports using probing questions (Brophy & Evertson, 1976; Clark et al., 1979). Effective teachers probe students' responses for clarification, for support for a point of view, or to stimulate thinking (Hollingsworth, 1982; Brophy & Good, 1985; Weil & Murphy, 1982).

Research shows, however, that probing is far from ubiquitous or even frequent (Newmann, 1988; Sahin & Kulm, 2008; Pimentel & McNeill, 2013). Surface-level thinking questions make up perhaps 80 percent of classroom discourse (Airasian, 1991; Barnettte, Walsh, Orletsky, & Sattes, 1995; Gall, 1984; Kloss, 1988; Marzano, 1991). In a study of secondary science classrooms, Pimentel and McNeill (2013) found that even teachers who expressed that "teacher-driven discussion was not ideal… rarely used probing questions or tossed back students' ideas" (p. 367).

These studies suggest there isn't as much probing going on in U.S. classrooms as we'd like to think. It is true that teachers are asking questions, looking for a few good responses, and are seemingly satisfied with the first draft answers. But who is pushing back? Who has permission to ask *Can you say more? How do you know? What is the evidence to support this claim?*

Probing requires pushback—from all directions. It turns out that not all agree on the effects of probing moves. Researchers agree that the effectiveness of probing likely depends on how and in what context probing is carried out. Wright and Nuthall (1970) found that probing questions neither helped nor hindered student learning. Gall and associates (1978) reached the conclusion that when probing—defined as a teacher asking a follow-up question to improve a student's initial response—was studied together with *redirection*, there was "no effect on learning." Wow, we say as formative assessors, really?

Francis (1982) and Dillon (1978, 1983) argued that teacher questions—including probing questions—can in fact inhibit classroom discussion. They found that student contributions to discussion increased when teachers used alternatives to questions (Dillon, 1979). Teacher statements that paraphrased student contributions, offered an opinion, or described their state of mind, such as, "I'm not sure I see what you mean," increased student input to discussions. So how teachers probe really matters, and what works with one group of students may not work with another.

Teachers know this. And they understand how difficult probing well is, even when that teacher is experienced and knows her curriculum and students well. Some education research has been dedicated to developing discipline-specific probes and probing techniques to aid teachers. Yip (1999) offered secondary science teachers a sequence of probing questions to use in response to questions from students that lead to the students constructing their own answers. Coupled with Moyer and Milewicz's (2002) findings that "competent" teacher probing demonstrates great attention to students' work and responses, we can draw inspiration from these applied studies that aim to inform classroom practice.

Research Backs Priming for Probing

Research supports the necessity of two kinds of priming for probing: teachers priming themselves by examining their *stance* toward probing, and teachers priming their students for specific probing experiences that they can expect in class. Dillon (1984), like Bridges (1979), maintains that teachers' attitudes, dispositions, and commitments to classroom discussion—including a teacher's *stance* that probing is necessary to help every student bring important contributions to light—are essential to the *amount* and *kinds* of student talk that happens in classrooms. In other words, a narrow focus on techniques or lists of good probes that facilitate classroom discussion is secondary to teachers' attitudes, dispositions, and commitments to inquiry.

Bridges (1979) uses the concept of "presuppositions of discussion" to articulate the role of priming—although Bridges does not call it priming—for deeper student talk. Among the necessary conditions for priming:

- commitment and follow through in putting forward more than one point of view on a subject;

- willingness to examine multiple points of views;
- intentions to develop knowledge, understanding, and judgment on the matter under discussion;
- reasonableness, peaceableness, and orderliness of the classroom environment;
- respect for truth, freedom, and equality; and people (p. 24).

Many of these prerequisites are embodied in the Habits of Mind. Central Park East Secondary School's relentless focus on Perspective and Evidence required all teachers, students, and staff to examine "From whose point of view is this being presented?" and "How do we know?" Using essential schoolwide learning targets such as the Habits of Mind allowed teachers and students to participate in and promote deeper classroom discussion—across grade levels and departments. Embedded in science, math, language arts, history, service learning, and physical education courses, these high-leverage Habits of Mind invited probing with these follow-up questions: "Can you say more? Can you give another example? Can you show me how this works?"

Despite educational researchers' and curriculum consultants' desires to provide ready-made scaffolds for teachers (e.g., end of chapter questions), these scaffolds can only reach so far into the formative assessor's world. Agreements that help foster healthy, vigorous classroom dialogue must be built among teachers and students—and revisited—day in, day out. Agreements that invite persistent, concrete next steps on how to revise an assignment or project must be won one classroom period at a time. Agreements on why we are probing and what it means for, as Socrates put it, "living the 'examined' life" will have to prevail over satisfying the desire to just get it over with or to beat the clock.

If we don't change our stance toward teaching and learning, then our students will see through the game and fall back on doing school. In a world of "Can we move on now?" it is easy for formative assessment, like its big brother summative assessment, to appear as a command, a hoop, just one more checkbox on the list of things to do to make the grade.

Teachers and students together possess the power to rewrite the scripts of classroom assessment, take risks with responding to probes, and try out for themselves the power of follow-up moves: *Can you say more? Now explain it to a friend. I am not sure I get it yet. What's your evidence? We need to back this up. I care enough to have you explain it one more time.*

Next Steps and Opportunities

As with other formative assessment moves, not much attention is given in the literature to how different students experience the cognitive, affective, and cultural demands of probing. It's worth noting that the studies we cite did not focus solely on probing. Findings related to probing—the challenges involved, the kinds of probing that affect student achievement, and how teachers gain skill in probing—must be teased out more carefully. Meanwhile, those becoming formative assessors can break new ground, create new spaces for inquiry, and pioneer new probing moves, techniques, and strategies for inviting deep reflection in the classroom learning space.

 FORMATIVE ASSESSMENT TIPS

The formative assessor is in the habit of asking probing questions so that students will learn to ask more questions about any given response: she is modeling the ways in which questioning all initial thinking helps us learn more about "first draft" responses. We want to move from the provisional to the substantial answers eventually.

Going Deeper With Probing

Although we may have been born curious, many of us learn that probing is rude, offensive, even selfish. Much of our socialization encourages limits on probing. Probing seems pushy.

However, as those mastering assessment moves are learning, probing is necessary to size up where students are stuck, when they are treading water, and what's needed to help them go the extra mile. To the extent that schools can be settings where adults and kids make their learning processes public and take intellectual risks together with one another's support, learning deepens. This takes probing.

Let's pause for a moment. We don't presume to know your subject as well as you do. Your experience with teaching reading, writing, and oral presentation skills matters. The research, for example, on how kids learn (e.g., "why things sink and float"), coupled with your experience teaching all sorts of learners is valuable to us on this journey. So jump into the work of creating your own "go to" probes for the unit or lesson. For those who like to get into the mix with sentence frames, we provide a few examples of "go to" probes in Figure 4.2 that are aligned with the Habits of Mind and standards.

Figure 4.2   "Go To" Probes

Habit of Mind/ Learning Target	Initial Pose	Follow-up Probes
Evidence	What do we know?	How do you know? Can you state your source? How credible is this? Are you sure? Can you back it up with more evidence?
Perspective	Whose point of view is this?	Are there other perspectives? Whose perspective is missing? Whose perspective seems to matter most?
Connections	How are things/actions/ events/ideas connected?	Which connections cause other events or ideas? How are these things connected? Is there a relationship? What else influences these actions or events?
Supposition	What if _____?	Is there another possibility? Could events have turned out differently? What are the alternatives? What effect might it have? What other hypotheses can you formulate?
Relevance	Why does this matter?	Who cares? How is it relevant to our lives? What effect does it have? Will anything change as a result of studying this material?

We leave it to you to decide what to incorporate into your formative assessment practice in your learning community, based on your schoolwide learning targets. You may have a district policy or school initiative that leans towards well-known taxonomies. The sorts of probes we offer here may or may not make your list of "essential," "higher-order," or "deep" questions.

But we know from research and personal experience that the Habits of Mind can set up challenging learning targets for any classroom. We also know that when traditionally underserved and disadvantaged students are in the habit—across grade levels and subjects—of responding to these requests, they can and do achieve great things. A study of CPESS high school graduates found high rates of both college-going and persistence toward degree, two key outcomes to support students of color in low-income communities (Bensman, 2000).

You might ask: but how did a small public school in East Harlem achieve such results? Although there are many possible answers, just one sticks out for us—now. At Central Park East Secondary School, teachers, students, staff, and the principal used probing routines everywhere, every day, for every child. Students were, one might say, primed for probing. Over time the community learned to view probing as a valued routine—perhaps not exactly natural, but in context, not offensive or rude. Deeper exploration using the Habits of Mind—and always living up to a commitment to support students' social and personal well-being, and to support the whole child—became the norm. Self-evaluation, peer feedback, and teacher judgment all relied on these common understandings about probing.

It was not uncommon to see a student and administrator in the hallway engaged in deep exchange: "Well, how do you think that makes other people feel when you don't take going to class seriously? So, when you do that, what are the effects of that on others around you? Is there another viewpoint on this? What does it mean to understand yourself through somebody else's eyes? So if you were in my position, what's the next thing you would need to do?" (Duckor & Perlstein, 2014, p. 24).

Students learned that a follow-up question, a probe, was not a personal attack, but rather an invitation to use their minds well. When students experience this—as you and we know they can—they have moved beyond "doing school" to engaging in earnest reflection. Isn't that one of the reasons we became teachers, to witness and guide such shifts in our students?

A culture of probing makes it possible for a learning community to experience respect for opposing points of view and intellectual vigor together, and helps students learn to become critical thinkers and problem-solvers, which is what a democratic society needs. "School," Debbie Meier and Paul Schwartz (1995) asserted, "must be a place where students learn the habits of mind, work, and heart that lie at the core of democracy. Since you can't learn to be good at something you've never experienced—even vicariously—then it stands to reason that schools are a good place to experience what such democratic habits might be" (p. 28).

Like Dewey, these school administrators and the educators they supported knew that probing isn't just good for students' thinking and teacher decision making—it's good for democratic institutions and life.

Planning for Probing: Guiding Questions

The following questions will guide you in going deeper with your probing. They emphasize the reasons for probing deeper and how you can make it happen in your classroom.

1. Why are these learning targets important and how will my probing questions advance the lesson?

Initial questions posed need to aim toward important learning targets. Probing, too, needs to align with important learning targets.

As you know, deciding upon important learning targets for your particular students and classroom context isn't easy. In the posing chapter we recommended using the Habits of Mind as an overarching frame to help you make sense of the standards in your discipline and define learning targets carefully.

Even so, you'll still need to articulate *why* the particular learning targets matter. You'll need tools such as the Question Map or Formative Assessment-driven lesson plan to help articulate your probes—whether they are presented as statements or questions or do nows. Planning, trying out, and revising your probing strategies will help you come up with better probes.

Next comes sketching out probing questions regarding the unit's learning targets. Revisit your Question Map. Place an essential question at the center. As you draft probes to support and elaborate on the various targets/nodes, group the probes first. Groupings you might consider:

- probes based on the Habits of Mind (essential question-based probes),
- probes for common misconceptions or learning progressions regarding a topic/concept (research-based probes),
- probes related to the processes students will engage in as they work toward the unit learning targets (metacognitive probes),
- probes that students might ask of another's work-in-progress (social probes), and
- probes tied to anchoring activities, texts, labs, or problems (task-based probes).

2. What kinds of things will the students initially say or do with the probing questions that I need to anticipate?

First, we need to know about the learning environment. Will students be working by themselves? In pairs? Will students be writing—on tablets, paper, or other media—in response to probes? How many opportunities to draft or articulate a response to probes are students allowed in the lesson segment? Will there be several "turns of talk" or rewrites involved? What scaffolds can—or should, given your students' needs and backgrounds—accompany the probing questions?

These questions deserve deeper reflection, in part, because they help the formative assessor anticipate what is likely to happen in the moment when you try to enact your best plans. Here is an example of what the real work looks like when you are making FA moves in a peer-to-peer writing lesson segment. We invite you to consider the possibilities.

 IN THE CLASSROOM

A 9th grade class is working on writing to persuade. They've already warmed up the concept "persuade" together. Now working in pairs, they are writing the mayor about homelessness in their area.

Manny and Thao are partners. Manny is an officially designated English learner and hesitant to speak English. Thao, too, is bilingual, but not shy. Each pair is drafting a topic sentence. Many seem stuck. The teacher gives everyone a graphic organizer then asks them to pause and breathe deeply.

She asks, "What did we say a topic sentence does? It helps us to communicate and develop an argument. How is an argument different from an opinion?"

Eventually each pair will post their draft work to the class online forum. Right now, the activity requires students know the difference between *opinion* and *argument*.

"Let's look again at the word webs we created yesterday where we considered *opinion* and *argument*." She highlights the most important descriptors.

"Let's hear from someone why the topic sentence helps us to begin the argument." She uses "equity cards" to choose whom to call on. "We'll hear from at least three people. [Pauses 5-8 seconds] Okay, let's look at the sample topic sentence [points to the document camera]. It's time to use our Writer Goggles." The teacher mimes and pretends to put on her Writer Goggles. "Remember," she says, "these goggles are a writer's best friend." She points to the poster at the Writer's Workshop Wall, *Probing questions are a writer's best friend*.

"Everyone have theirs on? Carl? Sandra? Roberto, I see yours are on!" Students giggle. "So, how did Enrique build his topic sentence? What words do you see that he included? Why did he choose those words? Pair-share, and we'll discuss."

[Pauses for 1-2 minute pair-share. Circles the room to see who is ready to share out and asks at each table for a volunteer.]

"Now, let's look at some of your topic sentences. Any volunteers?"

Thao raises her hand, then drops it. Manny fears they'll get picked. He doesn't want to speak, nor have their sentence critiqued. He sees Tina, Cassandra, and Ricardo have their hands up.

⊟ *Continued*

"Thao and Manny, please come up and show us your draft."

"Ours isn't really finished," says Thao.

"Ours is!" shouts Devi.

"It's okay if you didn't finish. Many of us have not finished yet. Remember our agreement at the beginning of this year? We will share, and we'll trust that others will respect our work. First drafts deserve respect and support from other writers. We are in this together."

Manny and Thao come to the document camera and put their sentence down for all to see. Thao fidgets. Manny grins from nerves. Eyes are on them, their sentence, the teacher. What will the teacher's next move be?

Will she correct the sentence?

Instead, the teacher refreshes a probing routine. She points to a poster at the Workshop Wall: *Can you say more? If not, we will help you!* And another poster: *First drafts deserve a closer look.*

The teacher reminds everyone about their purpose for writing and why they're probing. "We're probing to help you develop a topic sentence that will kick-start your argument. The mayor and city council must hear your voice. You can persuade them that you have a solution. But first, we need a topic sentence that grabs attention and helps focus your audience."

Before they delve into Manny and Thao's sentences, the teacher invites Luis's team to read aloud what they wrote: "Homelessness is not the problem, the politicians are when they don't serve the whole community."

The teacher notes that Devi's team wrote, "We cannot come together as a city unless we start cleaning up our backyard."

Then she asks Manny and Thao to share their draft topic sentence: "Homelessness is bad because it hurts the community." Manny did it!

But the probing isn't done yet. The teacher invites the class to use the Warm and Cool Feedback Protocol. "What makes this a good topic sentence and how can we improve it? Remember, I want us to provide Manny and Thao with "warm" feedback first and then "cool" feedback next so they can take next steps to improve their topic sentence. You have three minutes to write your feedback on sticky notes and bring them up. I'll read them aloud for the class. Manny, Thao, you write warm and cool feedback for your sentence, too."

The students pair up again; the room buzzes. The teacher circulates and observes the treasure trove of soft data in these drafts, and makes a few mental notes about what she hears and sees: *has an opinion; still not sure why it hurts the community; using*

Continued

"because" sentence starter but seems stuck; what do you want the mayor to do? and qué es las problema (she wants us to write about)?

By observing carefully, the teacher sees some teams revising their own topic sentences. Others seem stuck, not quite taking a stance with the prompt. The feedback protocol might be inspiring their revision. She probes a team, "I notice you're revising. Tell me about what you're doing."

"Well, ours was actually a question," comes the reply. "We didn't like how it sounded."

"I am not sure I understand yet. What do you mean? Say more," the teacher probes again.

Part of the power of probing with this peer-to-peer feedback (Writer's workshop) protocol is that students can see how others have approached the task and use this information to inform their own work. This protocol also allows the teacher time to size up her next FA moves, including deciding which probes might work best to address the responses she is getting.

The simple but challenging prompt embedded in the writing task, *"What makes this a good topic sentence and how can we improve it?"* opens space for safe probing in a writers' community. Their work together reflects work in the world outside school. We all need good editors.

We highlight that this teacher's sampling strategy brought to the students' attention a rich array of skill variation in the sample topic sentences they considered together. For now, we foreshadow her bouncing moves, as they relate to posing, pausing, and probing around the class, by noting this combination can help teachers to prioritize and focus on what to address, given the current level of understanding. Effective formative assessors move around, size up things, listen carefully, and probe where it makes sense to probe. They are good at letting go—of anxiety, preoccupations, and presumptions about learning the material—temporarily. The focus is on listening to more students, better.

Each FA move that the teacher orchestrated in this 9th grade classroom—the topic sentence task, the share out, and request for peer feedback—invites students to provide evidence of their reasoning processes about what makes a good topic sentence. Of course, more probing on students' initial writing samples is necessary. And this further probing will be related to what bins a teacher uses to categorize student work. How teachers bin students' initial work samples depends largely on the mental models available to them, which we explore more in Chapter 7.

For now our goal in mastering formative assessment moves is to see that students need more and better opportunities to elaborate, explain, and justify their answers—and that probing helps them do that.

3. At each turn of this lesson, which kinds of bins are anticipated by my probing questions and which ones aren't?

Improving your probing requires visualizing likely responses to initial questions, task demands, and problems students are working on during class.

The goal will be to anticipate student responses that fit in several bins and map out ways to categorize and sort student understandings that you are likely to encounter in a particular lesson or unit topic. As a formative assessor, our purpose is to see patterns and to explore student thinking—not to reproduce bins of *correct* and *on topic* responses that satisfy our need to feel effective.

For those learning to become formative assessors who can gauge "where the students are" and "what comes next," you will have to come up with a wider range of possible ways to handle student responses. You will need to get in the habit of building new bins to hold *incorrect*, *unorthodox*, and *off topic* student responses. Why does this matter? Because, with this set of anticipated responses to questions you pose or prompts you deliver during instruction, you can better decide on which probes that will push for deeper student thinking.

Note that we've taught adolescents, too, and we well know that formative assessors need to prepare themselves for student responses that belong to *off color* and *go to the office* bins. Such responses are inevitable. So be prepared to prime and corral the restless, juvenile wanderings. Tagging all responses—which we encourage you to do in Chapter 6—may foster a welcoming, open learning environment, but it doesn't make much sense to probe on the ones that signal "I need attention" or "Look at what I can get away with." Not now, anyway.

Anticipating these kinds of responses, however, helps us not be so shocked or disappointed when they appear. It also leaves us with more options from a classroom management perspective. Priming for probing also means setting rules of engagement. You need a plan for more than *unorthodox* or unusual responses to your posing-pausing-probing moves.

Guiding Routine: Apply the Predict-Observe-Explain Model to Your Probing Moves

Try applying the Predict-Observe-Explain (POE) routine, borrowed from science instruction, to your probing moves. It's deceptively simple and highly effective for improving practice. Here is an example of the three steps:

*In response to this probe, I **predict** the students will say…*
*Based on this particular probe, I **observed** that the students actually said or did…*
*My **explanation** for the difference between my prediction and my observation is…*

The POE routine works so well because it supports your own development of Conjecture, one of the Habits of Mind, by asking *What if students say this or that?* Then it encourages you to collect Evidence, *Do students actually respond that way? What does the soft data tell me? Are my binning strategies helping me to anticipate a few, most, or all the range of responses?* Most important, the evidence part of the POE routine spurs you to reflect from different Perspectives: *Who took the risk? Where are the students struggling most with elaborating? Why did they respond (today in 3rd period versus 5th) the way they did? What if I tried another probing approach (rather than call and response) with my English learners or my kinesthetic learners or my silent Sallies and Bobs?*

Developing solid probing moves will require you to think through such questions in advance of teaching a lesson or unit. The POE is a nice mental model to help you get started with new probing habits. Visualizing student responses is not easy. It takes time and experience to internalize all the student voices and patterned "typical responses" that become part of our teaching experience—years, in fact. But we can start now. If you say "Not yet," we'll probe with "Why wait?"

Principals, Procedures, and Practices

How probing happens matters. Consider the differences among probing student thinking using

- oral exchange only
- written "dialogue" only, or
- a mix of oral and written methods.

Which modes work better for whom? For what kinds of curricular material or lesson activities? At what particular points (openers, transitions, closings) in the lesson? Which probing strategies take longer? Which help us give students better feedback? Which seem to maximize engagement?

Let's probe a little further together by imagining a student, Javier: why might Javier struggle when we ask "Can you say more?" If he shrugs and sinks back in his chair, what's our evidence that his lack of response in 5th period life science means he didn't study or doesn't care? How could we find out if there is more behind Javier's thinking about natural selection than our questions (quick write and pair-share posing moves) revealed? Are we digging into cherished beliefs or uncharted territory that clashed with other mental models of "how the world works"? The formative assessor does not shirk these questions, nor rush to judgment when students resist answering our follow-up questions. Time to step back, get curious, and approach the learning challenge from another angle.

Brianna, a teacher we worked with a few years ago, likened the trade-offs of different in-class probing methods to many students' preference for texting over talking:

> Texting gives students chances to draft and revise what they want to say. This is especially true in high-tension or romantic situations. Talking, on the other hand, is immediate. You can't think about your answer for 10 minutes. I know that if probing is not done well, it can give students that same feeling of panic they would get if they had to call their crush's house and ask for a date. To put it more academically, probing [on the spot, verbally] can raise their affective filter.

Fortunately, teaching today seldom limits us to either/or modes. There are so many modalities for our students to listen, speak, read, and write. Finding the perfect pitch method for probing may be beside the point.

Let's not presume to know which of our students prefer oral versus written probing—and when. Rather, we can prime for probing by checking in with our students at the beginning of each unit (not just in late August and early September!). Let's invite them into agreements about what works better in which kinds of situations. Situations they perceive as high tension, as Brianna suggested, may call for different methods of probing than situations our students perceive as low tension. Because perceptions differ, it's important to explore them. Then offer choices.

Students find choice motivating. When we involve students, we'll likely wind up having access to better evidence for making decisions about what to teach, reteach, or even preteach. The more we learn about how real students in a particular classroom approach the material, the better we can guide them through the bottlenecks, cul-de-sacs, and eddies that will inevitably mark students' progressions toward understanding a conceptually difficult learning target such as genetic mutations, natural selection, and the theory of evolution. Every subject has its equivalent intellectual challenges; we must be ready to acknowledge places where probing is paramount and also vulnerable to becoming a stumbling block.

Try adapting the following supported probing protocol for your subject area. Note the warming up (activation of prior knowledge) and mix of oral and written modalities (differentiation of instructional media) that seems best given what you have likely learned so far about your students. Let's remember, too, that we know from research on learning that *all students* need opportunities *to work out their thinking verbally*. (Again, we see how the FA moves are interlinked.) Making space for pausing and think time while pursuing your probing moves is a critical part of helping students to retrieve and encode information into long-term memory and, most important, putting them on the path toward building stable, meaningful, well-formed schema that serve a purpose.

Supported Probing: An Example from a Middle School Science Class

How can a middle school science teacher know whether a student truly understands why things sink or float? One answer can be found in the FA moves framework, which is connected to a well-researched example.

First, do a warm-up with a brainstorm/word web. In this case, write the word "float" in the center of the board and say, "What comes to mind when you hear the word *float*? There are no right or wrong answers."

Write the question or prompt, "Why do things sink or float?" Next, ask your students to do a think-pair-share. After that experience, request that they do a quick write. Collect the results and select (randomly or strategically) a few responses. With these informal pieces of assessment evidence in hand, it's time to probe: "Nam, I like this response to the question, can you say more?"

Research on misconceptions about buoyancy (Yin, Tomita, and Shavelson, 2008) reveals that students typically think that big, heavy things sink and small light things float; that hollow things float; and that sharp edges make things sink. After asking students why some things float and others sink, the teacher might ask, "So who thinks things float because they're hollow? Can you say why? Turn to your partner and ask them for an example of a hollow thing that might sink."

Supporting probing by priming, pausing, and providing oral and written scaffolds helps teachers collect evidence about their students' thinking and where they might be getting stuck in common misconceptions. The better evidence our supported probing yields, the better opportunities we have to help students on their progression toward understanding conceptually difficult material. We tell our budding formative assessors in teacher education programs: to probe on 'big ideas' around buoyancy such as mass, volume, density, and relative density will require planning and discussion with your colleagues and a little research. Nobody succeeds by just winging it. Probing moves take time and care to craft.

Mastering formative assessment moves is not a "7 step" program. The FA moves framework we present is not linear nor isolated to making one move at a time. As we've noted as part of the NRC's logic of assessment design, posing-pausing-probing combos are essential to uncovering and observing the complexity of student thinking in each lesson. Priming your students for these combos is also essential. Supported probing takes time and requires trade-offs. And there will be bumps along the journey. The upside, however—better evidence, more equitable engagement, deeper learning, even increased teacher satisfaction—are well worth the time and effort.

Probing Your Learning Ecosystem

As with the posing of good initial questions, probing causes students to stretch, to feel a little pain, to scratch their heads and occasionally, stare into space. We can almost guarantee your students are not yet in the habit of reading, hearing, and handling such probes in your subject area. You can count on students freezing up, experiencing confusion, asking for help, or wanting to be rescued.

Priming individual students—and your entire classroom learning community—for probing is critical. It's your turn to go deeper now. Figure out ways you need to *prime for probing* by probing your learning "ecosystem." Yes, let's borrow a few concepts from our colleagues across the hall and use a paradigm for understanding "systems." Of course, it's just a metaphor (trigger warning). You don't have to be a science teacher to think outside the box:

- How are the classroom "adaptation" and "selection" dynamics lately?
- Is there ample space for all "species" of questions—and responses—in the learning "environment"?

- Can everyone "adapt" to changing cognitive demands of the higher- and lower-order probes?
- Who is at the top of the food chain and loves to "munch up" the *what* questions?
- Who avoids the *why* questions?
- Who prefers the *how* questions?
- Are some students more "specialized," occupying "niches" of response modalities (e.g., oral, written, kinesthetic)?

What will it take to restore balance to the ecosystem when someone feels threatened or bored? Together we can generate all sorts of paradigms and metaphors to illuminate the dilemma. Probing is not necessarily a natural act, one that we are immediately comfortable with or pursue without a push. Lately, there is so much focus on classroom management technique and more efficient ways to gather, store, and use knowledge. Probing has been ignored. Many view it as useful only if it produces a higher test score or better grade. Although we acknowledge, along with the experts, that probing moves and the other formative assessment practices can contribute to student achievement, that's not the sole reason to support it. Probing matters because it makes us more human.

Watch Out for Pseudo-Probes

As we search for direction and control of the lesson, the questions we select may be influenced by what's in our minds, how we are feeling, and whether this is a "good" or "bad" day. On days where we feel fatigued and frustrated, it will be easy to fall back on old habits. We've all done it.

"Guess-what's-on-my-mind" questions proliferate when we are under stress. We pose a question to our students while holding a particular, correct answer to our question at the forefront of our mind. It's a waiting game as we seek to hear the one right response.

Our probing moves can devolve into a game of guess what the teacher is thinking—even when that game is not necessary for the lesson to proceed or good for student learning. We pseudo-probe to get at least one student to say out loud what we have in mind (the "correct" answer). It's a human, social reaction to the complex demands we confront as teachers. We want to see results, to gauge achievement, to feel we made a difference. (Parents and administrators may be watching—forming a cheerleading squad and pointing toward the goal post.)

Pseudo-probing can become a pattern, especially for beginning teachers who are learning the game of doing school as others watch. Taking our probing to the next level requires breaking away from this pattern. Probing well asks that we open our minds to really hear students' responses, and not dismiss responses as we continue on the quest to the right answer. It means taking time, setting up routines, and making it clear that formative assessors value *process* as much as product.

Consider these questions and make a note in the margin: What situations make it more likely you'll pseudo-probe? What will it take to let go of this practice? Who can support you? How? If you're a coach to teachers becoming formative assessors, how can you discuss pseudo-probing in nonjudgmental, supportive ways? What role can you play in helping uncover alternatives to what those becoming formative assessors may not (yet) see as a problematic situation worth addressing? We share a cheat sheet as an FA Tip.

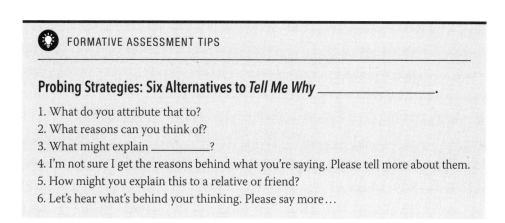

FORMATIVE ASSESSMENT TIPS

Probing Strategies: Six Alternatives to *Tell Me Why* _____.

1. What do you attribute that to?
2. What reasons can you think of?
3. What might explain _____?
4. I'm not sure I get the reasons behind what you're saying. Please tell more about them.
5. How might you explain this to a relative or friend?
6. Let's hear what's behind your thinking. Please say more…

Misconceptions and Challenges

Probing student responses in public school today is difficult for several compelling reasons. Factors related to *context, climate,* and *control* can explain why we see so little posing-pausing-probing exchanges in schools. Part of the challenge resides, as Debbie Meier and reform-minded educators note, in the structures of schools. The comprehensive high school, for example, is designed for social efficiency and maximizing tracks of learning (Kliebard, 2004). The middle and elementary schools less so. Yet school structures and conditions are not the only barriers to better posing practices. Other challenges (and opportunities!) reside in how our beliefs play a role in shaping what we take as possible, even necessary. Misconceptions and p-prims (intuitive ideas based in "everyday" teaching and learning experiences) with probing abound. We address a few and invite you to add to the list as we peel back the layers of time-honored pedagogical tradition.

Probing: Ellen's Case

Probing, whether oral or written, is feedback. Like other feedback processes, supporting students through probing helps. The more we can make these processes visible to our students, and the less they feel surprised, the better.

A challenge I have is making sure students get timely feedback on their writing—feedback they understand and can use to improve their work. I do rely on peer-to-peer feedback because my students certainly benefit from giving and receiving feedback to and from one another. Students need more than that, though. Probing and feedback from an adult who—in most cases, I'd like to think—is more expert than their peers does matter. Plus, I need the interaction with their writing, too.

My interaction with their writing needs to happen when they can still revise and still feel motivated to revise. Writing comments and probing their thinking when I'm grading their essays doesn't cut it. The kids barely read the comments and questions and practically no one revises—even though, technically, the option to revise is always there. It's on my syllabus.

So I have found ways to formulate feedback on their writing projects, give the feedback, and clarify feedback as needed—all within class time. Overall this works better for my students than my old methods. And I'm not facing stacks of essay drafts on Sunday afternoons.

Being disciplined and tightly focused is key to making this work. And my classes have to be able to function independently. Here's how it works: I dedicate the first third of class to getting students to work on a few specific aspects of their writing. For example, they'll check and revise their topic sentences, add commentary to quotes they have provided as evidence, or check for tense throughout their drafts. I give a minilesson, and then circulate as needed while they work. Sometimes students are paired up to help one another. They get a scoring guide.

I collect their work. Students watch a movie version of a text anchoring the unit or a relevant documentary as I read targeted portions of their drafts. Just portions.

I read for what the minilesson was on and maybe—maybe!—one other thing. Then I write on sticky notes a specific, positive reinforcement-type comment and a probing question. I'll write something like *That's it! Let's see if you can do similarly in your third paragraph* or *This revised topic sentence works much better, now add a quote in the body.*

My probes often urge students to expand: *What makes this evidence important to include? Tell us*, or encourage students to link their ideas, such as, *Please write out how these ideas are connected.* As I'm writing the sticky notes, patterns emerge. I find myself writing the same positive feedback several times in a row. Or using nearly the same probes—like, *How does this connect to your thesis?*—again and again. These patterns jump out. And they're important. They help me decide where to go next. Even if I'm not sure how I'm going to help my students link their content with their theses, I know that's where we need to go. And I can spend my planning period—or my afternoon run—figuring out how we can get there.

Before class ends I pass back their drafts. They get time to read the sticky notes. We have a process. *Can you make out my handwriting? What about what I've written confuses you? Where is clarification needed?* I take time to walk through this. I'll say: *I'm pretty sure some of my sticky notes will need translating. Let's hear from two that need translating.*

I pay careful attention to what needs translating. It's instructive. My students teach me where I need to improve my feedback. And, since I still have the opportunity to coach them through my feedback and my probes—the bell hasn't rung yet—I do. I've learned to set timers to make sure I stay on pace and protect this part of the process. My probes can't help students much if they can't read them or understand where and how they apply to the next draft.

By the time the bell rings I've acknowledged the work they did in the first part of class. I've also noticed patterns in their work and I use these patterns to think about what to reteach in the unit. Best of all, this process helps me to learn when and if my feedback strategies can use some tweaking.

⚠ Misconception Alert: Probing Always Means Asking Questions

Teachers, like the character Professor Charles W. Kingsfield Jr. in *The Paper Chase*, provide the template for probing. Using an exaggerated version of the Socratic method, they relentlessly pummel students with a barrage of questions. For each answer, there is another rapid-fire question, followed by yet another. In this dramatic setting, students and teachers joust to prove who has done the homework.

It turns out that we can probe without asking such prosecutorial "weeding out" questions. Research (Dillon, 1978, 1981) has shown that much like more traditional notions of probing, so-called *nonquestioning* moves by teachers increase students' verbal contributions. We know that during class discussions—including small group discussions—teachers' adroit nonquestions (statements such as "Socrates deserved to die," or "sharp metal edges make things sink," or "ratios are the same as proportions") can yield an array of student contributions that inform teacher decision making.

Such untraditional probing can also build community and encourage openness. Since probing-through-statements is, by its nature, usually invitational and inclusive and not just focused directly on only one student, many students experience such probes as more friendly than even the gentlest of traditional probing questions. Teachers who probe with nonquestioning moves become expert at listening. They choose where to insert their statements. They decide to what degree they want to be intentionally ambiguous in communicating to whom they're addressing the probing statement, especially when interacting with a small group. Some students seem to love trying to gain the spotlight when a probe sounds as if it's for the whole small group (but it's really for them). Other students need indirectly targeted probes just to feel safe. In some cases, a little ambiguity can go a long way. Formative assessors note which tactics seem to work when. Flexibility in approach, a burgeoning toolkit, keen observation skills, and commitment to reflecting on what works helps teachers to become formative assessors who can adapt consciously and intentionally to constantly changing circumstances.

Hattie's "teachers are to DIE for" strategies suggest that a variety of traditional and untraditional modalities may be effective in the diagnosis phase of formative assessment (Hattie, Biggs, & Purdie, 1996; Hattie, 2009, 2012). Probing as listening in/sizing up/intervening may be slower than probing as asking questions/listening for response/asking a follow-up question. Both types of moves are available to the formative assessor. As usual, the context, climate, and kids matter when making a choice of which type to deploy, when, and where in your curriculum planning. Never forget: we are professionals who must decide.

FORMATIVE ASSESSMENT TIPS

Why Posing and Probing Moves Are So Challenging for Beginning Teachers

Last semester Tito wrote: Posing is hard enough. How do I pick a good question for today's lesson? Probing seems easier. If I figure out a few good questions, no matter what the students say, I can always ask *why*. *Why* becomes the safety net when all else fails.

Asking why, however, particularly when asking one student, frequently triggers resistance. If not outright resistance, it induces at least a cognitive slowing caused by raising the student's affective filter.

We suggest that beginning teachers start here: (1) Recognize that using *why* is doing them no favors. (2) Remember that they have alternatives. (3) Ask them to commit to experimenting with these alternatives. (4) Acknowledge that it will take effort to add to their probing repertoire and help them respect the complexity and challenges of probing student responses. Beginning teachers should give themselves permission to slow down before launching a probe to give them access to their best thinking in the moment, so that they won't just hurl a *why* out there to keep the feeling of forward motion going during class.

Beginning teachers are desperate to keep the forward motion going. "My pacing in my teaching is sometimes slow enough as it is [without probing much]," they tell us. And, when they do have other probes in their toolkits, they still face plenty of challenges.

A 12th grade English teacher told us about his efforts to help a student, "I'd love to have more one-on-one private conversations to address Marlon's needs, if it can somehow be managed while also keeping 30 other students on task. These conversations take time. Drive-by probing, I've noticed, is not effective with Marlon."

Our preservice teachers struggle on the journey of mastering formative assessment. They confess, "When students resist my attempts at probing their thinking, it's frustrating. It feels like they're challenging me as a teacher." It can be ego-bruising. Sometimes teachers give in rather than persist in prolonging their suffering and the suffering they perceive from students.

An Algebra II teacher knows that students need to do the work. "Yet," she writes, "sometimes—and more than I like to admit—I handle resistance [to my attempts at probing] by caving and giving in. Today, for example, to help a student, I asked her if she remembers factoring by grouping binomials. She looked right at me, not really defiantly or anything like that, and said, 'I don't.'"

Continued

"Maybe she really has no idea, but that resistance to my probing allowed her to completely take the easy way out and not have to think at all. Like I said, I caved. I wrote on a piece of paper the work to factor that polynomial and just handed it over."

Preservice teachers learn that student pausing after a probe does not mean resistance, it's actually more often a sign that they aren't resisting. Many rely on (the mostly ineffective) "because it's on the exam" as a response to student "complaining."

Beginning teachers often interpret "I don't know" as resistance. That's even before they begin probing. A mature teacher-candidate wrote, "Student pausing is not resistance to probing. Usually it's if a student answers immediately and aggressively 'I don't know' that they are being resistant. I once had a girl throw back at me, 'I didn't do the reading.'"

When shadowing in the first phase of her teaching placement, one of our candidates witnessed a young Latina student say "I don't know, I'm stupid." The candidate was surprised how her mentor teacher handled the student's feelings, seeming to embrace the push back. "This particular mentor teacher told me that she needed to show compassion for feelings of inadequacy and low self-esteem and still 'hold them accountable for their answers,' otherwise they will use the same excuse, 'I don't know it.' And if I let it slide once, then the rest will use that as an excuse."

An art candidate we worked with in the student teaching seminar is learning to push forward: "I don't let students answer with 'I don't know.' If that is how they respond to a piece of art, I don't just say, 'okay' and move on. I probe them some more, often listing specific things about the art which they could choose to comment on. Worst case scenario I tell them I am going to ask someone else and then come back to them."

School leadership makes a big difference in building and sustaining probing moves. If the leaders in the school (principals, department chairs, and experienced teachers) do not explicitly and consistently value questioning, then we will see little evidence of the posing-pausing-probing cycle in classrooms. Probing takes time, effort, and support from school leaders who believe that the current standards require this work.

Rewarding teachers with praise, engagement, and constructive feedback about their probing practices is a necessary precondition for changing the mindset from "there is no time to probe—just get a few answers and move on." Research on growth mindset (Dweck, 2010) favors more probing of initial responses to important questions in the curriculum, in part, because benchmarking academic, social-emotional, and metacognitive progress requires us to see students on a continuum that emphasizes change and possibility.

⚠ Misconception Alert: Probing to Grab Attention and Manage Behavior

By now, everyone is familiar with the cold call. And they know when the teacher is using questions to gain control. We've all been in that hot seat:

> "Mr. Sanchez, can you tell me who invaded Poland in 1939?"
> "Uhh. I dunno."
> "Why didn't you take notes yesterday during the movie, Mr. Sanchez?"
> "Miss Washington, what is the lab procedure we are working on today?"
> Silence.
> "Miss Washington, pull out your worksheet. Can you remind the class please?"
> "Ms. Pham, I noticed you got the correct solution. How did you do that? Can you please come up to the front and explain it to your classmates?"

These pseudo-probing moves are not aimed at any particular learning target. There is no attempt to use a scaffold, create wait time, or develop a mechanism for sharing with different modalities in the classroom. By now, the priming-for-probing agreements are usually broken or in disrepair. No one feels safe.

A common misconception about probing for attention is that it is effective. People who are scared or feel embarrassed are often silent. Silence looks like a quiet, orderly, well-functioning classroom learning environment. In fact, effective probing can look very messy and can be loud and lively.

The grand inquisitor-style teacher, not unlike the Harvard law professor so aptly portrayed by John Houseman, wants to control the class so he probes students to grab attention. When a teacher is desperately trying to regain a voice, cold calling becomes the "go to" move. We see again and again how teachers sacrifice short-term tactical gains for long-run strategic and sustainable agreements.

Control is only part of the puzzle. We cannot simply call for better classroom management techniques that aim to control student behavior without teaching those same students to learn to use their minds and hearts well. Though we can easily imagine how beginning teachers tend to see most posing and probing moves through the fateful lens of crowd control ("Johnny, are you listening?"), experienced teachers should know better.

In order to maintain focus and feel successful, teachers can and typically will avoid opening classroom discussions they can't control. Considering that many classroom learning environments have not yet established norms of respect, trust, and forgiveness when things go awry, it is not surprising that we see so little probing (i.e., elaborating, explaining, justifying, reasoning) in the lesson. It's just too risky.

We have said that formative assessment consists of a patchwork of moves, which are sewn together as a sort of quilt and bring students together in the learning enterprise. But what is the purpose of probing? Isn't posing good questions enough? What are the goals of the formative assessor who asks lots of follow-up questions and offers feedback in the classroom? Ask Ellen (see the case study in this chapter).

 FORMATIVE ASSESSMENT TIPS

Reframing Probing for Success

Probing. What comes to mind?
Stand still. Brace yourself. Here it comes.
Deep space.
Ouch, that question hurts.
Please don't call on me. I dunno (and leave me alone).

Probing moves in all these colorful connotations remind us that deeper engagement with thinking involves risk. When we make probing moves with our students, we are leaping into uncharted waters and heading into new realms. We are inviting students to employ their Habits of Mind—to search for answers that go beyond surface, first response.

News flash: We are not playing prosecutor or police chief; nor are we conducting an autopsy or operation. Instead, we're asking, "What's behind the curtain?" Like scientists and engineers, we are asking, how exactly does this work? We are digging deeper, peeling back the layers, looking beyond appearances. The "correct" answer often falls apart upon closer observation and examination.

Probing is an indispensable part of the formative assessor's toolkit. Nonetheless, it is plagued with potential problems, dangers, and difficulties, including responses such as, "I don't know," "Leave me alone," "Why are you picking on me?," and "I told you that

Continued

I don't know." This is tricky terrain. We must navigate carefully, look for safe havens and harbors that minimize resistance and invite authentic exploration.

We formative assessors need our questioning practices to excite the imagination.

It is unlikely that we can rely on the literature on "questioning" to build, nurture, and sustain this practice in our formative assessment-driven classroom. Although there is lots of attention on the purposes of probing (the power of "essential" questions, for example), there is less focus on the problems, dangers, and consequences of going deeper in checking for understanding in classrooms and schools without establishing a shared foundation for inquiry. Students may resist. Parents may become alarmed. Principals may become concerned. Priming for probing is needed, even in schools that explicitly value inquiry or signal an interest in critical thinking skills.

Linking Posing and Probing with a Question Map

It is hard to imagine posing without probing. In a genuine dialogue, there is a give and take of information, thoughts, opinions, and feelings. Probing is a way to find out more. A question like "So where are you from?" often evolves into sharing experiences or questions about the geographical area. Like posing, probing can be cognitively demanding work. At times it is also emotionally taxing for the teacher and the students. "I'm from New York." "Really? Whereabouts?"

Having a probing routine ("Prepare your sticky notes" "Time for Q&A" "Ready-set-let's-go on the Gallery Walk") can help you direct traffic. It helps you to anticipate twists and turns in the road, however unfamiliar or rugged. As before, you may want to map out the probes that naturally follow after the questions posed—to individuals, in small groups, or the whole class.

There are the critical things to do to develop preplanned probing strategies and prompts. (You can use the draft Posing Map you developed in Chapter 2.) This new and improved map will help you probe with intention, care, and support for your particular students.

You already have your essential, guiding question at the center of the map. Remember that each node around the guiding questions represents a key learning target aligned with standards. Your nodes might include Evidence, Perspective, Connections, Speculation, and Relevance. Or something more content-specific such as Mass, Volume, and Density. Or even a cross-cutting set of learning targets such as Conventions, Structure/Organization, and Communication. The point is that, for each node, you will have questions or statements that can be posed in the unit and probed upon as lessons unfold.

The next step is to take the major nodes and branch out with secondary and tertiary probing questions. For your content and your particular students, what connects these nodes? Draft questions worthy of being considered again and again over the course of the unit. Take advantage of your students' interests and culturally relevant topics to find themes that will capture and sustain their interests (Ladson-Billings, 1995; Gay, 2010; Paris, 2012).

Revise the question map by focusing on the "nodes" and "links" on the map. Now that the map is more filled out than the one you drafted for Chapter 2, do you need to change its boundaries before you use it with your students?

Prioritize. Align your priorities with goals for your students. Are there common themes or different ones requiring new maps? Should you color code for question types (open ended or closed, statements or queries, verbal or written) or by levels of difficulty using a taxonomy? Are there more maps to develop based on future units or coursework in the upcoming school year?

Most important, make this a living document. Mark up and annotate the question map as you use it throughout the unit or semester. What questions and nodes do you predict will get the most action? Which ones align well with the current standards? What new nodes are needed to support students as they ramp up and circle back to these questions? Jot down notes before the lesson or after to keep a running record of what worked and what needs better delivery so you can formatively self-assess your posing and probing moves.

 TEACHER VOICE

Priming for Probing: "Re-" is almost a four-letter word

I can think of some positive and negative feelings that come with the "re-" prefix. Let's start with the bad news. Students who have a fixed mindset (as opposed to a growth mindset) will view the prefix as failure of the first attempt or assignment and view it as more work. Depending on how you prime the student, "re-" can be most liberating. My master teacher, when he talks about intonation, primes the kids and lowers their

Continued

affective filters by asking "if you're out of tune, are you a bad person? No, you just have to fix it." In this scenario, "re-" is liberating because it gives the student (who probably has more of a "growth" mindset) another chance to get it right. "Re-" is a very formative prefix in this regard.

—Jerry, a beginning music teacher

Learning to Look Back: Reflecting on the Just-Taught Lesson

Every lesson is provisional. It is a draft. You may want to treat your lessons as a first, second, or final draft. We remind you that perfection is not the goal, but neither is giving yourself a pass.

We believe that to improve your formative assessment practice, you must get in the habit of visually rewinding the lesson, playing it backward and forward. Hit the pause button. Freeze frame the action. Most important, we ask you to use the FA moves framework to see what is working and what can be improved in your assessment practice. In our research with teachers in professional development settings, we have found that time for reflection is crucial to revising the lesson and reworking it for the next round (Duckor & Holmberg, in press).

Formative assessors, like their students, will benefit from self-assessment and peer feedback to the extent it is positive, specific, timely, and content-related. The FA moves framework allows you to see what is worth seeing, and to forget what is trivial or distracting (such as "My tie was crooked" and "The kids make a lot of noise, especially Johnny"). Take one move and use it to break down, parse, and redirect attention on what matters.

These days many states require teachers to assemble a portfolio to obtain a credential and provisional license. Gina, an aspiring art teacher, used our classroom assessment and evaluation course to videotape her Phase II student teaching lessons, annotate her FA moves in a 5-minute clip, and reflect on how to improve each one with a set of brief commentaries. Thinking through her instructional practice and being guided by the FA moves framework allowed Gina to focus on the nontrivial, substantive aspects of her probing strategies. She now has the foundation for a state-approved portfolio and is one step closer to being hired in this profession.

Like many of our graduates, Gina feels overwhelmed by the state standards and requirements for the teaching profession. By the time she hits her final semester in our credential program, she reports feeling burned out, exhausted, and ready to "just do school" and "whatever it takes to get a grade." But somehow, each semester, we manage to push past these feelings and get back to making moves. It's a struggle—for teacher educators and their students.

By the sixth week of class, Gina makes a presentation to us all. She shares her experience: "Probing my students by asking for more elaborate oral responses is similar to asking them to revise their written responses. In both cases, it is like pulling teeth." Gina notes that in both instances the students are being asked to reflect on something that is already established. From their point of view, the assessment event is over. "I said it" or "I wrote it," so there is nothing more to be said or done.

Although Gina acknowledges that writing responses can take more time than providing oral responses, there is a benefit in the art classroom. She describes asking her 3rd period students to work in pairs and examine the drawings as part of a final project. She asked students to discuss and respond to the following questions:

1. Describe one interesting line you see in your classmate's drawing. Draw or write a description of the type of line.
2. Does the line you chose support the overall composition of the drawing? Why or why not?

As she told us that evening, Gina noticed a connection between probing and academic language:

> This worked well because students were able to see their classmate's artwork and use their academic language that pertains to this unit. After they located a line they found an interest in, the second question dives a little deeper into their discussion. The second question asks students to look at the overall image and address if the lines they see are supporting one another. This also allowed me to check in with students and see if they understand what composition is and how this knowledge is applied to the drawings they are making in class.

It is clear that oral and written probing moves provide different opportunities to check on students' understanding. Reflecting on her Thursday lesson (which we ask all teacher candidates to do as a weekly blog), Gina wrote:

During a demonstration this week I showed students how to make a duplicate of drawings using a light box. In my demonstration I explained to students that it was important to align the two drawing papers so that all the lines you add to the duplicate are in an identical arrangement as the original line drawing. After I showed students how to operate a light box, I paused and asked students to tell me how to do it step by step. When students reached the point where they were telling me to put the papers together, I asked students, "Why would I align the papers together to match?" I then asked students to pair-share with one another and be prepared to share out. After 30 seconds I restated the question and responded to raised hands. One student answered, "You don't want it to be wobbly."

I repeated what that student had said and asked if someone could expand on that. Another student raised his hand and said, "Because you want them to be similar." I acknowledged that comment and asked if we could hear from one other person. Another student raised her hand and explained that you don't want the papers to be crooked. I restated all three responses by saying, "Okay so you said you want to align the papers together because you don't want it to be wobbly. You want them to be similar and not crooked."

This serves as an oral probing example because I engaged students by breaking down the steps within the demonstration and asked them why I would do certain things and how do I know I am doing them right. This allowed me to gauge students' understanding and see when I could move on or see if I needed to approach a specific concept in a different way.

We share this example for several reasons. Gina is a student teacher in her early twenties who is learning to become a formative assessor. Her recognition that she and her students learn "by breaking it down" tells us she is integrating learning theory with assessment practice. The act of chunking the task and finding segments and episodes for self-study is a major leap on the path to becoming a formative assessor. Gina is on her way, at her own pace.

In a signature assignment for the course and her "teaching event," we asked Gina to revise this and several other lessons by thinking about what worked and what did not and how to add more moves to bring about her lesson objectives. We also invite beginning formative assessors like Gina to probe deeper into their own instructional choices by providing annotated comments online:

- Which habits of mind, heart, and work did this lesson segment foreground?
- Which kinds of academic language supports did the lesson assume?

- Did probing about "line choices" seem to advance student understanding? Who specifically benefited from the probe?
- If you could reteach this lesson, which probes might have scaffolded which specific skills to address the larger questions of the unit/discipline?

As teacher educators and formative assessment coaches, we want Gina and her preservice colleagues to see each and every lesson as fluid and open to redirection. Learning about formative assessment is a systematic process to continuously gather evidence about teacher learning. Since we are all teachers in this profession, the same rules apply. First draft lessons (and enactments in the classroom) are just that. Time to revise and rethink "what's next."

Putting It All Together

This book does not promise simple solutions. Learning how and when and why to use initial and follow-up questioning strategies in your classroom is a part of your unique journey as a formative assessor. Probing is as much a craft as a science. We've pulled together tips and suggestions but there is no substitute for trial and error.

Without a solid repertoire of probing moves in your FA toolkit, you may lose the opportunity to go deeper with the big ideas, to engage student thinking, and to monitor individual and group development in your own classroom.

But in the end, it's your classroom—and you must make probing moves happen on your terms, at your own pace. Of course every teacher needs to devote time and resources to think more about the purposes of probing. We hope that your school leadership team has the vision and commitment to support your learning. The exercises at the end of the chapter can kick-start these efforts. In the meantime, let's keep moving forward.

We believe that the Habits of Mind (Connections, Perspective, Evidence, Conjecture, Relevance) are helpful guides to probing deeper into student thinking. But any attempt to uncover things hiding below the surface is potentially dangerous. Socrates, Jesus, Copernicus, Galileo, Joan of Arc, Lincoln, Ghandi, and Martin Luther King Jr. all paid a price for probing and pushing beyond conventional limits of what is known and could be said during their time.

Ironically, we may be condemned to lead the "unexamined" life by the very structure and function of modern schooling and the educational system. Remember that Socrates is reported to have chided his peers for busying themselves with the pursuit of wealth, the customary trappings of success, and putting all attention on daily matters while celebrating conventional wisdom. Part of his message to the Athenian youth: ask questions, dig deeper, uncover reasons for what you do and why you do it.

Today's schools should be places where young minds flourish, where capacities are discovered, and where lifelong networks are built. We know that, for many children, school is a gateway and the bridge to a better life. For others, roadblocks and detours abound. The question remains whether the right to a good education is synonymous with the right to question the education offered in the name of the public good.

The realists among us know that, in the rush to compete, to advance ahead of other nations, and to increase the productivity of the next generation, we may be forced to leave many features of a good education behind. In this "hardball" future and increasingly "flat" world, it is clear that *not everyone* needs to go deeper. Specialists, high-paid professionals, and technical experts are counted on to know more. The rest of us, not so much. Instead, we get some version of a public education that has no time for asking: "Can you elaborate?" "Would you explain this more?" "Can you say more?" Instead, we are asked "Did you copy the information? Is everybody done yet? Don't forget to turn in your test before the bell rings."

But there is hope. The demand placed on students from 21st century skills to academic standards opens up all sorts of new avenues for probing—to know more, to explain it better, to go deeper into the real world. Probing, like rewriting or restating a position or rethinking a hypothesis, is a request to say more, to explain, and to be more specific about initial ideas. What could be more necessary or needed today?

If education reformers and policymakers are serious about public education, they will put FA moves into the mix as they seek to raise both standards and the meaning of the high school diploma. Embedded in this approach to learning and teaching outlined in these chapters is the hope that we all get better because we know what it means to go deeper.

Checks for Understanding

Probing challenges us all. It is hard to go deeper and to allow students to elaborate and broaden their responses to initial classroom queries. The following questions, prompts, and tasks are designed to help you advance your probing skills and take the ideas and thoughts in this chapter a few more steps forward. You can use the prompts in Warm-Up Prompts as self-checks and ideas in Try-Now Tasks as conversation starters and exercises for independent study or group work.

Warm-Up Prompts:
- Why probe?
- Can there be lessons without probing? Explain.
- For safe probing to occur, what has to happen first in your classroom?
- What are your top 3 "go to" probes on your Question Map?
- Why is priming for probing important?

Try-Now Tasks:
1. Use the Habits of Mind—*connections, perspectives, evidence, speculation,* and *relevance*—to decide on key questions and probes for a unit. For each habit, write a key question. For each key question, write 2 or 3 probes.

Challenge task: Cross-reference the themes of your probing questions (the Habits of Mind) with district or state standards.

2. In an interdisciplinary team, do the activity in question 1 for cross-discipline learning targets.

3. Review the Principles, Procedures, and Practices section in this chapter. Now imagine you are setting expectations for your classroom in the first week of school. You will need your students to help define the tone, values, and supports to bring a formative assessment-rich culture to life. The students can and must set expectations with you, but they must also envision ways to repair and mend agreements when things fall apart.

List as many probing agreements as you can, prioritize them, then choose 1-2 to share with your students tomorrow. Plan a lesson that primes the pump for probing and supports this discussion.

4. Use a Four Corners exercise. Ask your colleagues to move to the four corners of the room based on these probing-related themes:

Corner 1: Warm-ups and icebreakers
Corner 2: Tools, scaffolds, and technologies
Corner 3: Statements and sentence starters
Corner 4: Values and beliefs

Each group assigns a leader and scribe, then creates a list of examples related to its theme. The groups combine their four lists into a single visual and discuss, debating the merits of each example. (Note: This task can be used with students as well as teachers.)

Challenge task: Have one person in the group explain why a particular procedure may support effective priming in the classroom. Allow another person to push back and say why these moves may not work—for whom and why does it matter?

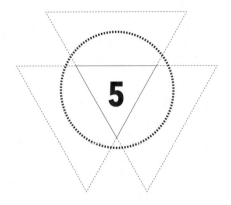

Bouncing

It was sobering to learn that during the entire period I'd heard from only three students. There are 29 in that class.

Mirabelle, math teacher

Focusing on bouncing means taking responsibility for the amount and kinds of information I get—and most important, who I get it from.

Arturo, physical education teacher

Everyone in schools is talking about data. Data systems. Data management. Data mining. In an era of accountability and high-stakes testing, we are expected to use more and more quantitative indicators. Some now talk about "big data" and how we can gather more information from students while they are being tested, using a web-based testing platform, or their smartphones to interact with testing companies' products and services.

Traditional paper and pencil assessments, including online standardized tests, produce lots of data because they take large samples from the student population. These instruments also have a very broad reach and can cover vast swaths of student sub-populations, giving the appearance of equity and inclusion. It is true, as any summative assessor will tell you: standardized tests allow us to summarize trends and to establish proficiency targets for the system.

Scores on benchmark assessments, the number of homework assignments completed, the letter grade earned if corrections are made to a test or quiz—these "public" numbers give us confidence that something has been mea-sured. In the aftermath of No Child Left Behind, we learned that the data points matter to school administrators and policymakers. These summative assessors prefer "hard, objective" data over the "soft, idiosyncratic" data generated by non-standardized assessment tools and teachers. Exit slips, word webs, quick writes, so the argument goes, are no match for the multiple choice and short answer items designed by experts (Bennett 2011, 2014).

So far, teachers have felt compelled to play this game. But we know that most teachers also value so-called "soft" data and cherish the just-in-time information that can be garnered through rich formative assessment practices. It's time to speak up for what interests us:

- We want to know how the kids' energy and concentration levels are affect-ing this morning's lab and what we can do now to move things forward;
- We want to know, after using a set of probing questions, which particular hand signals and gestures led to better positioning on the field or which feedback technique worked best with a struggling student in the band room;
- We want to know which specific rubric elements "landed" in the next writ-ten draft and which ones didn't, why, and for which students;
- We want to know who got stuck in the transition from the "I do" to the "we do" portion of the art lesson, who had trouble focusing today on the objective for the group project, and how to re-pose the guiding question so everyone can make progress.

In this chapter, we introduce the concept of bouncing to increase the depth and breadth of data points available to the formative assessor. Whether we're talking hard or soft data, there are no shortcuts to sampling from a wide vari-ety of data sources (oral, written, kinesthetic responses) during instruction. A sample of student thinking that is too small, too narrow, and not representative, helps us little in making good instructional decisions—and helps the kids even less with next steps.

That's where bouncing comes in. Formative assessors know that bouncing moves aim to widen the net of observation so the teacher can get more robust data to use during instruction and the learning segment. Bouncing moves help teachers like Mirabelle and Arturo on their journeys to becoming formative asses-sors by teaching them to strategically sample evidence of student understanding (and not just focus on the two to three kids who always do the work in class).

Bouncing puts the focus on what students say and do during class time and helps us gain access to more and better information about student thinking *during the learning process*. Bouncing forces us to examine our data-sampling strategies.

What Is Bouncing?

Bouncing. What comes to mind?

A ball. E-mail. A check. Tigger. Bouncing suggests movement: springing, hopping, ricocheting, rebounding, reflecting, and rallying. Bouncing implies energy, enthusiasm, dynamism, liveliness. Such bouncing does indeed happen in classrooms. But the kind of bouncing formative assessors mean is bouncing that facilitates sampling student thinking.

Definitions and connotations of *bounce* can help us with key and nuanced concepts related to bouncing in the classroom learning space. Doing a Google search on *bounce* reminds us that in many contexts, "bounce" is "exuberant self-confidence," as in, "the *bounce* was back in Jenny's step." Synonyms: *vitality, vigor, verve*. We certainly do want our students excited about learning, as educational psychologists who study motivation will tell us.

The combinations of potential bouncing moves are also worth considering in this chapter. Person to person, idea to idea, fact to fact, machine to person, person to machine—our goal is to widen the sample of student responses with all permutations of bouncing. Why? To gather evidence in order to make an instructional decision that advances student learning during the lesson. As formative assessors who bounce questions on the fly, we want to know: *Can we stop here? Is it time to check for understanding? Should we move on to the next activity? How many of us have grasped the objective? Who needs help making the leap?*

Other synonyms that Google lists for *bounce—rebound, spring back, ricochet, jounce, carom*, and *reflect*—suggest the motion, challenges, and complexities inherent in the bouncing action of *whatever it is* that bounces off, bounces back, or bounces around our classroom learning space. Let's explore some of the features of bouncing knowing that it is a move that requires patience, practice, and a new approach to speaking and listening to our students.

Bouncing Is Intentional, Systematic Sampling

Bouncing moves aim to intentionally and systematically sample a variety of student responses to better map the terrain of student thinking, understanding, and performance in a class. The goal of sampling—with the aid of bouncing moves—is to help teachers make sound instructional decisions grounded in the best evidence they can gather during instruction. Bouncing moves increase student engagement and bring more voices into the classroom learning environment.

Bouncing commonly happens via a call-and-response routine. During whole class instruction we see the teacher posing a question to the whole class. As the question hangs in the air, the teacher typically selects who gets to answer. Students with their hands in the air—or who aren't paying attention—often get called on first.

The problem with this common scenario is that the sample size is very small. We don't learn much about different student approaches to the topic or question when fewer than 10 percent of the students respond. We maintain that

- *How* students get called on—whether randomly, by recognizing the first hand in the air, or by choosing a student who hasn't participated in a while—matters when bouncing.
- How *many* students are called on matters when bouncing.
- *Which* students get called on—is there a pattern of calling on only the most talkative students?—matters when bouncing.

A more productive alternative to a typical call-and-response routine is the bouncing move "Call and Pivot." With "call and pivot" bouncing moves, teachers purposefully circulate around the classroom—from group to group, individual to individual. By bouncing themselves around the room, teachers can widen the net of observation, making more student thinking visible. Learning to listen in as students talk and work in groups, a formative assessor can gather valuable information about the depth and breadth of student approaches to an activity or task.

Sometimes the teacher poses a key question to the whole class, invites students to pair and share in response, and then *strategically* moves about the room, bouncing herself from pair to pair, listening in, and drawing conclusions about the level of understanding. In this example, bouncing helps us move beyond the appearance of learning; it focuses attention on who is stuck, who is moving along with assistance, and who can work independently during the lesson. Moreover, when connected to other moves, bouncing is a major time-saver. It guides the teacher's strategy for checking for understanding by providing a plan.

The teacher, who has mastered bouncing in group work settings can usually listen to—and perhaps prime, probe, and prime again—more than half her class's first-draft thinking in a short time, and do so before she redirects attention to the assignment and deliverable for the day. We maintain that bouncing is a prerequisite for checking for students' prior knowledge and for delivering on the promise of checking for understanding, day in and day out. Call. Pivot. Walk and Bounce—this is a new routine worth trying out.

 FORMATIVE ASSESSMENT TIPS

Becoming a Formative Assessor Means Moving Beyond Old Paradigms

If we see bouncing through a sage-on-the-stage paradigm of pedagogy, the teacher is the center of attention. The sage shines the spotlight, the student responds. Sage comments, then bounces the spotlight to another student.

In the best of circumstances, the teacher bounces the spotlight to several students, attempting to collect a range of student responses with which to make well-informed instructional decisions. In the worst case, the light shines on a few and no one sees a thing.

It's time to put forward a new paradigm of pedagogy—the guide on the side.

Why Bounce? For Whose Good? For What Good?

Some definitions of classroom assessment focus on getting hard quantitative results to teachers, parents, or administrators. The prevailing logic seems to be that the quicker the cycle of eliciting student responses—and turning them into numbers, graphs, and charts—and reporting this data happens, the better the formative assessment information will be to support "data-driven" decision making.

We concede that quantitative results (what appear to us as scores, points, numbers) are necessary in the school system. The question is if those results are sufficiently robust for teachers who need just-in-time qualitative information about student learning as it unfolds in the classroom.

Teachers have a different mandate and set of questions that drive their interests in data. We rightly ask: *How does the summative data inform the difficult choices we make as teachers in a particular lesson segment or transition? How does the numeric score inform pedagogical choices such as where to provide specific feedback, to whom, where, and when? What does a percentile or proficiency rating tell me about what to reteach, when to scaffold academic language, or how to coach, for example, a language learner through being "stuck" with a big idea or intricate procedure?*

To get answers to these questions, formative assessors need to refocus on moves that make student thinking visible in real time at grain sizes that are meaningful to teachers. Bouncing moves can help us to gather more instructionally sensitive, soft data about student learning as it unfolds *during* class.

Teachers want data that can help us make sound inferences and wise instructional choices on the fly. We want data not just about individual students' thinking and performance—but about group dynamics and school climate that influences our daily lessons. We want data that is representative of each period and each group of students—helping us make connections, see patterns, and be more effective in the next lesson. No matter how someone labels or markets or packages up the term "data," the formative assessor is most interested in samples that help us differentiate instruction and provide better feedback *during a lesson.* This takes learning to make bouncing moves—many of them, in all sorts of new and different ways.

 FORMATIVE ASSESSMENT TIPS

Maxim: All else being equal, the better we sample a set of student responses by bouncing strategically and consistently, the better chance we have of getting a representative and more reliable picture of student thinking on the day's lesson topic.

Bouncing Sits Within the Interpretation Vertex of the Assessment Triangle

So far, we have established that formative assessors are intentional in their classroom assessment designs. Borrowing a few principles from a panel of educational assessment experts at the National Research Council (2001), we have agreed that the logic of formative assessment is not that different from other approaches to assessing student learning. The assessment triangle is our guide too.

First, we identify what is worth assessing. We prepare a clear, well-defined set of learning targets to guide our lesson and unit plans. We care about how students learn and which Habits of Mind they bring to bear on authentic learning tasks, problems, and projects in our classrooms. The first vertex—student cognition/learning—is (and must be) the foundation of all formative assessment practice.

Next, we pair those learning targets and ideas about how students learn with a host of observational strategies, each aimed at gathering evidence of learning. We pose questions, then pause, and probe to elicit, coax, and make the current level of student understandings more visible to all. We set up clear, agreed-upon routines and practices that students come to see as normal, embedded assessments that support both instruction and learning. Our range of questions, prompts, and activities, aligned with specific instructional and curricular goals, are part of the FA toolkit. We purposely scaffold and tailor these routines and practices to maximize opportunities to meet students in their particular zones of proximal development.

We now turn to bouncing (which is also connected to tagging and binning) moves that serve the *interpretation strategies/modalities* vertex in the NRC's Assessment Triangle. Whether pulling equity sticks, using a randomizer app, or plain cold calling, bouncing demands that we sample the classroom learning space. To locate misconceptions, to uncover prior knowledge, to identify differences in the current level of understanding—we must widen the response net—and recognize when we have not. To make a reliable and valid interpretation of where student understanding is and where they need to go to next, we must have systematically sampled.

Bouncing moves allow the formative assessor to modify sampling strategies, take stock of the limitations of any given inference about students' abilities and skills, and most important, check what the evidence allows us to say or do with our soft data. As with all other moves in this book, our goal is to be purposeful, intentional, and aware of the pitfalls that come from being too hasty and rushing to judgment. The key idea in the next chapters is learning how to interpret and validate the data you have on student learning, and when necessary, to return for more.

 FORMATIVE ASSESSMENT TIPS

Formative assessors are bound by a covenant that places a priority on eliciting student responses that help them gauge learners' current levels of understanding and their need for support *in the actual moment of classroom instruction*. Skillful bouncing is needed to make this happen. The testing event is a snapshot, helpful for doing autopsies. Bouncing, on the contrary, works in the living classroom where the action is live.

Systematic, intentional bouncing in the classroom learning space helps us answer these questions: Which students have shared with the class and which ones haven't yet? What are the major misconceptions and procedural errors in play during this activity? How representative is this particular student response for the class as a whole? Am I dealing with an anomaly or a trend in student thinking with Alice's response?

Those becoming formative assessors need to be clear about how their bouncing moves link together with the other two major moves, tagging and binning. Each of these aspects of the interpretation vertex of the assessment triangle (Figure 5.1) will require planning, coordination, and practice.

Figure 5.1   Bouncing and the Assessment Triangle

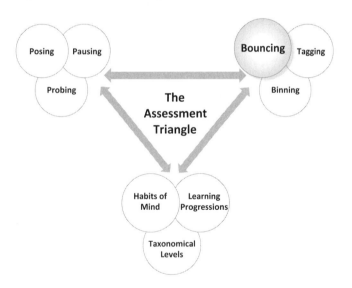

We can't skirt the facts on the ground: if our bouncing moves do not lead to better tagging and binning procedures and protocols, then our instructional decision making about what to do next will be compromised. No need to worry, though. We will explore a few basic bouncing moves (e.g., equity sticks, gallery walk, pass the stuffed animal) to improve our chances of landing on representative samples of student thinking, one lesson at a time. But first, we delve into what the experts tell us.

What the Research Says

Educational research tells us surprisingly little about the mental models teachers use to determine which students to approach, call on, or not call on. The research focus on asking good questions, using wait time, and probing for more in-depth explanations has come at the expense, it seems, of explorations into teachers' understanding and use of sampling strategies.

We do know that teachers' bouncing practices vary. Some seem to effortlessly increase the student response space and sample from it well. Others struggle. Experience, skill, depth of content knowledge (Carlsen, 2015), and disposition likely play roles in explaining why there is so much variation in bouncing techniques. Misconceptions (e.g., cold calling yields insight into most students' thinking) and p-prims (e.g., cold calling gets the ball rolling) may too. Recall that a p-prim, an intuitive idea stemming from our experience, is more like a preconception than a misconception—we all have them.

Cognitive demands on teachers are high as they work out who, when, and which on the fly questions will drive their lessons. Cognitive load theory (which we explored in Chapter 3 on Pausing) suggests that the working memory of teachers *and* students is likely to be limited in capacity and duration. As teachers launch, orchestrate, monitor, and adjust a lesson, they will need processing time to make sense of the current levels of student understanding that they are witnessing to guide their next instructional moves.

When it comes to bouncing, tech assists including clickers and vote counting apps may help to reduce extraneous cognitive load. Usually, however, these devices do little to aid in uncovering students' higher-order thinking or support requests for further elaboration and sense making (Hunsu, Adesope, & Baylyn, 2016; Kay & LeSage, 2009). Too often, these tech devices artificially constrain the response options (with predetermined "choices"). They may also promote the illusion of strategic sampling of student responses by relying upon a random default settings. As we shall discuss, random sampling is not always better or more useful to the teacher interested in equity and diversity.

For students, these tech assists look like another form of multiple choice testing. For teachers, knowing who voted for which answer does not tell us much about *why* they voted this way. No technology magically provides the cognitive, affective, and social-cultural sense making required for teachers to know what to do or say next when students are stuck. And for formative assessors to "sense make" in diverse classrooms, they need evidence—beyond polling for opinions by clicking a button. Students need to speak, verbally process, and elaborate on initial drafts of ideas in the classroom.

Research tells us that students' willingness to speak and how they get "the floor" or "in the zone" to give oral contributions in classrooms is influenced by many factors, including

- physical space and class configuration,
- student groupings (whether by ability or skill),
- socioeconomic status,
- gender, and
- language.

Wollman-Bonilla (1991) found that ability grouping affected the length and quality of students' contributions to discussions. Hemphill (1986) noted that girls from middle-class and working-class families use conversational overlap differently: either to make a bid to speak, or to show support for the speaker. Although these studies are insightful, we found little research that unpacked how bouncing to these different groups of students affected the quality and quantity of assessment-rich information that teachers might use.

We were surprised to learn that some research argues for cold-calling, a novice move in our eyes. The act of calling on students who do not volunteer is common. Dallimore and colleagues (2012) found that in classes with high cold-calling rates, significantly more students answer questions voluntarily, and the number of students voluntarily answering questions increases over time. Further, they found that in classes with a culture of high cold-calling, students' comfort with participating in class discussions increases; in classes with low cold-calling, students' comfort with participating does not change. Although their research findings show that "cold-calling can be done fairly extensively without making students uncomfortable" (p. 305), we leave it to you to decide to what extent these findings might be applicable to your kids, context, and curriculum. You might start by asking: how much do I get out of situations where someone cold calls on me and I am "volun-told"?

Research on typical bouncing strategies shows that they may not be warranted or in the best interests of the community learning. Take one example of the most common discourse pattern in classrooms, the Initiate/Respond/Evaluate (IRE) routine. Wells (1993) has documented that 70 percent of all discourse in secondary classrooms follows this routine. The teacher "Initiates" a question, a single student "Responds," and the teacher immediately gives a verbal "Evaluation" to that response (Mehan, 1979; Wells, 1993). In the next chapters we explore better options for uncovering student thinking for those learning to become formative assessors.

More recent educational research in this domain has focused on teachers' *elicitation* practices—actions teachers take during class to elicit evidence of students' knowledge and understanding—and "teacher responsiveness." Pierson (2008) has conceptualized "teacher responsiveness" as the extent to which teachers focus on student ideas in moment-to-moment interactions. Implicit in such observations is the notion of bouncing.

Pierson analyzed teacher talk and categorized teacher responsiveness as "low" or belonging to either of two categories of "high." The two categories of "high responsiveness" were distinguished by teachers' main purpose in responding: either to identify students' ideas with the intention of correcting them (High I responsiveness) or to understand students' reasoning on its own terms (High II responsiveness). Low-level teacher responsiveness, on the other hand, was characterized by teacher responses that exhibited limited connection to students' thinking.

As teacher educators interested in development and learning trajectories in formative assessment, we recognize that not every "productive," "responsive," or "high level" move by a teacher (however coded by researchers) will be fully captured in analysis of teacher-student talk. We maintain that researchers and practitioners agree on the importance of teachers being able to incorporate elements of students' ideas and reasoning skillfully into their oral responses to students and that scarcely little research has thoroughly explored how teachers develop these skills—from preservice to induction or beyond.

An exception is the work of Jacobs, Lamb, and Philipp (2010) in the area of elementary mathematics instruction. Jacobs and associates' study involved teachers who had participated in a professional development endeavor that extended beyond four years, which also contributes to the noteworthiness of their longitudinal research. They found that teachers do not routinely begin their careers with expertise in *attending* to children's mathematical solution strategies, *interpreting* children's mathematical understanding, or *deciding how to respond*. Teachers begin developing expertise in the first two of these three skills through teaching experience. Typically teachers get better at *attending* first, then they begin to improve at *interpreting* second.

Jacobs, Lamb, and Philipp also found that teaching experience does not correlate with expertise in deciding how to respond on the basis of children's understandings. That is, just having taught longer does not necessarily mean that teachers know better how to respond to children in the moment, nor know what "next steps" are likely to help advance children's learning. Not surprisingly, Jacobs's team found that professional development that supported teachers' attending, interpreting, and deciding how to respond to children's oral or written mathematical strategy explanations did seem to positively influence teachers in developing expertise in all three skills.

Their research has provided the most "nuanced story" of the development of teacher expertise in "professional noticing" of children's mathematical thinking—by attending to, interpreting, and deciding how to respond—to date (p. 192). Important as this research is, it does not address a critical aspect of bouncing moves, or the broader problem of sampling (error, bias, and fairness) raised later in this chapter.

Ateh (2015) conducted a study that analyzed two high school science teachers' elicitation practices over the course of an academic year. She specifically chose the two teachers from the participant pool of a larger, ongoing study of science teachers at 10 comprehensive high schools in Northern California because both teachers had stated, while watching video of their own teaching, that they had "used elicited evidence of students' knowledge to make instructional decisions that enhanced students' learning" (p. 118)—examples of "substantive" formative assessment practice according to Coffey, Hammer, Levin, and Grant (2011). But Ateh found a "mismatch" between their perspectives of their formative assessment practice and her analysis of what transpired between the teachers and students in class. Ateh found that, too often, these teachers' elicitation practices were "characteristic of low-level elicitation" (p. 112).

Educational researchers continue to document a hard, generally "known" and accepted truth: effective, "substantial" in-class formative assessment is needed, difficult to do, and still relatively rare in many K–12 classrooms.

That doesn't mean there aren't models of good teaching to learn from in experts' classrooms. Dr. Deborah Loewenberg Ball is widely known for teaching—and her self-study of her own experiences of teaching mathematics with 3rd grade students—in ways that reflected close attention and responsiveness to their thinking. Ball (1993) did not call what she or her students were doing in class "formative assessment" nor did she consciously enact "bouncing" (the concept and term had not yet been conceptualized nor articulated yet). However, a closer examination of her oft-cited article, "With an Eye on the Mathematical Horizon: Dilemmas of Teaching Elementary School Mathematics," published in *The Elementary School Journal* in 1993, through the lens of the FA moves framework presented here gives us insight into the complexities of teachers' decision making regarding bouncing.

Ball's article focused on the dilemmas of teaching, including the frequently occurring tough calls teachers make as a matter of course: "Often I must grapple with whether or not to validate [students'] nonstandard ideas" (p. 387). Black and Wiliam (1998) would refer to these as "unorthodox responses." Since we are reading Ball's research through the lens of the FA moves framework, we view Ball as anticipating and expressing the real challenges of bouncing to better sample a wider range of student thinking. Of the sampling dilemma, she writes:

> Sometimes my problem is that it is very difficult to figure out what some students know or believe—either because they cannot put into words what they are thinking or because *I* cannot track what they are saying. And sometimes, as in this example [the now-famous "Sean numbers" example; "Sean numbers" are numbers that, according to Sean, were both even *and* odd], students present ideas that are very different from standard mathematics…. Although Sean was, in a conventional sense, wrong—that is, six is *not* both even and odd—his claim was magnificently at the heart of "doing mathematics" (pp. 387–388).

Ball's focus was not explicitly on the percentage of students who were reached by her "bouncing" strategies. But we see them as having played a key role in orchestrating and uncovering student thinking during the class discussion about "Sean numbers." (The class named numbers made of odd numbers of "twos" after Sean in their next mathematics lesson.) Ball did, however, "aim to develop each individual child's mathematical power through the *use of the group*" (p. 388).

By our back-of-the-envelope analysis of Ball's report of the day when as class began "Sean announced that he had been thinking that six could be both odd and even because it was made of 'three twos,'" 32 percent of her students (7 out of 22 students in her class that year) either came to the board and questioned or explained or vocally weighed in during the first "Sean numbers" conversation (pp. 385–387). Without calling it bouncing, we suspect that Ball thought deeply about "ways to construct classroom discourse such that the students learn to rely on themselves and on mathematical argument for making mathematical sense" (p. 388). We argue that bouncing as a concept—and an accessible practice—can play an influential role in helping make that happen and that Ball's research bears our hypotheses out.

Deborah Ball and other expert teachers using "bouncing" techniques are operating at a level well beyond the bouncing moves we typically see novices enact in mathematics classrooms. As an expert teacher, she demonstrates a disposition toward inquiry and self-examination. As a formative assessor who anticipated the power of not merely checking for understanding but exploring student schema and p-prims, Dr. Ball's work deserves our attention.

Bounce Smarter, Sample Strategically

We favor approaches that increase the student response sample taken by setting up visible procedures that take advantage of random selection. Bouncing smarter means sampling on students without intentionally raising affective filters or promoting cognitive overload. There are immediate implications for our advice (alert: we may be challenging your sage-on-the-stage comfort zone).

We say, as gently as we can, no more teachers "pouncing" on students who aren't volunteering. No deploying "tough" questions as a classroom-management technique. Let's refrain from using pouncing strategies—like A.A. Milne's exuberant Tigger—to catch students who are misbehaving or not paying attention. Instead, we favor making your bouncing routines visible, sharing them with your students, and reaching agreements on how to increase the circles of participation. Sampling student thinking strategically means employing moves that feel more systematic and less arbitrary, less "gotcha" and more invitational to all.

We note that strategic, intentional bouncing moves will maximize the purposeful selection and recruitment of volunteers while potentially attending to populations of kids that tend to be *undersampled* in too many classrooms today. There are many ways to identify these students in your classroom.

Educational psychologists typically bin them into categories such as "quiet," "shy," and "introverted" and leave it to teachers as to how to actually approach "them." Students with IEPs, those from different racial or ethnic backgrounds, or those with language proficiency struggles (what summative assessors call "subgroups") may need us to bounce more purposefully to support their needs. But let's not fall into the "us" and "them" labeling trap: "We" are in this together and we bounce purposefully and with compassion because it helps us all to know where we are and where we want to go next in the classroom.

It is common to rely on a notion of teacher's intuition when deciding which students to call on and when. However, it turns out this may not always be the best guide. Communications scholar James McCroskey (2015) cautions:

> When asked what one should do to help a child that is quiet, the most frequent suggestion of the teachers with whom I have worked is to give [quiet students] more speaking experiences. While this approach may be helpful to some people, it is very likely to be harmful to most. Not all quiet children are alike.

No wonder teachers return to calling on the eager beavers! The pull of feeling like a successful teacher whose students know the correct answers is strong. Sampling silent Sallies and Bobs, who may be stuck or falter—especially when we are being observed and evaluated—is a dangerous move in the eyes of beginning teachers trying to look good. To complicate matters, researchers and formative assessment experts don't give us much guidance. We ask: *And what about bouncing to the cynical Sams or angry Andrews in 6th period? How am I supposed to sample 75 students on track and field? Why should I take the time to have all my students tag their responses to the wall when I can just hand out a quiz and "bounce" to all 37?!*

We agree. Good questions. It's enough to make us want to throw up our hands, too. It can take so much energy to just think about it—and more to actually bounce well.

Some teachers use extrinsic rewards (e.g., tokens or stickers) to increase participation and put a bounce into the classroom learning environment. Boniecki and Moore (2003) found that the amount of directed and nondirected student participation increased while a "token economy" of extrinsic rewards for participation was in place and returned to baseline after removal of the token economy. It is difficult to tease out the causes and long-term effects of these sorts of positive reinforcement regimes. But most agree that various bouncing strategies influence students' behavior differently. Armendariz and Umbreit (1999) found that students' disruptive behavior decreased dramatically when response cards were used and increased again when conventional hand raising was reinstated.

One thing is clear: the "business as usual" approach to sampling student responses is not working for "underachieving students, whether male or female"

(Myhill, 2002, 2006). Finn and Cox (1992) found that students who are not active participants in classrooms are at greater risk for dropping out of school. Common sense tells us that being invisible, sitting in the back of the room, having the teacher pass us by each day because we take too long to say what we think is going to have an effect. The case for bouncing to increase students' active participation while building up a better picture of the current levels of our students' understanding during the lesson is strong on its own merits. Let's now explore the problems, issues, and orientations necessary for smarter bouncing.

Going Deeper With Bouncing

We agree that increasing students' active participation in classes is a critical feature of democratic education. Bouncing helps students find their voices in our classrooms, but the bouncing moves outlined in this book need to be about more than "just" engaging students. The *sampling* aspect of bouncing, which underpins the interpretation vertex in the assessment triangle, is of core importance to teachers who are learning to become formative assessors, and thus make better instructional decisions based on sound classroom assessment evidence.

Going deeper with bouncing requires we explore the issues and challenges of sampling that are particular to the classroom learning space. We need to do the following:

- recognize and work with sample bias, measurement error, and unreliable observations;
- explore the drawbacks and limitations of common bouncing patterns;
- take action to establish new patterns and "course correct" when routines falter; and
- think about and act wisely on the limits of inferences made from on-the-fly observations.

First, let's talk about the role of sample bias in the classroom learning space.

Sample Bias

Intuitively we know that sample bias happens. When an organization conducts a survey of public opinion, let's say on predicting U.S. election results, but only uses one social networking site such as Twitter to do so, clearly the range of responses depends on who has an account with the company. Though Twitter accounts are certainly popular and are widespread in the United States, the "American public" in this survey sample is not well represented, in part, because the survey is restricted to account holders.

Now let's pretend the organization, after conducting its survey of Twitter account holders, says "According to our exhaustive survey, the people in the United States believe that ..." or "Overwhelmingly, we found that U.S. citizens favor..." or "People in the United States feel...." Would you trust these statements? Would you agree with the sampling methodology? Would you wonder—even just a little—how the polling organization controlled for bias before reporting their results?

It turns out that sampling bias happens in the classroom learning space, too. We may sample the prior knowledge of *only students who raise their hands*, a parallel to the Twitter users example above. We may sample *only students who respond* to our questions nearly immediately. (Even if we have the intention to check back in with students who need more time to respond, we don't always.) Perhaps, while circulating during group work time, we may sample *only students whose nonverbal body language communicates* to us, "I'm open to conversation right now."

 TEACHER VOICE

Beginners on Pros and Cons of Bouncing and Wait Time

I've found that bouncing can be the easiest formative assessment move as well as the hardest.

It can be the easiest if the classroom is primed right. Students have to know what procedures to expect. Students need to understand we really are going to ask questions of *everyone*. Bouncing in a class that is not primed brings lots of blank stares.

Wait time with bouncing gets into the hardest part of bouncing. During wait time, I used to get students pointing out that other students were ready. "Call on them."

So many students are used to sitting in class without being called on. They've been able to wait teachers out. Some students, it seems, will do anything to not talk in class.

Bouncing is a culture you have to build in class. And if you don't do it right, it's like pulling teeth and taking prisoners.

—Don, preservice U.S. history teacher

How aware are we of the different types of classroom sample bias? We know from experience that it is easier to call on students who volunteer, are verbally facile, are extroverts, communicate interest in the topic, respond quickly, give responses that are easy to understand, ask questions, or emanate positive energy.

These characteristics describe the eager beavers in our classrooms, those kids who make it easy to create and sustain feedback loops. No wonder sample bias often skews toward these kids' experience of the lesson!

Formative assessors, however, need samples that are more representative of their entire classroom population. Checking in with only the "Twitter users" will influence the inferences we can soundly make about the whole class. Instructional decisions based only on responses from those students with accounts do not have the opportunity to be as robust as instructional decisions that are based upon more representative samples. So, what's a formative assessor to do?

One answer: try the stratified random sampling approach.

 FORMATIVE ASSESSMENT TIPS

Stratified Random Sampling

As formative assessors, we need a wide and diverse range of student responses. We can carry out bouncing strategies that aim to get us a more "representative" representative sample. How? By identifying which students, by groupings, need to be a part of our sampling design.

In a modified stratified random sample response design, the teacher checks for understanding with a sharper focus on students from particular populations such as English language learners (ELLs), special education (SPED), or accelerated (GATE). For example, she might have a few cups to store the equity sticks in different groupings/configurations. Each day, depending on her purposes and her choice of focus students, the teacher pulls names at random from the different intentionally configured cups.

There are no predetermined limits on which groups the teacher chooses to sample or which techniques for sorting and calling she uses in her classroom. The point is to gather data or responses, from each of these cups. With this more representative sample, based on differentiated student needs, teachers can make instructional decisions grounded in smarter data.

What might the different cups or buckets be—beside the familiar ones based on well-known categories? That's your decision. Maybe you want to start with just one of your classes for a particular unit? Or maybe with the shy students? Or students taking the class for a second time or struggling with different modalities of verbal communication?

Continued

Gathering responses from one or two stratified buckets is probably better than having a one-size-fits-all approach to bouncing, but each teacher has to make a move that regularly gets them student response data from *all* the buckets they deem important for a particular unit and class.

Measurement Error and Unreliable Observations

Summative assessors who work in the standardized testing world know that measurement error happens. When we use score data, the evaluation of any student's *true* ability, skill, and capacity is always compromised. Testing experts use the concept of reliability to express the degree of uncertainty about the dependability of these observed scores. We teachers do the same every time we question: *Is this really Juan's best performance? Are we getting an accurate indication of what he really knows and can do? Did Jackie's mood, energy, lack of sleep, and missed breakfast interfere with her best efforts on the test this morning? Was Bikram's first draft on the lab really his best work?*

As well-intentioned as we are, whether as professional test makers or classroom assessors, we will miss data points that fill out a picture of true ability and skill level—whether it's a picture of an individual's performance or of the entire class's. All sets of observations—standardized or not—will contain a degree of measurement error, which leads to a degree of mischaracterization about our students.

To complicate matters, the questions, prompts, and tasks we use to assess our students can succeed and fail for reasons having little to do with students themselves. Poorly written questions, confusing instructions, and language laden with cultural and linguistic assumptions can push us into the shadows from what we truly hope to evaluate in the classroom. Too many classroom assessors hide behind those shadows, perpetuating the myth of the accurate score, the reliable GPA calculator, and other so-called objective grading practices (Guskey, 2002; Winger, 2005).

Most of us try to construct fair tests, reasonable homework assignments, and unbiased questions and tasks for class activities; however, measurement error still happens. Our points, check marks, and grades are an attempt to approximate the true score assigned to each and every student; we presume these numbers represent the actual level of student understanding. But we never know the true score. Ask any expert. Formative assessors, like summative assessors, must admit that our judgments about students' current level of understanding are at best provisional. Sometimes we have a degree of confidence about those true scores, other times not so much.

It's Hard Work to Establish New Patterns (Or, "How I Took the Risk and Let Go of Old Patterns")

Cold calling seems to work. It's a pattern we know and see all the time in classrooms. Despite the potential pitfalls with this bouncing move, we notice that most teachers (beginning and experienced) use the question-as-flashlight approach to shine light on the eager beavers, and to wrestle control back from the lesson "haters." Cold calling and other teacher-directed bouncing techniques seem to satisfy a need to dominate the classroom learning space. Before getting ahead of the how-to-sample-better story, let's examine the traditional Q&A model more closely and explore a few of its problematic characteristics.

"For Volunteers Only" Is Inequitable and Leads to Skewed Results

First, many teachers are in the habit of making participation in their classrooms voluntary. Only a small group of students deeply and actively participate, soaking up the offerings of the learning environment in the process. This results in two significant problems: the teacher's evidence base for decision making is much smaller than it could be; and there are many other kids who could be engaged more directly but become invisible as the lesson proceeds. The majority of student ideas and beliefs recedes as volunteers take up more and more space in classroom discussion.

You are probably familiar with the sobering implications of this imbalance of student engagement. Others have referred to it as the multiplier, or Matthew Effect (Gladwell, 2008). The deeper, more direct engagement of a few kids often leads to their greater success as compared to their quieter, less engaged classmates. This comparative success—and attention from the teacher—leads to greater effort (often from both the teacher and those students), which leads to still greater success—a *small* reinforcing feedback loop that could, with some changes, include many more students.

Missing Misconceptions and Chasing Missed Opportunities

Second, even when student participation is not voluntary, but proceeds in a random fashion, a few good eager beavers can still soak up the action. Now, it is the randomizer app that cold calls on students. In this traditional Q&A model teachers *still* tend to elicit responses *only from a few students*. Hence, these technologies consistently misrepresent the full range of student thinking on a topic. This means, inevitably, that teachers miss out on finding misconceptions or digging deeper into preconceptions.

You have probably experienced what's problematic about not uncovering misconceptions or procedural errors or firmly held opinions early in a unit. Failing to bounce out the gate, to sample across the classroom, to "pass the stuffed monkey" to more than 10 percent of the class means that students' thinking goes undetected—for hours, days, or even weeks. Before you know it, lots of students are failing quizzes and unit tests. You are handing out zeros and *F*s. Now becoming a formative assessor takes on a whole new meaning. Bouncing is a new habit that breaks up old cycles and brings about opportunities for early intervention.

Good Intentions Are Not Enough, Nor Is the Quest for the "One Best Answer"

The third problem with the traditional Q&A model for sampling is too often the result of good intentions. In an effort to connect with students and lead them toward a learning target, the back-and-forth among the teacher and students frequently takes on a "guess what's on the teacher's mind" quality. If not an outright guessing game—which we have observed many times and have played on occasion in our own classrooms—then at least a situation where the teacher is working for a *predetermined response. A response. One.* Not the wide range of responses formative assessors need in order to make valid, sound inferences on the current levels of understanding to meet students where they are.

Becoming a formative assessor means becoming aware of when this search for the one best correct response is happening, having other bouncing options at your disposal, and trying out routines that improve your sampling odds. Improving bouncing moves requires self-regulation and a metacognitive stance toward your teaching practice. A professional development conversation with your colleagues about how and why teachers sample the classroom (for whose good and for what good) could make student thinking more visible in your classroom and school.

FORMATIVE ASSESSMENT TIPS

Surfacing Misconceptions Early in the Unit

Earlier we gave the example of a physics unit focused on buoyancy and specifically the question, "Why do things sink and float?" Research on misconceptions about buoyancy (Yin, Tomita, Shavelson, 2008) reveals that students typically think that big, heavy things sink and small, light things float; that hollow things float; and that sharp edges make things sink. Similar work on facets of understanding in physics (Minstrell, 1992, 2000) have been worked out, as have new breakthroughs on student learning progressions in math (Clements & Sarama, 2014; Lehrer & Kim, 2009). These findings can guide our choice of observational strategies, but we must still attend to the mode of interpretation based on good samples of student thinking.

If we know that major misconceptions related to concepts of mass, volume, and density exist for this topic, but we constrain our sampling to only one or two students' responses, we may miss the opportunity to surface these beliefs and hence address these misconceptions across the classroom. Bouncing well matters.

To make good instructional decisions for students on the fly, teachers need good information on the current level of understanding of the group. So after asking students why some things float and others sink, the teacher needs to bounce the question across the room to pick up more responses. She can widen the net by probing and bouncing: "So who thinks things float because they're hollow? Can you say why? Take two minutes to explain what you think to your table partner and then write down two to three sentences explaining why. We will share these responses out on the document camera to look for patterns."

Mastering FA moves allows us to go deeper and wider with samples of student thinking at the same time. We think that a mix of lesson openers, quick writes, and exit slips can move the formative assessor toward more evidence-based decision making in the classroom. But first, we will need to think through our bouncing moves to employ sampling strategies that help to form a clearer, more reliable picture of what most students know and can do.

Assessment for learning demands no less.

We argued in Chapter 2 on Posing and Chapter 4 on Probing that formative assessors are in the habit of planning, enacting, and reflecting on the questions, tasks, and prompts they use to elicit student thinking. Unless you are the undisputed expert in your field and able to retrieve questions and size up every student's needs on the spot, however, we suggest taking the unheroic route by preparing a few questions in advance of lessons. Questions that are planned in advance of the unit, that are aligned with visible learning targets in the Cognition vertex of the assessment triangle, and that spiral back throughout the semester are most likely to help your students learn to use their minds well.

Planning for bouncing, as for posing and probing, can also help prevent mishaps that result from teachers' well-intentioned, often improvised efforts to engage students. Students, like most humans, do not like to experience learning in the form of surprise attacks, swarming probes, and inchoate, seemingly random queries that demand an immediate answer. When we skip the planning phase, our bouncing quickly descends into pouncing, and the students know it.

For those committed to mastering formative assessment moves, priming for bouncing requires us to plan lessons that anticipate where particular groups of students will likely fall down and when particular individuals are likely to freeze up as we bounce questions and thoughts around the classroom.

 TEACHER VOICE

My Efforts to Focus on Bouncing

I started out strong. I started using equity sticks for my bouncing for the first few weeks. But as the semester progressed, I got lazy with continuing to train myself to use equity sticks every time. Pretty soon, once-in-a-while turned into never.

I've renewed my commitment to using equity sticks to bounce even though the kids groan when I take them out. I think it's because they know there is actually a chance they will be called on. Too bad. I think they're getting used to it. But even if we get stuck—or I forget—I don't want to stop with the equity sticks. I know to bin well, a teacher needs to bounce well. For me, using equity sticks is key to bouncing better.

—*Aaron, social science teacher*

Recognizing and Working with Limits of On-the-Fly Observations

Let's be honest. Even when we try to sample around the classroom, in the theater, in the gym, or on the field, our capacity to capture, record, and study even most, if not all, student responses is limited. Too little student thinking is made visible by the idiosyncratic and inconsistent nature of our sampling strategies.

Despite our good intentions, we may be searching in the dark for clues about our students' abilities, skills, and capacities. On-the-fly observations suddenly don't seem so cool, fair, or useful.

Going deeper and getting smarter with bouncing requires recognizing—and working productively with—the limits of the inferences we can draw from our on-the-fly observations.

 FORMATIVE ASSESSMENT TIPS

FA Fact: Poor sampling leads to poor inferences. We can't know what's next if we haven't figured out the current level of understanding.

How can we make valid or reliable inferences about Javone's current level of understanding when we spent 55 minutes talking to Hannah, Alexis, and Noah? How can formative assessment be formative when it fails to obtain a sample of what the kids are thinking about a topic through a class brainstorm or word web that checks for prior knowledge? How can we claim the student response space has been represented without being explicit—and intentional—about our strategies, procedures, and checks for who shared and who didn't? There is an old adage in educational measurement circles, "Garbage in, garbage out." Is poor sampling on student responses any different? Not for the formative assessor.

To make these points a little clearer, let's put two sampling strategies and stances toward bouncing into sharper relief. The one stance is depicted by the *Q&A bouncer* who mostly uses pouncing techniques to get it done and tends to move on after a few correct answers are supplied. The other stance is the *FA bouncer* who is working on new moves, and different configurations for sampling a wider response space to better understand student thinking. Figure 5.2 helps us imagine these two types of assessment stances in action.

The question for all of us on the formative assessment pathway is which type of bouncers are we—on our best days, worst days, and the ones in between? We will freely admit to switching stances ourselves. Somedays, it just feels easier to play the Q&A role and say to the class "get it done."

Figure 5.2   Assessment Stances: Pouncing and Bouncing

Q&A Specialist *Pounces*	Formative Assessor *Bounces*
Only "voluntary" participation → too few students engaged and sampling feels like targeting and "gotcha" → most are "volun-tolds" Unsystematic, arbitrary, appears more biased	Mixes voluntary and random participation → lots of students engaged → if involuntary, primes for "pass" or "lifeline" Systematic, intentional, visibly more equitable
Too small a range of student responses → focuses on correcting answers → misconceptions left uncovered at the class level	Wide range of student responses → works to surface prior knowledge → misconceptions explored at class level
Teacher works the room for a close-ended, predetermined response → can fall into "guess what the teacher is thinking" game → teacher not open (and therefore temporarily unable) to meet students where they are at turns of lesson	Teacher is committed to meeting students where they are → makes visible procedures for tagging all responses → works iteratively to probe on ideas including misconceptions → uses open-ended questioning protocols frequently at important turns in lesson
Questioning strategies are untethered from learning targets → lack of differentiation in observational tools → more focus on task-oriented queries than taxonomical levels of understanding	Questioning strategies are purposefully related to learning targets → wide array of observational tools and strategies → plans questions, uses question scaffolds, addresses priming for "higher" and "lower" order questions/prompts/tasks during lessons and units
Little planning of priming for bouncing → students feel unprepared, surprised, experience confusion and anxiety when and if participation occurs Bouncing moves are disconnected from other moves and do not advance any broader, more complete picture of student thinking	Lots of planning for priming for bouncing → students feel ready, aware, and prepared to share ideas → procedures for repair if sampling strategy fails Bouncing moves are connected with other moves to support checking for current level of understanding at multiple levels—individual, group, and whole class

Linking Bouncing to Other Moves

Bouncing is integral to *tagging*; both moves can lead to more valid and reliable *binning* (we will get to *tagging* and *binning* moves soon). So if we fail to bounce, we actually reduce the sample space of student responses, which reduces the tagged response data available for interpretation. With this "restriction of range" (i.e., number of student responses heard, seen, read), our binning strategies become compromised. It's hard to interpret misconceptions when you haven't detected them. It's difficult to talk about students' prior knowledge and experience with a big idea or conceptually difficult material if you have not yet sampled it. Put another way: we can't make good instructional decisions or figure out our next steps in the lesson when we don't have credible soft data. Working on your bouncing moves can go a long way toward making your students' thinking visible enough to learn from it.

Getting Beyond Pouncing: Moving the Ball Around the Court

Let's learn to pass the ball. By visualizing our classroom questioning strategies as a basketball court, maybe we can better see the need to bounce the ball from player to player. No one likes it when someone hogs the ball and fails to bounce it around the court, mostly because it rarely leads to a win. A few superstars on any team are welcome. But a good basketball game, like successful classroom teaching and learning environments, depends on teamwork. Each player has a role in bringing the game to life. The ball must bounce around the court—lots of times, to many players—before we identify the winners.

Formative assessment, like a good basketball game, is not just about racking up points or celebrating the number of slam dunks in a classroom time period. It's about the movement of the ball (good questions, rich tasks, smart probes) across the room to better coordinate learning for all.

Beginning teachers often pounce on the first hand raised in response to their questions. It is exciting to see that you can command and control the audience with a query. "You mean they will answer my questions if I just ask them?!" It's a powerful feeling. Teachers crave attention. We like having a captive audience. It feels good that someone "got it."

Many novice formative assessors are initially content to experience the Q&A routine with a few eager beavers. The eager beavers are fun and usually cannot wait to participate. They are willing to risk a public response. They gladly supply a raised hand or excitedly blurt out an answer. They keep the ball moving, pass it back to the teacher, and give us the impression that "we got game."

Teachers who work to elicit *the* correct answer from their students seem to have an unbreakable bond with the few willing students who have that answer. Too often, the symbiotic relationship leads to a false sense of feedback. When asked after a lesson, "So who seems to understand the objective of the lesson?" beginning teachers typically recall the answers that the hardworking, engaged students supplied.

Beginning and experienced teachers who are on the formative assessment journey need ways to broaden the circle of inquiry. We offer tips and proce-dures, of course, but let's refocus on why we bounce. The most important reason is to increase your sample size. Formative assessors can use equity sticks, index cards, or other tools to generate responses from individuals and groups through-out the classroom. Those who are learning to become formative assessors can make notations on a seating chart to widen the net and keep track of patterns of participation. By increasing the breadth and depth of student responses, the teacher is better able to draw meaningful conclusions about the current levels of student understanding, including the bottlenecks, pit stops, and places we all get stuck.

Without consistent procedures and visible practices related to bouncing, or spreading questions throughout the classroom, there's not enough evidence that the majority of students in a class have actually engaged in thinking through a topic. We know from research on academic language and English language development that providing opportunities for students to articulate their thinking—in a variety of productive modes—is essential (Abedi & Herman, 2010; Abedi, 2010). This practice also makes it more likely that all students will feel included in classroom conversations (Zwiers, 2007a, 2007b).

Principles, Procedures, and Practices

Because bouncing strategically supports making valid inferences and sound instructional decisions, make it your mission to know why you're bouncing as you do. Bounce with intention and awareness. Don't let your moves reflect only happenstance or old habits you picked up from "doing school" (Lortie, 1975).

Try "bouncing yourself" through the classroom to listen to at least half of your students as they pair-share in a group work activity. Try just listening—not coaching. Try getting to every area of your classroom, especially those hard to reach pockets. Listening can be a good way to sample vulnerable or shy students' talk without shining the spotlight on them (yet). Try bouncing by *snaking* (turn-taking "snakes" through the seating arrangement), *whipping* (student responses "whip" around the room), or *popcorning* (students decide when to speak, so responses can "pop" from anywhere). Experiment with the upsides and downsides of each method for various poses and probes and the kinds of sampling you want to achieve. Does the unit get harder at a particular point? Are there well-documented p-prims, preconceptions, and misconceptions in this topic? How can you quickly spot check who is struggling with the big idea or discrete procedure? Which sampling strategies make the most sense at which turns of the lesson?

IN THE CLASSROOM

Do the Math to Maximize Student Response Space

In the complex world of bouncing moves, we are listening for and trying to capture the maximum number of responses to widen the student response sample size. Like we found with pausing, a main purpose of bouncing is to increase the sample of responses for any given question or task. By bouncing systematically, we increase the likelihood that more students can and will add their voice to the classroom.

Let's go back to our pausing example from Chapter 3. We imagined we had 36 students. We said that on a typical day, Devi, Christy, and Alex will respond within a fraction of a second and raise their hands, which led to 3 responses out of 36 possible student responses. We noted that in this scenario only 1 out of 12 students in the classroom respond. Of those three responses, two were correct and one was a misconception. The problem is (and yes, there are many problems in this scenario) we still don't know how many other students shared that misconception. More than half? Less than half? Was it precisely that misconception? Or slightly different?

If this is too complicated, then let's simplify. A little technology should help. We hear the teacher say: "Okay everyone, please use your clickers now. Vote if you agree with (A) Devi's solution, or (B) Christy's, or (C) Alex's. I see from the results on my computer that several of you still haven't voted. I'll wait. Okay, it looks like Devi's solution is the most popular."

In the best of all worlds, the kids can self-diagnose accurately, they do not guess, and they can explain why they voted for Devi on a principle other than she always gets it right. It turns out Devi had the misconception this time (she confused the word *materials* with surface area and volume). But the students who voted for her solution may or may not have shared her misconception. They may know that she usually gets things right and has an *A+* in the class. Technology can mask bouncing problems as much as reveal them.

For a low-tech option, what if the teacher had three coffee cups and she polled the kids instead? After asking Devi, Christy, and Alex to explain their reasoning at the document camera (if a visual is necessary) and assigning a coffee cup to each answer, the other students are asked to drop their popsicle sticks (identified with their names) in the cup that corresponds with their answer.

Based on the results, the teacher pulls a stick and asks a randomly chosen student to explain his or her reasoning and how it supports the solution. Not only has the response rate improved by bouncing more systematically, but the students now have the opportunity to elaborate on each solution and explore its strengths and weaknesses, which can help them to meet Standard 3 of the Eight Standards for Mathematical Practice, "Construct viable arguments and critique the reasoning of others." (CCSSI, 2010).

Continued

Bouncing strategies like these and others in this book are intended to feed many birds with one seed. These moves

- Address the use of academic language and the practicing of particular registers of mathematical/specialized subject matter discourse, which are learning targets and criteria for success.
- Take the advice of experts on the need for wait and think time.
- Connect to the real world and standards by inviting students to collaborate, discuss, and weigh options to solve problems.
- Help create classroom learning environments that support equity and inclusion, but also demand engagement with high-order skills from more than the eager students while still sharing the floor with them.

Try Questioning Your Beliefs About Why You Bounce as You Do

We invite you to think about how improving bouncing often takes adjusting not just our practices, but our beliefs as well. Fortunately, trying out new practices can help us to examine beliefs—and test them against experience.

Trying new bouncing practices might challenge and dislodge unhelpful and potentially harmful beliefs: *The shy ones don't want to speak. This one doesn't know the answer and always gets it wrong. That one didn't do the homework and always falls behind. These kids are too lazy to share or when they do, I can barely hear what they are saying.*

Rather than overgeneralize and play to your worst fears, try on a new bouncing practice, reflect with your students on its worth, tweak the procedure as needed, and rededicate the class to having everyone participate. Tell them what's bothering you about pouncing. Show a picture of Tigger (not Professor Kingsfield). Ask your students "What is to be done?" We predict you'll be pleasantly surprised at what you and your class discover together.

Some of your students will be delighted to be included in the FA-driven classroom where dialogue is at a premium and bouncing is prolific and productive. Others, not so much. You will get through the unease, however—together. Remind your students: no pain, no gain. Bouncing is like pumping iron. Feel the burn.

💡 **FORMATIVE ASSESSMENT TIPS**

Celebrate victories among the inevitable setbacks with your students. Ask them to reflect on specific bouncing practices that are working well for them. Remind them that as they get better and better at bouncing, they are growing up and getting ready to go out on their own. Make connections to the worlds of work, college, and life. Doctors bounce medical opinions to their colleagues. Construction workers bounce ideas off structural engineers. Retail sales people bounce different products and services to their customers, explaining the benefits and costs. In society, we need to hear from everyone to make good decisions. Bouncing helps to create feedback so people can be heard. Our democracy may depend on our citizens being able to discern the difference between pouncing and bouncing.

What time is it? It's time to persevere, to try new social skills, to speak up and listen better. It is the 21st century and global communication skills and capacities are at a premium. Try making your learning community's stance toward bouncing explicit, intentional, and public. Show how bouncing is connected to all sorts of exchanges and that to be players in a democracy and the global economy we have to step up.

Post positive statements of these values and beliefs around the classroom. We all need reminders. Colorful images can support class agreements.

Here are some sample class agreements about bouncing.

- We agree that it's okay to pass the ball (or the stuffed monkey)
- We always return to a person if he doesn't want to answer right away
- We seek new opinions and more voices daily
- We avoid hand-raising until a peer is finished speaking
- We believe everyone has a voice, and make it true
- We take turns
- We understand that listening well takes time and effort
- We check: Did everyone have a "say" today? Who's next?
- We acknowledge that bouncing helps everyone exercise their right to a good education

Orchestrating bouncing moves in your classroom can feel like directing traffic, hosting a dinner party, mediating a conflict, and navigating a maze—all at once. Having sentence starters ready for a variety of bouncing routines can help you be present for teachable moments. Planning for bouncing means you can put your cognitive powers (attention, memory, effort to encode and retrieve information) on other moves such as probing or tagging when you need them most.

Ultimately, your attention needs to be on making sense (what we call Binning in Chapter 7) of student responses. But before you can start tallying, noting reactions, making connections, inferring patterns, and improvising your own responses to student responses, you need ways to quickly increase the sample size.

Supports for Bouncing That Include Your Students' Needs

Priming for bouncing before the unit begins:

- As your teacher/mentor, I really need to know what you all are thinking in this unit. If you don't understand or aren't sure, I need to hear your voice so we can improve.
- How will I know you're ready to share when things get tough or we get stuck? Can you give me a signal? Should we "check in" at the end of each week?
- Thank you for all your effort and contributions this week. Your enthusiasm is wonderful. Let's see if we can get others to be this enthusiastic next week. Who hasn't had a lot to say yet? What can we do as a class to help you share your ideas more next class?

Priming for bouncing during class time:

- Before I select someone to answer, I'm going to give everyone more time to think.
- For this challenge problem, we're going to hear from everyone.
- I want to hear from someone in this part of the room now.
- Let's hear from someone who hasn't spoken yet today.
- There's probably a range of opinions on this. We can find out by checking in. To do that, first we'll _____.
- Who is thinking something different?
- I'm not sure what is meant by _____.
- What are some other possible ideas?

- Let's have some folks add to that.
- This could be a good question for the class. Let's get the whole class in on it.

Involve the Already Active and Vocal Students to Support New Voices

Got an eager beaver? Talkative or easily bored student? Assign her as scribe (more on this in the next chapter on Tagging). We say take students' energy and passion and harness it. Differentiate with subtasks that engage the students who tend to talk a lot. Focus your energy on bouncing to those students who are not yet in the habit of speaking up and still outside the response space. Widen the loop as you reposition those who have already added to the discussion. Enlist the eager beavers into the process of expanding the discussion outward.

Try Keeping Records

How could you be bouncing differently to get better, more robust classroom data? A good place to start is by collecting all the soft data available in each lesson. Focusing on this treasure trove of observations (from daily word webs to exit tickets) will help you answer this question.

Are your "go-to" bouncing routines yielding what you'd like them to yield? How do you know if you can trust the evidence? Is your memory of the student responses from the popcorn exercise that good? Without running records of the streams of soft data to examine, review, and look over, how can you determine to what extent a bouncing routine is working to uncover student thinking and increase your understanding of where the kids are today, yesterday, and the day before?

Before we go further, keep in mind that bouncing will look different depending on your reason for bouncing. Bouncing to check that students understand instructions is one thing. Bouncing to uncover prior knowledge on the concept of *ratio* or *thesis* is another. When reflecting on a choice of sampling strategies to capture the soft data, it may also help to note the differing contexts and purposes for bouncing based on research. Bouncing at a particular juncture in a well-established learning progression may require a different approach than for the more generic levels on a taxonomy. Again, it all comes down to the cognition vertex and the path a formative assessor takes to respect and honor important learning targets that form part of the assessment triangle.

Bouncing: Sydney's Case

For bouncing, I often use equity sticks. For each class, I've got a cup of wooden tongue depressor sticks, one with each student's name. Using equity sticks helps me—helps *us*—hear from students who, given a choice, won't volunteer. I'm a big believer in *Students need to talk to learn*, and *A teacher's job is to help students listen to, respond to, and learn from their classmates' ideas*. It's important that the ways we bounce help me to sample, probe, and get students talking with one another and with me.

The students can't see it, but I put small color-coded dots on one end of the sticks: yellow for English language learners, light green for students with IEPs, orange for so-called "middle achievers" with no diagnosed learning issues, and light blue for students who consistently give strong responses no matter the topic.

Of course there's overlap. I've got English learners who are really strong in math, and so on. Still, the dots remind me that to get a good read on where a class period's understanding is, I need to sample from all kinds of students. The coding helps me be strategic, purposeful, and systematic in my bouncing.

There's another benefit to using equity sticks (the physical, actual sticks versus an anonymous, hand-held randomizer app on my smartphone): the sticks support a good visible routine, which is pose, pause, pull a stick from the cup, and probe. I've used index cards, too. I like when the students see what I am up to.

When I open a lesson or make a transition to an activity, often I pose the question, protect silent think time, and have everyone pair-share. Then I shake the cup of sticks. The noise grabs their attention and says, wordlessly, "Come on back from your pair-share, we're about to hear from several of you." I find the physical presence of the sticks does this better than any app. Whenever I can signal, lead transitions, and reinforce norms without talking, I do. I use my air time judiciously.

When I'm pulling equity sticks or cards, there's always the option to pass. (I don't really like the "volun-tolds" cold-call game.) But students don't often pass. I think it's because our class is a safe place for tentative or "trial balloon answers" as we call them.

As a math teacher, I focus on how students have arrived at an answer, not just what the answer is. I bounce to hear explanations [of their thinking]. They know that. It's how we do math class together. I make a point to affirm and build on students' contributions. My kids see that. What they say gets used in class, respectfully. I think this also plays a role in the "pass" option getting exercised less often than it otherwise might.

I probe too. When equity sticks are part of bouncing, I'm careful about probing since the fact that I'm using equity sticks means I can't know whether the student in the spotlight would have volunteered. This matters. In general, I think that students who have volunteered to respond are more at ease with public probing than students who have not volunteered to respond. But it's hard, maybe impossible, to know for sure.

I bounce differently for different purposes. I use the equity sticks when that kind of entirely random or partially random selection (when I use the color coding) makes sense. My decision often depends on where we are in a lesson.

Sometimes I decide ahead of time which students I'm going to call on and in what order—for example, when I'm having students come up to the document camera or dry erase board to demonstrate how they solved or approached a problem. In these cases, I've already gone around the room as students were working. I know who has solved the problem and how. It wouldn't make sense for me, and wouldn't match my purposes for the students' learning, to pull names at random. Since I've already sampled student thinking, how I bounce at this point in the lesson is more for the students' benefit, not my own. I want all the students to see the different ways the problem has been approached and for us to begin to make sense of this together. As students demonstrate and we discuss, I count on all the other FA moves to help us.

We usually build from more common, concrete operational solution methods to more abstract or uncommon solution methods. My 6th graders are transitioning from arithmetic to algebraic thinking. How I bounce in this part of the lesson is supposed to serve all my students in interacting with and being able to link these different ways of thinking about and solving math problems.

Whether the students are passing the class dolphin, or I am using the sticks in a cup—the larger point is the same and my students know the routines by now. We all get sampled for our ideas, solutions, and strategies. Making sense of mathematics as a class is as important as individual growth and progress.

Prioritize your bouncing moves—one routine at a time. Your professional goals are your own. You know best where and how you could best spend your energy for next steps. New teachers in particular do well to focus on bouncing effectively regarding students' understanding of content. This helps them build their pedagogical content knowledge (PCK). PCK is specialized knowledge experienced teachers have for their subject matter and the knowledge and skills they have in relating content to their students' learning (Shulman, 1986, 1987).

PCK is not only a thorough understanding of a subject's fundamental principles, but also an understanding of the kinds of difficulties students might encounter, and having the creativity to address these difficulties in ways that deepen student learning. The better new teachers bounce, we contend, the faster they can build PCK. This book reminds us again and again that there are no shortcuts to uncovering and supporting student learning. A focus on mastering FA moves and integrating them with PCK can make a big difference.

 FORMATIVE ASSESSMENT TIPS

Think Local, Go Global

Got bouncing problems in a humanities curriculum? Make it a social issue inside your educational world. Use your classroom to illustrate the significance of the "silent majority" for societies and governments. Look up at the Habits of Minds poster on the wall. Point to Connections and Conjecture. Re-pose: What happens to a society when only a few speak? Who decides for all when only a few go to the microphone? What kind of governments come to power by drowning out the voices of the people? Maybe it's time for a pair-share and quick write: what is the connection between how we behave in school and the kind of government and society we can expect to live in? Or an exit slip: are we training to be powerless in this classroom so we can train ourselves how to be "good" citizens for others? Address the challenge of silence, apathy, and disinterest—no matter which subject you teach. The students are waiting on the adults to get real.

It's Your Turn to Reflect

Bouncing ideas, exchanging opinions, and exploring student thinking are core principles of the FA moves framework. In a society increasingly unable to engage with people from the other side of the fence, we need to recommit to the values and norms of formative assessment for our children. Take a moment and examine your own beliefs and attitudes toward bouncing. Is it natural and normal for you? Is it awkward and strange for you? Are you a Tigger who loves to pounce on Pooh? Were you a silent Sally or Bob in your school? Which classes made you want to be an eager beaver and which ones made you slink to your seat and hide in the back while hoping to be saved by the bell?

We have offered suggestions for smart bouncing, but you and your colleagues are in the best position to come up with and customize bouncing practices for your context. What works in the art classroom or on the dance floor may not work in a science lab or mathematics class (Mewborn & Tyminski, 2006). You're familiar now with the principles behind bouncing and how sampling strategies relate to the logic of assessment design. As you innovate bouncing procedures with your colleagues, we encourage you to widen the circles involved and help one another learn from the range of suggestions and ideas bouncing back and forth among you.

Misconceptions and Challenges

⚠ Misconception Alert: Bouncing and Revoicing Are the Same

A lot of teaching assumes that revoicing what students say in the classroom provides a bounce to the discussion. By amplifying student voices, the teacher is trying to increase the confidence and effects of individual responses to a question. Like an echo chamber, what a student just said gets bounced by the teacher— and perhaps added to and amplified—for everyone to hear. Revoicing is good practice, but we wish to distinguish it from sampling strategies aimed at gathering more and better student data on the fly.

Bouncing moves (and tagging moves, which we discuss in the next chapter) look to improve the representation of classroom responses, so as to identify more patterns in how students are approaching the material. Bouncing puts a premium on increasing the sample while including a representative range of student thinking—not merely restating what this or that student said about a topic.

How are bouncing and revoicing related? Bouncing is not revoicing, but a teacher can choose to revoice what a student says while bouncing. Researchers O'Connor and Michaels (1993) drew on Goffman (1974) and his concept of *animation* to identify a strategy they named *revoicing*. Revoicing is when a teacher gives students an "expanded voice" by saying out loud to everyone what the student has said. In the process of bouncing, it may help to animate and amplify students' voices, but we need to move the ball around the court regardless.

⚠ Misconception Alert: Bouncing Only Works for Motivated Students

One of our quieter teacher candidates observed that bouncing seems connected to motivation. He noticed that it's hard to bounce in part because classroom preps differ, by grade level and curriculum track. In his case, the difference in motivation and engagement was acute. He told us:

> To give everyone an opportunity to participate, I announce to the class that I want to hear from those students who have not yet spoken. What follows

is that the eager beavers stay quiet and eventually a quiet student speaks up. This procedure, however, does not work in every class. It may work for my seniors who are AP students and do all of their classwork, readings, and homework, but not with my 7th period sophomores for whom school is not one of their top priorities in life. They just don't seem as motivated as the others.

Let's unpack the word "motivated" for a moment. Do we mean "motivated students"? "Motivated teachers"? Both? What is motivation, anyway? And what "causes" motivation? In other words, where does motivation come from, for whom? Part of the misconception about effective bouncing depending on high levels of motivation is due to an unexamined assumption.

Motivation is an effect, as much as a cause, of student participation. Cognitive behavioral therapists, such as David Burns (1980), contend that motivation comes from action, not the other way around: motivation does not come first, action does! You have to prime the pump. Then you begin to get motivated, and the fluids will flow spontaneously. It works like this:

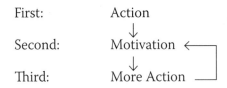

Beginning teachers see differences in their students' willingness to share publicly. They ascribe these differences, often without being fully aware of it, to personality types and noncognitive indicators. Beginners are keenly attuned to what experts call "grit," "locus of control," and "self-concept" in the students they are called to teach. In these teaching placements and internships, our candidates don't perceive lots of examples of perseverance or positive academic mindset. The teacher candidates become frustrated when their students' affective dispositions and noncognitive orientations seem to get in the way of their best efforts.

What these new teachers do not see (yet) is that these behavioral differences are more often the result of conditioning than intrinsic qualities of kids. The students, in many cases, are mirroring the behaviors, norms, and attitudes of the school system itself. They feel "batch processed" and they act that way toward their managers. Different ways of "doing school," it turns out, are also related to different tracks in the curriculum. The AP seniors are on track for college and they are operating from a different frame of reference. Hence, they may react to different behavioral cues and signals than those "for whom school is not a top priority."

Differences in age and maturity must also play a role in the "motivation" to participate in bouncing moves. Naturally, even "the same" bouncing procedures will unfold differently when used in different classes and contexts. Experienced teachers often meet this reality with a "can-do" orientation, without subscribing to the misconception that "bouncing only works for the motivated." A reason for this is that experienced teachers are accomplished at adjusting and repositioning a practice. They tweak off-the-shelf "solutions" and avoid one-size-fits-all strategies for their particular students.

It's common for beginning teachers who are learning to formatively assess to think something is not possible due to their own apprehensions of the challenge. Novices tend to believe bouncing fails because they

- Have not seen a bouncing move work with their particular students.
- Have unrealistic expectations that a new procedure should meet success immediately for all under differing conditions.
- Have not yet acquired skills in how to set their students up for success by instantiating and adapting new practices to changing circumstances.
- Have limited notions of what bouncing is and how it relates to their own perceptions of student traits and dispositions.
- Have difficulty seeing the general challenges associated with sampling student responses (e.g., restriction of range, measurement error, reliability, and bias).

We never shame or blame novice formative assessors for these beliefs or preconceptions. It is, so to speak, their current level of understanding formative assessment. Nor do we pretend that a teacher who rises to the top of a learning progression will never fall back on old habits or have difficulty maintaining a particular level of sophistication with a move. As contexts, kids, and the curriculum change, we can expect the formative assessor to change, too. Rather than look down on the beginner and celebrate how much further along we are as experienced teachers, let's open up new avenues and vistas for seeing the problem of bouncing from the new lens of sampling strategy and design.

To address these and many other common p-prims, it's time to go back to the drawing board. All formative assessment-rich classrooms need procedures and practices to widen the net of participation so we can better understand all students' beliefs, opinions, and ideas.

Revisiting the FA toolkit is part of our advice to a novice classroom assessor. The other part of our coaching strategy is to explore teachers' reflection on their moves-based practice. One student teacher during his Phase II placement in a high school serving predominately Latino/Hispanic students wrote:

> Let he who is free of pouncing cast the first stone. Although bouncing is the ideal, we are all guilty of pouncing. Taking this class has made me aware that we need to be prepared with a set of questions to lead classroom discussions, and to call on students as equally as possible, instead of allowing the same 3 or 4 students to respond to the questions. This is sometimes difficult to handle, especially if you want to move on to the next step on your lesson plan; it is always easier to have the same students respond to your questions in order to move on.

We know this student teacher and many others like him well enough to realize he cares deeply about students who are at risk. He is a first-generation college student interning at a high-needs school. He, too, felt ignored by and invisible to his instructors. He has a commitment to social justice but knows that pouncing works for now. Classroom management is central at this juncture in his development; formative assessment less so.

Rather than become embarrassed for or frustrated with those teachers that still pounce, or hold up the "best practices" baton to correct their behavior, we choose to offer formative feedback:

- Perhaps next week's unit presents a fresh start. Let's try to generate a loop with a solid opening question. Ask the kids which method they'd prefer: stuffed monkey, "equity" sticks, or popcorning.
- We get it. So what does it take for you to persevere with bouncing when you lose motivation? Does blaming the victim of pouncing seem fair? What's the deeper issue here?
- Remember when we modeled using sentence starters in class. What if you primed for bouncing first? Maybe start by asking the eager beavers to take the lead, ask for volunteers and scribe?
- Let's make a plan. First, a list. Which actions in the classroom propel you toward feeling more confidence with bouncing? Second, let's observe the kids in another learning space: in the gym, in the science lab, or in band

practice. Can these same students bounce a ball on the court? Or share ideas with an experiment? Or play in a band after school? What might it take for them to do the same in your classroom?

Bouncing happens everywhere. Your students know how to use social media (Twitter, Instagram, YouTube) to bounce all sorts of things. It's just a matter of making it happen in your world—with them—one day at a time.

The Change Is Big and Necessary

Priming for bouncing is not easy with a bevy of students used to hearing the few and ignoring the many. Students know from years of experience that teachers are in the habit of pouncing on the first hand up in the classroom. The majority of students are in the habit of letting the minority of eager beavers "do school" for them. Yes, posing "the right question, the right way" matters and implementing a "no hands" policy may work in the short run (Wiliam, 2014). But we need to push more on the meaning of bouncing moves and go a little deeper with research. The truth is we still don't know that much about breaking the chain of a few students providing cover for the many.

We ask the formative assessment experts and educational researchers: *Who will undo all the years of conditioning that shuts down the feedback loops in our classroom before the bell rings? How can a group of disenfranchised people socialized to shut up suddenly open up? How is the educational system designed to reinforce rather than reset the dynamics of tracking and delivering "just enough" freedom to some so they (or their parents) can speak out and move up? Why should children trust a teacher enough to speak up, and why should they believe that adults are actually interested in what they have to say when they finally feel able to speak?*

These are tough questions. We do not pose them to mystify or shirk our responsibilities. But let's be clear which habits we are inviting and which ones we are undoing. The FA moves framework is a beginning. It can clarify our stance, but school structures and priorities must support rather than impede the democratizing stance inherent in the FA moves framework.

Just as we introduced the posing moves in Chapter 2 that help you to focus on learning goals, curriculum targets, and the stuff that is worth knowing about your subject, we now need to introduce bouncing moves that any beginning formative assessor can try while acknowledging that they may fail to widen the circle of inquiry beyond. For now.

Posing and probing moves in your classroom are useless if no one takes the ball to bounce ideas, solutions, first draft responses, and runs with them.

Those students who sit there quietly in their seats—the silent Bobs and Sallies—are harder to reach than the FA experts imagine. Is this a Goldilocks quest where we hope for the "just right amount of participation"? Can we really strike a balance and achieve the golden mean where all students, including those at each extreme and in the middle, can play a role in sharing their thoughts? Are bouncing moves just another flight of fancy whipped up by the academics and corps of professional development specialists? Maybe "bouncing" is just the latest flavor of the month in the endless cycle of "reforms" (Cuban, 1990) that are abandoned once the new one arrives?

Time will tell. For now, we note that there is so much attention on the outliers in these discussions about how to best engineer exchanges. Yes, we know a vibrant, thoughtful, rich exchange among teachers and students, students and students, even administrators and students when we see them. We have a few examples, mostly from STEM subjects, of classroom formative assessment in action (Ball, 1993; Furtak, Ruiz-Primo, Shemwell, Ayala, Brandon, Shavelson, & Yin, 2008; Franke & Kazemi, 2001; Hammer, 1997; Lampert, 2003; Warren, Ballenger, Ogonowski, Rosebery, & Hudicourt-Barnes, 2001; Warren & Rosebery, 1995). But many of these bounce-rich exemplars are taken from the elementary and middle school years with less attention on how sampling across a wide range of students occurs in the high school classroom. The fact is we don't know very much about the middle range students who have learned to play the game of doing school. The majority of our students, who are neither eager nor silent, just slip through the cracks.

Educational reformer Ted Sizer (1984) referred to this phenomena in *Horace's Compromise*, a book that describes classrooms and schools dedicated to the path of least resistance, where teachers (and students) complacently accept the fact that learning is about learning to do school. Sizer and his colleagues at the Coalition of Essential Schools challenged us to care about the forgotten middle. One way to take up this challenge is to rethink how we assess—for whose good, for what good. The trick is not to become cynical about reaching more students or to fall back on being a summative assessor to catch those who don't play your game.

If putting a pedagogical bounce into your teaching practice is too much to ask, then we should not be surprised when Jenny and Raymond tune out, get kicked out, and eventually drop out. For those of us formative assessors who want our students to get excited about learning, and know we can assess better, it is time to increase the sample size and raise the volume on those hard to hear voices.

Learning to Look Back: Reflections on a Just-Taught Lesson

Our teacher candidates are steeped in the basics. They know the tricks of the trade when it comes to describing classroom learning environments that are inclusive and equitable. By the time they get to our course, they've heard of equity sticks in methods courses. They have learned about popcorning, snaking, and other strategies for increasing participation in their multicultural, language literacy, and educational psychology courses. A few of our advanced candidates have tried these tactics in their teaching placements. A few are "in the zone" with the sticks, the cards, and marked-up seating charts. We get to hear their war stories and their personal variations on the bouncing theme.

But others sit quietly next to these budding formative assessors and are not so convinced. By the end of the credential program, having run the gauntlet of preparation courses, a few student teachers feel safe enough with (or exhausted by) their university professors to push back.

"Hold on, I am not so sure about what you are calling bouncing. *It hasn't worked for me. My mentor doesn't do it. What's the evidence it really works?"*

At this point in the classroom evaluation and assessment course, we know things are working because push back is a form of engagement. The Habits of Mind are in gear. Our beginning teachers are moving up Bloom's Taxonomy. It's one thing to know a fact or procedure related to instructional methods. It's quite another to apply those methods to different classroom contexts, curriculum, and kids. And it is quite another thing to begin to think strategically about which formative assessment moves to experiment with and for which students—and to think about when things fail, why and what can be done next time.

By now it should be clear that the purpose of reflecting on the just-taught lesson is to "re-experience" and rethink what is actually addressable and actionable. Using the FA moves framework, we can guide your attention to what matters for the teacher learning to become a formative assessor. We present the concept of sampling strategies under the umbrella of bouncing moves. It gives us all, as Pamela Grossman calls it, a "grammar of practice" to share and play with as teacher educators (Grossman & McDonald, 2008).

Before moving forward, let's breathe. To be clear: sampling student thinking is not easy. It requires making difficult instructional decisions. There are trade-offs and compromises with listening to some, but not others. Not everyone can or must be heard at every moment of the lesson. We hear our beginning teachers. Growing pains in this profession are real.

Being purposeful and skeptical is critical to gaining traction on any learning trajectory—for teachers, too. In the parlance of educational psychologists, a few of our student teachers are moving beyond *declarative* knowledge about what sampling means and *procedural* knowledge of how to use equity sticks effectively; they are also applying *schematic* knowledge of the entire FA moves framework and *strategic* knowledge in deciding which strategies are likely to work depending on the context, student needs, and curricular demands. These teacher candidates are moving through the formative assessment realm, making connections, and seeing how it is all related back to the bigger picture.

Once you have some traction in a discipline, it's good to ask: "Wait a minute. Why should I use a quick write during my science lab when I can use that activity to warm up the concept of 'diffusion' at the beginning of the lesson, and circle back at the end of the period with an exit slip?"

Recently, we invited Maria, an English major who was placed at a fairly affluent suburban school in Silicon Valley, to reflect on her just-taught unit on personal narrative. Maria decided to focus on more purposeful sampling strategies, based on an observation she made early on:

> In the past I have had trouble trying to include bouncing in my lessons. Unless I am actively thinking about it in the moment or put it into my lesson plan, I tend to forget. Lately I have been experimenting with using a plush toy as a means of getting my less willing students to talk. I toss the toy to one student who speaks and then throws it to another student, and so on. So far it is working nicely with my freshman class, who tend to be very vocal and all want to share at once. It's adding more structure to the discussions, and students are now becoming more respectful of their peers.
>
> The discussions have become much more student-centered and less teacher-centered, and I am happy to see that they are beginning to feel comfortable posing their own deeper questions for the rest of the class to answer. It's also serving to bring out answers from my ever-so-quiet girls. Both of my classes have a majority of boys, and the boys tend to drown out the girls.

The plush toy is forcing the girls to give an answer, and to speak loudly and clearly, forcing the boys to listen to what they have to say. I hope that this succeeds in building confidence in the girls in my class, as well as helping the boys be more patient with responses and response times.

Maria has taken the bouncing challenge. She is playing with a sampling method that we discussed earlier in this chapter. Though Maria probably doesn't describe it this way to her mentor teacher, what stands out for us as her university teachers is her sense of the need for equity. Bouncing moves are no longer an academic abstraction; Maria can actively use sampling techniques to address the need for a plurality of student responses. In a diverse public school classroom, we can expect different students will feel empowered to speak. Others will hang back and watch the action. What is to be done: get out the tin buckets, coffee cups, plush toys, or stuffed monkey. It's time to put a bounce back in our steps and move a little closer toward the goal.

Teachers like Maria who are aiming to master formative assessment moves will design a sampling strategy to widen the net. They may focus on gender identification or language or ability groupings for a particular class period to balance participation. They might tackle sampling challenges around specific learning targets (such as students' reading, writing, oral communication skills) with their colleagues. Or, they might consult with school counselors, paraprofessional staff, and after-school providers about students who seem stuck and unable to bounce, and ask what seems to work best for these kids.

In department meetings and professional learning communities, these formative assessors are not content to play grading games. They fight for the time, resources, and attention needed to advance student learning. This means standing up for assessment practices that uncover more student voices and help us to get a better, more reliable picture of student thinking during instruction. These classroom assessors are united in a struggle for making learning visible, in part, by resisting technologies that hide that learning or merely box it up into tidy, neat packages.

By focusing on the interpretation vertex of the assessment triangle and starting to see the importance of having a classroom sampling strategy, Maria is thinking more and more like an action researcher who is studying what works and what doesn't to widen the net. She is acknowledging the limits of her evidence and looking for a firmer basis to develop instructional next steps.

We want all teachers to gain a more representative, balanced view of their students' thinking—to move beyond chalk and talk, question and answer, and pouncing routines that skew what teachers know and can do with soft data. To do that, we have to adopt Maria's stance toward her own pedagogical practice.

We could, of course, inquire into the buckets or cups that Maria chose to use this semester in Phase II student teaching. As part of lesson debriefing we might ask her and her mentor teacher about the equity sticks: Are you ready to explore other buckets (e.g., ELL, Latino, kinesthetic learners) to hold these sticks? Are there any connections between these students? Do their learning styles and issues overlap? How do we ensure that all students feel safe and no one feels singled out when you pull the sticks and cards?

Knowing that Maria is *at a particular level* of pedagogical development with her bouncing practices allows us to better serve as guides on the side. We do not need to dominate the conversation during her reflection on the lesson. Nor do we see it as productive to demand she bounce to this or that student, in this or that group, with this or that designation or label. Rather, we see her bouncing moves on a continuum of professional growth, and we note her progress with breaking down the sampling, looking at ways to widen the student response space, and connecting her concerns for social justice and equity to her teaching practice (Guitérrez & Rogoff, 2003; Noguera, 2008).

Like many of our credential candidates, Maria has learned that part of becoming a formative assessor is changing up our game and the familiar routines we take for granted. She is experimenting with configurations and groupings of FA moves to see if she can learn more about her students' thinking. She wrote at the end of the semester: "I am hoping that by bouncing in this way, the girls in the class will be able to find their voices easier, and that our discussion will also become much more student centered. We'll see how it goes!" That sense of hopeful expectation and the attempt to shift to a student-centered pedagogy is a big step in her teaching career. The utterance "we will see how it goes" is what we formative assessors live for.

Putting It All Together

As we've just highlighted, deep bouncing moves are intertwined with other moves. It's complex and often quick paced. We can make a move, start dancing, then trip and fall before the music is over. Falling down is inevitable. Getting up is the real challenge.

As teacher educators, we want beginning teachers to learn. This means, as Piaget and others remind us, we can expect teachers who are learning a new craft, skill, or concept to go through a process of assimilation and accommodation. The constructivist approach to learning recognizes the need to move beyond concepts such as assessment for learning with novices and to start building scaffolds and supports toward deeper pedagogical practice. Experience is key. So is patient coaching.

We'd like to know those teachers learning formative assessment moves are trying out new ideas, making mistakes, and reengaging bouncing moves through practice. Only by applying what they have learned in their efforts to get better at sampling student thinking—*and knowing that they are supported by mentors when things go awry*—can teachers improve in the domain of formative assessment.

To build up a mental model (new schema) for bouncing, those learning to become formative assessors need time, experience, and guided practice. That's how all people learn.

The real challenge for anyone seeking to master formative assessment moves is to develop a mental model or schema for sampling and widening the student response space. Bouncing is a placeholder we use to build up new connections in this FA domain for beginners. If there is going to be a deep shift in classroom assessment practices, we need a new language to describe these new practices as we slowly replace the old ones.

But on our journey we shouldn't get lost in the narrow pursuit of technique to the point that we leave the road to broader understanding. Bouncing presents more to think about than meets the eye.

Checks for Understanding

The following questions, prompts, and tasks can help you broaden and deepen your bouncing. Remember the point is to examine your sampling strategies for gathering student responses (oral or written). The following questions, prompts, and tasks are designed to help you advance your bouncing skills and take the ideas and thoughts in this chapter a few more steps forward. You can use the prompts in Warm-Up Prompts as self-checks and ideas in Try-Now Tasks as conversation starters and exercises for independent study or group work.

Warm-Up Prompts:
- Why bounce?
- What are the consequences of skipping over the *priming-for-bouncing phase* of formative assessment?
- Who seems to thrive on *pouncing* vs. *bouncing* in your classroom? Who does not? What are some ways to accommodate these differing participation styles productively?
- What *bouncing agreements* have to be in place in your classroom to maximize the number of student participants? What is your personal goal for the number or percentage of student responses? How can you monitor that goal?

Try-Now Tasks:
1. On the first day of a new unit, jump right in to this activity with no lead-in or fanfare. Write the word *bouncing* in the middle of the board. Ask, "What comes to mind?" In 30 seconds or less, write down all responses on the board.

2. On the second day, explain to students that it's time for a word web. Remind them that word webs are warm-up tasks that help us to start thinking about a topic. Put the word *bouncing* in the middle of the board. Ask your students to write on a sticky note what *bouncing* brings to mind and then to place their responses on the board (can use other media, if preferred). Take approximately 2 minutes.

3. On the first day of the next week, pair students up to discuss their responses before writing to the prompt "We bounce because..." Have a student from each group state one reason/agreement. Appoint a scribe to capture these reasons/agreements on the board, poster paper, or shared software such as Google Doc. Give up to 5 minutes.

4. Give an example of a bouncing move you made this week. What worked? What didn't work so well? For whom? List 1 or 2 next steps to better prime for bouncing.

5. Are bouncing and pouncing compatible? Discuss.

6. Ask teachers to gather into Four Corners, connected to themes related to "bouncing back" (resetting expectations, making agreements, what to do when things fall apart). Focus on:

Corner 1: Warm-ups and icebreakers

Corner 2: Tools, scaffolds, and technologies

Corner 3: Statements and sentence starters

Corner 4: Values and beliefs

Each group assigns a speaker and a scribe, then creates a list of examples related to its theme and ways to support bouncing moves. Share out and, as a whole, reach consensus on a department or school-based plan about how and when to check back in on bouncing agreements and ways to assess progress. (Note: This task can be used with students as well as teachers.)

Challenge task: Have one person in the group explain why a particular procedure may support more effective priming for bouncing in the classroom. Allow another person to "push back" and say why these moves may not work—for whom and why it matters? Pick a focus "student" and use a fishbowl approach to discuss the challenges and ways to work on them.

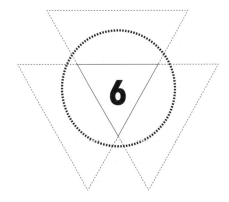

Tagging

If I want to support a classroom environment where students believe their voices matter, then we need loosely structured opportunities for *all* ideas to be heard—and represented. That's tagging.

Kaila, science teacher

At the end of a class tagging session—with our prior knowledge of a topic all up there—I've put a *C/S* next to our work. *C/S* stands for *con safos*, or "with safety." During the heart of the Chicano Movement, Los Angeles street artists would add the *C/S* to finished messages to let their fellow free thinkers know how to approach a message with a community purpose.

If we are building a community of learners, the *C/S* not only makes sense, it's critical—especially for students used to their ideas, prior knowledge, and experiences being overlooked, unexplored, even discounted.

Carl, high school English teacher

Formative assessment deals mostly with soft data—the stuff of classroom learning that resists easy labeling and quick categorizing: students' questions, first draft thoughts, fuzzy notions, puzzled looks, *I don't know*s, unfinished utterances, and off-the-wall responses. Tagging—and moves that support tagging—are about eliciting, recording, honoring, and using soft data in the classroom learning space well. With thoughtful attention and procedures aligned to our purposes, we can advance the cause of tagging for learning.

A challenge in dealing with soft data is holding it in one place. Unlike hard data—the numbers, scores, and points—soft data is hard to capture, upload, and store. Many of today's "assessment solutions" promise to help us record, analyze, and make sense of classroom data. But these solutions remain silent about a more important problem. How do formative assessors have their "soft" data ready and accessible, *when they need it* to make sound inferences and valid interpretations?

Before we explore and answer this question, let's make it clear: tagging student responses during the lesson is paramount—not recording the scores and points and grades after the lesson.

This is not a radical statement. Nor does it require a leap of faith.

We know from years of research that formative feedback is key to advancing student learning in the classroom. Neither numbers nor points, scores nor grades, help those committed to assessing for learning provide that formative feedback. Grades, for example, merely communicate to students and parents and colleges who is on top, who is in the middle, and who is at the bottom of a distribution (Winger, 2005). In fact, research shows that students tend to ignore feedback when accompanied by a grade (Black, Harrison, Lee, Marshall, & Wiliam, 2003) so we are spinning our wheels when we try to blend the two assessment purposes.

Although grades matter a lot to summative assessors, they miss the point for formative assessors. We need to evaluate current levels of understanding during the lesson. We need to make student thinking visible at each turn of the lesson segment. We need assessment procedures and practices—beyond quizzes, tests, and homework—to capture what students are saying, doing, and thinking about the academic content and conceptually difficult material.

This requires tagging and lots of it.

Like all classroom teachers, we acknowledge the reasons we put numbers, scores, and points on student responses. The grading game is part of doing school. Although collecting hard data helps the school system function, this student evaluation method is not likely to get us where we want to go. Formative assessors need higher quality, just-in-time information about learning as it emerges minute by minute. Real assessment for learning depends on high-quality feedback, but that feedback depends on capturing, recording, and making public what we know now about the kids.

A core purpose in making formative assessment moves is to be able to give our students on-the-fly feedback, but to do so we need to make their thinking visible. Tagging student responses is a nonjudgmental act: it says "all ideas, solutions, strategies, beliefs and notions are welcome." Labeling students' responses ("13 out of 20," "satisfactory," or "B+") preempts and defeats the purpose of tagging. In taking tagging moves seriously, we suspend judgment, faithfully record student thinking first, then evaluate it later to make a decision.

This chapter puts attention on a less told part of the formative assessment story—the softer, more fleeting, ephemeral parts—where the action really is for those seeking to become formative assessors and improve their interpretation strategies (what we call "binning" moves) in real time.

Tagging slows down classroom action. Tagging helps make soft data visible, honorable, manipulatable, and available for revisiting during the lesson or the next day. As Kaila and Carl point out, tagging practices can play a significant role in fostering classroom community *for learning*. Tagging can also help create a safe harbor for student responses. Most important, tagging is part of why we bounce; it helps us widen and record the student response space, so we can be smarter and more balanced in deciding what to do next.

What Is Tagging?

Tagging is publicly representing variation in student thinking by creating a snapshot or running record of a class's responses. Most often tagging is *scribing* what students say—writing it down—in a place and via a method that allows all in the classroom learning space to see, process, and record it for themselves.

Students, not just teachers, can scribe—by recording their classmates' contributions—during a tagging routine. Tagging could involve students writing, drawing, or posting representations of their thinking—sentences, phrases, diagrams, pictures, symbols—themselves. For example, when students write thoughts on a sticky note—whether in paper or digital form for all to see —that's a form of tagging.

Key aspects of making tagging moves:

- Tagging aims to represent **the full variation** present in student thinking around a topic, question, or problem during the lesson.
- The recording of this variation is **visible**, **public**, and potentially **save-able** (retrievable, storable).
- These running records **reduce extraneous cognitive load**, freeing up mental resources for processing other requests (e.g., probing questions) and **increase germane cognitive load** (e.g., scaffolding participation).

Tagging. What comes to mind? *You're it!* Graffiti. #. The dreaded price tag.

A Google search on tagging brings up *to attach a label to*; *to mark, ticket, identify,* and *flag.* Also *to categorize, classify, designate, describe.* Graffiti artists tag. Google's definitions also include *tag on*—to join, tack on to, to add—and *tag along*—to follow, to trail.

Tagging in the classroom learning space is about scribing, noting, and creating records, a practice societies have long depended upon, especially to help make commerce and civic life work with a high degree of precision and dependability. More than 5,000 years ago, Sumerian scribes imprinted clay with cuneiform to capture and represent ideas. The content and particulars of the scribing we do in our classrooms today is related, but strives for a different kind of accuracy.

We aim to capture and represent accurately the wide variation in our students' thinking. Our tagging strives to welcome and capture *all* contributions—even unorthodox and incorrect ones—because there is much to be learned from these student responses as we make adjustments during the lesson.

Tagging in the classroom learning space is also related to graffiti. Students sometimes express emotions, assert their identities, and convey strong social and political messages as part of classroom tagging, just as some graffiti artists do when they tag. As formative assessors, we emphasize the creative and useful elements of tagging student responses in the classroom learning space that allow us to *mark*, *identify*, *tack on to*, *describe*, *trail,* and *follow* student thinking so the thoughts won't evaporate and ideas won't get lost.

In Chapter 5 on Bouncing we noted that student thinking can spring, ricochet, hop, and jounce across the room during lessons. With all that movement, it is no surprise we often fail to tag. Words jump around the classroom learning space. Relatively few get publicly recognized. Certainly our bouncing practices can influence this, but all too often myriad valuable learning opportunities are lost. If we focus on tagging moves, those learning to master formative assessment moves can do a better job of representing student thinking, building confidence that students' prior knowledge and beliefs also matter when tagging.

Why Tag? For Whose Good? For What Good?

We tag to encourage full participation. To help ensure that students' thoughts are heard and recognized. To support opportunities for all to engage with a wide range of student thought. To document evidence and gather it in one place to support teachers' decision making. To make it possible to revisit students' first draft thinking. To help activate students' prior knowledge. To slow down and make visible quick, verbal action. To better remind everyone where the class has been. To foster connections between the spoken and written word. To assist students in using their Habits of Mind publicly.

Tagging helps make thinking visible. The advantages of making thinking and learning visible are many and well-documented (Hattie, 2009, 2012). A tagging-rich environment is crucial for developing and maintaining a classroom culture of healthy formative assessment. Tagging all student responses that can be elicited with a powerful prompt or question reinforces this message: *This classroom is a safe place to take intellectual risks.*

 FORMATIVE ASSESSMENT TIPS

To tag well, you have to preserve student speech—not run over it with your own interpretations or beliefs or opinions. There is a time for making sense and processing the information (i.e., by binning the student responses) later.

Formative assessors must avoid increasing the lesson pace and ignoring signs to reteach the lesson. Instead, they must carefully observe student thinking. At this moment in the FA moves framework, our aim is to tag to let students speak for themselves in their own voices—without judgment.

Tagging Helps Deepen Teacher Expertise

The process of tagging student thinking is also important because it supports teachers in developing pedagogical content knowledge (PCK). As we noted in the last chapter, PCK refers to the special knowledge and skills teachers have about how to teach certain content to particular groups of students, including what aspects to emphasize and why. Knowing how to teach history (whether you are a history major or historian) takes time, experience with students, and reflective analysis to help develop deeper engagement with the curriculum. After all, teaching aspects of the Industrial Revolution to 4th graders differs greatly from teaching aspects of it to 8th or 11th graders.

We suspect that beginning teachers' skills at formatively assessing students are closely associated with their levels of PCK. More research is needed, but for now we've noticed that tagging helps novice teachers develop their "listening ears."

Without clear, purposeful tagging procedures, it is hard to maximize opportunities to pose, pause, and probe, let alone to interpret and bin student thinking (which we discuss in the next chapter). Tagging can help teachers learning formative assessment moves start to make the most of their experiences interacting with students around particular content. But it's a move that must be integrated eventually—not left to practice in isolation.

In our capacity as university educators in a credential program, we encourage our teacher candidates to use the formative assessment moves—and improvise with them—in real time as much as they can. We provide opportunities to video record minilessons, to replay the FA action, and rethink in the company of classmates what is working and what needs more work. Tagging can provide beginning teachers with much-needed cognitive processing time, opportunities to adjust pacing, and moments of think time to see where the lesson is headed. Tagging moves, as we remind our novices, can also free up "mental disk space" to attend to classroom management issues and other noncognitive and socioemotional concerns we sometimes see in the video. Tagging is a friend—it serves many purposes for the classroom teacher.

 FORMATIVE ASSESSMENT TIPS

Think About a Learning Environment without Tagging

- *Disappearing thoughts and failure to encode*: When student responses, thinking, contributions, misconceptions, and wild card ideas are left untagged, they disappear. Some of these understandings are unlikely to be encoded in anyone's long-term memory.
- *Jogging memory and activating prior knowledge*: Getting students to interact with untagged ideas can be challenging. It's hard to hear and remember who said what. Activating prior knowledge without a running record in the classroom makes it difficult to know where we were and where we are now.
- *Maintaining and directing attention*: Word webs representing students' ideas about a topic reduce cognitive load so that students can put active working memory toward processing relevant information and elaborating on their understandings.
- *Interacting and meaning-building*: Tagging holds student responses where everyone can interact with them—again and again—during the lesson. Students make meaning and connections via tagging routines; this strengthens nodes and increases the likelihood of information storage into long-term memory.

Tagging Helps to Record Formative Feedback, Student Misconceptions, and Moments of Contingency

Besides helping teachers create space, time, and a place for student contributions—a "safe harbor" for honoring all student responses—tagging plays other important roles. When ideas are tagged—represented and accessible to the class—teachers can better support students in exercising their Habits of Mind. By making tagging moves, formative assessors help students revisit beliefs, reconsider opinions, make connections to other topics or subjects, explore perspectives that differ from their own, consider and question evidence presented on the board, ponder the relevance of various responses to the topic/question, and ask, "What if?" of the ideas recorded as they are referenced later in the lesson.

Tagging also plays a critical role in supporting revision, a culture of "*re-*" as we like to call it. Re-considering, re-imagining, re-designing, re-writing—all these stances are absolutely necessary for formative feedback to occur among teachers and students and for the next steps we offer to be useful for them.

For classroom assessment to *become formative* for students, we will need them to tag their own performances and work products, too. Self and peer assessment are critical pieces of the FA puzzle (Wylie & Lyon, 2013). A gallery walk with visible warm and cool feedback tagged by students on examples of classmates' work is a perfect example. So is an annotated organizer to tag personal bests and potential next steps to improve performance. Students can digitally tag "tips" and "shout outs" on group projects to record their feedback and keep a running record of next steps for improving drafts.

When tagged student contributions stay up on the classroom walls, dry erase boards, overheads, and interactive whiteboard over time, teachers and students can better see how a lesson activity progresses, or how student thinking is evolving over time. Misconceptions—welcomed, faithfully tagged, and revisited—have opportunities to get worked on, visibly, together. Researchers who deal with conceptual change (Smith, diSessa, & Roschelle, 1993/1994) invite us to record all conceptions ("pre-," "mis-," and the like), spend time with them, and challenge and rechallenge them. All manner of initial understandings tagged at the beginning of a unit can be periodically revisited. Students can see that what we first defined as "function" or "adaptation" or "tone" later became more fleshed out by the end of the unit—just look at the wall.

Lastly, tagging plays a special role regarding "moments of contingency" in the classroom learning space. These are moments in which the direction of instruction depends upon what students are revealing (Leahy, Lyon, Thompson & Wiliam, 2005). By slowing down action and helping make student thinking visible, tagging supports teachers in creating moments of contingency and leveraging them for learning.

 FORMATIVE ASSESSMENT TIPS

Tag Now, Evaluate Later

Effective tagging depends on teachers temporarily suspending displays of outward judgment and holding back from evaluating student responses. When tagging, a teacher's focus needs to be on eliciting, welcoming, and recording student responses without bias. Teacher judgment isn't absent during tagging, it is just not expressed. There is time to build bins, sort responses, and decide who needs support. For now, relax and let tagging provide the running record to remember what's next and why.

Tagging's Place in the Assessment Triangle

At first glance we might want to place tagging moves (not to mention Bouncing) in the *observation* vertex of the assessment triangle. When students speak, we record—tag—their words on a medium that is visible, accessible, and shared. When students write, we invite them to publish their writing to a medium that is trusted, public, and judgment-free. The same goes for when our students sing, or run, or paint in the classroom learning space. Tagging helps us observe them better and to give attention to what is significant in their performances.

We argue that tagging—like bouncing—moves are actually a part of the *interpretation* vertex. Without thorough bouncing and tagging, we can't really trust first impressions about what our students know and can do. In Chapter 5 on Bouncing we discussed implications of sampling and how our inferences about "what to do next" in a lesson are compromised if we fail to gather data on students other than the eager beavers. A related challenge is presented in this chapter as we struggle to capture not only who or how many responded to a question or problem, but also to record—tag—and use that information to make better, more valid instructional decisions.

Formative assessors must put a premium on noting and documenting observations of student thinking—that is, tagging—*before* they work to move lessons in productive directions. Tagging faithfully what students actually say helps us to move closer toward achieving the learning targets or gaining traction on a misconception. Both tagging and bouncing moves are fundamental prerequisites to what's available to interpret and how likely our interpretations of soft data will stand up to scrutiny. This is why we assert they are located within the *interpretation* vertex of the assessment triangle.

Too often the literature on formative assessment—and the common practice of formative assessors—puts an emphasis on binning: on categorizing, evaluating, and judging the worth of student thought. FA experts can inadvertently put the pressure on novices (including teacher candidates) to evaluate, differentiate, and offer feedback. The received wisdom seems to be to teach them how to evaluate, interpret, and decide what to do next *immediately* in a lesson.

The first order of business for those learning formative assessment moves, however, must be working to get as complete and accurate a snapshot of student thinking as possible. By emphasizing bouncing and tagging, we are moving in the right direction with beginners. Teacher candidates, in particular, need permission to learn how to listen first, act later.

Making schema and prior knowledge public makes it easier for students to learn from one another's ideas. As Figure 6.1 reminds us, the wider the variation represented by our running records, the sounder the inferences teachers can make, the better teachers' decisions regarding adjusting instruction can be, and we hope with experience and time, the faster teachers gain relevant PCK in their subject areas.

Regardless of how a specific episode of tagging is carried out—via a high-tech app or a low-tech chalkboard, or whether the teacher does the recording or students do the scribing—tagging's main purpose is the same. The formative assessor is attempting to *observe* (most frequently by listening carefully), and then gather and document these *observations* as evidence to inform instructional decision making.

We must step back for a moment, before moving into how tagging is connected to the larger FA moves framework. Let's remember that, unlike the summative assessors' world that produces grades, proficiency bands, and other hard data for public consumption, the evidence generated by formative assessors isn't prepackaged. It has to be recognized, collected, and captured by some medium, which teachers usually decide upon ahead of time. A dry erase board, a school yard blacktop surface, a piece of butcher paper, a pack of sticky notes—any or all will do.

Figure 6.1   Tagging and the Assessment Triangle

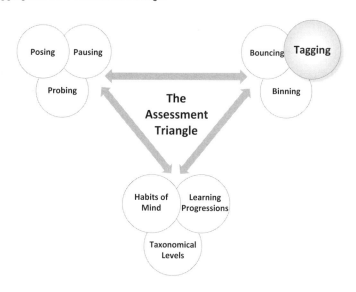

For tagging to be guided by the assessment triangle, it also needs to be well-supported by the other formative assessment moves—besides bouncing. Many of these moves—such as probing—require improvising. Priming for tagging is key. Together, planned and improvised aspects of tagging make up the loosely structured opportunities for all ideas to be shared, as Kaila mentioned in the beginning of the chapter.

Tagging and the Other Moves

In our moves-based framework, tagging is situated between bouncing and binning. We see tagging as a *pre-binning* exercise, which we will discuss more in the next chapter. For now, let's say that tagging is necessary but not sufficient for making sense of student thinking. Let's also recognize that tagging has its own unique learning progression for teachers. No one is born an FA expert. Everyone was once a novice. Mastering formative assessment moves will require tapping into your own zone of proximal development (ZPD) and adjusting expectations and providing supports and scaffolds to improve your tagging practices.

Tagging's potential as a practice of classroom formative assessment is directly related to how skillfully a teacher primes, poses, pauses, probes, and bounces with her students. It will not be possible to faithfully or meaningfully record (via a scribe or some "magical" technology) what has not yet been articulated by more than a few eager students. Likewise, it is not much use reducing cognitive load by using a collective word web populated by sticky notes if no one understands how to approach the question/problem. Note that "skillful priming" to support the tagging of responses to a posed question that significantly overshoots students' ZPD (or for which students have no frame of reference) will have limited value. Probing two or three student responses doesn't help if we are missing data from 50 percent or more of the class.

At this point in our journey, it should come as no surprise: the better the FA moves work in concert toward worthy purposes, the more *formative* formative assessment practices are for students—and for their assessors, too.

 IN THE CLASSROOM

The Power of Tagging: Low-tech, High-leverage Lesson Openers to Get the Class in Gear

Teachers picking up the language and practices of the FA moves framework may begin to think:

I can use a word web to check for prior knowledge and increase the student response space with nodes around the big idea: *"What's the first thing that comes to mind when you see or hear the word 'ratio'?"* The responses (nodes) from the web can serve as a running record of our present understanding at this point in the unit. I can probe on responses (nodes) and add more depth to the web now or by revisiting it next week. I can circle and link responses to "ratio" before pressing for a formal definition. I can use what we've tagged in this lesson segment to form bins (e.g., bins of "proportions" and "fractions") for use later today or this week.

The beauty of this new thinking about tagging—the whole procedure can happen within 5 minutes at the beginning of any lesson.

What the Research Says

Our own research supports the idea that formative assessors rightly practice and value tagging sessions that begin with open, welcoming posing and priming, such as *"What comes to mind when you hear the word* contrast? *There are no right or wrong answers.*" In such wide-open tagging sessions *all* responses are written and noted. They are especially useful for activating students' prior knowledge, identifying what constructivists call schema, and building a ramp to examine conceptually challenging material that is about to unfold in the next lesson segment.

Other research tells us that more constrained tagging procedures for recording student thinking yields benefits, too. Schwarz and Glassner (2007) found that when middle school students were engaged in online class discussions with specific parameters, they generated longer, higher-quality threads of discussion and argumentation with explanation compared with significantly more open online discussions on similar discussion topics.

We know that tagging student contributions helps teachers facilitate better discussions, although classroom teachers and researchers approach this work differently. For teachers, tagging sessions often produce community word webs, mind maps, or concept maps. Assessment experts and researchers have documented some of these methods for producing hard data to substantiate claims about student learning (Herl, Baker, & Niemi, 1996; Yin, Vanides, Ruiz-Primo, Ayala, & Shavelson, 2005). The point for us is that—whether conceptualized quantitatively or qualitatively—tagging routines and artifacts are powerful tools for those learning to become formative assessors.

Chinn and Anderson (1998) tagged student contributions to whole class discussions by studying classroom videos (post-lesson enactment) to create "causal network diagrams" and "argument network diagrams" of discussions. Such detailed records can be used to generate quantitative measures of the quality of the class discussions and of individual student contributions to them. Chinn and Anderson also reported that when teachers were shown the diagrams, they were inspired to try to elicit more evidence, perhaps by probing students about their assertions during discussions.

Such detailed, exacting records are beyond the scope of classroom teachers' independent daily practice. But, interestingly, Chinn and Anderson (1998) reported an incident where a researcher *did* tag a live class discussion in a kind of shorthand and was able to show the "abbreviated argument network diagram" of the discussion to the teacher *during* class. The teacher expressed that she highly valued experiencing the student discussion in this more visual way.

This *is* something teachers can potentially learn to do for themselves as they work on their tagging moves. Many argue that teachers already tag in their minds, without writing things down. We argue that teachers (and their students) are more likely to benefit from support (logistical, observational, and professional) as they try to make classroom dialogues, turns of talk, even note-taking visible to all. In addition to more research on tagging practices of teachers, we need more resources for teachers who are ready to capture their soft data and put it to use.

We are not alone in making and standing behind the claim that tagging matters. Supporting teachers to make visual "representations of the macrostructure" of discussions, as Chinn and Anderson call it, "provide[s] schemata that can help teachers conceptualize discussions in new ways" and "help them have many more insights into how to improve discussions and how to improve students' reasoning" (p. 363). Tagging has a role to play in making this happen.

Tagging in Mathematics

Research on mathematics teaching supports the idea that tagging supports student learning. Although researchers before us have not called it *tagging*, math teachers have a tradition of tagging student thinking and making student thinking public.

The National Council of Teachers of Mathematics (NCTM) has long advocated this research-supported practice (2000). Magdalene Lampert and Deborah Ball's well-known work (1998) has illustrated how student thinking and understanding can be furthered by students' "making math public" by representing their work and ideas on the board, by sharing, and by engaging in "instructional dialogues" (Ball, 1993; Leinhardt & Steele, 2005).

Math teachers in Japan practice *bansho*, a concept and practice similar to tagging, that refers to effective use of the blackboard:

> In Japan, the blackboard is used extensively in lessons: to keep a record of the lesson, to help students remember what they need to do and to think about, to help students see the connection between different parts of the lesson and the progression of the lesson, to compare, contrast, and discuss ideas that students present, to help to organize student thinking and discovery of new ideas. (Takahashi, 2006)

Pjanić (2014) highlights an important benefit of keeping "all that is written during the lesson on the blackboard without erasing it." *Bansho* gives the teacher and students a perspective-taking opportunity, a "birds-eye view of what has happened in the class at the end of each lesson" (p. 90).

Learners also have an easier time comparing multiple solution methods when they appear on the blackboard simultaneously.

Tagging and Concept Mapping

Research supports the practice of tagging to build concept maps that assist learning in the classroom. Aguirre-Munoz and Baker (1997) have asserted that assessment that features concept mapping could especially help English language learners (Aguirre-Munoz & Baker, 1997) because it is a "less discourse-dependent" method of gauging students' understanding. We also know that tagging students' ideas via concept maps highlights relationships and links among ideas, and can represent complex ideas rather quickly.

Although there is much research about the scoring of individual students' concept maps (Herl et al., 1996; Ruiz-Primo & Shavelson, 1996; Rye & Rubba, 2002; Yin et al., 2005; McCloughlin & Matthews, 2012; Richmond et al., 2014), educational research on collaboratively generated concept maps and how teachers might use them on the fly to make instructional decisions is scarce. Our own informal observations of preservice teachers across eight subject areas shows a simple word web is a place for teachers to start tagging when launching a lesson. Sometimes, it's enough to gain a foothold when climbing a mountain, whether one is engaged in assessment *for* or *of* learning. The formative assessor does not have to worry about grading these student-generated word webs. The point is rather to check for understanding routinely and use the informal tools at one's disposal to get traction.

Tagging with Technology

Now, a few words about technology use while tagging. Researchers have found that technologies used to support tagging can foster increased student participation and engagement, whether the technology is interactive whiteboards (Smith, Hardman, & Higgins, 2006); clickers (Hunsu, Adesope, & Bayly, 2016; Kay & LeSage, 2009), tablets, or bring your own device (Grant et al., 2015).

Researchers also note that for claims of increased student engagement, motivation, and achievement—and even "behavioral gains"—*to be sustained* (emphasis ours), these technologies need to be used in the context of "interactive pedagogy" (Glover, Miller, Averis, & Door, 2007; Knight, Pennant, & Piggot, 2005; Higgins, Beauchamp, & Miller, 2007). Once again, the success of a particular technology solution is inextricably linked with the kids, the context for learning, and the type of curriculum and instruction.

Formative assessors everywhere will not be surprised by Higgins, Beauchamp, and Miller's finding (2007) that *teachers are the critical agents* in mediating technology, such as interactive whiteboards, to promote productive interactions aimed at learning targets and lesson objectives. We agree with the experts: no matter the technology used to tag, teachers are the critical agents in building toward and sustaining a classroom rich in formative assessment. Teachers set the pace, the purpose, and the plan for tagging moves. It's up to us to size up how technology advances make student thinking visible—and where and when to hit the pause button.

Going Deeper with Tagging

Open Versus Constrained Tagging: Purpose Drives Everything

Tagging happens on a continuum from wide-open, anything goes, no-right-or-wrong-answers sessions, to more constrained, "a few flavors welcomed here" and "let's keep it on topic today" sessions.

Where a tagging session falls on this continuum usually depends on a teacher's purposes. We say usually, because what actually happens (and therefore where a tagging session falls on this continuum) may depend less on beginning teachers' purposes and the opening question posed and more on their skills at priming and bouncing to elicit a range of student responses. A poorly primed and bounced tagging session won't be "wide open" if only 4 out of 32 students offer responses. Tagging 1/8 of the student response space to a powerful question ("Is the United States a democracy?") will compromise inferences about what students believe, think, or know.

The degree of openness of a tagging session should relate to a teacher's purposes for a particular lesson. For example, to elicit students' prior knowledge, teachers might do well to orchestrate "anything-goes-on-the-board" tagging sessions during lesson openings or to help with transitions between lesson segments. For a unit on probability or statistics, the tagging procedure might start with the teacher writing the word *bias* in the middle of the whiteboard and asking, "What comes to mind when you hear the word *bias*? There are no right or wrong answers. Remember, we want everyone's ideas and opinions to get us started."

The teacher would bounce and tag, coaxing, cajoling, and scribing responses from over half the students in the class in four to seven minutes. She would scribe "out there" responses and similar sounding responses as well as use tally marks to honor repeated responses.

Such a wide-open tagging session differs from a more-constrained tagging session that might happen toward the end of a class when a teacher says, "Let's record all the reasons you came up with to support or critique the claim 'The poll data favors the incumbent.'"

Here, the teacher wants to see how far students have gotten with an in-class task and to have students recognize the variety of reasons they have generated as a community of learners. The teacher wants everyone to benefit from seeing and hearing one another's reasons before class ends. This recognizes and honors their work and sets the groundwork for tomorrow's lesson on *sampling bias*.

The message from the formative assessor: *I care about your ideas as they develop in this lesson, over the unit, and throughout the semester. I will tag and scribe to see how your ideas change and grow as you learn more about this important topic.* Tagging also provides the teacher a record of evidence to use in adjusting her plans for the next lesson. She can study this treasure trove of soft data (perhaps using a smartphone to capture the word web) and think more about patterns and preconceptions that are worth addressing over time.

Tagging That Supports Improvised Instructional Moves

At other times, a teacher initiates a tagging procedure in response to a student need that he perceives on the fly. In other words, a student introduces the concept that needs consideration—by the teacher, by other students, by the class as a whole.

For example, in the course of a lesson a student may ask, "What's *surface area* again?" The teacher responds by pausing the lesson and getting everyone to consider this student's question, perhaps beginning by having students think, pair, and share with their elbow partners (Duckor, Holmberg, & Rossi Becker, 2017). He runs tagging procedures that elicit and publicly recognize many student responses. The teacher probes a bit further into a few answers. In the process, the formative assessor learns much about his class's present understanding of the concept and definition of *surface area* and *materials* and all his students have had opportunities to use new academic language in an authentic context. Tagging can reveal and highlight the academic language demands of the lesson for beginning and experienced teachers.

Democratic Tagging, Marginalized Students, and Other People's Children

Research shows that marginalized students benefit from schools that are organized to amplify, not suppress, student voices and thinking (Boaler, 2002; Delpit, 1988; Freire, 1970; Plaut & Sharkey, 2003). Tagging practices in classrooms, theaters, band rehearsal spaces, courts, and fields have a role to play in this work. Democratic, supportive tagging says: *It's okay to share, to risk, to* not yet *know something but remain committed to learning about it in this community. We will hold one another accountable and support one another at the same time.* How many adults, let alone children, have bought into this belief or even heard it expressed—inside or outside today's classrooms?

Students learning to be citizens and workers must be guided and supported by a school community (Dewey, 1902). School staff and teacher leaders who support the community of learners will not only offer reasons to exercise duties and fulfill obligations, but will also model and practice what it means to act equitably, civilly, and fairly. They will come to meetings ready to tag all ideas. They will listen hard and record faithfully what they hear. These leaders will facilitate, scribe, and represent the current levels of understanding with students, teachers, and parents.

We do not exaggerate the principle behind tagging: the success of our democratic experiment as a country may depend on how far and how deeply this modeling and practice inhabits and reverberates through the classrooms, hallways, offices, and school yards. Tagging helps make ideas, and the process of considering them, visible in communities. As Carl suggests at the opening of this chapter, these classroom moves can be a significant contribution to democracy with a small "d."

When a teacher comes from a different class or ethnic or cultural background from her students, when she teaches, as Lisa Delpit (1995) has written, "other people's children," tagging can support the teacher's process of learning more about her students. Tagging puts the teacher who is learning to become a formative assessor in a position to listen and learn from her students' prior knowledge and beliefs. You need not argue about how power dynamics animate who gets to learn which lessons while doing school to accept the claim that tagging is a powerful procedure. It allows us to walk the walk of formative assessment and not get lost in debates about who rules the "system." It is our decision to tag or not to tag—each and every day.

To foster connections necessary for deeper learning, a teacher has to see how students are thinking about a big idea. Tagging can also help reveal just what and how much the teacher does *not yet* know about her students. Getting this out in the open, respecting it, examining it, and working with it is important for keeping things real. It's key to becoming a formative assessor.

 FORMATIVE ASSESSMENT TIPS

Tagging and Students' Zones of Proximal Development

To get at the challenge of teaching to students' needs, researchers focus on concepts such as the zone of proximal development (ZPD). ZPD describes the region between what learners can do without direct assistance and what they can do with minimal scaffolding and support. Within her individual zone of proximal development, a learner can accomplish particular tasks and feats with minimal guidance. Over time, we remove these supports so that the learner can function independently with a high degree of autonomy.

Tagging helps teachers toward clearly, consistently, and publicly describing what learners' needs might actually be. Significantly, tagging creates a running record that both teacher and students can revisit and reflect upon as skills develop over time.

We see tagging moves as another part of the FA toolkit that helps teachers figure out more about their students' zones of proximal development.

Tagging for All

Generally speaking, a teacher needs to get enough student responses such that a wide range of student ideas, associations, opinions, and misconceptions is tagged. But how much is enough? How many students' ideas do we really need on the board? Are all beliefs worth recording publicly? Isn't it a mistake to represent "mistakes" and "misconceptions" for all to see? Won't other students take them up as "correct"? Or, at the least, get confused by them? By tagging such a wide variation of responses, won't we be creating more challenges for ourselves and our students than is necessary or wise?

When it comes to tagging, there is no magic number of student responses to record. Nor is there a rule of thumb for when to delete "incorrect answers" from the session or censor your students' opinions and thoughts. Nonetheless, research shows that too many beginning teachers fail to reach a robust, let alone representative, sampling of student responses in any given lesson. Some are crippled by the fear and anxiety of the "unorthodox" and "off color" response.

The formative assessor's commitment to "tagging for all" is critical to the promise of tagging as a practice that embodies democratic (perhaps even scientific) values. This implies that, in many ways, tagging needs to be felt and seen as an end in itself. Process is as important as product: *how* student responses are obtained is as important and as valuable as the *what* that emerges from the tagged data gathered in your lessons.

 TEACHER VOICE

Some of my students are desperately eager to be heard—immediately. Others want to watch their peers take a risk first before they'll jump in. You have to prime the tagging or it's going to go south.

—Cara

Distinctions Among Oral Tagging, Revoicing, and Tagging

When novice teachers who are learning to become formative assessors take their first forays into tagging, they will repeat what a student has just said, usually so that everyone in the class can hear or hear it again. Beginning formative assessors call this "verbal tagging." Though there was no public written representation of student responses during their lesson, they will report, and often with pride, "I *verbally* tagged today!"

"Verbal" tagging is an invention on their part. We refer to this *pre*-tagging practice—because that is what it is—as *oral tagging* since it features spoken language only, nothing written, as their use of the modifier "verbal" might imply. We also celebrate when it appears (as it does every semester, though we do not introduce it to teacher candidates as a concept) because experience has led us to believe that from this point forward in their growth as formative assessors it is only a matter of time before they leap into orchestrating "actual" tagging sessions during their lessons. In addition, striving to repeat students' words accurately verbatim is laudable, a skill teachers need to develop, and—we add—not easily done!

We gently remind the beginners, however, that oral tagging does not reduce cognitive load, activate working memory, or record the students' ideas for use later. Tagging *can*, of course, and these potential benefits are among its greatest strengths.

Tagging, to put it bluntly, differs from revoicing in many ways. There is much more to revoicing, say O'Connor and Michaels (1993) and Gray (1993), than a teacher repeating a student's words in a "teacher voice" so that everyone can hear. Although revoicing may be beneficial by giving students an expanded voice in classroom discourse, too often it is accompanied by intentionally changing, adding to, and revising students' original words. Teachers will "voice again" what students have said to correct them and to "academicize," if you will, their words.

Teachers socialize students into academic or discipline-specific ways of thinking and acting with revoicing that highlights, reformulates, and repositions students' words. When revoicing, teachers may highlight only certain aspects of an utterance, such as by saying, for example, "Michelle, you said, 'Learned *by osmosis.'* or "Ryan, I heard you say, *distribute.*" Or teachers may reformulate student words into more academic terms: *So you hypothesized the 'perp' was guilty based on your interpretation of events as an eyewitness?*

Revoicing, according to experts, also includes positioning a student's ideas explicitly and "visibly," so that the student can claim or disclaim that position. Students are often not aware of how their words imply a position on a topic. The teacher points this out through revoicing. A teacher might say, for example, "So then, Javier, you don't agree with Leslie that if the 'perp' wasn't at the crime scene..."

But again, there is a distinction. Revoicing does not require that anything be written down. Like oral tagging, revoicing routines may increase extraneous cognitive load while denying everyone a visible running record that makes all ideas, opinions, and misconceptions public for careful examination. Tagging does this and more.

Here is an example of how we, as teachers of beginning teachers, have revoiced in our own classes. As a teacher candidate has told us about her teaching day, we have responded with, "So you *primed* that way in an attempt to *lower your students' affective filter?*" Or, "So when you invited all responses, not merely correct ones, you were *activating your students' prior knowledge?*"

These are definitely examples of revoicing with purpose, and good to do on occasion, but they are not instances of tagging moves that widen and record the student response space. Because we have not publicly represented the student teacher's contribution for all to access and use later in the lesson, it's not tagging. Tagging creates a visual record. See Figure 6.2 to explore the differences.

 TEACHER VOICE

Moving Beyond "Tagging 1.0" Moves

I've been trying to get in the habit of visually tagging student responses on the white-board because I heavily rely on verbal tags. Having it written on the board shows students that I am making an effort to consider their responses and to show their effort to the class. It took time to get comfortable writing while trying to orchestrate the discussion. Now I allow for students to scribe for me. This keeps them involved and makes them feel like they are more a part of the learning going on in the classroom.

—Karen, elementary school music and art teacher

Supporting Multilingual Learners During Tagging

Students working to gain fluency in English may need special supports before, during, and after tagging. Research shows that language learners and students with special needs benefit from rehearsing what they will say out loud to support them in meeting the academic language demands of a particular lesson or unit (Zwiers, 2007a, 2007b). Teachers can—and should—for example, facilitate pair-sharing and the use of sentence starters or graphic organizers for these oral language rehearsals.

Formative assessors will go further. They may need to develop norms around defining words that pop up during tagging sessions that are new to language learners and other students. Side conversations and direct translations can be encouraged, and may include allowing students to use their mobile devices to look up new vocabulary. The particulars of supporting students are context-dependent and based on the particular language learner's designation.

Adapting tagging norms and procedures to support all learners, regardless of their language proficiency status, is key. We are reminded by our colleagues that academic language demands and cognitive processing needs are cross-cutting pieces of the lesson planning puzzle. We add explicit and visible tagging procedures for those learning to master formative assessment moves and teach in linguistically, culturally, and economically diverse K–12 school settings. A good lesson plan will integrate all of these facets.

Figure 6.2   How Tagging Differs from Revoicing

Key Aspects	Tagging	Revoicing
Who leads it, does it?	Teachers and students scribe classroom responses	Only teachers revoice classroom responses
What is the process?	Written and visual documentation	Oral and aural modality
What does it result in?	Public records of student thinking	Amplified student voice, opportunities for students to clarify their position
How is it related to sampling of student responses?	Coupled with bouncing, tagging strives to represent a wide variety of responses	Can work well with a few—or even single— student contributions
Does it promote students' speaking and listening skills?	Yes, since ideas and opinions are articulated, recorded, and made visible to all	Not necessarily, because the point is reamplification, "academicization," and making students' positions visible
Effects?	Slows pace, increases "think time," and allows for encoding and retrieval of information	Socializes students into using voice and allowing teachers to "support" speech, especially academic language of the discipline
Where does the power in the practice come from?	From *not* only amplifying words but also recording them for all to see or hear; assists in probing and reposing to check for understanding	From amplifying, to the extent possible, students' words; may support confidence and feeling of having one's words attended to by teacher and foster academic identity
How is it related to binning?	Occurs prior to binning moves; is descriptive in nature; expands the response space; increases available soft data to evaluate and analyze for next steps	Descriptive or evaluative depending on how much the teacher inserts her own voice to reshape student responses

Let's not get too overwhelmed by the call for more tagging to meet our students' academic language needs. As a tagging session commences, the formative assessor can facilitate the processes and mechanisms for adding new vocabulary to word walls or updating running lists in students' notebooks. Teachers can probe on tagged responses with short scenarios that require students to meaningfully use the new vocabulary, giving students another near-time exposure to the new word, phrase, or sentence frame. The goal here is to act upon the recognition that there are particular language demands inherent in every lesson and that tagging procedures can unpack those demands, segment by segment. The skillful formative assessor is not only aware of these learning opportunities in the lesson plan, she allows the particular tagging procedure (and medium) to help her students build more complex, nuanced understandings. A move in the right direction is to embed tagging-for-academic-language supports into multiple parts of the lesson, gather up the soft data that is on the proverbial wall, and figure out what's next.

 FORMATIVE ASSESSMENT TIPS

A quick clarification: Is tagging simply making a recording? Or must tagging always involve a degree of transformation and hence interpretation, however subtle, of student responses? We maintain that tagging is the act of publicly recognizing student responses while attempting to record those responses without bias. Tagging communicates respect for student thinking, beliefs, and ideas. The teacher acts as a neutral party committed to sharing all ideas with the class on behalf of a particular student. Temporarily, the teacher is not a scorekeeper or coach with an agenda. When teachers provide a safe harbor for all student responses, students can trust in the teacher's role as an advocate for unorthodox ideas or tentative notions.

Principles, Procedures, and Practices
Start by Eliciting and "Word Webbing" Prior Knowledge

For teachers newly focused on making tagging moves, we recommend a concrete procedure: word webbing students' prior knowledge one lesson at a time. Part of the rationale is to remind the formative assessor that students need to be primed nonstop. Word webs tell our students used to doing school that we will be exploring new ways of working and learning together in this classroom. Everyone get ready.

Many find the formative assessment moves strange and uncomfortable at first. Students may not be used to pooling their knowledge (or raising questions) in one public place. They love to watch teachers put others in the spotlight—being at the other end of the beam, not so much. Tagging is a public act where everyone's contribution is suddenly visible. The public, semi-permanent nature of tagged content excites and motivates some students, scares and baffles others. So priming and repriming, gently, matters for the effectiveness of tagging. It will take more than a few first tries, in addition to stamina, to put up with the inevitable "fails and chokes" at the wall.

Teachers can take responsibility for making tagging useful and meaningful to students. Going into tagging sessions with clarity of purpose and a commitment to helping students see the value in the tagging sessions sets teachers up for success. Find real-life examples. The kids tend to buy into pedagogical practices if they see people they admire do it well. Tagging is no different. Buy-in matters.

A piece of advice: make it easy. Class brainstorming is the most obvious place to start tagging. It is also, we acknowledge, for many teachers, a dangerous activity. But so is teaching and learning. Think of others who struggled to change old habits and ways of thinking. Recall the lessons from Socrates, Galileo, and Martin Luther King Jr.

For many of the mentor teachers we work with, the messages are mixed. Each semester our teacher candidates mention their worries that opening a lesson with a brainstorming exercise could invite chaos. *What if students say bizarre, off-topic things? What if they joke? What if I can't write fast enough (and students get bored) or can't spell well enough (and students laugh at me)? If I transcribe their misconceptions, won't that just reinforce them? If I write everything, won't other students start learning the wrong things?*

As teacher educators working with beginners in the profession, we remind them about the lessons from educational psychology. Schema, like Rome, aren't built in a day. Constructivist approaches to teaching make room for students' notions, beliefs, and knowledge (however rudimentary or inchoate) about a topic. If we review the professional teaching standards and the research on how people learn, it becomes abundantly clear: our job is to check for our students' prior knowledge routinely, consistently, and dynamically.

In practice, most of us don't tag regularly. Why? Because it is risky. That's one reason. It's time-consuming. That's another explanation. Another is that checking for prior knowledge in a classroom full of children (try doing it on the blacktop or in the gym!) requires social skills and solid norms for group functioning that may not yet be in place. Teachers and students who choose to tag together will need time and practice to get skillful at enacting this particular formative assessment move.

That said, we note that word webbing works in any subject and for most age groups. We recommend webs over lists or t-charts because webs are nonlinear. They do not imply a predetermined hierarchy. All responses can be represented without sending the unconscious message that order and structure and ranking matter most. The goal for tagging student responses, particularly when checking for prior knowledge, is to keep things open. A flow of ideas and beliefs is key. (You can impose order later when it's time to bin for feedback).

The formative assessor needs to be strategic in planning which big ideas in the unit or curriculum are amenable to this or any other procedure. In Chapter 2 on Posing, we saw that James's opening pose, ("What comes to mind when you hear the word *vector*?") met with crickets (student silence). The entry bar was set too high. Students were confused and withdrew. James's pose couldn't really be bounced. James stood at the chalkboard, eager to scribe. He paused, but his pausing was not going to fix the situation. No amount of pausing will save us if we have overshot our students' levels of understanding.

As James said, "The silence was painful." No wonder we don't tag publicly. Better to give quizzes or tests, which are very private affairs.

As uncomfortable as moments like these may be for us, they are a necessary step on the path to becoming a formative assessor. Missed opportunities can inspire us to improve. James's example did. Our whole class of teacher candidates worked together to solve the *Vector* puzzle that night. We put our attention on moves that make a difference but remain hard to put into practice. We honored James's struggle as our own and figured out how to say aloud *What if?* and *Try this*, and *Not yet*.

Illustrations of competent tagging practice can inspire us too. Let's see how a high school math teacher in training, Serena, elicits and tags her students' prior knowledge by word webbing it on the whiteboard (see case study, pp. 224–225). Her entire process takes fewer than three minutes. Now that's inspiring!

Word Webbing Versus Quizzes: A Tale of Two Tagging Procedures

Before launching into a key concept in a unit, teachers have at least two options for checking for prior knowledge: they can administer a traditional quiz that functions as a pretest, or they can use a word web. (There are more options, but let's simplify for now.)

The benefits of giving a quiz—assuming the items on the quiz perform reliably and as intended—are numerous. We get a *more standardized and hence constrained assessment event.* Each student has time to respond under the same conditions and the questions are the same for everyone. On quizzes, every student gets a point score, which later can be turned into grades. A teacher can look at the distribution of grades across the class and gain a sense of students' prior knowledge on a topic or unit.

Because we have defined tagging and tagged material as that which is publicly shared, we cannot say that students' individual quiz performances are an example of tagging. Student responses to assessment items typically remain private.

A word web functions quite differently than a quiz (see Figure 6.3). Word webs are not designed to keep student answers private. When bouncing moves are functioning well, each student has time to respond under the same conditions and the questions or prompts are the same for everyone. No grades are assigned with a word web and the teacher doesn't indicate who has the right or wrong answer.

With the word web-tagging procedure, there is no preconfigured scoring sheet or technology to assign points to student responses. The word web is a process that unfolds in real time and hence is not easily standardized or scripted or benchmarked. At its best, the word web represents everyone's contribution and captures the student responses space much like the quiz does.

Figure 6.3   Final Word Web Tagging

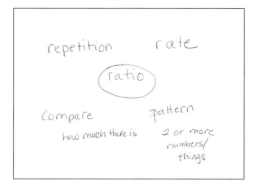

Tagging: Serena's Case

Every math teacher I know emphasizes: *doing math is much, much more than getting the right answer*. Teaching math ought to align with this belief. We math teachers espouse this; however, it's easier said than done.

A critical moment in my development as a teacher came when I tried out a method that helped me embody this belief and some important corollaries: *Students' prior knowledge matters tremendously*; *Everyone needs to be engaged*; and *Teachers help students foster connections to aid conceptual understanding*.

In my experience it makes no sense to start by formally defining a word, for example, *ratio*. To check for prior knowledge, you must roll the die. No exceptions. My go-to method of introducing a term or phrase of academic language is to tag a word web of students' prior knowledge, in this case, a concept in proportional reasoning.

My big moment happened when student teaching algebra 1 with 28 kids from 9th through 11th grades at a large, urban comprehensive high school where students spoke more than two dozen languages. The class was untracked.

We had just finished a warm-up problem involving scoops of ice cream and average consumption of ice cream by season. The problem was meant to hook students into the concept of ratio as we began a new unit. I sought to discover and validate students' prior knowledge of *ratio* before we worked to come to a common understanding of the concept of *ratio*. This exchange took two and one-half minutes:

ME: OK, so here we have a ratio—actually Vi told me it was a ratio—that expresses a comparison between these two quantities of ice cream scoops, okay? All right. So, we're going to do a little brainstorm before we establish what a ratio really is, okay? So, when I write the word *ratio* on the board, okay, I want to ask you guys—I want some help defining it. What do you think of when you hear the word *ratio*?

BERNICE: Compare.

ME: Compare. What do you think, Conrad? What do you think of when you hear the word ratio? Anything that comes to the mind.

CONRAD: [Speaking softly] How much there is.

ME: How much there is? Okay. [tags] How much there is.

REYNALDO: A pattern.

ME: I heard a pattern. Is that—yeah, pattern. [tags] Thank you! Okay, anybody else got any ideas?

MATEO: Repetition.

ME: Repetition. [tags] Did you have an idea, Leon? No, *nothing* comes to mind when you think of ratio? Not even scoops of ice cream now? What?

LEON: A rate.

ME: A rate, yeah. [tags] And how about, what are we comparing?

ALESSIA: Two or more numbers.

ME: Two or more numbers, that's good; two or more numbers, excellent. [tags] Any other ideas? Are ice cream scoops in terms of numbers? We can write them in terms of numbers, right? Or we can just say ice cream scoops. Or maybe just say two—two or more things. We could say number or things. Okay, well, all these are really good ideas. Any other ideas that people want to throw out there? Ok, so—so far we have a ratio. It seems to tell how much there is, right? By making a comparison of two or more numbers or things, okay. So, let's go ahead and write a definition.

If I were to teach the same lesson today, the tagging session would probably go a bit differently. And yet, essential aspects of the values of tagging were in place at the beginning of my journey into formative assessment.

For example, tagging demonstrates to students that what they say is worth putting up on the board. It's sharing the "knowledge space" in the classroom, on the whiteboard. This helps with classroom community. Today I would invite students to pair-share, write their initial responses on sticky notes, and then walk up to the board to tag it. Then I'd have a student help read what others wrote. That move frees me up to see patterns and bin responses on the fly without also having to do all the prompting and scribing.

I have learned to accept that we tag all student responses—not just the right answers. It's tempting to think that so-called wrong answers will be contagious and spread like an epidemic. But I've learned to be patient, even if it looks—at first—like that might be happening. I had to let go of some fear about this, gain some perspective, grow my understanding of how students learn and construct new schema over time, and learn ways to productively use incorrect answers and the thinking and beliefs that go along with them. Tagging students' prior knowledge—regularly, routinely, and with different methods—is part of my journey into soft data and its potential uses during my lessons.

The aim of the word web as a formative assessment tool is tagging actual student ideas, beliefs, and opinions—not summarizing or neatly packaging them into predetermined categories. When we have a broad distribution of actual, real-time student responses, we know that tagging has occurred. But only part of the work for the formative assessor has begun—the results or data from the word web must be woven into the next steps in the lesson. The word web as a check for prior knowledge helps to direct other instructional choices and moves. Unlike the quiz, it doesn't wait to be graded. The word web, and other tools like it, are embedded assessments that inform instruction (Wilson & Sloane, 2000).

A formative assessor can choose intentionally and with purpose between a quiz and a word web (or any other assessment tool) when introducing key concepts in a unit. Each tool is potentially useful to widen the observation vertex of the assessment triangle. But only once the formative assessor knows the strengths and weaknesses, or the affordances and constraints, of a tool can he hope to advance the cause of formative assessment.

The two assessment activities differ markedly. Quizzes cannot be shared. We do not have the opportunity to build off others' ideas during the test event, nor can we explore misconceptions in real time.

Our faith in quizzes and tests—as instruments to get to the bottom of things—is hard to shake. When checking for student understanding, there is a strong desire to use what we got from our own teachers when we were young. Plus, tests seem objective. They are easy to administer and score. They allow for comparisons within and among groups of students. Results can be posted online!

But these traditional classroom assessment tools may not get us the information we really would like, and the processes of quizzing and testing may be even less helpful to learners than some alternatives. If assessment for learning means anything, it should invite us to make moves such as bouncing and tagging. Only by gathering all the soft data at our disposal can we drive lessons forward in ways that are responsive to the learner.

Here is the good news: we have a choice. We can mix up the formative and summative assessment routines in our classrooms. We can add new moves to the FA toolkit (word webbing is just one). We can experiment with different tagging configurations and procedures according to our students' needs. We can also learn to think harder about the trade-offs with degrees of tagging. *Who disengages when tagging slows down too much? How quickly can I get these students re-engaged with another move? Am I publicly recording all the voices or just a few? Am I capturing enough soft data to help launch the lesson, set the hook, pivot to the next activity, and tie up the loose ends by the time the bell rings? How am I/ how are we using this data—minute by minute? Where is the "low hanging fruit" (troves of soft data) we've yet to discover as a class?*

TEACHER VOICE

It's the Little Things That Get in the Way of Tagging

My handwriting is poor—even in the best of circumstances. When I'm writing student responses on the board as fast as I can, as I'm tagging, my handwriting is appalling. I could use technology. Or a student could scribe. But sometimes I just need to be the one writing stuff down. At least it feels like that.

Maybe if I had students scribing more often it wouldn't feel like such a big deal to yield control of the whiteboard. Sometimes control of the class feels so fragile and hard won. Once gained, to relinquish that control is like giving Excalibur over to, well, a teenager.

In order for us all to benefit from tagging, I need to do so in a way that we can all read and understand the words. I also see that my struggles with tagging are about more than my bad handwriting.

—*Sam, high school social science teacher*

Enlist Students to Create and Adjust Tagging Agreements and Procedures

Tagging cannot succeed without student buy-in. Take an inventory of agreements. Link bouncing and tagging moves and remind your students neither can happen without priming. Are the scribes scribing or goofing off? Do they prefer high-tech or low-tech media? Does anyone have a suggestion for a method that is more efficient? More visible? Easier to save and share? Is tagging making people feel more or less safe? What can we do about it as a community?

Reassure students that there will be days and times when they will be energized and happy to share, as well as days and times when they will be reluctant and tired. Feelings, all feelings, though respected, do not keep a learning community from getting the work of learning together done. Class agreements about why and how tagging is valued play an important role bringing the FA moves framework to life. Post these agreements proudly where they can remind everyone why and how to take the time and effort to tag and tag well.

Got tagging problems in your classroom? Let's go back to our Habits of Mind: Evidence and Conjecture. Ask the kids: What would happen if all our recording devices disappeared? How could we know what anyone thinks about an important topic if we never recorded it? If a tree falls in the forest and no one is around to hear it, does it make a sound?

Ask yourself: Are tests and quizzes the best way to show and record what all my students know and can do with the curriculum? What if I never used another standardized test or uploaded a result online? Would it be impossible for parents, counselors, or school administrators to know if my students had mastered the material? What's my evidence (soft, classroom-based data) for learning in my classrooms and can we make it more visible to the public?

Enlist Students to Scribe to Get It Done

Make taking the risk to be a scribe safe. Remind students that tagging is cognitively demanding. The more unfamiliar the content being tagged, the tougher the challenges. Misspellings will happen. Awkward silences will ensue. Someone will goof off. This is all part of the process. But tagging is a life skill. People who run meetings, campaigns, or professional sports trainings do it all the time.

When students tag, the classroom dynamic shifts. Teachers get to observe their whole class in action—an opportunity not to be missed. Strengths formerly hidden may shine. A student known for her serious demeanor may reveal herself to be a ham. Another student may gallantly "rescue" a classmate when it's not the teacher leading. Question: Whose behavior seems to change, and how, when you start tagging tomorrow? What you notice might surprise you.

Scribing students build leadership skills in front of the class. They challenge themselves to be facilitators as they improve their listening and recording skills. Whether keyboarding or writing with a marker, scribing students also gain the experience of expressing professional care and curiosity in their classmates' ideas ("Did I get that right?" "Can you say it again?" "Is this what you said?"). Trying on and exercising this professional persona is especially important for students who have formed judgments (and perhaps strong or negative opinions) about one another. Scribing gives students opportunities to practice seeing one another in another light.

Students being served by student scribes may give more honest, uncensored responses to a peer than they would to a teacher. Many learning benefits can accrue from this, including what a teacher can potentially do with this more accurate, if raw, snapshot of student thinking. Contributing students may have to speak louder when they give responses to a student scribe rather than a teacher. Teachers can be amazingly accommodating of the most soft-spoken students. Having to learn to speak up may seem like a small achievement to educational policymakers and outsiders, but it's an important skill in a culture that not only equates well-projected voices with confidence but where some voices tend to dominate and drown out others.

Add a Scribe Helper/Facilitator to Get Tagging Moving

For younger students, or students needing more support, consider having two students work together: one to do the scribing, and one to be a scribe helper. The scribe helper can serve as facilitator, manage the turn-taking, and assist with the listening, clarifying, and repeating. The scribe helper can repeat a student's response as the scribe is writing on the board. This can especially help scribes for whom it is challenging to simultaneously hear new content, process it in working memory, and write it neatly or type it accurately. We venture that everyone struggles with doing all these tasks at once, so assign roles to make tagging a success for all. Like the pair-share or table partner, this tagging buddy system creates a sense of safety and builds confidence that we are in this together.

Prime Everyone: Coach the Class Ahead of Student Scribing/Helping Routines

Scribes, scribe helpers, and all class members can benefit from brief coaching sessions before the tagging begins. Remind students, "What do we do again in the case of long responses?" One possible answer is that the scribe can ask, "How shall I write that down?" and pause.

Invite the scribe to try out a few probes. Tell the scribe, "A student just gave you a one-word response. It's a word you've never heard before. What can you say?"

Coach your scribes, especially those who have trouble holding in judgmental comments, to say *thank you* after each contribution. With all the class listening, remind the scribe and the scribe helper:

- Take care and time in writing/typing what each classmate says. You have time. Your careful attention to detail shows respect. Making spelling mistakes is okay.
- After a burst of responses, contributions may slow down. This is okay. It's your job to ask (again) for more responses and to pause patiently. More students may get ideas once they've had a chance to read what has already been tagged.

- Follow our classroom norms for calling on classmates.
- If someone offers a response in Spanish or Vietnamese, ask them how to spell it or invite them to tag it. Honor all responses and remind everyone that we learn more when people share in ways that meet their needs. Making connections to languages other than English can be a powerful learning experience.

Plan a Tagging Session's End

Plan a tagging session's end: What will you say, do, highlight? What will students do with the word web, for example? How will you handle transitioning into the next part of the lesson? Why does it matter to remind your students: "We will revisit this word web at the end of today?"

What's tagged should be celebrated and treated as a snapshot of the state of student understanding. It should be digested and not ignored. The tagged "data" is ripe for manipulation once you've recorded it faithfully. Sometimes you will want to grab a marker, highlighting certain aspects of the data, color-coding it, reorganizing it, or focusing in-depth on one piece of the data that surfaced during the share out.

Math teachers can tag prior knowledge around terms like *ratio* before turning to formal definitions for the students to copy in their notebooks. Music teachers can tag prior knowledge about barbershop quartets and harmony before modeling both together in a new unit on musical genres. PE teachers can tag "What comes to mind when you hear *pickle ball?*" on a movable whiteboard rolled in for the session.

Formative assessors know that a tagging session's end is really just a beginning, as they prepare to transition into the lesson's next segment. It provides a segue into the next activity. It can be part of the cycle of *I do, we do, you do*. Tagging practices embedded in lessons help us pace and customize content while we check for understanding and redirect instruction toward learning goals.

Misconceptions and Challenges
Polling Isn't Tagging

With the advent of new educational technologies, polling has become popular. Clickers, gestures in accordance with "hands up in the air if you agree," and "show me your stoplight cards"—these polling moves are too often focused on making tidy boxes of messy learning outcomes. They are binning strategies in disguise. They appear to gather opinions, ideas, and beliefs. But more often than not, they provide what assessment experts call distractor-like answer choices that don't always serve teachers well. If discovering and meeting students where they are is our goal, then we will need other procedures.

Polling students or categorizing responses into boxes (A, B, C, or D) certainly does have a place in classroom instruction. Binning student responses into predetermined categories can help teachers make decisions about next steps. But it is not tagging. And the predetermined categories may play a role in "helping us" miss out on eliciting important (what Black and Wiliam call "unorthodox") information from our students that would enable us to make even better instructional decisions.

Polling is really a sorting and stacking procedure, like the purpose behind standardized testing formats. Polling allows one to track "buckets" of information (i.e., student responses) and order them on a scale from better to worse, higher to lower, poor to advanced. As we maintain in the next chapter, polling has its place in teachers' efforts to bin student thinking, but polling cannot be mistaken for faithfully recording all student voices. Put sharply, polling is judgmental.

Tagging is not polling. Polling technologies will distort how we hear student responses by limiting them into bins. A challenge is that we cannot always know in advance of the teaching and learning moment if we have exhausted all the possible responses to a query, problem, or prompt. Nor can we be sure that we have accounted for all the nuance and complexity of those responses.

For example, self-report surveys (via clicker or a pencil) are notoriously problematic in social science research. *Reference bias* and *desirability bias* are nearly always in play, and can really influence the inferences that we can, with integrity, make about our students' knowledge and skills (Duckor, 2017). By limiting the response choices in advance, we have herded our students' thinking into three to four "answers." Inherently, these few answers cannot honor the complexity of the classroom learning space. Most often—and problematically so—the "correct answer" guides the poll-savvy instructor; she is not that interested in learning more about the "incorrect" responses. Too often, these polls are designed to answer the all-too-familiar pacing question: "Can we move on?"

Yes, we need order, structure, and ways to quickly make sense of the world inside the classroom. We crave solutions and efficiency. Less work means more time. But then again, we also need to be careful about the ways we—perhaps inadvertently—close down our students' thinking before it's even begun. Rather than rush to judgment (with the help of "smart tools") maybe we should walk over to a desk and ask, "That's interesting. Can you say more?"

 TEACHER VOICE

Too often we label student responses before we hear them. We fail to see their meaning, in part, because we never take the time to record them. We dismiss student thinking we see as falling into *Throwaway Bins*—such as wrong or incorrect answers, off-topic responses, crazy comments—before taking the time to observe and dig deeper. At a minimum, tagging slows down action. It gives everyone the space to breathe before we tackle what to do next.

—Lorri, a college advisor and teacher in a
nationally recognized after-school program

Representing Student Thinking Accurately Is Challenging

Listening well and scribing faithfully are key to successful tagging—and neither is easy to do. In observing many lessons and participating in lesson debriefs, we have noted that beginning teachers make subtle shifts in reporting back what they have just heard from their students. We see it clearly in video playback sessions, lesson study circles, and clinical field observations. The teacher asks students a question, the response is barely audible, so the student teacher "repeats" what he has heard. Okay, why not?

What's particularly interesting to us, however, as teachers committed to helping others become formative assessors, is how a teacher's act of "repeating" a student's response often reveals (inadvertent) misrepresentations of student thinking (e.g., Coffey, Hammer, Levin & Grant, 2011). We frequently see differences between what has been said by students and what is represented and attributed to them by teachers. Sometimes the differences are stark. Let's call it an Accuracy Gap.

The Accuracy Gap will be a persistent and problematic feature of formative assessment on the fly—especially when tagging procedures and routines are absent. This is because formative assessment procedures, unlike summative ones, place a premium on the teacher-as-instrument. She has to record, process, and analyze the streaming classroom data. She has to hold all the information gathered on the fly in her memory banks and be able to retrieve it at a moment's notice. This is a Herculean task for even the best formative assessor.

One way to close the Accuracy Gap is to place a premium on getting what students say down on paper, or into the computer. Tagging can slow verbal exchanges down to good effect, creating better opportunities for clarifying, sizing up, and accurately determining where we are and need to go next. The Accuracy Gap won't disappear, but it will become something everyone in the classroom learning space begins to take responsibility for. Respect for ideas and connection with others will, inevitably, increase.

 FORMATIVE ASSESSMENT TIPS

Insight Corner: Tagging is About Describing, Not Evaluating

Tagging takes the place of private notation (revoicing aloud or in one's head). Its medium must be public, accessible to all. The intent of tagging is to form a better picture of the collective thinking of the group. Tagging takes its inspiration from the art of describing, recording, transcribing, and representing—not evaluating or judging.

Learning to Look Back: Reflecting on the Just-Taught Lesson

We listen hard to teachers in our service territory and professional development efforts. When we ask them for difficulties in using formative assessment, no matter the district or grade level, they respond: *Formative assessment takes too much time, is too much extra work, is too challenging with unmotivated students, makes it difficult to make connections between data and individual needs, requires too many resources for planning, and is hard to do on the fly.*

Experienced teachers know this too well. The novices feel it acutely. One of the teacher candidates pithily summed up the difficulties by saying, "It's a practice that takes time to master."

Yes, indeed. In the limited time we have with the teacher candidates in our credential program, we strive to unpack the "it" of formative assessment with them. We do so by breaking down formative assessment into flexible moves that can be practiced, discussed, and looked at from many different angles.

Fred recently returned from industry to teach math in high school. He is a self-described teacher from the "old school." He reminds us that mathematics is a challenging subject that requires mental discipline and commitment.

There are, as we learned from Fred over the semester, right and wrong answers in his subject. "The idea of partial credit," he told us, "is 'nice,'" but lots of kids in Fred's classroom won't make it to college by our "schemes" for giving extra credit. Fred grades the students' work objectively and fairly on a weekly basis so they will know where they stand.

It's hard to argue with Fred's logic of classroom assessment. We have found, though, that it is not necessary to do so. The bigger challenge for us is opening a door, gaining a foothold with new teachers, trying to meet a person with strong opinions where they stand.

Fred, like many others in our credential program, does not always see the point in devoting all this time and effort to a stand alone assessment and evaluation course. Why not just focus on making grading more efficient to reduce workload? Talking about priming, posing, pausing, probing, bouncing, tagging, or binning is "interesting," but, he points out, "we need to manage all the data." Parents and principals and employers need to know whether to hire or fire, accept or reject, punish or reward. Fred knows many of his students, like his two grown children, want this kind of "real" feedback. It made them the success stories they are today.

We hear our beginning teachers (especially those from the "old school") tell us they ask plenty of questions, and they get answers they need from students on tests, homework, and quizzes. They also remind us they are busy and "under pressure" to post grades every day. No one is asking to see "soft data"—only the "bottom line."

But Mr. Steinbrenner, as the kids call him, surprised us with his reflection a few weeks into our course.

> I've used a form of tagging and scribing to capture students' mental experiences in my Algebra 2 classroom. After a presentation, I'll ask students to individually work a problem related to our classroom discussions. The problem is usually short and by cruising the aisles I can see how they've grasped the material. When I find a student with an especially nice solution, I ask her (or him) to write it on the board and walk us through the thought process. I

especially look for opportunities to call on students other than the usual contributors. I'll capture good thinking wherever I can find it, though.

I like to present my class material in Microsoft PowerPoint chart presentations. My charts often pose questions that students will be expected to answer before we move forward. Sometimes responses are either profound or confusing. I'll ask the student to write their response on the board both to assure understanding of the point and to facilitate a review.

Despite his initial strong preconceptions about classroom assessment and the role of grading in motivating students, Fred had many breakthroughs in the course, but not when or how we quite expected. We contend that Fred has decided to scale the mountain; he wants to become a formative assessor. We do not yet know which route he will take, or whether he will need others to set fixed lines along the way. Compared to other climbers on the mountain, he may need a longer period of acclimatization at base camp. He may get restless there. As his coaches and guides, we tried to extend his thinking about tagging and all the other moves that can reveal new ways of teaching and learning. At times, we appealed to his intuitions and interest in mathematics. Random sampling, probability, the odds of gaining a favorable outcome in representing student thinking—all are made more likely by tagging.

When Fred wrote, "I'll capture good thinking wherever I can find it, though," we wondered if he was in the habit of binning before tagging. That is to say, by limiting his student response sample space to examples of "good thinking," was he missing an opportunity to teach toward "other" thinking in his mixed-ability classroom?

We consulted with our methods faculty across campus about Fred's approach to classroom teaching and assessment. In a meeting where we share anonymously without using real names, we formed a "fish bowl" to troubleshoot "what is working and what is not?" across our teacher education curriculum. Our focus in these professional conversations is never on individuals. We present cases without personal identifiers. Our colleagues recommended we probe more on "Teacher X's" characterizations of student thinking beyond "good thinking."

Our colleagues in the math department were curious how we thought tagging could help this teacher and others to take more risks and let students present solutions to word problems on the dry erase board. We shared what we'd seen middle school teachers do in a local school district with tagging different solution strategies and asking students to work through the problem collectively as they probed on procedural fluency (Duckor & Holmberg, in press).

Having multiple perspectives on teaching practice is critical to our success as a program. We all agreed that by looking through the dual lens of math content demands and formative assessment practice, a finer distinction than the search for "good thinking" was in order. *We wondered if Fred was writing about his perceptions about his students' conceptual understandings, or their procedural fluency, or their skills with explaining, organizing their thoughts, and communicating in his register? Was the teacher candidate thinking that "good thinking" simply referred to correct answers and solutions he could share with the whole class? Or was he interested in productive misconceptions or typical procedural errors that many students would benefit from having represented in a public, visible way?*

Our job as teacher educators is to troubleshoot assumptions and preconceptions about assessment with beginning teachers, to triangulate with mentor teachers and field supervisors about what they see happening in the clinical placement with assessment practices, and to probe deeper on what everyone too often takes for granted. Formative assessment is not just another technique. It is a research-based practice with proven outcomes. Formative assessment is a powerful ally for teachers learning to connect with students and to make connections to higher-order thinking and 21st century skills.

We also work as teacher educators in a large, diverse public university program to connect the dots with teacher candidates; what they have learned in their educational psychology, classroom management and learning environments, language and literacy, and multiculturalism courses does indeed apply to the challenges of assessing for learning. We try to show how to break down the barriers, transfer between silos, and begin to see the teaching profession in a new light. Taking a lesson from the Buddha, as much as from Socrates, we invite beginners to see that ultimately, it's all connected.

We have no reason to discount Fred's experience with "doing assessment and school" as it was done to him. Rick Stiggins (2002) and others have pointed out that many do succeed with the "old school" approach to teaching and learning; homework, quizzes, and tests is how some students may in fact learn best, benchmark their progress, and achieve solid results in school. We note that Dewey and others rightly caution us about this stance as educators:

> At [many] schools, great faith was placed in standardized tests that typically assessed lower-order thinking skills, using items that were easily

administered (Newmann, Bryk, & Nagaoka, 2001; Resnick, 1987). And often teachers' own tests at these schools were not very different. They too reinforced a curriculum focused on mastery of often-trivial declarative knowledge which students were not expected to actually use in thinking about questions that arose outside of the classroom. This "mere absorption of facts and truths," as Dewey (1900) presciently observed, "is so exclusively individual an affair that it tends very naturally to pass into selfishness" (p. 29). The pervasive atmosphere of judgment and failure enforced by such assessments thus became a self-fulfilling strategy and heightened the reproduction of social inequality in schools (Duckor & Perlstein, 2014, p. 23).

Whether or not you agree with Dewey, let's remind ourselves of the purpose of this book: to coach those who are aiming to become formative assessors by meeting them in their zone of proximal development—as teachers and not the students they once were. Fred's reflections on his lessons is a starting point for the FA conversation.

We, of course, would prefer to triangulate his recollections with direct observation. Does he do what he says he does? Is there a gap between his recollection on the just-taught lesson and what others experienced in the classroom that day? But Fred has a mentor teacher who can help with that. He also has a university supervisor who can help clarify and probe on what is working to bring about more visible learning for all and which moves need more practice.

Fred has just one more semester with us. Soon he and all our other teacher candidates hoping to join this profession will be climbing new mountains, on peaks (and valleys) far from our view. Our aim is for Fred to want to revisit his practices of formative assessment again and again—not to judge him as if we had a crystal ball or knew his future prospects as a classroom teacher in general, or formative assessor in particular.

What we do know is that if this generation of teachers has neither the capacity nor the skills, not to mention the passion and confidence, to become formative assessors, the battle for this profession will be lost. The statistics on persistence and retention of public school teachers are sobering. Becoming a formative assessor is another aspect to being a teaching professional—it means knowing what you do and why you do it. Now more than ever before, teachers must know how to communicate with others outside their field about evidence-based practice. We see FA as a way to stay engaged and increase your chances of success at these efforts.

Student teachers like Fred keep us real. We thank him for his perspective on classroom assessment. We nudge him toward new horizons. He pushed us to share and better communicate a common vision for teachers. By pushing back, he provides us the opportunity to ask the tough questions:

- What if we try to tag and it fails to make most students' thinking visible?
- How is student tagging likely to differ from teacher tagging and what works better over time?
- What is the evidence that our tagging procedures are actually working to engage more students? To provide a more representative sample of ideas or solutions?
- For whom does tagging seem to work best? How would we know? Are there other viewpoints on the efficacy or effectiveness of this method of instruction and assessment?
- What have studies on tagging—by grade level, subject area, student population—shown?

Fred wrote, "Sometimes responses are either profound or confusing." He is so right. And more often than we'd like, our tagging moves run into a wall or seem to improve at a glacial pace. We ask enthusiastically, "Can someone share their solution on the board?" But we meet silence. And more silence. No one volunteers. We cold call on Juan; he says, "I don't know." Nothing is tagged. So we are tempted to call off the hike. The mountain is too high, the learning curve too steep.

But we suspect that the Fred in all of us is, in fact, learning to listen, to gather, to record. With him we are on the path to tagging. He may move slower than we like. He might not make it easy to walk alongside him. But it's time to gear up and join him on the trek. Otherwise, what kind of teachers *of teachers* are we?

Putting It All Together

Let's recount and connect the dots: tagging happens in lively classrooms with continuous and sustained give and take between students and teachers. Tagging is a vigorous, active process that involves established norms of trust, respect, and passion for classroom conversation. The teacher is the guide. All students are invited—and supported in these invitations—into conversation.

Students may learn to scribe and to represent their classmates' and others' ideas. In a classroom rich with tagging, students and teachers are invested in the assessment *process*, not the testing event. Classroom community practices that value tagging moves demonstrate how much students' opinions and thoughts matter.

Tagging and bouncing are closely related—not identical, but symbiotic. Each influences the potential of the other. Tagging is a skill. It is also a mindset. Inherent in tagging is a value in meeting others on their terms and taking the time to observe what they say.

Students, like teachers, need to learn how to capture, record, and make sense of real-time discourse. We know from Vygotsky's work on learning, language, and mental tools that authentic classroom discourse is a part of the puzzle; we will need to scaffold, assist, and practice our tagging moves, together.

Whether they are meeting one-on-one, in a group, or in a bigger community, it is critical that our students learn how to see a variety of perspectives. It would be short-sighted and odd if we as teachers did not emphasize the need to represent the complexity of ideas, beliefs, and opinions about our subject matter. That may be the most significant "so what" of all. Why bounce? Why tag? Because it shows we respect the democratic process in public education for all children.

Formative assessors in K–12 classrooms not only bounce and tag, they support students in developing bouncing and tagging skills. These skills will be useful long after the bell rings. The children in our classrooms are becoming lifelong learners who will participate—already participate—in a diverse society and an increasingly complex global community. Helping them gain skills in widening the net of conversation and including and honoring multiple viewpoints and many, many voices will be paramount to their—and society's—abilities to adapt to changing circumstances.

In this book, we argue that each and every move (Priming, Posing, Pausing, Probing, Bouncing, Tagging, and Binning) is conditioned by the others. This means, for example, that the formative assessor has to learn to bounce and to tag in tandem. Bouncing without tagging is a missed opportunity—an effort that records nothing students have said or done with the lesson material. Tagging without first bouncing is also a missed opportunity—it's time spent capturing a too-narrow-to-be-meaningful slice of data. The quilt is incomplete, the dance stilted, the work inefficient, if we don't work tirelessly to connect the FA dots.

Learning to coordinate the seven FA moves toward a common curricular goal is our recurring message. The goal of this chapter on tagging is surprisingly simple: to increase *our knowledge as teachers* of our students' knowledge, beliefs, and ideas. In large part, we are simply learning to think about student thinking more reflectively by recording it more faithfully. But to do so, we need to first think about what we say and hear every day in the classroom. Thinking is hard to do without having supports (mental, tech, or other tools) to capture student ideas. By now it's fairly clear, tagging helps you to express genuine curiosity in your students' ideas by honoring their contributions.

At this point in the journey to becoming a formative assessor, it must be obvious we are deliberately slowing down the classroom learning action and going deep into particular practices that link instructional and assessment moves together. Within each chapter, you have probably noticed that there are major and minor moves. The majors, such as Bouncing, are supported by minor (equity sticks), even micro (pass if you want), moves. Our hope is to show what is required for mastering formative assessment moves. If you only work on tagging student responses rigorously and regularly, we can rest assured that you have gained a valuable new skill.

In many ways the journey has just begun. We are now ready to move onto the Binning chapter. We have the data from the classroom, now it's time to sort, categorize, and make sense of it—for next steps, for making adjustments and course corrections, for figuring out what our students are telling us about the learning experience while we work to enact it.

Checks for Understanding

We can all improve the tagging that happens in our learning environments. Deliberate practice can help. Technology (low and high) supports can assist. Assigning new roles and trying out routines can move the ball forward. We present these checks for understanding to guide your individual and community efforts to develop this especially cognitively demanding FA move. You can use the prompts in Warm-Up Prompts as self-checks and ideas in Try-Now Tasks as conversation starters and exercises for independent study or group work.

Warm-Up Prompts:
- Why tag? For whose good? For what purpose?
- What are the consequences of skipping or ignoring the priming-for-tagging phase of formative assessment?
- Which students are noisy, bored, or "too eager" in your classes? What would it take to enlist them as scribes? Describe how you would approach these

students and what agreements need to be in place to monitor and support their success.

- What agreements have to be in place in your classroom to faithfully record student responses? How will you deal with unorthodox, off-topic, or R-rated responses?
- When is it time to invite the silent Sallies and Bobs to the front of the room as scribe helpers? What would it take to enlist them and other "quieter" students as scribes? Describe how you would approach these students and what agreements need to be in place to monitor and support their success.

Try-Now Tasks:

1. Examine the pros and cons of tagging. Make a t-chart: one side for the cons (every reason tagging is a waste of time, resources, effort, and energy; how tagging can get misused, disrespected, and misunderstood). On the other side, list the pros (possibilities for student and community growth from intellectual risk-taking, deeper learning, connection, and reflection). Predict how your perspective on tagging might evolve if you continue to embrace the challenges, complexities, and benefits of its practice in your learning environments over time.

2. Consider the concern of a new teacher on your staff who tells you, *I love the idea of recognizing every student's contribution. What about students who copy down everything that's on the board? It seems to me that without cues from the teacher about which parts are the most important, students can get overwhelmed by the amount of their peers' answers and tune out.* What might be a productive way to respond?

3. In a PLC, run a word webbing session on "problems with tagging." Appoint a scribe and scribe helper. Draw "Problems with Tagging" on a visible medium. Prime: *So let's think together about some of the problems with tagging. We will brainstorm in pairs and then report some thoughts back to the whole group.* Pose: *What's the first thing that comes to mind when you hear "Problems with Tagging"?* Pause. Remind everyone: *There are no right or wrong answers.* Repeat the question. Invite responses.

4. Give an example of a tagging move (e.g., with dry erase board, poster paper, or Smartboard) you made this week. What worked well? What did not work so well with this move? Decide on one or two next steps to better prime for tagging. Pick one warm-up activity you can do in less than five minutes.

5. Imagine you are resetting expectations for the learning environment three weeks into class, and just before you start a new unit. To rebuild the foundation necessary for the formative assessment-rich classroom culture you seek, the community needs to redefine the tone, values, and supports to make it come to life. Relationships have fallen down and agreements about tagging, scribing, and public posting of responses need repair. Plan a lesson segment for your students that includes a Four Corners exercise on tagging that uses these themes:

Corner 1: What is working well?

Corner 2: What's not working?

Corner 3: What can we do to start tagging more?

Corner 4: Why does tagging matter?

Each student group assigns a leader and scribe for its corner, then creates a list for ways to reprime classroom practices and culture related to tagging, given the question they are considering. Have the groups combine their four lists. Discuss a plan to check back in three weeks on agreements.

Challenge task: Have one person in the group explain why a particular procedure may support more effective priming for tagging in the classroom. Allow another person to push back and say why these moves may not work—for whom and why it matters?

Binning

I grade with points and letter grades, including *F*s. At first, *F*s are Incompletes. At the end of the grading period, if they're still Incompletes, that's when they turn into *F*s. That's how we do it at my school.

Cyrus, middle school social studies teacher

To provide students feedback without assigning grades to their work, I write in the margins and use stamps. Students ask, "What did I *really* get? What does a stamp mean?

Belinda, Spanish teacher

Paul Black and his colleagues (2003) wrote, "Overall teachers seem to be trapped in a 'no-man's land' between their new commitment to formative assessment and the different, often contradictory, demands of the external test system." They add, "Their formative use of summative tests had enabled them to move the frontier significantly, but further territory seemed unassailable" (p. 21).

We reframe this important insight by juxtaposing two competing demands on teachers' work in the classroom today: *binning for grading* versus *binning for feedback*. These competing demands—and the stance toward classroom assessment they demand—on teachers' time, attention, and resources are likely to produce a sort of cognitive dissonance. There is a gap, so to speak, between the ideals of classroom formative assessment and the institutional grading practices that ignore them. How we cope with this gap (this dissonance) as a community of formative assessors living in a summative, accountability-based world is instructive.

But first let's clarify a few things about what is summative and what is formative in the struggle for classroom assessment. To do so, we step back and look at the bigger picture to see what is really going on.

We maintain that binning—interpreting, categorizing, and evaluating student learning experiences—is as inevitable as death and taxes. As teachers charged with making critical instructional decisions day in and day out, we have to bin.

In this chapter, we pose three essential questions to those learning to become formative assessors:

1. When do you bin summatively? That is, when do you rely on *binning for grading*, by using letter grades, the familiar "*A* through *F*" categories used to evaluate performance?

2. When do you bin formatively, that is, when do you engage in *binning for feedback*? Which bins maximize the potential effect of your oral, verbal, and written feedback to students?

3. How do the ways you *bin for grades* and *bin for feedback* differ? Which students benefit most from one strategy and which students benefit most from a combination? Are you sure grades and feedback go well together? What's your evidence?

Of course, there are more questions than answers on this controversial topic. We are not saying, "To grade or not to grade, that is the question." Rather, we are reminding ourselves that formative assessors cannot hide behind statements such as, "I do both." Both binning strategies may have their place in the classroom: only one has been shown to improve student outcomes (Hattie, 2012).

But before we get too tangled up in controversy, let's probe a little deeper together. Let's explore the binning strategies we use—and the stances we take as summative and formative assessors—and try to unpack what those purposes mean for learners in our classroom. It is too easy to hover at 35,000 feet in these discussions and to forget "learner" means an actual child, with a name and family background, a unique learning style, a zone of proximal development in affective, academic, metacognitive, and other areas that are comprised of bundles of skills and capacities. So again, before we get too excited, let's remember eventually we will need to dive down into the real work by convincing our students—not one another—that any of these stances *actually* work to promote learning.

To start, we know that summative assessors are in the habit of looking for points, scores, and numbers to communicate the meaning of results. They point to the demands of standardized testing, accountability, and social expectations to explain their perennial use of grades and score results. Parents and colleges demand a GPA. Many students are "grade driven" and the summative assessor gladly (and at times grudgingly) concedes "test scores" are a fact of life. We live in a competitive society. Grades and test scores help to sort the winners from the losers.

Those with a summative assessment mindset see binning—for grading—as the fundamental purpose of classroom assessment. Summative assessors explain that numeric scores are "objective," letter grades are transferable, and hard data from tests is more reliable—and hence more generalizable—than alternatives. We need to know who is excellent and who is not. Grades are a time-honored way to make these distinctions.

Lately, summative assessors in the testing world promise a lot. They have introduced terms like "interim" assessment to persuade policymakers that their summative data can be used formatively. They say: "We can provide teachers with proficiency bands and rankings to help make better decisions in the classroom or department." Shepard (2009) and others (Herman & Baker, 2005) have written extensively on the promises and challenges implicit in this approach. Stiggins (2002) draws the distinction between assessment *for* and *of* learning and has also pushed back on the case for "having your cake and eating it too" approach.

We wonder for those working to become better formative assessors how much traction is to be gained by arguing about the best uses of standardized test data. Clearly everyone wants in on the promise of formative assessment to improve instruction. Of these efforts to blend assessment purposes, James Popham (2008b) writes:

> The sorts of periodically administered tests being peddled with great zeal these days by commercial vendors—vendors who often plaster a "formative" label on such tests—are also not formative assessment. Sometimes referred to as "interim" or "benchmark" assessments, these tests are typically administered every few months or so as part of a districtwide assessment program. Such periodic tests may be useful in evaluating schoolwide or districtwide programs, and may also predict how well students are likely to perform on a subsequent accountability test—but there is currently no body of research

evidence attesting to their worth. Moreover, to refer to such tests as "formative" constitutes either verbal carelessness by a commercial firm or, more likely, downright deception. (p. 18)

Formative assessors, on the other hand, tend to advocate for their binning stance by highlighting the commitment to oral, written, and other forms of feedback to communicate next steps in lesson activities. Those with the formative assessment mindset note that students learn best when feedback is positive and nonjudgmental. Rather than communicate through grading, formative assessors see the value in specific, timely, content-rich, and addressable feedback for their students in real time. Those with a formative assessment mindset share a clear pedagogical disposition and a relentless commitment to the notions of "not yet" and "next steps."

Formative assessors know that numeric scores are not descriptive, letter grades are abstractions based on mathematical procedures, and that taken as a whole, "hard" data from tests are rarely valid for particular instructional purposes such as reteaching in the moment, or deciding where to stop and review, or checking for prior knowledge 25 minutes into the lesson. The fact remains: points, scores, and numbers do not operate at a "grain size" to do much instructional good. For teachers and students, these signals are best treated as indicators of achievement. Use the numbers to tally grades at the end of the unit, but don't expect they'll provide any concrete, addressable next steps during the instructional cycle, or help with the daily work of teaching and learning that occupies the central concern of this book.

Clearly, there are significant differences among the aims, purposes, and consequences of formative and summative assessment. We argue that *binning for grading* versus *binning for feedback* is how most educators experience this tension in their classrooms. How we face this tension matters—for our students, schools, and communities.

As teachers learning to become formative assessors, we can choose to do different kinds of binning. Finding a balance between summative and formative purposes will be a challenge. We need to bin consciously, strategically, and more publicly.

We hope this chapter aids in this quest, in part by clarifying what's at stake and providing a way forward.

What Is Binning?

Binning is looking at evidence (such as student work, speech, action, *and* inaction) and sorting, grouping, and categorizing this evidence according to some organizing principle. For many teachers, the organizing principle is guided by notions of how to differentiate the correct from the incorrect response. We are conditioned to reflectively bin—to recognize, distinguish, and place student responses into bins. The nature and use of those bins will vary. But one thing is certain: we will bin, it's how we think.

Binning is an *act of interpretation* and, ultimately, an evaluation of student understanding. It is based on observations gathered from hard and soft data in the classroom. It resides in the third vertex of the assessment triangle and is supported by bouncing and tagging moves. When we categorize a student response "wrong," "major misconception," or "careless mistake," we are binning. What a teacher does with this evaluation of the quality of student thinking or performance is up to her. She may offer feedback to a student. She may not. The point is, the teacher has formed a judgment. To make an instructional decision, we have to judge what students know and can do.

To unpack this universal move—of judging the quality of student thinking—we need to take note of the flavors of binning. There are two types of binning phenomena we've observed over the years: one covert and secretive, the other overt and shared.

Covert binning of student responses is private, mysterious, not visible to students. When teachers engage in covert binning strategies, students don't know what bins are being used on their work or performances. They may guess. They can hope to see the grading scheme. But mostly only the teacher knows which bins were used and why. Confusion, controversy, and suspicion exist—for students, with parents, and even administrators.

Overt binning of student responses, on the other hand, is public and visible to all in the classroom learning space. Teachers and students know *what* bins are being used, *how*, and *why*. The students may struggle or try to make sense of outcomes, but they are not left wondering why they got a certain grade or how they were supposed to improve. At student, counselor, and parent-teacher conferences, teachers who use overt binning strategies are clear about their standards of judgment; they have tools that reveal how and why they distinguished among student responses and performance levels. There is a trail of feedback visible in student work and ample evidence that the students put the *public* binning procedures to use *during* instruction and over the unit.

Two Stances, Two Strategies for Interpreting Students' Thinking

By now, it's no surprise that we'd like to see more binning for feedback in the classroom learning space. Why? Because feedback can be put to use in the immediate service of student learning and progress. Bins that don't lead to action, to feedback, or to encouraging next steps with our students aren't very productive from a formative assessor's point of view.

We know from research that many teachers take this stance. They already see the power of formative feedback to transform their learning environments. But progress is slower than researchers and formative assessment experts might expect. Binning-for-grading habits are deeply entrenched in school practices. Social and cultural expectations and pressures favor grading—not feedback.

It will take an overt, visible, continuous demand from teachers who share their "best binning-for-feedback" strategies to move the ball toward the goal post: formative assessment for all and not just the lucky few. But we are sober enough to know: beginning teachers will at first struggle to see the value of moving beyond the binning-for-grading paradigm they've been acculturated to over decades of doing school.

The next generation of teachers—with the coaching and mentoring from the present one—hold the promise of mounting a campaign for formative assessment practices. We have the research, we know the evidence, and we've seen kids turn around once their work is recognized as worth a comment, given a few suggestions, and allowed the opportunity to revise. Now it's time to take a stance.

Binning for feedback is worth fighting for. Binning for feedback practices work to make binning overt because this is a natural outgrowth of teachers taking action to help students understand success criteria, or learning targets. Core to the definition of formative assessment is that students achieve clarity about where they're heading and that we address the student learning with actionable next steps so they can reach their potential.

Okay, get ready. Controversial statement in play: we maintain that *binning for grading* performs an autopsy on performance and dutifully reports on the results, whereas *binning for feedback* holds a learner's progress as paramount and subject to change. Binning for grading "marks" the body of knowledge and territory a learner has achieved, whereas binning for feedback requires attention to the trajectory of the living learner and constant calibration of the needs of the person in the moment. Binning for grading is an ending, binning for feedback a beginning. The former signals where you stand, the latter where you are going and need to move next.

Let's be real honest: binning for feedback is much harder than binning for grading. Binning for feedback requires a level of intention and care that binning for grading does not. Sunday night's stack of papers may seem daunting but reading through them and assigning grades is not. Deciding how to coach for the next drafts on Monday morning, how to provide scoring guides and exemplars, and how to orchestrate student peer-to-peer "warm" and "cool" feedback sessions each period for a week—now that's challenging.

The kinds and levels of teacher and student engagement required by binning for feedback are significant. Priming demands are high on binning for feedback, too. It is likely that your students are not used to being treated as writers, historians, scientists, and other types of professionals in the classroom. No one ever asked them to rewrite a draft of their fruit fly lab as if they were making a conference presentation or behave as peer editors as if they were planning to publish in a journal. Binning for feedback moves, especially when they invite peer and self-assessment routines, takes a lot of practice. Everyone must be ready to tackle the challenge and step up the level of the game.

Often teachers—unless they have lots of experience coaching athletes, musicians, graphic artists, or actors—are more accustomed to binning for grading than they are to binning for feedback. Grading, for many, is synonymous with classroom assessment. When we ask: "What's the first thing that comes to mind when you hear the word assessment?" the responses pour in. "Grades" always makes the top of the list. But giving grades and giving feedback are not the same.

Becoming a formative assessor asks that teachers bin for formative feedback—consciously, intentionally, and with great care. Formative feedback matters to student outcomes (Hattie & Timperley, 2007). As we now know, through years of study and our own personal experience, formative feedback can change what it means to be a student and get a good education. We remember those teachers who took the time and energy to say "not quite, try again, let's look at it again." They believed in us—enough to mentor with formative feedback—not merely summary judgment and symbols.

In thinking through our own particular binning moves in this chapter, we don't want to leave the impression that it's all up to you. Yes, we said that binning student responses is how we think. Binning (the act of interpreting and judging) is a cognitive process that teachers use to make sense of classroom data. We can become more metacognitive in our binning stances. But binning practices also involve complex cultural, historical, and sociological processes—for teachers and students.

At the macro level, binning emerges in real time and historical contexts, through traditional classroom assessment practices we've imitated or received, like tools passed on from generation to generation. Ultimately, we cannot ignore the fact that binning—for grading or feedback—is conditioned by the school environment and the larger ecosystem that we inhabit as educators living in a democratic, highly competitive society.

At the micro level, binning for feedback in particular asks for complex coordination from the teacher who is thinking, in real time, about what to do next. It occurs under pressure. To support better, more effective real-time binning strategies, we need to unpack the relationship between received and preconditioned binning strategies and what and how we think about new, less familiar ones.

Evaluation of our students' thinking, skills, and habits happens in many contexts—inside and outside school. The habits, values, and mores of a larger community are likely to shape teachers' and students' expectations about what is worth binning—for whose good and for what good?

In the end, we may find out that the journey to becoming a formative assessor takes us down two roads: one, paved with our own concept of the meaning of the public good in education; the other, strewn with good intentions that mostly fall apart under competing demands from the "system."

Either way, binning will be there. It's what we do.

Why Bin? For Whose Good? For What Good?

As we learned in Chapter 6, unlike tagging moves, the goal of binning is not merely to describe and faithfully represent student thinking in your classroom. By constructing bins, you wish to *evaluate and interpret* the quality and nature of student responses in order to make an instructional decision. Your bins are the key to unlocking the information and soft data you gather each period. Whether minute by minute or at the end of each day, how you bin will reveal what you perceive as possible for your students.

If you are mostly focused on binning for grading, the focus will be on normative or criterion-based achievement of the students. So-called standards-based grading is an attempt at meaningful, criterion-based binning, but too often it devolves into the same dilemmas as grading on the curve. If grading is your focus, sorting, ranking, and placing students in bins on a distribution will dominate your assessment practices. If you are mostly committed to binning for feedback, all attention will center on degrees of progress and next steps to improve students' understandings and skills. Differentiating, customizing, and monitoring the delivery and uptake of formative feedback will take precedent.

Implicit in all binning strategies is the hope to locate a student (by examining her responses to queries, work tasks, and other "exhibitions" of mastery) along a trajectory or taxonomy of learning outcomes. Some bins contain the hope of learning trajectories, others rely more on fixing locations in a classification system. The *A* to *F* binning framework fixes students in a particular place, in ways well understood by society, the media, and popular culture. It seems making the grade has seeped into all aspects of our lives. Social media and big data sites use all types of grading schemes to signal the best, most popular, or trending of nearly anything you can imagine. Policymakers and politicians enjoy mocking up report cards to evaluate different people and institutions. It makes them feel like teachers.

As formative assessors who have studied the research on evidence-based practices that support learning, we know these grading schemes won't get us very far. If, for example, we decide to prioritize student growth and progress on mastering the concept of relative density or the use of plot devices on story development, we will have to develop feedback strategies that explicitly support students on their individual learning trajectories, lesson by lesson, unit by unit, perhaps even year by year. We must stand behind the educational research, not play the game of fair and balanced vote counting. We know that specific, timely, actionable, criterion-based next steps and oral and written comments will take all our students farther in the learning process than a thumbs-up emoji, a "*C+*," or "good job."

The habits of binning for feedback intend to support student growth and learning, visibly, consistently, with a trail of evidence that follows their responses and work. The message is that for a meaningful, productive feedback loop to form, there must be give and take—and incorporating feedback about a first draft is part of the process of ensuring that next steps are taken. The message to students who inhabit classrooms where binning for feedback occurs: "Expect to revise your lab analysis, your graphing solution, your free throw, your enunciation, your brush stroke—all your first draft answers, responses, and thinking about today's topic. It's how we learn in this classroom!"

The formative assessor notices what is—and what is not—helping her students to grow and to become more competent writers, scientists, mathematicians, artists, historians, musicians, readers, athletes, and Mandarin language users. As a coach and guide, the teacher who is pushing for students' personal bests is acutely aware of how feedback can advance or sidetrack a student's progress in a lesson, unit, or course. There is a quiet but persistent voice reminding the formative assessor: *not all feedback is formative.* Ask any student who is spinning wheels, going backward, losing traction, or just plain stuck.

To meet the formative feedback litmus test, the formative assessor has to admit to falling short sometimes: "Just redo this part," "Read the instructions again," "Good effort." We all know the easy bins from the hard ones. Old assessment habits die hard. It's okay if not all your feedback to students is formative. But knowing when it is or isn't is what matters at the moment. Remember, the journey has just begun.

 FORMATIVE ASSESSMENT TIPS

To be **formative**, feedback needs to be used, understood, and processed by students to *revise* their performances so they can take another step toward the learning target.

Not all feedback, however—even feedback that gets used by students—is actually effective. One case in point is Casey, a 6th grader who used her 9th grade brother's "feedback" to revise her composition. He told her, "Replace *because* with *due to the fact that.*" This certainly was a clear next step that she could tackle by herself, just not a good one. Calls for "search and replace" and these sorts of "corrections" are not particularly formative. At this stage in her development as a writer, Casey needs more.

Students come to our classrooms having received plenty of ineffective feedback, inside and outside school. Certainly it was well-intended. Yet, as the late Grant Wiggins (2012) reminds us about *effective* feedback, "Advice, evaluation, grades—none of these provide descriptive information that students need to reach their goals" (p. 14).

What Makes Formative Feedback Effective?

The consensus among teacher education and professional development experts is that the most effective feedback to students is neither general advice nor praise. Specifically, Grant Wiggins discusses (Wiggins, 2012, p. 13) effective formative feedback as

- goal-referenced,
- tangible and transparent,
- actionable,
- user-friendly,
- timely,
- ongoing, and
- consistent.

If binning for feedback—effectively—is harder than binning for grading, why do it? Because effective formative feedback spurs action and learning by the student. We see revising, reworking, and rethinking our students' current position in a learning trajectory as the hidden story behind effective feedback. Schools, classrooms, and teachers that value feedback and revision and create space for rethinking ideas and activities along a trajectory will send very different messages to students than those that don't. Yet sustaining reengagement with tasks and ideas in the classroom is challenging.

So we say, "It takes a village to give, take, and incorporate feedback." Agreements and supports in the learning environment need to support sustaining reengagement so that revision becomes pervasive, even the norm, at school. Central Park East Secondary School knew this well.

A large part of what made Central Park East Secondary School special was that the entire structure of their work together was organized to support their primary goal: helping urban adolescents of color learn to use their minds well and providing them with opportunities to practice, share, and revise their work product. As we noted in Chapter 2 on Posing, CPESS fostered clear agreements and explicit scaffolds and supports for students in the daily learning environment. They picked schoolwide learning targets that were coachable and subject to improvement. They sustained engagement and reengagement with the Habits of Mind (Connection, Perspective, Evidence, Supposition, and Relevance) in part by making these "meta bins" transparent. By providing rubrics, scoring guides, and lots of feedback on current drafts, the students and teachers at CPESS could agree on expectations and calibrate progress.

Everyone in this East Harlem school "got the memo" that *This is a place to improve, to grow, to excel. But first I/we need you to look at my/our feedback and ask what else you need to do to move forward.*

 FORMATIVE ASSESSMENT TIPS

Our Message to Those Mastering Formative Assessment Moves:

As you pick and choose how you proceed on your journey, we encourage you to Rethink. Revise. Rework. Reflect. Redo. Rewrite. Reread. Recognize that a learning community works together through a process that requires next steps to become more skilled, more proficient, more knowledgeable day by day, week by week, year by year. Formative feedback and uptake isn't a "one off." It's a lifetime commitment to learn something well and to coach others learning with you.

—*Melissa, Teacher Lead, Astoria Unified School District, Oregon Public Schools*

Binning Is Sense Making

Teachers bin student thinking because binning helps process this raw classroom data. To avoid information overload and to make meanings that stick, we must categorize, sort, and interpret the student response data. Remember that data comes in many guises and forms for the formative assessor.

From things our students write (i.e., quizzes, labs, reports, tests, projects) to things they say and do that never get written down (i.e., utterances, comments, body postures, and movements)—there are so many variables in play. Teachers are not sponges, nor are we capable of soaking up all the information and data flying around the room on a given day. Add the developmental, affective, and dispositional factors that come with sorting out who has this or that idea, belief, or misconception—and it is no wonder that we shut down.

We bin to impose order on the controlled chaos of classroom teaching and learning.

Teachers cannot be expected to bin on the fly during every class discussion, nor do we always get it right as we move around the room trying to figure out who needs what kinds of support and when it is needed. Instead, we go back to well-established procedures for binning student work and managing the flows of information. We use stamps. We add points. We assign grades. In a word, we survive.

These traditional classroom assessment methods have great advantages—they help us impose limits and order on the potentially wide-open student response space. Tests and quizzes are effective allies for this purpose. With a test, we can slow down the assessment action, control the assessment environment, and get answers to who knows what is going on with the material and who does not. We all relish the silence and calm that envelops a classroom of test takers. It's a welcome break.

Whether you are a university professor or a kindergarten teacher, the desire to bin efficiently and effectively is relentless. Classroom assessors—from K to college—have devised several binning strategies using widely available tools:

- answer keys
- partial credit scoring keys
- rubrics
- scoring guides

As we go deeper with binning moves, we'll consider the affordances and constraints of each of these strategies for interpreting student thinking and skills. We will also keep in mind the tools, purpose, actions, and procedures that accompany particular binning stances. Here is a thumbnail sketch to get us started and help organize our thinking about the challenge ahead:

	Tool	Items/ Responses	Purpose	Action/ End User	Procedure
No bin	Activities	Quick writes; End of class whip-around responses, for example, "Tell us one thing you're still wondering about."	Informal; general impression	Teacher, though students' learning may benefit	Varies, frequently unsystematic

(continued)

	Tool	Items/ Responses	Purpose	Action/ End User	Procedure
1 bin	Checklists	Single component task or product check, for example, "Was the homework started?"	Informal; general impression	General impression for teacher; May return to student	Check mark; Sticker; Star; Stamp
2 bins	Traditional answer keys	Component review or check for mastery (e.g., test items)	Semiformal	General information; Return to students	Dichotomous scoring: correct or incorrect
3 bins	Partial credit answer key or scoring guides	Multifaceted performance (e.g., procedural and conceptual fluency)	Semiformal	General feedback; Return work with next steps; May request test correction and revision	Polytomous scoring with at least 3 levels; typically accompanied by points (e.g., 0, 0.5, 1)
4 or 5 bins	Analytic Rubrics	Complex, multifaceted performance (5-step lab, research paper, tennis game, solo violin performance)	Formal	Analytic feedback; Return work; Request revision; Identify specific elements for improvement	Partial credit scoring with 4-5 levels of performance AND 4-5 learning criteria based on Standards/ Learning targets; may include point values

Binning and Its Role in the Assessment Triangle

With this chapter, we now complete our trip around the National Research Council's (2001) Assessment Triangle. In our adapted version of the triangle, binning is the core of what the NRC calls the *interpretation* vertex. See Figure 7.1. For formative assessors, the validity of interpretation of student data generated in the classroom depends, in large part, on the quality of bouncing-tagging-binning moves. When working in unison, these FA moves help us to improve the soundness of the inferences we draw from soft data (from student comments "Uh, I don't know" to "A comparison between things and numbers"). Flexible binning strategies, together with effective bouncing and tagging procedures, will enable us to make better, more informed decisions on where students are currently and what's next in the lesson. They can also be used to make interpretations about what students know and can do more public, visible, and actionable. Students can use these bins to take action.

Figure 7.1   Binning Triangle

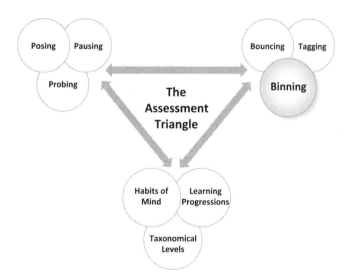

If the *cognition vertex* of the assessment triangle is meant to help us set coherent, meaningful learning targets in the curriculum and the *observation vertex* is meant to be a public space for collecting evidence and gathering data from students, then the *interpretation vertex* is the place to bin responses to evaluate if our students are on the mark with those learning targets or if we need to make adjustments to instruction.

Although bouncing and tagging moves strive to faithfully represent student responses, binning schematizes, orders, and helps us make meaning of student responses. Formative assessment moves can help with deciding next steps for instruction, but only if we have validly interpreted the meaning of our data. The effectiveness of formative feedback, in that sense, depends on the meaning and accuracy of our binning strategies. If we have binned a student's response based on the initial learning targets and solid observational strategies, then we can reasonably expect to advance the work of assessment for learning in the classroom.

Formative assessors know there are no shortcuts to aligning our binning strategies with the first principles of assessment. The logic represented by the assessment triangle, like it is for educational assessment experts, can be a guide and critical friend that keeps our eyes on the prize. But we must realize that being flexible, strategic, and adaptable in our binning moves is key. One size does not fit all.

What the Research Says

The research literature tells us little about how teachers learn to bin better. We know that teachers favor binning for grading despite the issues they face when it fails to produce optimal results (Guskey, 2004). We don't know why teachers use these binning strategies (What are the mental models, the p-prims, and belief structures that help such strategies to persist?). We also know about feedback, specifically factors influencing feedback, ways of thinking about feedback, and the prevalence of different kinds of feedback in teachers' classroom practices. But again, we'd like to know more about why some teachers excel at binning for feedback and why others do not. Maybe we need more research on teacher learning progressions related to binning—as a mental model and cognitive processing device, a socially sanctioned practice with job-related rewards and punishments, and a cultural tool with deep symbolic value and ritual significance to its participants.

Binning for Grading

"Doing school" likely influences how teachers bin, and how *students* have come to see binning for grading as the primary purpose of learning. The classroom assessment mindset that prevails in most schools reflects the wider view of grades as commodities. As Winger (2005) and others suggest, if binning strategies promote grades as commodities and not as a reflection of learning, then we can expect perverse incentives and behaviors to ensue.

As many beginning teachers will tell you: *The kids want the grades, they haggle over them, they don't care about my advice, they just want the* A. The problems with grading are well-documented in the literature. We have known for years:

- **Learning and grades are disconnected.** Grades may or may not measure what teachers value most. Winger (2005) points out that grades often measure attendance, compliance, class participation, and homework completion.

- **Grading isn't essential to instruction or learning.** As family and community members who have helped children learn important life skills without giving them grades, we've all lived this. Frisbie and Waltman (1992) and Guskey (1994) corroborated our personal experiences with extensive research. In most schools, however, students, parents, and principals expect grades to be reported. So, too, do guidance counselors, coaches, grandparents, siblings, friends, college admissions officers, and potential employers.

- **No one method of grading serves all purposes well.** Austin and McCann (1992) and Guskey (1994) have argued that when schools attempt to use grades to communicate students' achievements, provide incentives, support student self-evaluation, identify students for special programs, and evaluate program' effectiveness, they end up achieving none of these purposes well.

- **Grading is inherently subjective.** Subjectivity isn't always bad. Teachers' deep knowledge of their students may translate into accurate descriptions of what students have learned. But subjectivity is a problem when—as commonly happens, according to Hills (1991)—boys' grades are disproportionately negatively influenced by teachers' perceptions of their behavior. Sweedler-Brown (1992) found that poor handwriting has negatively affected teachers' judgment of students' work. We start to worry when grades signal more than achievement, and start looking like prizes awarded to those students the teacher likes most.

Before discussing what we know about binning for feedback, it is worth noting the letter grade *A* to *F* bins are relatively recent cultural phenomena, if we look back on the history of schooling dating back to the Greeks or Chinese (Zhang, 2008). Since the early 1900s, reformers in the U.S. context sought to standardize the reporting systems across the nation's schools (Johnson, 1918; Rugg, 1918). The graded school, and the evaluation systems that followed its emergence, have emphasized accountability and accreditation as part of modern state school systems (Ball, 2013). Modern school bureaucracies, it seems, need to make the grade.

There have been notable exceptions (which survive in today's "Pass/Fail" and "Credit/No Credit" bins), but these alternative grading schemes have not met the cultural demand to communicate who is relatively better (or worse) in society. The Narrative Evaluation System is an interesting hybrid where instructors write evaluations that accompany marks of pass or fail. A few public and private colleges experimented with narrative evaluations, mostly in the 1960s and 1970s, but the Narrative Evaluation System failed to take root in mainstream public schools, where, as Winger put it, "commodities" must be traded. Central Park East Secondary School promoted a version of the narrative evaluation system for mid-semester student/parent meetings, but in the end, it also produced graded transcripts for colleges.

The *A* to *F* grading system in public schools is not tolerant of minority opinions and alternative approaches to assessment—it demands conformity. Grading in the U.S. public school systems has reflected societal values for well over a century, says historian Larry Cuban (1993).

Binning for Feedback

As Stiggins (2002) and others point out, grades are not the type of feedback that formative assessors use to guide student learning. If instructors intend to practice assessment *for* learning rather than assessment *of* learning, then research unequivocally demands separating letter grades from next step comments and requests to revise. The two ways of communicating are fine, but should not be mixed together.

Each year we have a fresh crop of beginning teachers in our preservice programs who demand to see the evidence that supports these incredible claims. But first they hit us with the "protest" questions: *What, why can't I give grades and feedback together? When I tell a student she got a C+ and offer the suggestion to rewrite the thesis—what's wrong with that? Are you serious—keep the grade book and the comments in separate places and focus the students first on revision? Are you mad?* Perhaps.

It turns out that when grades are given at the same time as comments, students frequently focus on grades and ignore the comments (Butler, 1988; Black, Harrison, Lee, Marshall, & Wiliam, 2003; and Pulfrey et al., 2011). When students see a grade and lots of comments scrawled across papers, labs, or projects, there is a tendency to drop them into the figurative and in some cases, actual trash bin. Rarely do students say "Gee, I got an *F...* let me see why and how I can improve." Graded feedback doesn't move the ball forward. Formative assessors come to face these facts.

We have known for more than two decades that of all the possible influences on student achievement, formative feedback is among the most powerful. John Hattie's well-known work (1992, 2009, 2012) found that some practices such as goal-driven, criterion-based, scaffolded feedback appear to be more powerful than others. Formative assessors will have to experiment with new strategies for incentivizing students to take up and utilize our formative feedback. But one thing is clear: without priming, binning for feedback moves will fail. If there are no second chances in your classroom, why would anyone want to listen to or read comments? "What's done is done" is the message—not "Let's see what you can do with more practice."

Kluger and DeNisi's (1996) review of studies on feedback found that feedback improved student performance 60 percent of the time. Researcher Paul Black and others (2003) have noted, however, that when "feedback" was not helpful, it was because the feedback "turned out to be merely a judgment or grading with no indication of how to improve " (p. 18). In other words, it wasn't effective feedback, according to Wiggins's (2012) definition, and that explains many of the cases where it did not make a difference.

Not surprisingly, the difficulty of a task also influences the effectiveness of formative feedback. Shute (2008) found that students' prior knowledge and aspects of the task interact with characteristics of the feedback in complex ways to influence formative feedback's "success at promoting learning" (p. 153). Praise for completing a task appears ineffective. Rather, learners need more learning-, task-, and process-related information (i.e., scaffolding, tools, and academic language supports) to advance their work on conceptually difficult material. Rewards and punishments, carrots and sticks, candies, and "time outs" to manage trips to the bathroom do not move the needle on student learning. Feedback related to content and learning goals does.

Common sense tells us that socioeconomic status, ethnicity, gender, and culture must play a role in the experience of formative feedback for students in the U.S. classroom. Research supports the idea that gender differences likely play a role in the efficacy of our binning-for-feedback strategies. Dweck and Bush (1976) note that girls' performances after negative feedback from adults tend to deteriorate more than boys.' Interestingly, when peers (versus teachers) were giving the "failure feedback," Andrade (2013) reported that "boys attributed the failure to a lack of ability and showed impaired problem solving while girls more often viewed the peer feedback as indicative of effort and showed improved performance" (p. 28). Perhaps of no surprise to elementary school teachers is a study of 4th graders by Yurdabakan (2011) which found that girls assess their classmates' learning levels and group work contributions in ways that more closely match their teachers' judgments than boys.'

It seems that ethnicity may play a role in building a formative assessment culture, but we have few conclusive studies. In a longitudinal survey, Blatchford (1997) examined the effects of gender and ethnicity on self-assessments of academic attainment. Blatchford found that as "students grew older, White students (especially girls) were less positive and less accurate in their self-assessments of academic achievement than Black students." Students in Blatchford's study were from mostly working class and relatively disadvantaged backgrounds in multiracial schools in inner London.

We note that U.S. and Canadian classrooms differ ethnically, linguistically, and demographically in nuanced and significant ways from school contexts and demographics in, for example, the United Kingdom. We need more cross-cultural studies on formative feedback practices for different populations of students to ensure we aren't overgeneralizing and sweeping the complexity of binning moves under the carpet.

Lots of research has categorized feedback by whether it is teacher-led, or generated by students in self- or peer-assessment contexts. For now, there is no definitive consensus on *which* practices, in *which* configurations, with *which* subjects, are the most influential on student outcomes.

 FORMATIVE ASSESSMENT TIPS

Corno and Snow (1986) corroborated what many experienced teachers already know: interrupting a student immersed in trying to solve a problem or task on his or her own can impede learning. Those learning to become formative assessors take note: sometimes it's best to scaffold and monitor progress at a safe distance. It helps to hold back a bit before directing your feedback to an individual or group that has been released into an activity. Try to give students ample time for independent practice, then strategically seek cues for support for the next step when they are ready.

Sometimes we can point to well-grounded research on binning strategies and draw out "truths" to better inform our FA moves. Other times we will need to rely on inspiring examples of teachers doing what matters—even if researchers haven't yet measured the extent of the effectiveness of these instructional practices or whether, in fact, those practices can transfer to other learning environments and situations. But this is not a time to wait and see. Researchers are not going to magically release us from responsibility for our own assessment practices. The students are waiting for our judgment. They need us to help evaluate their prospects—their emerging skills and budding knowledge of the topics we love to teach. Hopefully we can approach and examine our binning moves with integrity and care. After all, we have the power to make a real difference—day in and day out.

Going Deeper with Binning

Let's look more in depth at a few of our choices when it comes to binning in the classroom. The formative assessor will recognize each of these examples: the answer key, the partial credit scoring key, the analytic rubric, the scoring guide, and, yes, the checklist. She may or may not yet have thought through the particular affordances and constraints of each approach. This chapter provides opportunities to look at familiar and not-so-familiar binning strategies ("mental tools" as Vygotsky would recognize), so we can begin to openly examine options and discuss them more thoughtfully.

Our focus is naturally on *binning for feedback* and the extent to which the tools can yield better inferences about student thinking and performance. But we also recognize that some of these tools support binning-for-grading strategies, and that these uses occupy the imagination of many teachers who want to make a difference in the lives of their students. Before deciding how each binning strategy relates to the formative or summative purposes of classroom assessment, let's examine each.

The Answer Key

When dealing with traditional quiz and test data, many teachers use the answer key. It helps to define outcomes and impose order. The answer key has a set of predetermined right and wrong answers. We can quickly and efficiently evaluate student achievement. Here is an example of a typical fixed-choice item on a social studies/geography test. The corresponding answer key provides two bins—correct and incorrect. Though there are five choices for students (A, B, C, D, or E), the answer key bins a student's choice either correct or incorrect.

What is the capital of Germany?

A. Berlin (correct bin)

B. Bonn (incorrect bin)

C. Brussels (incorrect bin)

D. Johannesburg (incorrect bin)

E. None of the above (incorrect bin)

The answer key makes this type of question easy to score. When binning for grading, one only needs to process, sort, and bin the student responses data. Many schools have machines that score these quizzes and tests. Two categories drive the assessment framework: correct and incorrect answers. It's fast, efficient, and the number of correct answers is tallied to produce the summative indicator, the letter grade.

The Partial Credit Scoring Key

The partial credit scoring key, a modified version of the answer key, can open up areas for alternative scoring of student responses. It can alert teachers to minor and major misconceptions. If used "formatively" in a quiz, for example, it might allow teachers to bin and sort student misconceptions on a Friday, to allow for reteaching the information on Monday, and to design new lesson activities through the next week to reinforce a concept (or facts) *before* the final unit test. Let's use the previous example to illustrate. Note there are still five choices for students, but the partial credit answer key bins each choice uniquely, not just as either "correct" or "incorrect."

What is the capital of Germany?

A. Berlin (correct bin because "current capital")

B. Bonn (partially correct bin because "historically true prior to unification")

C. Brussels (misconception bin because "capital in neighboring country")

D. Johannesburg (major misconception because "off continent" with German-sounding name")

E. None of the above (incorrect bin because likelihood of "guessing")

Unlike the first example, there are many more bins for teachers (and students) to work with in the partial credit scoring key. This approach to binning student thinking opens up more uses of test/quiz data. Much of the initial excitement around developing ordered multiple choice items (Briggs, Alonzo, Schwab, Wilson, 2006) with these partial credit scoring protocols was based on a promise of better uses of standardized test data. Classroom assessors can take advantage of these item formats and use information gathered during instruction to modify or refocus on content. The key to success lies in a rich, productive set of potential student ideas, including misconceptions and plausible meaningful "distractors" as the assessment experts call them.

Some classroom teachers like the idea of partial credit, in principle, but struggle with the effects of giving partial credit in the real world with the example above. They don't necessarily see how we can award credit for misconceptions (answers B & C) or just plain guessing (which is more likely for answer E). Each answer/response does elicit information about "the current level of student understanding" and an argument for evaluating different mental models (e.g., the "continents schema" still needs work). Although researchers can and do separate grading practices from scoring procedures, most teachers don't. Classroom teachers tend to focus on points and who deserves more or less of them. It's difficult to reset expectations on binning for feedback (versus grading) even when sharing these sorts of examples.

But for those learning the craft and trade of formative assessment practices, it's time to move beyond the stale debates about "How many points to award?" or "Who deserves a higher score?" Let's try to go in a different direction. The next time you decide to check for understanding with a quiz, see how many of these types of items you can write and which ones will provide you with a breakdown of who is still laboring with a misunderstanding. Probe. Ask for an explanation or justification. See whether or not these new items offer more insight into student thinking, in part, by honoring and exhausting it. We like these sorts of "fixed-choice+" items—where the "+" is your asking for explanation or justification—because at least they open up the possibility for meaningful dialogue *during* classroom instruction as you debrief "results."

The Rubric

When looking at data generated by performance assessment—in English, art, science, history, music, PE, world language, even math—teachers use rubrics to impose order on and make sense of the diversity of student "open-ended" responses. Performance assessments can be scored in different ways, but a common one involves the use of an analytic rubric, consisting of a predetermined set of elements or criteria. Analytic rubrics, in addition to establishing learning criteria, also provide the levels of performance. Implicit in the progress levels is the idea of "less to more" of the skill. Here is an example of a 4x4 matrix (or analytic rubric) for binning student responses with a science lab assignment:

	Needs Improvement	Emerging	Proficient	Advanced
Hypothesis/ research questions				
Lab set up/ procedures				
Evidence/ data collection				
Analysis of results/ conclusions				

As with the partial credit scoring key, the analytic rubric is a tool that helps the teacher evaluate the learning criteria/skill, the performance level, and score it. Rubrics, like all matrices in education, allow us to process, sort, and bin the student response data. Typically these matrices are criterion-referenced (standards-based, in some cases) categories.

The student gets points for each level in a given category (e.g., Lab set-up/ procedures or Analysis of results). In theory, these rubrics help us to differentiate "where students are" and which next steps they need to take to make progress. Students may be shown the rubric in advance so they know the grading or feedback procedures associated with an assignment or project. Note: The progress levels used in this example are purposefully upgraded. We see no *a priori* reasons to impose an additional evaluative structure such as *A* = Advanced; *B* = Proficient; *C* = Emerging; *D* = Needs Improvement; and *F* or *Incomplete* on top of the binning system. For now, let's attend to what this analytic rubric structure implies and aims to do for teachers.

While it takes a little more time to accurately sort everyone's work into each box, the rubric is a faster and more efficient method of binning than reading and rereading every student response while seeking to get an overall impression (e.g., Very Good). Many argue that analytic rubrics can produce a summative indicator (e.g., a letter grade) that is "fair" and "reliable." Despite their popularity among researchers and teachers, a few questions remain: *How formative can these rubric tools actually be? For whom? Under what conditions? And how would we know if they delivered better feedback, ensured and supported its uptake, and made a difference in the revision process?*

The Scoring Guide

The scoring guide is an alternative to the rubric. It is a simpler binning strategy for teachers and (like rubrics) can be used by students for peer- and self-evaluation. Scoring guides, however, tend to contain less verbiage and dysfunctional detail that might overwhelm students (Popham, 1997). The scoring guide, like the partial credit scoring key, is a good tool for awarding partial credit. But it is much more: it has great potential for binning for feedback during instruction when the teacher needs to check for understanding with a lighter touch.

Level 3	Complete and accurate
Level 2	Contains at least one major conceptual error, misstatement, or omission
Level 1	Attempts to answer but with major errors or omissions
Level N/A	No response or off-topic
Comments/ Explanation	

Similar to the rubric, the teacher can process, sort, and bin student response data into this graphic organizer. Scoring guides can also provide a clear, articulated justification for partial credit on constructed response tasks, short answer items, and try-now activities. We like how this tool reduces extraneous cognitive load on students while increasing the germane load by reinforcing the importance of providing comments to explain their reasoning.

There are powerful examples of students using scoring guides to shed light on the grading process and to communicate more clearly about expectations for improvement (Roberts, Wilson, Draney, 1997). We explore these examples later in the chapter, but for now it is important to recognize these tools as methods for binning for feedback (or grading). To be formative, for use by students to self and peer-evaluate their work, however, the focus will be on *levels*, not *points*. Teachers who use scoring guides can scan "results" by response level and see patterns and trends to make decisions about the current levels of student understanding in their classroom.

Scoring guides tend to focus less on criterion-referenced or standards-based categories to drive the assessment framework in classroom assessment (compared with, for example, analytic rubrics), but they can be aligned with progress variables in the curriculum. The scoring guides can also allow students to bin their responses (products, performances, "first drafts") in a new way, without the stigma of letter grades and with a focus on revision.

The Checklist

We include the checklist in this chapter not because we favor it. We don't. The checklist is neither a rubric nor a scoring guide. It tends to combine the best and the worst of binning strategies. Yes, it is fast, efficient, and can produce a raw score. But it is also vague, arbitrary, and not tied to much in the way of higher-order thinking or evaluating and differentiating skills development.

We have seen the checklist used in physical education, science, and language arts. It's like a procedural scorekeeper: did this, didn't do that. Check marks are converted to points and points to grades. The binning-for-grading cycle is complete. But not much more is accomplished than task management (a worthy learning target if it is revealed at the outset) and awarding points to those who remain "on task."

We contend that each of these binning strategies and tools has its own affordances and constraints. As educational assessment experts know, an assessment procedure or tool's *purpose* will govern the validity of its uses. It is no different for binning moves. You can make a binning move with a scoring guide—it's up to you to make it *formative* or *summative* for your students.

There is no one-size-fits-all classroom assessment solution to categorizing and evaluating student thinking. Pick your tools and procedures with care.

To start the cycle anew and reboot our binning moves, let's try this approach to planning the next series of lessons for a unit. We have to *think first* (How might we bin student responses?), *act next* (How do we bin for formative feedback with particular tools), and *think back* on what is and is not working in our classroom (How can we bin for feedback more effectively or efficiently to close the gap on learning?) Once you get up and running with a binning-for-feedback system, you can add nuance to the challenge, especially for the silent Bobs, cynical Sams, forgetful Freds, and disconnected Dans who are "not yet" ready for the formative assessment-rich classroom culture.

As formative assessors, we must acknowledge that each assessment move (and corresponding binning system) is provisional and subject to review. This means that we need to check on our assessment procedures and tools and revisit their usefulness and purposes regularly.

Results from rubrics, for example, require ongoing validation if we are to use them formatively. Too often we toss them into the classroom and treat them like answer keys. Using rubrics to provide scores, rather than timely and specific feedback to inform next steps for a revision process, is a particular use. But that use (with the corresponding points) is not valid for formative assessment purposes. Points, scores, and grades are NOT formative feedback. Not the kind of assessment experts recognize, anyway.

Of any binning system that you decide to use, ask:

- For whose good does the bin "correct" or "proficient" serve?
- For what good will the bins and categories be put to use (e.g., continuous improvement or benchmarking)?
- Who decides which scoring categories and bins are best for promoting habits of revision?
- Does the bin make a difference in tangible outcomes? For whom? How?

The partial credit answer key can aid the formative assessor, *if* it helps identify trends and patterns linked to how students think about a topic. The analytic rubric can support the aims of assessment for learning, particularly *if* it affords tangible opportunities for revision of students' work. The scoring guide can get us started with unpacking challenging tasks, *if* it guides feedback that is specific, addressable, and augmented with next steps for the student *during the instructional cycle.*

FORMATIVE ASSESSMENT TIPS

Expert Formative Assessors Advise:

When considering our binning tools and supports, we need to **prioritize feedback** and how binning tools support **feedback loops**.

Although students take their own next steps to learn and move toward deeper understanding, teachers take responsibility for generating feedback loops in the classroom learning space: feedback loops that demonstrate evidence of give and take, action and reaction, offer and acceptance of feedback.

Tools that make this process more visible are welcome, those that obscure it are not.

—*Reta Doland, Curriculum Coach, Le Grande Unified, Oregon Public Schools*

Binning for Substance and a Deeper Purpose

Students engaging in feedback loops and what qualitative educational researchers call "turns of talk" in the classroom about subject area content isn't enough. If student-to-student and student-to-teacher dialogue about content stays on the surface—if it is mostly about "content as correct information" (as research has demonstrated it frequently is)—then students' learning won't be deep enough. The deeper learning called for in this book asks for more.

Students need to engage with teachers and with one another in ways that support them as they try on the disciplinary thinking of that subject. *How do scientists consider evidence*? (Scientific evidence is evidence that serves to either support or counter a scientific theory or hypothesis.) *How do mathematicians argue*? (An argument of a function is a specific input in the function, also known as an independent variable.) *How do musicians elaborate*? (Musical elaboration is the development or expansion of a musical idea or theme.)

For teachers, especially teachers in middle and secondary schools, becoming a formative assessor means not just understanding how experts in your subject engage in disciplinary thinking. Becoming a formative assessor means being able to orchestrate the classroom learning space so that students—visibly—are scaffolded as they try on and engage in that kind of thinking too, in developmentally appropriate ways.

For example, if you are teaching world history and formatively assessing it, this would mean supporting students to make "live" arguments, weigh "real" evidence, interrogate "actual" sources, and push back on competing views and interpretations during lessons.

Don't merely act as if you are assessing history "content" while posing, pausing, and probing with students. Don't settle on pat answers or clicker responses to assess for learning. The logic of formative assessment and the first principles of assessment require teachers to exhibit a set of dispositions and skills that promote inquiry and skepticism—not superficial acceptance of "correct" answers. It's not that different from what goes on in the scientific community when practitioners ask probing questions or demand more evidence. Being a formative assessor requires a critical stance.

If you take the time to ask, "Who caused WWII?" or have students write "3 reasons the Treaty of Trianon failed to keep the peace after WWI," or probe on "Why did Hitler invade Poland?"—then set up a framework for how historians tackle such intractable questions. Make the unit "problem based" or "project based." Have your students set up a poster gallery walk, identify the essential questions related to the causes and consequences of war, evaluate the quality of the reasons and justifications provided by different teams, and devise a set of probing questions that everyone will do for an exit ticket or peer scoring guide before they sit for the unit test.

Your formative assessment bins should go beyond the stale notions of "correct," "partially correct," "major misconception," or "off topic." (In the first chapters, we admittedly relied on these overused bins to move us forward; now it is time to dig deeper into what each discipline reveals about student learning progressions.) Instead of searching for incorrect answers or obsessing on how much partial credit to award "Bonn" or "Brussels," ask your students to engage in the work of historians during your assessment rounds. Consider together with your students as you debrief the gallery walk: What counts as "a good argument" for historians? Who is the "we" writing this history? Which sources do they find problematic (fake news, propaganda, official pronouncements)? How will "our" perspective (and bias) influence the evidence presented or case made for war? What differentiates a reliable source from an unreliable one?

By engaging in these sorts of back and forth conversations, there is the potential to assess your students' factual declarative knowledge *and* to evaluate the use of those facts by your students as they learn how to make arguments in history.

A Word of Caution

Learning to be a formative assessor does little good if we simply reproduce the mistakes of summative assessors and fail to seize on the real work of learning. Hovering at the surface and asking trivial questions on the fly does little to advance our students' exercise of their Habits of Mind. For our respective subject disciplines, we need time, resources, and support to dig deeper into what we might now call "high-leverage" bins. Work in STEM fields has produced insight into student learning progressions that can help us map formative assessment moves into our teaching (Alonzo & Steedle, 2009; Black, Wilson, & Yao, 2011; Lehrer, Kim, & Schauble, 2007; Lehrer, Kim, Ayers, & Wilson, 2014). But for most of us, we will need to build better, more substantive and attentive binning strategies on our own. Using the FA moves with our students can help us do that.

If we expect formative assessment to support the college and career prospects of the children and youth we teach as they move toward becoming scientists, historians, musicians, writers, engineers, lawyers, computer scientists, nurses, counselors, and practitioners of other professions, then we will have to go deeper. Posing better questions, pausing for deeper reflection, and probing for more sophisticated explanations is a start. But we will need other content experts and experienced practitioners to help us decide "what makes a good question" and how to best position it at a particular turn in the lesson, unit, and even curriculum.

The problem is that many content experts don't know enough about classroom teaching to make their ideas useful to those becoming formative assessors; and many teachers haven't been exposed to the latest research to integrate it into their formative assessment moves. We hope to see more collaboration and dialogue between these different groups going forward—for now, we will focus on trajectories of practice that animate our daily work as teacher educators in a large, diverse preparation program.

Becoming a Better Binner Takes Time

Getting better with binning takes time. Teacher learning takes time. The same is true for our students.

We observe our students for a very limited time. We see a tiny slice of their lives each day. Some of us get 55 minutes, others 90. Despite occasional peeks into the developmental window, we don't know—at age 6, 11, or 15—who will grow up and work in this or that profession. "The system" may encourage us to peg children as "good" or "bad" or "mediocre" students and move them along particular tracks.

But the point remains: we don't know the paths our students will take or professions they will choose. We almost never have the required evidence to determine what will happen to which students—in a particular class, let alone in school or in life. Yes, we make predictions. But they remain predictions.

Too often we assume that grades, scores, and points predict future performance in college, on the job, in the world at large. There are studies that try to establish the link, but correlation does not equal causation. There is no necessary connection between past performance and future results, as the Scottish philosopher David Hume—and our stockbroker—remind us.

As classroom assessors, we can try to assume that rubrics (and the points we assign) capture the true level of student performance on a project, task, or assignment. We can get caught up in the calculation of points and the bins we've created to assess student learning. These matrices and graphic organizers provide comfort; we get a sense of accomplishment figuring out who goes where, in which little box. But shouldn't we hold back and slow down a little rather than wield these all-too-human scoring tools with abandon?

Common sense tells us there is plenty of bias in how rubrics are used and we know there is a fair amount of inconsistency in applying them to student work. The concept of rater-reliability should remind us of the fallibility of human judgment. Formative assessors, like summative assessors, are dealing with probabilities and not certainties when it comes to evaluating students.

The success (or failure) of a particular formative feedback binning strategy is no different. We can't perfectly predict which ones will work. Success is perplexing, even inexplicable. When, for example, our formative feedback fails to produce the desired effect in our students we can fall into despair and frustration:

- How can this student resist my suggestions—they're for his own good?
- Why would someone throw away a second chance to improve a grade?
- What does a student expect to get on the assignment when she fails to meet me halfway?
- How can a student get better without revising and resubmitting work?

As always, our students can play unique and powerful roles in helping and hindering our attempts to bin their thinking and performances. They resist. They buckle. They defy categorization at times.

It should come as no great surprise that teachers *are* binning students, daily. We pigeonhole them. We judge them. We grade them. Students have learned over the years that our job as teachers is to bin them first, and ask questions later. It is no wonder students have trouble believing the formative assessor when she says: "It's all about the learning, take a look at my feedback, and we will focus on next steps and not your grade, until finals." They look at us incredulously. *Really?*

The CPESS Example:
Binning for Feedback in the Middle School Math/Science Classroom

In Chapter 2 we talked about Central Park East Secondary School (CPESS) in East Harlem. An urban high school whose founder, Debbie Meier, won the first MacArthur "Genius Grant" bestowed to a K–12 educator, reminds us that among the many purposes of public education, one is to teach students to use their minds well. Debbie, like so many of the teacher leaders at the school, was steadfastly committed to student success. The Habits of Mind figured prominently in that vision. But so did formative feedback. Because *teachers* at CPESS were in the habit of using their minds well, too, the binning strategies employed focused on revision, next steps, and the process of developing one's skills as a classroom learner.

In a video made by the students of Central Park East Secondary School, "Graduation by Portfolio," (Gold & Lanzoni, 1993), we get a chance to peer into the world of a math/science teacher who is an expert formative assessor. We watch as she moves around the classroom, sizing up individual students' zones of proximal development, and providing just-in-time formative feedback throughout a lesson on "how and why pitch changes" in a unit on the physics of sound. The video cuts back and forth to different students, some at the computer, others at the chalkboard, still others in small groups working on the lesson objectives.

But the teacher also knows when to allow students to struggle, to pause her own comments, to honor when and when not to scaffold the next step. Without condescending or coddling her students—nearly all of whom are African American or Latino—her demeanor is professional, focused, and persistent. Her questions are direct. She probes on the students' responses. She is patient, positive, and firm.

When sharing this video with our teacher candidates, we often stop to pause and reflect. The students in this video case study provide one another with rich formative feedback—an impressive amount. We see Betty providing her table partner, Danni, with specific, positive, task-oriented feedback on the first hand-written draft of the assignment (called an "exhibition" at CPESS). When Danni is ready to crumple up her paper, Betty cautions and supports her peer not to throw away drafts: "You can use that—just reword it."

Danni is also providing feedback to herself, as she struggles to keep engaged with the topic. "Okay, I just have to relax and explain myself," she coaches herself, when her frustration is starting to get the better of her. She continues to use a wide lexicon of Tier I and II academic language throughout the recorded exchange: *tension, pitch, increase, vibration, Tau, therefore.* For viewers, it is both exasperating and exhilarating—watching learning happen, at the learner's particular pace! Our student teachers never fail to recognize how exciting it is to watch this "formative" assessment process unfold, for these kids, in these circumstances, with this conceptually difficult material.

Every teacher in this country has had these moments. We've all experienced the "aha" or "now I get it" that makes teaching so rewarding. We'd like more of these moments of FA-in-action, but it's hard without the support from school leaders, district officials, and policymakers who prefer the mile-wide, inch-deep approach to teaching and learning that emphasizes coverage over comprehension. Times are changing and some lessons from the past are re-emerging. Still, planning time, professional development resources, and leadership that supports "thinking outside the box" will be necessary to embed FA moves in the 21st century curriculum. Ahead of her time, Debbie Meier knew that. We do too.

For now, let's keep priming ourselves. *How do we get more formative feedback flowing into the lesson? Who are the Bettys and Dannis in our science classrooms? How do they interact in other subject classrooms? Is there space in the other disciplines, including physical education, math, music, and history for these formative feedback-driven "pair-shares" and "table talk" moments? What do we as a faculty know about these two students and countless others who risk sharing how they solve equations and the words on a first draft? What does it take to coach, scaffold, and support our students to get in the habit of talking aloud, using academic language, and trying to make sense of conceptually difficult material?*

Our faith in quizzes, tests, and homework as instruments to get to the bottom of student understanding and learning in the classroom has fooled us. None of these assessment tools produces the level of discourse or reveals the complexity of student understanding that is evident in the exchange between Betty and Danni. Yes, CPESS had other infrastructure to support these students. Behind the scenes, there were rubrics, exemplars, and focal questions. But what makes this exchange between these two young women so extraordinary, decades later, is how ordinary and abundant formative assessment moves are in this teacher's practice. Again, it just looks like "good teaching."

The "new" education standards, along with the policymakers who promote them, promise room for evaluating students like Betty and Danni in more authentic ways than before. Advocates tell us that the new standards-based tests will have items to capture what these two girls know and can do, for example, in science and mathematics. Supporters of these tests claim that we are moving closer to "smarter, balanced, 21st century" measures.

Putting our Habits of Mind lens back on, we are curious to see if and how the conceptual understanding and procedural fluency skills like the ones witnessed in the "Graduation by Portfolio" video will be assessed by these brave, new summative tests. Will summative assessors really be able to show what these girls from East Harlem and others like them know and can do—inside a classroom or science lab or workplace? What is the evidence that these new and improved test items measure complex understandings, application of skills, or non-cognitive outcomes such as persistence any better than the old standardized tests did? For whose good are these new "big data" tests developed, marketed, and deployed? And perhaps most importantly, who decides which is more valid, reliable, or fair?

In the meantime, as these summative and interim assessment reformers work at 35,000 feet with politicians and policymakers, we will get back to assessing for learning and binning for feedback and next steps that support a cycle of inquiry *in our classrooms*. Let's start from ground level and review a few more examples of formative assessment moves that promise better binning.

Principles, Procedures, and Practices

We offer an illustration of overt binning for feedback by sharing the results of a special collaboration among University of California–Berkeley curriculum developers in the Lawrence Hall of Science, assessment developers from the Graduate School of Education, and—most important—the field test teachers and students they worked with in a Kentucky school district. Together, as part of the Science Education for Public Understanding Program (SEPUP) initiative, the team designed a yearlong middle school science curriculum called "Issues, Evidence, and You" (IEY) that innovated a comprehensive, integrated system for assessing, interpreting, and monitoring student performance. Among the many "firsts" in this federally sponsored project, we note the use of different binning moves and strategies to support student learning were among the most important "take aways" for teachers, students, and parents.

The IEY curriculum was ahead of its time. It focused on student decision making, the uses of evidence, and how to evaluate scientific argument. We note that its approach anticipated that of the Next Generation Science Standards by nearly 20 years. The overt binning for feedback that teachers and students used, as we discussed earlier in this chapter, is in direct contrast to the previously private and hidden processes that teachers had engaged in when scoring and grading student work. Suddenly why student work was valued and scored the way it was became public discussion—for and by students!

Teachers in the IEY/SEPUP project initially facilitated the scoring of student work, then gradually released the scoring process to students. As students gained competence with explaining and justifying their reasons for assigning scores, they became more knowledgeable about the curriculum topics. This process allowed them to elaborate and build more meaningful connections to the curriculum.

With overt binning strategies in play, teachers and students know what bins are being used, how, and why. Overt binning-for-feedback processes are social and visible in the classroom learning space. They are the opposite of subjective, private, and arbitrary grading practices. Binning-for-feedback moves, as this project reveals, often work best in small-group configurations: groups of students—with teachers' scaffolding and guidance—consider student work together and talk about why each work fits into which bin. It is powerful to watch as students themselves work toward becoming formative assessors in the classroom as they ask why the response deserves a "3" on the scoring guide, or what it might need to look like in order to score a "4," or what next steps could be taken to help get the work there. At each of these turns in the lesson, we observe them engaged in a process experts call "assessment moderation" (Wilson & Sloane, 2000).

Assessment moderation, or overt binning for feedback, as we call it, is the opposite of "traditional" classroom grading scenarios such as doing test corrections or quiz review. As the IEY team explains in a video titled *Moderation in All Things: A Class Act* (Roberts & Sipusic, 1999):

> Traditionally, grading has been a private matter between students and their teacher with feedback arriving in the form of teacher comments in red ink.

While privacy minimizes embarrassment, it obscures the deliberative process the teacher uses to value student work. Because of this veil of privacy, students may not fully understand the criteria for excellence their teacher uses to grade their work.

Introducing an overt binning-for-feedback process (although they didn't call it that in the 1990s), the narrator of the video continues:

We describe a social moderation process that lifts the veil of privacy by promoting open discussion about the quality of student performance. During moderation teachers meet and discuss scores given to samples of student work. Using criteria specified in a scoring guide the teachers reach agreement on the appropriate scoring level for each paper.

When discussing this video with our teacher candidates, we remind them that the scoring guide is the anchor and pivot for the classroom discussion. It allows feedback to have a specific, targeted direction. It provides a scaffold for peer-to-peer feedback, so that students have clearer criteria as they struggle to develop the practice of formative feedback. Here is a sample scoring guide, the one used for evaluating the Understanding Concepts (UC) learning target in the IEY curriculum (in the video):

Score	Recognizing Relevant Content: Response identifies and describes scientific information relevant to a particular problem or issue.	Applying Relevant Content: Response uses relevant scientific information in new situations, such as solving problems or resolving issues.
4	Accomplishes Level 3 AND extends beyond in some significant way.	Accomplishes Level 3 AND extends beyond in some significant way.
3	Accurately and completely identifies AND describes relevant scientific information.	Accurately and completely uses scientific information to solve problem or resolve issue.
2	Identifies and/or describes scientific information BUT has some omissions.	Shows an attempt to use scientific information BUT the explanation is incomplete; also may have minor errors.
1	Incorrectly identifies and/or describes scientific information.	Uses scientific information incorrectly and/or provides incorrect scientific information; OR provides correct scientific information BUT does not use it.

0	Missing, illegible, or is irrelevant or off topic.	Missing, illegible, or is irrelevant or off topic.
X	Student had no opportunity to respond.	

Assessment moderation discussions amongst teachers, according to researchers (Roberts & Sipusic, 1999),

> Lead to useful classroom innovations as teachers compare their approaches to teaching the same science activities. In addition, teachers often find it useful to have their students participate in moderation. While this process was originally developed to benefit teachers… students also benefit from participating in the moderation process.

As we "listen in" and watch the SEPUP video today, we are struck by how much classroom assessment innovation occurred in these Kentucky schools and how the UC–Berkeley/SEPUP project anticipated the current science standards by decades. The video evidence shows that binning-for-feedback practices are well established in these middle school classrooms. Teachers masterfully prime and reprime the routines, values, and norms of assessment moderation and peer feedback. They inspire and model for us what it means to be a formative assessor who has taken it to the next level.

Let's dig a little deeper into the classroom exchange to make sense of the work. In the video we see a diverse group of middle schoolers discussing samples of student work. First the teacher primes the procedures and purpose of the exercise. They have already examined the student work together in small groups and are now ready to share in a whole-class discussion.

Each group has decided upon a score for the work sample; they use the scoring guides to assign X, 1, 2, 3, or 4. There are "discrepancies," naturally, in the scores they've given. The teacher reminds them that the purpose of this peer assessment exercise is to resolve the discrepancies in scores through discussion. Resolving discrepancies in scores through discussion, as experts tell us, is a basic element of assessment moderation, which was initially developed to improve rater agreement (reliability). In the classroom context these moderation sessions, as the teachers note, are a powerful form of peer feedback that helps students revise their work and improve it.

Here is the science task that students were examining and asked to respond to in the *Moderation in All Things* video clip:

Activity 16: A student conducts an investigation to see which is more concentrated, a sample of acid or a sample of base. He finds that it takes 4 drops of acid to neutralize one drop of base. Which is more concentrated, the acid or the base? Explain your answer. You may wish to include a diagram.

Here is a transcript of the turns of talk that animate FA moves in play in a video clip from *Moderation in All Things: A Class Act*:

Teacher (priming): It's important to state your reasons for assigning the score you did using the scoring guide. Tell me why you wanted to look at (exemplar response) G.

Student: OK, as a group we gave it a 3, but I gave it a 2 because I didn't think, I mean, it uses a diagram but I don't think it explained it as well as it would have to get a 3… and Jeff thought that too, but the other two guys thought it was (3).

Teacher (probing): Instead of telling me why it didn't get a 3, tell me why you gave it a 2, using the scoring guide.

Francine: Well also, it doesn't have like all the information that the other 3 and 4 had given.

Teacher (priming-posing): OK. Let's look at this. It says in the scoring guide it has some omissions, what do you feel is omitted from this? What in your mind before you read these (exemplars? Scoring guide?) when you were starting to answer these questions what in your mind do you think was omitted?

Francine: Well, I mean… I just thought… (gestures with her hand)…

Teacher (probing-priming-pausing): Yes? You have to be able to tell the writer of the question what they omitted so they can… what if I came up to you and said, "Well, I just don't know, but you need to add *something* else to your paper."… If I can't tell you specifically, how are you going to make your paper better? So, you need to tell this person—or us—how can this person improve? What did they omit?

Francine: Well, there wasn't anything about the particles or anything… um (pause)

Teacher (bouncing): Let me have Emily help you. Emily, since she has her hand up.

Emily: They never said that the base is four times stronger than the acid and I think they need to. They showed in the diagram… what's the diagram [in Figure 7.2] showing you?

Teacher (bouncing): OK, there's your support… anyone else have a… Jeff?

Jeff: Well, the author actually didn't talk about, they said the base is more powerful, it would take four drops of acid to neutralize it but they didn't say why four drops. Why four drops, not a different amount of drops?

Teacher (repriming): We're coming down tough on these, aren't we? Tougher on these than maybe some of us are as teachers.

Francine: Can we do another one of these?

Teacher: Sure. Which one?

In another episode, the students in the SEPUP video at a particular table are trying to explain their reasons for assigning a *1* to a sample student response to an assignment (see Figure 7.2, p. 282). They use the scoring guides to justify the point award. The give and take among the students is reminiscent of how we practice reasoning by making arguments with evidence. The "take away" from these exchanges is that binning for feedback does not magically happen, nor can scores tell us what to think about the quality of student responses. We must as formative assessors struggle for the meaning behind the score, point, or number.

By examining other people's work—breaking it down, taking it apart, putting it back together—students get a sense of their own level of understanding. But the scaffolds, tools, and agreements must be embedded in the lessons and unit as part of classroom and department expectations. The SEPUP teachers and students have primed for binning and they hold one another accountable to more than "Because I said so" or "Ahh, that looks like a *B* to me."

Assessment moderation is a powerful process in which local groups of teachers come together to score and discuss student work. This process serves at least two purposes. First, it leads to more reliable judgments about the quality of student thinking (a key piece of the NRC's Assessment Triangle's message). By allowing for agreement among teachers as to the appropriate score level for a particular student response by building local consensus aligned to a set of standards of student performance, moderation also allows for more valid inferences. Second, and also as important, it provides a powerful tool for professional development that teachers can turn around and share with students in their classrooms.

Assessment moderation, like the peer review process in the professional world, teaches students an invaluable lesson. In the real world, professionals work together to establish standards of excellence. That is, they engage in the evaluation of scientific, academic, or professional work by interacting with others working in the same field in principled ways that follow recognizable structures and forms—*that can be learned*! Communities of practice can help their engaged members "socialize each other" into lasting, positive change. As Roberts, Wilson, and Draney (1997) write:

> One-shot teacher professional development has failed time and again to serve teachers' needs in our dynamic educational system; to be truly effective teacher enhancement must also be in-depth and long-term (Fullan, 1990; Loucks-Horsley et al., 1989; St. John, 1991). Changing assessment practices is no less difficult to promote and support, but we believe local assessment moderation provides teachers with ongoing support to this end (Roberts, 1996, 1997; Roberts, Sloane, & Wilson, 1996; Wilson & Sloane, 2000). (p. 15)

Figure 7.2   Sample Response to Science Task

Student Response

The base is more concentrated and a sample of the two would look like this:

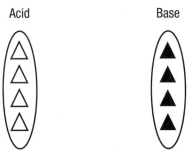

The base is more powerful and it would take four drops of acid to neutralize the base like this:

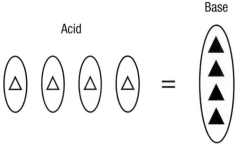

We see a third benefit to the process of assessment moderation in today's schools. Moderation foregrounds the powerful role that binning moves can play and asks us to differentiate assessment *for* learning from assessment *of* learning. By making explicit and public the role of feedback in the classroom learning environment, students are allowed to focus on the meaning of points while demanding that "we" (teachers, students, and staff) unpack the meaning of provisional numeric scores. Moderation promotes rather than obscures the real work of classroom assessment in a learning culture—where we all need time to process and get collective think time to go deeper.

When the students in the SEPUP project were asked about the norms and expectations that surrounded this classroom work, it was clear that everyone had been primed for using and incorporating the formative feedback from these sessions. Teachers who engaged in consistent, visible, public formative assessment moves such as binning for feedback made a lasting impression on their students. In a post-interview, two middle school students recalled:

> Student 1: Mrs. D is the kind of teacher that if you don't understand it, like just now, tons of people didn't understand, she'll sit at a table and she'll go through step-by-step the whole problem so that you understand, so you know the concept, and what you're expected to do.
>
> Interviewer: And what do you think of these scoring guides that you use for this class?
>
> Student 2: They really, really help, because like… they explain what you have to do.
>
> Student 1: The teacher gives us a chance to look at what we did wrong and redo things… then if we had trouble with it, so then you can really understand the labs you're doing (with her feedback). The work you're doing… once you go over it enough times and you really start to understand it, and then I think your final grade shows what you really know because you've gone over it so much.

We are inspired by the SEPUP project and other examples where the classroom learning space has become a place for the exchange of ideas. In each instance, teachers and students share a visible, sustained commitment to formative feedback. The students expect specific, evidence-based, "what are my next steps" feedback. Scores, points, and other representations are merely placeholders. The real work begins in moderation sessions, and the revision process that follows. In these examples, the notion of a work-in-progress honors and pushes the learner to the next level.

We share these examples knowing that our critics and critical friends may yet not be convinced of the power of FA moves. Are these exchanges the gold standard in authentic, 21st century scientific argument in today's schools? We doubt it. Are there better examples of feedback loops in STEM classrooms that engage in assessment for and of learning with proven results? Perhaps. Can't we—from the perspective of employers and college faculty—demand deeper engagement with disciplinary substance and procedural fluency in K–12 schools? Yes, of course.

We introduced you to the SEPUP moderation exercise for one reason. It is an example of a science classroom where the students and their teacher have attempted to make formative assessment (justifying the reasons for assigning a score) more than a ruse to cover the inevitable summative judgment (the search for letter grades). By opening up the classroom learning process, making thinking visible, we see these young middle and high school students doing the kind of work that we and others hope brings us closer to disciplinary substance and practice.

Clearly, our nation needs more scientists, engineers, and mathematicians. But its citizens also need a place where they can learn to share ideas, push back on claims and evidence, try to find adequate justifications for theirs or others' beliefs, and most pressing, discuss what they see and don't see as the benefits of an example, proposal, policy, or project that affects our democracy.

The Kentucky students and teachers, like those at Central Park East Secondary School, are deeply invested in the learning-by-assessing process that inhabits the disparate worlds of summative and formative assessment. We see hope for disciplinary substance in these exchanges. Moving beyond "grade grubbing" and "Can I have another point?" these students own their own struggle to learn. Rural, urban, suburban—it doesn't really matter for those looking to master formative assessment moves. Every formative assessor can reach for these subject-specific pathways and trajectories of learning in their own school. But they will need support from leaders who clear the way—for encouragement, for collaboration time, for the space and resources—to breathe new life into classroom assessment practices that have grown tired, even counter-productive.

We've culled a few lessons from the type of formative assessment work highlighted in the literature and these examples.

Here are a few benefits to share with people in your building about why you chose moderation with feedback for this unit. If parents or your principal asks for more traditional grading schemes than 1, 2 , 3, or 4 as modeled and discussed in the SEPUP example, no worries that you can prime them. Communicate that students in these feedback-rich moderation sessions can and know how to

- Use academic language in scaffolded conversations
- Be specific about claims based on written text and diagrams
- Improve their listening skills
- Experience building classroom community when they encourage class-mates' participation by saying things like, "What's your evidence?" and "I can see that point of view, but I think _____."
- Get real-time information about their own progress
- See concrete examples of their peers' work at each level of progress
- Develop conceptual understanding and build communication skills

Teachers modeling feedback-driven moderation sessions can

- Share the feedback process with students
- Use class time to monitor individual and group progress
- Self-evaluate the success of instruction
- Modify instruction based on these observations
- Promote changes in science or math instruction based on current standards
- Engage in professional development through collaboration with colleagues

 FORMATIVE ASSESSMENT TIPS

Add a Moderation Component to Your Next Unit

To make it more real world, we could set up a "Our School's Got Talent" or "Public Gallery Walk" simulation. Make it fun. First explain how adults (scientists, writers, musicians, artists, translators, and others) work under tight deadlines. Very often, they have to give feedback on projects with quick turnaround. Appoint teams to the project. Remind everyone that each group is tasked with providing one or two positive, practical suggestions on the work samples. Display examples on the wall. Do a gallery walk. "We have 15 minutes to get things done." A scribe can capture the warm and cool and next steps feedback with a high- or low-tech device. Then have team leaders present their observations about "areas for improvement" and where the class needs to go as a whole. Close the exercise with a "for this week" request for revisions based on today's feedback. Set a due date for the next drafts.

Deep binning for feedback will eventually require everyone to believe that *revision matters* in all subject areas. No longer can English language arts or PE teachers be the ones to carry the water. Too often, the word "revision" has been associated exclusively with rewriting papers or running around the track once more. Not true. Revision is universal. It's a fact of college and professional life. It has no special home in one person's class or subject matter or grade level. No need to monopolize; share the love.

Binning for feedback depends on all of our efforts. Revision is a process of *re-doing, re-thinking*, and *re-orienting* your proverbial "first drafts" or responses to assessments. The FA moves framework widens the perspective on classroom assessment; it's as much a *process* as an event.

Schools that communicate the agreement "to deepen feedback"—and the revision strategies, tools, and supports doing this implies—*within and across departments* will better support the formative assessor. Think big, but start small. One way to start is by beginning a dialogue about binning for feedback in your own classroom and with a few colleagues.

Invite Beliefs About Binning for Feedback into the Light

Students and teachers already have opinions about *binning for feedback*, even if they have never explicitly called it that. For example, students may believe that feedback is nearly always painful. Or that feedback only comes in two flavors: positive and negative. Teachers may believe that grades provide "feedback" because they signal "You'd better work harder next time" if someone receives an *F*.

Formative assessors should enact practices that work to dispel such false notions. But we've said before, and we mean it: no one is born an expert. Teachers, like students, have to learn a discipline and learning requires opportunities to uncover p-prims (or preconceptions) and misconceptions in any topic or field. We value novice teacher beliefs and experiences in the university preparation classroom. It's our job as teacher educators to bring them to light for discussion.

Moreover, we do not pretend to have all the answers. Beginners are right to ask: *What will we gain by giving and receiving feedback when it's almost always perceived as painful? When is a little "feedback pain" healthy? For whom? If we are working with super-sensitive students, how can we increase their—and our own—tolerance for "constructive criticism"?*

Discussing these kinds of questions can go a long way to building learning communities that support revision—in this case, of our own preconceptions about formative feedback and its uses in a lesson. We try to remind everyone that without revision (or reflection), binning-for-feedback moves are likely to fail. To uncover the truth about your own feedback beliefs and values, we came up with an organizer to get you started:

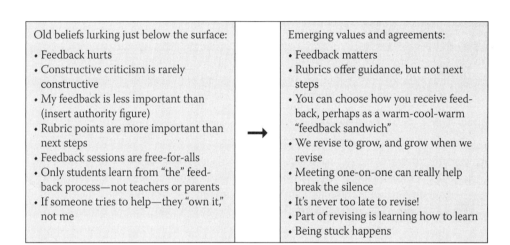

Old beliefs lurking just below the surface:		Emerging values and agreements:
• Feedback hurts • Constructive criticism is rarely constructive • My feedback is less important than (insert authority figure) • Rubric points are more important than next steps • Feedback sessions are free-for-alls • Only students learn from "the" feedback process—not teachers or parents • If someone tries to help—they "own it," not me	→	• Feedback matters • Rubrics offer guidance, but not next steps • You can choose how you receive feedback, perhaps as a warm-cool-warm "feedback sandwich" • We revise to grow, and grow when we revise • Meeting one-on-one can really help break the silence • It's never too late to revise! • Part of revising is learning how to learn • Being stuck happens

Even when students display intrinsic drives to learn and to complete tasks to the best of their abilities, giving and getting feedback in school settings can be fraught with emotion. Nearly all students need to be "wooed," to some extent, into giving and getting feedback and revising work in light of that feedback.

Try to help students better understand *why* they're engaging in feedback processes and *how* to approach them. Offer them guidance when their first approaches are not working well. Seek their input on what might work. Pull out the priming moves. Set the course toward *why* we do what we do—that's using our minds well.

When putting the formative in formative assessment, there's no "faking it." These assessment activities and processes are, by their nature, cognitively demanding and socially and emotionally complex. And it's nearly impossible to see our blind spots when teaching and checking for understanding. We all have them. Feeling hurried? Impatient? A tad confused or tired from coordinating all the overt, shared binning action?

Fortunately, for the most part, our students are forgiving—especially when we approach them with respect and genuine admiration for the miracles of experience and curiosity they are. There's no predicting what gems, gold, and amazing work they'll surprise us with when they trust we are a caring and committed audience. Believe your students when they say "Bring it on!" but be ready to repair when suddenly their confidence sags or bubble bursts: "You mean I have to write all that down—again!?"

Binning: Kayla's Case

Much of my work as a middle school science teacher is about teaching differently than I was taught. As I see it, the biggest difference is the open discussions we have in class about how and why student work gets scored as it does and our emphasis on revising, revising, revising.

When I was a student, scores were private, with two exceptions: when our teachers passed tests and quizzes back in descending order—top scores first, lowest scores last—and when they posted our graded compositions on actual cork bulletin boards.

Now, as I delve deeper into academic standards, I lead students through examining anonymous students' work, evaluating the work according to a scoring guide, and discussing the scores they've given together. In other words, I try to get them to experience the real world of scientific research, discussion of findings, and peer review. These are 21st century skills!

Naturally, students disagree about the "level" or threshold of the work samples. That's where the fun—and the learning—begins. Students get to chew on the criteria that I'm looking for in their work. As we discuss, they begin to understand the difference between 2 and 3 according to the "scoring guide." And as my students continue to talk, and question one another, and talk some more—a shift occurs. The shift is from the idea that the criteria we are looking for is not "my" criteria but is drawn from standards that the science community has set as to what makes a good lab report or explanation for chemical reactions.

Of course my 8th graders don't start the year calling it "the criteria." By the end of the year they do refer to the scoring guides—using the language in them—and realize it's not a game of points and grades. We don't shy away from academic language. Why would we? It gives them power and access to more powerful metacognitive thinking.

My middle schoolers love the power of assigning scores. This is a new role for them. To understand that this power is not wielded arbitrarily is another important experience for them to have. So much about their lives seems a mystery. So many decisions that affect them deeply can seem unfounded. They've been told so often, as an explanation for decisions, "because I said so." At the same time, their fairness sensors are better developed than they've ever been. So they're ready for grounding our discussions in evidence. I think for many students, it almost feels comforting to begin to understand the order behind the mystery of how and why student work gets valued the way it does. And that it is based in evidence that's discussable!

Through this process, which assessment experts call "moderation," the students also experience that understanding builds back and forth, from proposition and challenge, with interaction and communication with others. Some students take to this struggle for meaning easily, or so that's how it seems to me. Others—most, I'd say—need careful scaffolding to support their engagement with other students' work. This whole process of self- and peer-assessment is new for them (and to be honest, many of my colleagues in the department).

Moderation is a little abstract at first, but it puts them in the habit of listening for and using academic language. When it works, peer assessment gets them to apply and analyze the concepts we've discussed in class.

But we are evaluating science explanations and cross-cutting concepts such as analysis of evidence—not a favorite sports team, video game, or social media outlet. So I have to prime, prime, and prime again with my students. We negotiate norms around turn-taking, note-making, written and oral rehearsals before whole-class sharing out, offering reassurance to others, using sentence starters, and celebrating "first uses" of academic language.

Since the student work they're diving into is anonymous, there's no danger of hurting feelings. Sometimes their disagreements are strong, but that's different.

The entire process of moderation is the core of modeling the process of formative feedback—for students and for me. By examining others' (anonymous) work, they get a sense of their own level of understanding. I walk around and observe how they are processing the task and whether the scoring criteria are in play.

By being "forced" (and I realize for some of my students it feels like this) to produce specific advice to anonymous students on how work can be improved, my students begin to learn the art of formative feedback. Even if their advice is fast and loose initially, it's important that they're engaging in attempts to give formative feedback. It's how we learn. It's also how they get used to the culture of revision—which I point out is a scientific practice. No science journal accepts first drafts! And all important discoveries require peer review.

Revising is paramount—for my students and for the scientific community. Scores and points—of anonymous students' work or their own work—are merely placeholders in my classes. That is what we strive for together, anyway. We want to discuss, question, and make our feedback to one another as specific as we can and based on the evidence we have. Our moderation sessions are critical to beginning this work. What we learn together in the moderation sessions we carry into the revision processes that follow. We push each other to higher levels. I, too, get better and better at binning for feedback along the way.

Misconceptions and Challenges

⚠ Misconception Alert: Binning Beyond "Black" and "White"

When binning student work for summative purposes, we typically admit only two possibilities: correct or incorrect. We manage the complexity of student response patterns, as it were, through a rather narrow lens; black and white thinking dominates our binning practices.

Too often, when we write multiple choice questions for a quiz or unit test, we have in our mind the right and wrong answers, and we purposefully ignore the spectrum of possible, even plausible answers. The correct answer (bin) is the one that is counted right over all others. The incorrect answer (bin) is defined as the absence of the right response. What makes an answer right or wrong (except in cases such as 2 + 2 = 4) is likely to depend in large part on your frame of reference.

Even formative assessors can be trapped in the conventional dichotomous binning frame when shaping their assessment tools. When assessing for learning on the fly during a lesson, however, we will likely crash and burn if we fall back on these correct/incorrect frames of reference. From the students' perspective, being told the answer is "wrong" doesn't explain why or what to do next. Getting a zero on a worksheet doesn't show a student how or why to solve the problem. Receiving a check mark or star merely acknowledges task participation—not level of understanding.

The use of correct/incorrect bins without further investigation is an anathema to the principle of natural variation and scientific understanding. It forecloses any notion of difference or progression or the development of children's understandings over time. Formative assessors will want to change lenses and explore new frames of mind related to how we think (Gardner, 1983).

Neither the Scantron nor the red pen can save us from investigating the meaning of the different flavors of thinking and intelligences at play. "Polytomous" binning strategies admit variation rather than silence it. Formative assessors feel this tension between the dichotomous and polytomous mindsets, but often feel pressure to just play along.

Productive Bins Communicate Next Steps Needed

Some bins may communicate next steps. Most of the time, however, our bins fall short of communicating specific next steps needed to move the performance to the next level. They are, after all, bins: graphic organizers and matrices with tiny boxes to place student responses into for safe keeping. Hopefully, these bins represent important learning targets and are based on criteria/elements that help us better evaluate progress. But they do not speak for themselves. Bins are tools used by teachers and students to make sense of work. As the formative assessor knows, they provide a starting place for the conversation about what to do next. The rest is up to us.

 FORMATIVE ASSESSMENT TIPS

Bins Alone Do Not Communicate Fruitful Next Steps

Yes, some bins do hold more hope than others for directing us to feedback that matters. Yet, the supports around the bins, especially those that advance teachers' capabilities for orchestrating next steps for students to take, is too often missing. We need to practice binning for feedback with one another. And we need opportunities to retool and adjust when our binning strategies fail to bring about a classroom culture in which next steps matter.

Turning Challenges into Opportunities

As we come to a close, we focus on three challenges to binning for feedback going forward for your FA practice. We are sure you will discover more and we hope you will share them with us and others on the journey. For now, let's touch on a few challenges that we hope to turn into opportunities, but not before we wrestle with their meaning and significance as potential barriers to success.

First, when our expectations of giving and receiving feedback do not mesh well with our students' expectations and experiences, conflict and misunderstanding are likely to ensue. In fact, these struggles are inevitable. Teachers' goals around binning for feedback need to include making visible—to the extent they can—the frames, schema, expectations, and attitudes in play around these big ideas behind binning, feedback, and binning for feedback. Each concept is new and likely to face resistance. But not for long.

Second, binning for feedback well requires time, curricular resources, and specialized knowledge that can only be gained through teaching and classroom assessment experience. The moderation example in this chapter took weeks for the teacher to master—and she was a master teacher! A real challenge new teachers face with binning-for-feedback strategies that include using scoring guides to analyze student work is other teachers' buy-in. For many, formative feedback practices are not well supported by the school structure or social expectations embedded in a work day.

Third, adjusting and tailoring our bins for our students, their performances, and our pedagogical purposes is a huge challenge and highly demanding work, cognitively and emotionally. We have to build bins, then share them, then get reactions, and then go back to fine-tune them. Our students (and their parents) may be confused, anxious, or uncertain about all the focus on formative feedback when summative judgments affect their college and career prospects. Holding the line on competing pressures, knowing when to loosen the slack or when to tighten it, giving children the space to experience "moderation" and make mistakes—these are challenges for even the best among us.

Whether or not we are explicit about handling this component of the binning-for-feedback puzzle—with ourselves or with our students—negotiating purposes of education and what it means to have a good education will always be a critical piece of binning-for-feedback moves. Feedback is the deepest form of equity. We can't separate the two.

Learning to Look Back: Reflecting on a Just-Taught Lesson

Stacy is one of the best candidates in our program. She is eager, hardworking, and very attentive to her students. Both of her clinical teacher placements serve traditionally disadvantaged students. She is single, holds a job (30+ hours), and lives with her roommates from college. Her passion is to teach U.S. history and psychology. She knows that she has to be highly competitive to land a job in the Bay Area, especially in a subject area like history and social studies.

Stacy was introduced to the FA moves framework earlier than most in the credential program. At the end of a 6-week seminar, her university supervisor made a point of grounding the culminating 15-day "Phase I" teaching experience in the themes outlined in this book. She was invited, coached, and supported over a full semester to develop lesson plans, question maps, scaffolds, and procedures that created space for priming, posing, pausing, probing, bouncing, tagging, and binning. Her mentor teacher, though initially skeptical of this early introduction to formative assessment, nonetheless supported Stacy's efforts to plan good questions, do pair-shares to allow for think time, solicit responses with a word web, and to check for prior knowledge and identify misconceptions.

For the 15 days that Stacy took over the history class, she made tremendous progress with her FA moves. In our program, she developed a rubric with a classmate and explored formative feedback strategies for a poster project. All indications pointed in the direction of success. Her introduction to student teaching was an integrated one—she learned about how to better blend classroom management techniques, learning theory, and formative assessment during a unit on the Civil Rights Movement. She received high ratings from all who worked with her.

Summer passed and Stacy was now at a new placement for her fall "phase II" student teaching experience. In this new context and with a heavier teaching load, things were looking and feeling a little different. In a reflection about her grading practices, Stacy writes about her teaching experience:

> With the *A* to *F* bin, we are able to categorize the levels of how well our students did on certain assignments, or any other vague definition supplied to us at the beginning of the Guskey article ["Are Zeroes Your Ultimate Weapon?"]. As a future teacher, when I bin a student's assignment into the different levels of success, I will try to keep my scores focused on "improvement" and "ability." Granted that is almost as vague as the other definitions, and still is full of its own problems. I know I need to grade. I hope I have time to give lots of feedback with 150 students.

Three semesters into our credential program, it's as if Stacy really is living in Paul Black's no man's land. We see the struggle between the demands of formative and summative assessment rearing its head. Stacy is talking about herself as a "future teacher" during her clinical teaching placement! She is not quite sure how to balance the present with the future she imagines. She continues

> The benefits of the *A* to *F* binning process is that we don't have to work against the grain and use a new system. I have been using stamps as a way to not assign grades, but to provide feedback without any consequences. Of course, I am confronted with students asking what did they *really* get, and what does a stamp mean. I explain that I am just providing feedback to let them know where they are in terms of progress, and that they should read and take note of suggested areas of improvement. My beautiful explanation

is not what they want. They still press me: *Will we be getting a grade? Do we need to keep the assignment?*

My students who are excelling, and know how to succeed in school, benefit from the *A* to *F* binning. They know what to do, and how to fix it.

Gone are the references to the qualities of formative feedback. Wiggins's and Stiggins's advice from course readings and discussions has all but vanished in this reflection. No longer struggling to offer specific, timely, addressable, and next steps feedback on concrete assignments that might lead to revision of student work, she has fallen back on stamps. As a beginning teacher, Stacy's intention is perfect; she does care about her students' progress. But something is amiss. Reality is clashing with the ideal of becoming a formative assessor.

Overall, my ELL and IEP students are really struggling with the *A* to *F* bins. I have one student who is working hard, but not showing a whole lot of improvement. I try to provide as much feedback as I can, but when he gets his grades back he is frustrated.

Stacy knows that the school administration and her mentor teacher expects her to post grades every night—on homework, tests, quizzes, and worksheets. It is in her job description to provide grades for all her students, especially the ELL and IEP students who are most vulnerable. Feedback, as Stacy has learned, is optional. There is no box to check on School Loop (or another grading and accountability software at her school site) for the types or examples of formative feedback that the research and we know work.

Here comes the admission that says it all:

To be perfectly candid, I do not think anyone benefits from an *F*. Now I am sure the next question is: do I give out *F*s? I do. I don't know what else to assign. Maybe after class today I can think of a better method or a better bin. I do like the idea of giving an Incomplete at a certain point, and requiring the student to go back and fix it. The *F* bin stands for failure. A failure to do or know something. I do not think any of my students are complete failures at doing or understanding something. They just need to revisit either the content or the rules. As for now, I think I might change my *F* bins to *I*. The student will have to fix the assignment and talk with me so I can find out where the gap is, fix the misunderstanding, and then assign a new due date. Now the next question is what do I do when the student does not take the second chance? Is an Incomplete still sufficient?

Our teaching force struggles to play the game of "doing school." Some, we suggest, are quite content to leave the *A* to *F* system in place. Others, like Stacy, are still struggling to balance the worlds of summative and formative assessment, the demands of grading and feedback, the push and pull of "doing the right thing" on their professional identity and practice.

Beginning teachers in the United States are not simply suffering from externally imposed mandates on job performance. Yes, some states and districts continue to toy with the economist's vision of "value-added" and notions of teacher productivity as judged by their students' performance on standardized tests. Institutional forces will always place demands on teachers. There is historical precedence for society's desire to "correct" behavior through educational institutions, going back to Plato's academy.

But those learning to become formative assessors are also struggling with internal battles about which assessment pathways to take and protocols to adopt with their students—not just socially sanctioned or fashionable ones. Binning for grading versus binning for feedback is the historic challenge facing the next generation of teachers. The acceleration of social media, global technologies, and "big data" analytics will place tremendous pressure on formative assessors. We are being swarmed by new promises for how to evaluate student learning with machines. Teachers can lead or follow these trends. Time will tell.

Today, Stacy is a thoughtful, energetic, and hard working public school teacher. An active member of the AVID and GEAR UP programs at her school, she knows that her students get to college using their GPA and taking tests. She sees how students who are at risk and low-income struggle to go to college. As a white woman, who listens to progressive and conservative educators, she does not want to fall into the trap of the "soft bigotry of low expectations" by pretending that grades don't matter. Her students will need to learn how to make the grade to gain admission to college, to graduate from high school, to find work. Besides, as she can tell you from having attended a large, state university, professors aren't providing a lot of formative feedback in their assessment practice. They spend their limited time and resources grading midterms and final exams. Students in her world, Stacy realizes more and more, need to learn how to play the game of school.

It is easy to throw up our hands. Binning for grading is a very powerful force. It is the dominant mode of classroom assessment. Despite our best intentions in the formative assessment community, what do we say when Stacy says *Stamps are the only way I can handle 150 students*?

Schools like Central Park East Secondary School make room for summative and formative assessment. They reorganize teachers' (and students') work to build in time and resources for both assessment modalities. They provide release time, adjust course loads, and adapt school resources to meet the challenge of balancing both demands. Linda Darling-Hammond and associates have documented the costs and benefits of school restructuring that integrates formative and summative assessment purposes in middle and secondary education. Of these structural school reform approaches, Darling-Hammond (2006) writes:

> It is possible to create strong teaching on a wide scale in urban schools, as some states and districts have done, and evidence suggests that such investments can produce impressive gains in student achievement (see, for example, Darling-Hammond et al., 2005, on San Francisco; Elmore & Burney, 1997, on New York City's Community District 2; Wilson, Darling-Hammond, & Berry, 2001, on Connecticut). But these examples are currently exceptions to the rule. (pp. 14–15)

A body of institutional knowledge and case studies are available to guide policymakers who wish to support local change (Chittenden & Wallace, 1991; Miles and Darling-Hammond, 1997; Darling-Hammond, Ancess, & Ort, 2002). But, as with Stacy's experience in her own classroom, people and politicians are divided on the issues. And, as always, U.S. education reformers' memories are shorter than we'd imagine. The push for school "choice" has obscured the need for a careful examination of, as Black and Wiliam put it, "what's inside the black box." If the schools that parents are able to choose from aren't actually engaged in substantive formative feedback, how well informed is the choice? How can choice matter if these schools are not employing formative assessors who are likely to have the best, most sustained outcomes for children?

Traditional classroom assessment anchored by the triumvirate of tests, quizzes, and homework are meant to sort, period. As Stiggins concedes (2002), experience tells us traditional classroom assessment "works." Some kids do get into college and others do not. Some students excel into AP courses, and others do not. Some learners thrive on the carrots and sticks approach to teaching, others do not. In a world of limited prizes, not everyone can be a winner. Binning for grading is a time-honored tradition—it has worked for years. After all, nothing succeeds like success.

But still we fight on. We don't know how and when Stacy will reflect on her university lessons about the power of formative assessment. She has a few more hoops to jump through to clear her credential. Somebody will ask, perhaps in a job interview, "Do you provide formative feedback?" and she will answer "Yes." Maybe they will ask her why and she will cite the evidence to support the practice.

In the meantime, we teacher educators can gently remind her that she needs to provide evidence of her FA practice for her last portfolio in the credential program. We trust (knowing her well by now) that Stacy will find ways to provide that evidence—for the university faculty—and to reflect on the evidence's meaning and the next steps she can take to get better at these complex, high-leverage FA moves.

The bigger challenge, as we see it, is in the hands of Stacy's mentors. These are experienced teachers in her department and the induction support providers who are charged with providing her formative feedback on her progress toward a clear credential. It is their job now to coach her growth in becoming a formative assessor. We can help by keeping connected with our colleagues in the field. We also work to keep open the lines of communication with Stacy, and her classmates from our program, as they move through their careers.

One thing is for sure: Stacy will grow as a teacher. We can bet she will change instructional and assessment practices. She will play with ideas, moves, and strategies if they make sense. We'd like to know what she is learning and what insights she has to offer. We will invite her back to share with our next class of formative assessors. But formative assessment could lose its shine. There are no guarantees. By then Stacy will actually have more than 150 students. She will still be expected to report graded quiz and test results online each day. She will be expected to use the A to F system to serve students, parents, administration, and college admissions teams.

As time passes, Stacy may get stuck. It is possible that she will come to see all the talk about priming, posing, pausing, probing, bouncing, tagging, and binning as interesting but largely irrelevant to her daily work. Until FA professional development becomes the norm in her district or enters the conversation in her professional learning community, there is a good chance Stacy will fall back on established grading patterns and find shortcuts like everyone else. Who can blame her? After all, she is not a maverick or troublemaker. Having studied and taught world and U.S. history in our public schools, Stacy knows what happens to reformers and revolutionaries. It's not pretty and it rarely ends well.

Putting It All Together

It's one thing to demand that teachers need to evaluate, code, interpret, and decide what to do next in their lessons. It is another to support and coach them in an unfamiliar process, to shed light on it, to slow down and decode the major and micro moves necessary to bin effectively with particular students, in particular grade levels and curricular contexts.

Research tells us again and again: formative feedback—from yourself, your peers, and your teachers—is where the action is. But it takes time and practice to do this FA move well, let alone coordinate it with all the others. True, letter grades and point schemes won't cut it. But FA experts need to stop pretending (and posturing) about the minimal work required to give effective feedback. It's a lot of work and we will need help.

From our vantage point as teacher educators, it should be clear by now that we are most interested in where novices begin with specific classroom assessment practices and where the FA moves can lead them in the teaching profession. We watch day by day as they learn to cope with the gap between what they hear in the credential program and what they see in their teaching placements. For many, how they see their binning options are largely determined by what they observe in their placements: "My mentor doesn't do it, why should I?" For others, binning options are a source of anxiety tied to their status as nontenured teachers: "How can you expect me to 'choose' to become a formative assessor when I don't feel particularly free to do what I want in the classroom?" Still others feel whipped around by all the voices clamoring for teachers' attention today: "You are talking 'evidence-based practices' while I am trying to survive day by day." Never forget, teachers have to answer to all sorts of people—from politicians who expect results to businessmen who have products to sell. Add demanding parents and angry taxpayers into the mix—and teachers, understandably, feel pressured to cave in no matter what the research tells us.

Instead of becoming alienated from our teachers in training or the vast majority of unsung teacher-heroes who are working to master formative assessment moves, we must acknowledge the depth of the classroom assessment struggle. Experts in formative assessment (ourselves included) must confront the powerful sway that binning for grading has over everyone, even for those who wish to try another path. We must confront and address the tension between binning for grading and binning for feedback, between the uses of hard and soft data, between "commodities" (as Winger calls them) that can be exchanged in the education marketplace and those that cannot.

It would be irresponsible and all-too-easy to wish away the dominance of the *A* to *F* system and the power of grading, and to ignore the hold grading has over teachers' assessment practices.

We have come full circle with this seventh formative assessment move, binning. If posing questions is the alpha, then binning is the omega move for the skilled formative assessor. Yes, priming is key, but it always supports and shores up the other FA moves.

As we close this chapter and think about what's next, we offer a few recommendations. Some of these suggestions will require new approaches to seemingly intractable problems. Others will demand more collaboration between preservice and inservice stakeholders, where pooling expertise across a continuum of preparation, training, and professional development modules is at a premium. Working smart on teacher learning progressions that link these stakeholders will require careful, collaborative planning and follow through. Too many university research projects have suffered from this disconnect.

It would help beginning formative assessors if educational researchers freely shared the latest research on learning progressions—not only those aimed at how students learn but also how teachers learn. If we had access to a compendium of K–12 learning progressions that might guide instruction and assessment, we would have signposts and footholds in the content areas we teach. Luckily we have a few research-based examples of these progressions in STEM. In the science curriculum that deals with why things sink or float, for example, teachers can look into common student misconceptions related to mass, volume, and density. In chemistry, probability, and a few other STEM subjects, we have a better grasp on how student understanding progresses with conceptually difficult material at different grade levels.

But let's not oversell the case for learning progressions (the latest craze in "meta" binning) for our students or teachers. It turns out for music teachers, physical education teachers, foreign language teachers, art teachers, social science teachers, and history teachers, we know very little or haven't shared very much about advances in learning progressions research. Despite the best efforts of curriculum companies and test providers, we are far from having worked out how particular binning strategies are truly formative for students—or teachers.

How to build this teacher knowledge of different students' learning progressions, in relation to different topics and with different levels of background knowledge, is one of the most important formative assessment challenges. By failing to bin potentially productive responses (based on research on "misconceptions" or "p-prims" or "facets" in science, for example), we may circumvent the power of formative assessment to uncover difficult learning steps or bottlenecks that block student understanding. We agree teachers need to know, through practical training and more careful attention on student thinking and rich classroom learning experiences, where kids typically get stuck and why. Research on learning progressions is part of the puzzle. But only part. It takes time in the classroom and school site for teachers to gather these insights, make connections, and see patterns to improve their assessment moves.

Years of teaching, combined with moments for reflective professional development within a school, are more likely to reveal patterns and processes in student learning. Herman and colleagues (2006, 2015) have found positive relationships between teachers' pedagogical content knowledge (PCK) and their FA practices. So there is hope for deepening formative assessment's role in teacher preparation and professional development settings. Different subject area specialists and instructional coaches can help by providing resources that honor binning-for-feedback strategies. We need to develop more powerful binning strategies—with conceptual tools like learning progressions—but buzzwords and a few scattered examples are no substitute for the work ahead. It is unlikely we can use ready-made solutions to solve the problems of blending instructional and assessment practice until we know which moves are in play and which have yet to be observed. Money matters, as does training and support, to advance the FA cause. Will anyone hear the rallying cry?

In this chapter, we examined binning moves, tools, and practices so you could start to reflect on your own assessment and instructional practice. Although we devoted some attention to binning for grading, much of the literature speaks for itself, and does not require further exploration. Instead, we focused more on binning for feedback and tried to offer examples of minor and ancillary moves that carry the work forward in this area of high-leverage practice.

Checks for Understanding

We can all improve the binning that happens in our learning environments. Deliberate practice can help. These checks for understanding can guide individual and community efforts to take your binning for feedback to new levels. You can use the prompts in Warm-Up Prompts as self-checks and ideas in Try-Now Tasks as conversation starters and exercises for independent-study or group work.

Warm-Up Prompts:
- Why bin? Use a word web.
- Do students need to understand the different purposes (such as grading and feedback) of binning moves in the classroom? If so, how can we prime them for either type of binning while distinguishing the two? Make a list of agreements so your students will know what to expect from each modality—when, and why.
- Describe the difference between binning for grading and binning for feedback. Are there any similarities? Use a Venn diagram.
- What are the qualities of formative feedback? Use a word web. Then probe on the meaning of each node (e.g., timely or specific).
- Does "graded" feedback work? For whom? Cite evidence to support your response.
- Does "ungraded" feedback work? For whom? Cite evidence to support your response.

Try-Now Tasks:
1. Write the word "grades" in the middle of your whiteboard. Ask your students, "What comes to mind when you hear the word *grades*?" Tag responses on the board. (30 seconds or less).

2. Put "feedback" in the middle of the board. Ask your students, "What comes to mind when you hear the word *feedback*?" Tag responses on the board. (30 seconds or less).

3. Explain that it's time for a word web. Remind everyone that word webs are warm-ups that help us to start thinking about a topic. Put "grades" and "feedback" in the middle of the board. Give everyone two sticky notes to write down what comes to mind for each concept. Have students post their sticky notes near the concept it is associated with. Reflect on the similarities and differences between both word webs.

4. Think of a time you got an *F* on an assignment/quiz/test. Did the grade provide feedback to you? How so? What were your next steps based on the grade? Be specific.

5. Give an example of a binning-for-feedback move you made this week. What worked well? What did not work so well with this move? Make a list of one or two next steps to better prime for binning for feedback. Pick one activity you can do in fewer than five minutes to have students practice feedback with a peer. Consider using a scaffold such as a scoring guide.

6. Ask teachers to move into Four Corners. Explain that the objective of this activity is to help teachers and staff to teach students in *all classes* about the value of formative feedback. The guiding question: what is needed to prepare for binning for feedback this academic year?

Corner 1: Warm-ups and icebreakers about binning for feedback

Corner 2: Tools, scaffolds, and technologies to support binning for feedback

Corner 3: Statements and sentence starters to prime binning for feedback

Corner 4: Values and beliefs about binning for feedback

Each group assigns a leader and scribe, then creates a list of examples related to its theme. (Will you use scoring guides? Annotations via electronic documents? Rubrics with a comments/next steps section?) The groups combine their four lists into a single visual and discuss. Be sure to discuss what to do when learning communities get stuck, or fall down, or forget agreements.

Challenge task: Have one person in the group explain why a particular procedure may support effective priming for formative feedback in the classroom. Allow another person to push back and say why these moves may not work—for whom and why?

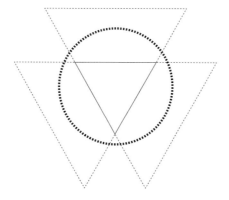

Conclusion

Traditional formative assessment in K–12 classrooms includes do-nows, polling technologies, and even quizzes. But FA is more than an interim assessment event or another high-tech tool for more efficient grading.

Throughout this book, we've heard from teachers who demonstrate that planning for, making, and reflecting upon FA moves is at the core of becoming a formative assessor. Formative assessors rely on verbs over nouns when thinking through classroom assessment practices. They can be seen *launching, orchestrating,* and *eliciting* student understanding in real time during the classroom period. They fully engage their students in speaking and listening routines, seeking collaboration and shared understandings in the classroom learning environment.

Formative assessors use the repertoire of moves to uncover prior knowledge, check for understanding, and delve deeper into misconceptions rather than to try to merely correct them. Formative assessors anticipate bottlenecks in the curriculum and welcome when their students get "stuck" in conceptually difficult material. They see the FA moves framework as a powerful way to make learning visible, especially in culturally, linguistically, and economically diverse classrooms.

Formative assessors are optimists and realists. FA moves require teachers to see the potential in all students for being able to deeply understand content and the potential in themselves to guide students to understanding. Teachers on the path to becoming formative assessors know that by consciously enacting multiple combinations of moves—over time and with practice—they get better at doing FA, and consequently at improving student learning outcomes.

Next Steps, Moving Forward

The FA moves can be stitched together in a multicolored patchwork quilt that becomes uniquely your own over time. Each patchwork block—a potential repertoire of moves—represents the possibilities for learning envisioned by teachers and students in a particular classroom, in a particular unit of instruction, with a particular lesson. It is up to you to design, assemble, and weave these moves together for maximum effect.

No one can prescribe or predict what your journey will be with the FA moves or what it will look like when you enact them each day in your school. Rather than tell you what to do, we have tried to share what we have learned so far on our journey with teachers, mentors, and colleagues.

Formative assessment will always be entwined with good teaching. It will be a part of positive, open, equitable classroom learning environments. It will draw from educational psychology and the science of learning. And it can be an integral part of your growth as a teacher if you commit to practicing the moves over time.

Where We Stand

Paul Black and his colleagues (2003) wrote, "Overall teachers seem to be trapped in a 'no-man's land' between their new commitment to formative assessment and the different, often contradictory, demands of the external test system" (p. 21). He presciently added, "Their formative use of summative tests had enabled them to move the frontier significantly, but further territory seemed unassailable."

We believe that there are new assessment and learning possibilities on the horizon. There is no reason to get stuck in no man's land—or between the worlds of formative and summative assessment. We are not condemned to cycle through stages of optimism, hypocrisy, complacency, and cynicism as we learn to cope with the gap between authentic assessment for learning and the reality of high-stakes testing. The cult of point spreads and the worship of normal distributions and benchmark bar graphs is ubiquitous. So-called better, faster, cheaper grading technologies and "assessment solutions" are proliferating across the educational system. But these trends need not exhaust our imaginations nor our efforts as educators committed to student learning in our classrooms.

There are many ways to deal with the demands of social and political forces that pressure our schools. Rather than get cynical or complacent, the message of this book has been to remind ourselves of the real work ahead: make a move and don't give up.

Part of the reason the book ends with the chapter on binning is to remind everyone that the power of formative assessment lies in generating and sustaining feedback for learning. We argue that binning for grading and binning for feedback is something we do every day, and to that extent, it is something that is within our immediate sphere of influence. For those who learn to do both well, finding the balance will be the challenge, and we hope this book aids in that quest.

Unfortunately, the literature on building, nurturing, and sustaining a formative assessment culture in today's classrooms is thin. We need more progress maps tied to teacher and student learning trajectories, more case studies about the nuance and flavors of each move during encounters with different subject matter content, and more stories from and testimonies by teachers about growth over time in these high-leverage practices.

There is more work to be done. Much to learn about teachers and teaching. And that is more than half the promise of becoming a formative assessor—on your terms, in your time.

What's on the Horizon

We promised at the outset of the journey to becoming a formative assessor not to inundate you with "how to" lists and magic formulas. So rather than tell you what to do or try, we instead shared some findings from our work with different teachers, in diverse subject disciplines over the years.

Employing a teacher learning progressions framework, we educators and researchers have a choice of where to direct attention and effort. When teachers shift from lamenting what their students can't do to focusing on changing their own thoughts and actions, they make leaps and bounds in their growth as formative assessors.

Let's agree as we go forward that our journey in becoming formative assessors has just begun, there will always be ways for us to go deeper and get better at a particular practice, and we can model for our students how we, too, learn daily as professionals.

Incremental change is good. Sustained commitment to improving our pedagogical practices, lesson by lesson, is even better.

What if your formative assessment-driven lessons were just like first drafts? *What if* beginning to improve your formative assessment practice required others in the community (teacher educators, school administrators, educational policymakers) to acknowledge your ongoing development toward becoming a professional educator in your school? *What if* all the stakeholders in education started seeing teachers ("expert and novice" or "experienced and newbie") as potential formative assessors who can benefit from positive, specific, timely, and content-related feedback on possible next steps for revising lessons? This paradigm shift might change the conversation and remind us what is ultimately worth fighting for—teacher and student growth.

Formative assessment is a systematic process to continuously gather evidence about learning. Labeling teachers as "novice" or "ineffective" or "needs improvement" is unlikely to produce much insight or improvement in the practices we've outlined in this book. We should use data on teachers as learners—not for summative evaluation but to improve teaching—to identify a teacher's current level of learning (about each of the FA moves) and to help the teacher reach the desired learning goal in concert with others.

Mastery of the formative assessment moves is a worthy professional goal for teachers, one grounded in evidence-based research on what makes a difference in student outcomes. In a formative assessment-rich school culture, teachers are active participants with their mentors and colleagues. They willingly share professional learning goals and understandings about how their own learning is progressing, what next steps they need to take, and how to take them in a community.

We follow Sadler's insight that the true purpose of formative assessment is to narrow the gap between where, in this case, teachers currently are with a particular move, where they can go with coaching and support, and how to narrow the spread between what is actual and what is possible "at the next level." Following Vygotsky's lead with the notion of the zone of proximal development, Sadler (1989) presciently writes of *all* students:

> If the gap is perceived as too large by a student [teacher], the goal may be unattainable, resulting in a sense of failure and discouragement on the part of the student [teacher]. Similarly, if the gap is perceived as too "small," closing it might not be worth any individual effort. Hence, to borrow from Goldilocks, formative assessment is a process that needs to identify the "just right gap." (p. 130)

To close the just-right gaps in your own teaching and learning, you must now take the leap in your classrooms and incorporate the moves into your practice. Throughout this book, serving as guides on the side, we have explored pathways to uncovering student thinking, to realizing the power of student ideas, beliefs, and feelings, and to unlocking the secrets of learning. The rest is up to you, to become what you know you can be, a formative assessor.

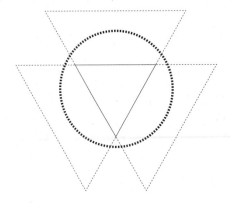

References

Abedi, J. (2010). Research and recommendations for formative assessment with ELLs. In H. L. Andrade & G. J. Cizek (Eds.), *Handbook of formative assessment* (pp. 181–197). New York: Routledge.

Abedi, J., & Herman, J. (2010). Assessing English language learners' opportunity to learn mathematics: Issues and limitations. *Teachers College Record, 112*(3), 723–746.

Aguirre-Muñoz, Z., & Baker, E. L. (1997). *Improving the equity and validity of assessment-based information systems* (Report No. 462). Los Angeles: National Center for Research on Evaluation, Standards, and Student Testing.

Airasian, P. W. (1991). Perspectives on measurement instruction. *Educational Measurement: Issues and Practice, 10*(1), 13–16.

Alexander, R. J. (2006). *Towards dialogic teaching: Rethinking classroom talk* (3rd ed.). Thirsk: Dialogos.

Alonzo, A. C., & Steedle, J. T. (2009). Developing and assessing a force and motion learning progression. *Science Education, 93*(3), 389–421.

Andrade, H. L. (2013). Classroom assessment in the context of learning theory and research. In J. McMillan (Ed.), *SAGE handbook of research of classroom assessment* (pp. 17–34). Thousand Oaks, CA: SAGE.

Anyon, Jean. (1980). Social class and the hidden curriculum of work. *Journal of Education, 162*(1), 67–92.

Apple, M. W. (1979). What correspondence theories of the hidden curriculum miss. *The Review of Education Pedagogy Cultural Studies, 5*(2), 101–112.

Apple, M. W. (2004). *Ideology and curriculum* (3rd ed.) New York: Routledge.

Armendariz, F., & Umbreit, J. (1999). Using active responding to reduce disruptive behavior in a general education classroom. *Journal of Positive Behavior Interventions, 1*(3), 152–158.

Artino, A. R. Jr. (2008). Cognitive load theory and the role of learner experience: An abbreviated review for educational practitioners. *AACE Journal, 16*(4), 425–439.

Ateh, C. M. (2015). Science teachers' elicitation practices: Insights for formative assessment. *Educational Assessment, 20*(2), 112–131.

Atwell, N. (1987). *In the middle: Writing, reading, and learning with adolescents.* Portsmouth, NH: Heinemann.

Austin, S., & McCann, R. (1992). *Here's another arbitrary grade for your collection: A statewide study of grading policies.* [Monograph]. Retrieved from http://files.eric.ed.gov/fulltext/ED343944.pdf

Ball, D. L. (1993). With an eye on the mathematical horizon: Dilemmas of teaching elementary school mathematics. *The Elementary School Journal, 93*(4), 373–397.

Ball, D. L. & Cohen, D. K. (1999). Developing practice, developing practitioners: Toward a practice-based theory of professional education. In L. Darling-Hammond & G. Sykes (Eds.), *Teaching as the Learning Profession* (pp. 3–31). San Francisco: Jossey-Bass.

Ball, D. L., & Forzani, F. M. (2011). Teaching skillful teaching. *The Effective Educator, 68*(4), 40–46.

Ball, D. L., Thames, M., & Phelps, G. (2008). Content knowledge for teaching: What makes it special? *Journal of Teacher Education, 59*(5), 389–407.

Ball, S. J. (Ed.). (2013). *Foucault and education: Disciplines and knowledge.* London: Routledge.

Barnes, J. (1982). *Aristotle.* Oxford: Oxford University Press.

Barnette, J. J., Walsh, J. A., Orletsky, S. R., & Sattes, B. D. (1995). Staff development for improved classroom questioning and learning. *Research in the Schools, 2*(1), 1–10.

Bennett, R. E. (2011). Formative assessment: A critical review. *Assessment in Education: Principles, Policy & Practice, 18*(1), 5–25.

Bennett, R. E. (2014). Preparing for the future: What educational assessment must do. *Teachers College Record, 116*(11), 1–18.

Bensman, D. (2000). *Central Park East and its graduates: Learning by heart.* New York: Teachers College Press.

Biggs, J., & Collis, K. (1982). *A system for evaluating learning outcomes: The SOLO taxonomy.* New York: Academic Press.

Black, P., Harrison, C., Lee, C., Marshall, B., & Wiliam, D. (2003). *Assessment for learning: Putting it into practice.* London: Open University Press.

Black, P., Harrison, C., Lee, C., Marshall, B., & Wiliam, D. (2003). The nature of value of formative assessment for learning. *Improving schools, 6*(3), 7–22.

Black, P., Harrison, C., Lee, C., Marshall, B., & Wiliam, D. (2004a). *Working inside the black box: Assessment for learning in the classroom.* London: Kings College.

Black, P., Harrison, C., Lee, C., Marshall, B., and Wiliam, D. (2004b). Working inside the black box: Assessment for learning in the classroom. *Phi Delta Kappan, 86*(1), 8–21.

Black, P., & Wiliam, D. (1998). Assessment and classroom learning. *Assessment in education, 5*(1), 7–74.

Black, P., & Wiliam, D. (2009). Developing the theory of formative assessment. *Educational Assessment, Evaluation and Accountability* (formerly: Journal of Personnel Evaluation in Education), *21*(1), 5–31.

Black, P., Wilson, M., & Yao, S. Y. (2011). Road maps for learning: A guide to the navigation of learning progressions. *Measurement: Interdisciplinary Research & Perspective, 9*(2–3), 71–123.

Blatchford, P. (1997). Pupils' self assessments of academic attainment at 7, 11 and 16 years: Effects of sex and ethnic group. *British Journal of Educational Psychology, 67*(2), 169–184.

Bloom, B. S., Hastings, J. T., & Madaus, G. F. (Eds.). (1971). *Handbook on the formative and summative evaluation of student learning.* New York: McGraw-Hill.

Boaler, J. (2002). Learning from teaching: Exploring the relationship between reform curriculum and equity. *Journal for Research In Mathematics Education, 33*(4), 239–258.

Boaler, J., & Humphreys, C. (2005). *Connecting mathematical ideas: Middle school video cases to support teaching and learning* (Vol. 1). Portsmouth, NH: Heinemann.

Bodrova, E. & Leong, D. J. (2007). *Tools of the mind.* Columbus, OH: Prentice Hall.

Boniecki, K. A., & Moore, S. (2003). Breaking the silence: Using a token economy to reinforce classroom participation. *Teaching of Psychology, 30*(3), 224–227.

Bridges, D. (1979). *Education, democracy & discussion.* Albany, NY: Delmar.

Briggs, D. C., Alonzo, A. C., Schwab, C., & Wilson, M. (2006). Diagnostic assessment with ordered multiple-choice items. *Educational Assessment, 11*(1), 33–63.

Brookhart, S. M., & Nitko, A. J. (2006). *Educational assessment of students.* (5th ed.) New York: Pearson.

Brophy, J. E., & Evertson, C. M. (1976). *Learning from teaching: A developmental perspective.* New York: Pearson, Allyn and Bacon.

Brophy, J., & Good, T. (1985). Teacher behavior and student achievement. In M. C. Wittrock (Ed.), *Third handbook of research on teaching.* New York: Macmillan.

Brown, A. L., & Campione, J. C. (1998). Designing a community of young learners: Theoretical and practical lessons. In N. Lambert & and B. McCombs (Eds.), *How students learn: Reforming schools through learner-centered education.* (pp. 153–186). Washington, DC: American Psychological Association.

Burns, D. D. (1980). *Feeling good: The new mood therapy.* New York: Avon Books.

Butler, R. (1988). Enhancing and undermining intrinsic motivation. *British Journal of Educational Psychology, 58*(1), 1–14.

Carlsen, W. S. (1992). Closing down the conversation: Discouraging student talk on unfamiliar science content. *Journal of Classroom Interaction, 27*(2), 15–21.

Carlsen, W. S. (2015). Closing down the conversation: Discouraging student talk on unfamiliar science content. *Journal of Classroom Interaction, 50*(1), 73–84.

Casteel, J. D., & Stahl, R. J. (1973). *The social science observation record: Theoretical construct and pilot studies.* [Monograph]. Retrieved from http://files.eric.ed.gov/fulltext/ED101002.pdf

Cervone, B., & Cushman, K. (2014). *Learning by heart: The power of social-emotional learning in secondary schools. Executive summary: What kids can do.* Retrieved from Center for Youth Voice in Policy and Practice website: https://edpolicy.stanford.edu/publications/pubs/1176

Chin, C., & Osborne, J. (2010). Students' questions and discursive interaction: Their impact on argumentation during collaborative group discussions in science. *Journal of Research in Science Teaching, 47*(7), 883–908.

Chinn, C., & Anderson, R. (1998). The structure of discussions intended to promote reasoning. *Teachers College Record, 100*(2), 315–368.

Chittenden, E., & Wallace, V. (January 01, 1991). Reforming School Assessment Practices: The Case of Central Park East. *Planning and Changing, 22,* 141–146.

Christenbury, L., & Kelly, P. P. (1983). *Questioning: A path to critical thinking* [Monograph]. Retrieved from http://files.eric.ed.gov/fulltext/ED226372.pdf

Clark, C., Gage, N., Marx, R., Peterson, P., Stayrook, N., & Winne, P. (1979). A factorial experiment on teacher structuring, soliciting and reacting. *Journal of Education Psychology, 71*(4), 534–552.

Clements, D. H., & Sarama, J. (2014). *Learning and teaching early math: The learning trajectories approach.* London: Routledge.

Coffey, J. E., Edwards, A. R., & Finkelstein, C. (2010). Dynamics of disciplinary understandings and practices of attending to student thinking in elementary teacher education. In *Proceedings of the 9th International Conference of the Learning Sciences, Volume 1* (pp. 1040–1047).

Coffey, J. E., Hammer, D., Levin, D. M., & Grant, T. (2011). The missing disciplinary substance of formative assessment. *Journal of Research in Science Teaching, 48*(10), 1109–1136.

Common Core State Standards Initiative (CCSSI). (2010). *Common Core State Standards for Mathematics.* Washington, DC: National Governors Association Center for Best Practices and the Council of Chief State School Officers.

Cora, R., & Liyan, S. (2013). The impact of using clickers technology on classroom instruction: Students' and teachers' perspectives. *Canadian Journal of Action Research, 14*(1), 21–37.

Corbett, H. D., & Wilson, B. L. (1991). *Testing, reform, and rebellion.* Norwood, NJ: Ablex.

Corno, L., & Snow, R. E. (1986). Adapting teaching to individual differences among learners. In M. C. Wittrock (Ed.), *Handbook of research on teaching* (3rd ed., pp. 605–629). New York: Macmillan.

Cuban, L. (1990). Reforming again, again, and again. *Educational Researcher, 19*(1), 3–13.

Cuban, L. (1993). *How teachers taught: Constancy and change in American classrooms, 1890–1990.* Research on Teaching Monograph Series. New York: Teachers College Press.

Cuban, L. (2009). *Oversold and underused: Computers in the classroom.* Cambridge, MA: Harvard University Press.

Dallimore, E. J., Hertenstein, J. H., & Platt, M. B. (2012). Impact of cold-calling on student voluntary participation. *Journal of Management Education, 37*(3), 305–341.

Damon, W. (2008). *The path to purpose: Helping our children find their calling in life.* New York: Free Press.

Darling-Hammond, L. (1996). The right to learn and the advancement of teaching: Research, policy, and practice for democratic education. *Educational Researcher, 25*(6), 5–17.

Darling-Hammond, L. (1997). *The right to learn: A blueprint for creating schools that work.* San Francisco: Jossey-Bass.

Darling-Hammond, L. (2006). Securing the right to learn: Policy and practice for powerful teaching and learning. *Educational Researcher, 35*(7), 13–24.

Darling-Hammond, L., Ancess, J., & Falk, B. (1995). *Authentic assessment in action: Studies of schools and students at work.* New York: Teachers College Press.

Darling-Hammond, L., Ancess, J., & Ort, S. (2002). Reinventing high school: Outcomes of the Coalition Campus Schools Project. *American Educational Research Journal, 39*(3) 639–673.

Davis, B. (1997). Listening for differences: An evolving conception of mathematics teaching. *Journal for Research in Mathematics Education, 28*(3), 355.

Dawson, T. L., & University of California–Berkeley. (1998). *"A good education is…": A life-span investigation of developmental and conceptual features of evaluative reasoning about education.* Retrieved from ProQuest Dissertations and Theses Full Text: The Humanities and Social Sciences Collection (Order No. 9922801).

Deci, E. L., & Ryan, R. M. (2000). The "what" and "why" of goal pursuits: Human needs and the self-determination of behavior. *Psychological Inquiry, 11*(4), 227–268.

Delpit, L. (1988). The silenced dialogue: Power and pedagogy in educating other people's children. *Harvard Educational Review, 58*(3), 280–299.

Delpit, L. (1995). *Other people's children: Cultural conflict in the classroom.* New York: The New Press.

Dewey, J. (1900/1990). *The school and society.* Chicago: University of Chicago Press.

Dewey, J. (1902). *The child and the curriculum.* Chicago: University of Chicago Press.

Dewey, J. (1916). *Democracy and education.* New York: Macmillan.

Dewey, J. (1920). *Reconstruction in philosophy.* New York: H. Holt and Company.

Dillon, J. T. (1978). Using questions to depress student thought. *The School Review, 87*(1), 50–63.

Dillon, J. T. (1979). Alternatives to questioning. *The High School Journal, 62*(5), 217–222.

Dillon, J. T. (1981). To question and not to question during discussion: II. Non-questioning techniques. *Journal of Teacher Education, 32*(6), 15–20.

Dillon, J. T. (1983). *Teaching and the art of questioning* [Monograph]. Retrieved from http://files.eric.ed.gov/

Dillon, J. T. (1984). Research on questioning and discussion. *Educational Leadership, 42*(3), 50–56.

DiSessa, A. A. (1983). Phenomenology and the evolution of intuition. In D. Gentner & L. Albert (Eds.), *Mental models* (pp. 15–33). New York: Psychology Press.

Dobbs, D. (2011). Beautiful brains. *National Geographic, 220*(4), 36–59.

Duckor, B. (2017, April). Got grit? Maybe… *Phi Delta Kappan, 98*(7), 61–66.

Duckor, B. & Holmberg, C. (in press). Increasing students' academic language acquisition and use: A case for supporting teachers to code instructional video through a "formative assessment moves" lens. In S. B. Martens & M. M. Caskey (Series Ed.), *The Handbook of Research in Middle Level Education: Preparing middle level educators for 21st century schools: Enduring beliefs, changing times, evolving practices.* Washington, DC: AERA Press.

Duckor, B., Holmberg, C., & Rossi Becker, J. (2017). Making moves: Formative assessment in mathematics. *Mathematics Teaching in the Middle School, 22*(6), 334–342.

Duckor, B., & Perlstein, D. (2014). Assessing habits of mind: Teaching to the test at Central Park East Secondary School. *Teachers College Record, 116*(2), 1–33.

Duhigg, C. (2012). *The power of habit: Why we do what we do in life and business.* London: Random House.

Dweck, C. & Bush, E. (1976). Sex differences in learned helplessness: I. Differential debilitation with peer and adult evaluators. *Developmental Psychology, 12*(2), 147–156.

Dweck, C. S. (2010). Mind-sets. *Principal Leadership, 10*(5), 26–29.

Easton, L. B. (2009). *Protocols for professional learning.* Alexandria, VA: ASCD.

Eccles, J., Lord, S., & Midgley, C. (1991). What are we doing to early adolescents? The impact of educational contexts on early adolescents. *American Journal of Education, 99*(4), 521–542.

Eccles, J., Midgley, C., & Adler, T. F. (1984). Grade-related changes in the school environment: Effects on achievement motivation. In J. G. Nicholls (Ed.), *The development of achievement motivation* (pp. 283–331). Greenwich, CT: JAI Press.

Elias, M. (2004). Strategies to infuse social and emotional learning into academics. In J. Zins, R. Weissberg, M. Wang, and H. Walberg (Eds.), *Building academic success on social emotional learning: What does research say?* (pp. 113–134). New York: Teachers College Press.

Erdogan, I., & Campbell, T., (2008). Teacher questioning and interaction patterns in classrooms facilitated with differing levels of constructivist teaching practices. *International Journal of Science Education, 30*(14), 1891–1914.

Farrington, C.A., Roderick, M., Allensworth, E., Nagaoka, J., Keyes, T. S., Johnson, D. W., & Beechum, N. O. (2012). *Teaching adolescents to become learners. The role of noncognitive factors in shaping school performance: A critical literature review.* Chicago: University of Chicago Consortium on Chicago School Research.

Finn, J. D., & Cox, D. (1992). Participation and withdrawal among fourth-grade pupils. *American Educational Research Journal, 29*(1), 141–162.

Flavell, J. H. (2004). Theory of mind development: Retrospect and prospect. *Merrill-Palmer Quarterly, 50*(3), 274–290.

Fliegel, S. (1994). Debbie Meier and the dawn of Central Park East. *City Journal.* Retrieved September 21, 2011 from http://www.city-journal.org/article01.php?aid=1414

Francis, E. (1982). *Learning to discuss.* Edinburgh: Moray House College of Education.

Franke, M. L., & Kazemi, E. (2001). Learning to teach mathematics: Focus on student thinking. *Theory into Practice, 40*(2), 102–109.

Freire, P. (1970). *Pedagogy of the oppressed.* New York: Continuum.

Frisbie, D. A., & Waltman, K. K. (1992). Developing a personal grading plan. *Educational Measurement: Issues and Practice, 11*(3), 35–42.

Frykholm, J. A. (1999). The impact of reform: Challenges for mathematics teacher preparation. *Journal of Mathematics Teacher Education, 2*(1), 79–105.

Fullan, M. G. (1990). Change processes in secondary schools: Toward a more fundamental agenda. In M. W. McLaughlin, J. E. Talbert, & N. Bascia (Eds.), *The contexts of teaching in secondary schools: Teachers' realities* (pp. 224–255). New York: Teachers College Press.

Furtak, E. M., Ruiz-Primo, M. A., Shemwell, J. T., Ayala, C., Brandon, P. R., Shavelson, R. J., & Yin, Y. (2008). On the fidelity of implementing embedded formative assessment and its relation to student learning. *Applied Measurement in Education, 21*(4), 360–389.

Gall, M. (1984). Synthesis of research on teachers' questioning. *Educational Leadership, 42*(3), 40–47.

Gall, M. D., Ward, B. A., Berliner, D. C., Cahen, L. S., Winne, P. H., Elashoff, J. D., & Stanton, G. C. (1978). Effects of questioning techniques and recitation on student learning. *American Educational Research Journal, 15*(2), 175–199.

Gardner, H. (1983). *Frames of mind: The theory of multiple intelligences.* New York: Basic Books.

Gardner, H. (1985). *The mind's new science: A history of the cognitive revolution.* New York: Basic Books.

Garmston, R., & Wellman, B. (1999). *The adaptive school: A sourcebook for developing collaborative groups.* Norwood, MA: Christopher Gordon.

Gay, G. (2010). *Culturally responsive teaching: Theory, research, and practice.* Teachers College Press.

Gayle, B. M., Preiss, R. W., Burrell, N., & Allen, M. (Eds.). (2009). *Classroom communication and instructional processes: Advances through meta-analysis.* London: Routledge.

Gladwell, M. (2008). *Outliers: The secret of success.* New York: Little Brown.

Glaser, R., Chudowsky, N., & Pellegrino, J. W. (2001). *Knowing what students know: The science and design of educational assessment.* Washington, DC: National Academy Press.

Glover, D., Miller, D., Averis, D., & Door, V. (2007). The evolution of an effective pedagogy for teachers using the interactive whiteboard in mathematics and modern languages: An empirical analysis from the secondary sector. *Learning, Media and Technology, 32*(1), 5–20.

Goffman, E. (1974). *Frame analysis: An essay on the organization of experience.* Cambridge, MA: Harvard University Press.

Gold, J. (Producer & director), & Lanzoni, M. (Ed.). (1993). *Graduation by portfolio: Central Park East Secondary School* [Motion picture]. Available from New York Post Production, 29th Street Video Inc., at http://vimeo.com/13992931

Grant, M., Tamim, S., Brown, D., Sweeney, J., Ferguson, F., & Jones, L. (2015). Teaching and learning with mobile computing devices: Case study in K–12 classrooms. *Techtrends: Linking Research & Practice to Improve Learning, 59*(4), 32–45.

Gray, L. S. (1993). *Large group discussion in a 3rd/4th grade classroom: A sociolinguistic case study.* Retrieved from ProQuest Dissertations and Theses Full Text: The Humanities and Social Sciences Collection (Order No. 9318201).

Graybill, O., & Easton, L. B. (2015, April). "The art of dialogue." *Educational Leadership, 72*(7). Retrieved from http://www.ascd.org/publications/educational-leadership/apr15/vol72/num07/The-Art-of-Dialogue.aspx

Grossman, P. L. (2005). Research on pedagogical approaches in teacher education. In M. Cochran-Smith & K. Zeichner (Eds.), *Studying teacher education* (pp. 425–476). Washington, DC: American Educational Research Association.

Grossman, P., & McDonald, M. (2008). Back to the future: Directions for research in teaching and teacher education. *American Educational Research Journal, 45*(1), 184–205.

Guskey, T. R. (1994). Making the grade: What benefits students? *Educational Leadership, 52*(2), 14–20.

Guskey, T. R. (2002). Computerized gradebooks and the myth of objectivity. *Phi Delta Kappan, 83*(10), 775.

Guskey, T. R. (2004). Are zeros your ultimate weapon? *Education Digest: Essential Readings Condensed for Quick Review, 70*(3), 31–35.

Gutiérrez, K., & Rogoff, B. (2003). Cultural ways of learning. *Educational Researcher, 35*(5), 19–25.

Hakuta, K. (2013). *Assessment of content and language in light of the new standards: Challenges and opportunities for English learners.* Princeton, NJ: The Gordon Commission on the Future of Assessment in Education. Retrieved from http://www.gordoncommission.org/rsc/pdf/hakuta_assessment_content_language_standards_challenges_opportunities.pdf

Hammer, D. (1997). Discovery teaching, discovery learning. *Cognition and Instruction, 15*(4), 485–529.

Harmin, M. (1998). *Strategies to inspire active learning: Complete handbook.* White Plains, NY: Inspiring Strategy Institute.

Harris, L. R., Brown, G. T., & Harnett, J. A. (2015). Analysis of New Zealand primary and secondary student peer- and self-assessment comments: Applying Hattie and Timperley's feedback model. *Assessment in Education: Principles, Policy & Practice, 22*(2), 265–281.

Hattie, J., (1992). Measuring the effects of schooling. *Australian Journal of Education, 36*(1), 5–13.

Hattie, J. (2009). *Visible learning: A synthesis of over 800 meta-analyses relating to achievement.* New York: Routledge.

Hattie, J. (2012). *Visible learning for teachers: Maximizing impact on learning.* London: Routledge.

Hattie, J., Biggs, J., & Purdie, N. (1996). Effects of learning skills interventions on student learning: A meta-analysis. *Review of Educational Research, 66*(2), 99–136.

Hattie, J., & Timperley, H. (2007). The power of feedback. *Review of Educational Research, 77*(1), 81–112.

Hemphill, L. (1986). *Context and conversation style: A reappraisal of social class differences in speech.* Retrieved from ProQuest Dissertations and Theses Full Text: The Humanities and Social Sciences Collection (Order No. 8620703).

Henning, J. E., McKeny, T., Foley, G. D., & Balong, M. (2012). Mathematics discussions by design: creating opportunities for purposeful participation. *Journal of Mathematics Teacher Education, 15*(6), 453–479.

Heritage, M. (2007). Formative assessment: What teachers need to do and know. *Phi Delta Kappan, 89*(2), 140–145.

Heritage, M., (2008). *Learning progressions: Supporting instruction and formative assessment.* Retrieved from Council of Chief State School Officers website: http://www.ccsso.org/Documents/2008/Learning_Progressions_Supporting_2008.pdf

Heritage, M. (2010). *Formative assessment: Making it happen in the classroom.* Thousand Oaks, CA: Corwin.

Herl, H. E., Baker, E. L., & Niemi, D. (1996). Construct validation of an approach to modeling cognitive structure of U.S. history knowledge. *Journal of Educational Research, 89*(4), 206–218.

Herman, J., & Baker, E. (2005). Making benchmark testing work. *Educational Leadership, 63*(3), 48–54.

Herman, J., Osmundson, E., Ayala, C., Schneider, S., & Timms, M. (2006). The nature and impact of teachers' formative assessment practices. CSE Technical Report 703. *National Center for Research on Evaluation, Standards, and Student Testing (CRESST).*

Herman, J., Osmundson, E., Dai, Y., Ringstaff, C., & Timms, M. (2015). Investigating the dynamics of formative assessment: Relationships between teacher knowledge, assessment practice and learning. *Assessment in Education: Principles, Policy & Practice, 22*(3), 344–367.

Higgins, S., Beauchamp, G., & Miller, D. (2007). Reviewing the literature on interactive whiteboards. *Learning, Media and Technology, 32*(3), 213–225.

Hills, J. R. (1991). Apathy concerning grading and testing. *Phi Delta Kappan, 72*(7), 540–545.

Hollander, E. & Marcia, J. (1970). Parental determinants of peer orientation and self-orientation among preadolescents. *Developmental Psychology, 2*(2), 292–302.

Hollingsworth, P. M. (1982). Questioning: The heart of teaching. *The Clearing House, 55*(8), 350–352.

Hunsu, N. J., Adesope, O., & Bayly, D. J. (2016). A meta-analysis of the effects of audience response systems (clicker-based technologies) on cognition and affect. *Computers & Education, 94*, 102–119.

Jackson, P. W. (1968). *Life in classrooms.* New York: Holt, Rinehart and Winston.

Jacobs, V. R., Lamb, L. L., & Philipp, R. A. (2010). Professional noticing of children's mathematical thinking. *Journal for Research in Mathematics Education, 41*(2), 169–202.

James, W. (1890/1950). *The principles of psychology.* New York: Dover.

Jimenez-Alexandre, M. P., Rodriguez, A. B., & Duschl, R. (2000). "Doing the lesson" or "doing science": Argument in high school genetics. *Science Education, 84*(6), 757–792.

Johnson, R. H. (1918). Educational research and statistics: The coefficient marking system. *School and Society, 7*(181), 714–716.

Kay, R. H., & LeSage, A. (2009). Examining the benefits and challenges of using audience response systems: A review of the literature. *Computers & Education, 53*(3), 819–827.

Kaya, S., Kablan, Z., & Rice, D. (2014). Examining question type and the timing of IRE pattern in elementary science classrooms. *International Journal of Human Sciences, 11*(1), 621–641.

Kazemi, E., Franke, M., & Lampert, M. (2009). Developing pedagogies in teacher education to support novice teachers' ability to enact ambitious instruction. In R. Hunter, B. Bicknell, & T. Burgess (Eds.), *Crossing divides, proceedings of the 32nd annual conference of The Mathematics Education Research Group of Australasia, Vol. 1* (pp. 11–29). Palmerston North, New Zealand: Mathematics Education Research Group of Australasia.

Keeley, P. (2008). *Science formative assessment: 75 practical strategies for linking assessment, instruction, and student learning.* Arlington, VA: NSTA.

Kirschner, P. A., Sweller, J., & Clark, R. E. (2006). Why minimal guidance during instruction does not work: An analysis of the failure of constructivist, discovery, problem-based, experiential, and inquiry-based teaching. *Educational Psychologist, 41*(2), 75–86.

Kliebard, H. M. (2004). *The struggle for the American curriculum, 1893–1958.* (3rd ed.). New York: RoutledgeFalmer.

Kloss, R. J. (1988). Toward asking the right questions: The beautiful, the pretty, and the big messy ones. *The Clearing House, 61*(6), 245–248.

Kluger, A. N., & DeNisi, A. (1996). The effects of feedback interventions on performance: A historical review, a meta-analysis, and a preliminary feedback intervention theory. *Psychological Bulletin, 119*(2), 254–284.

Knight, P., Pennant, J., & Piggott, J. (2005). The power of the interactive whiteboard. *Micromath, 21*(2), 11.

Kohlberg, L. (1970). Stages of moral development as a basis for moral education. In. C. Beck and E. Sullivan (Eds.), *Moral Education* (pp. 23–92). Toronto: University of Toronto Press.

Ladson-Billings, G. (1995). Toward a theory of culturally relevant pedagogy. *American Educational Research Journal, 32*(3), 465–491.

Lampert, M. (2003). *Teaching problems and the problems of teaching.* New Haven, CT: Yale University Press.

Lampert, M., & Ball, D. L. (1998). *Teaching, multimedia, and mathematics: Investigations of real practice. The practitioner inquiry series.* New York: Teachers College Press.

Leahy, S., Lyon, C., Thompson, M., & Wiliam, D. (2005). Classroom assessment minute by minute, day by day. *Educational Leadership, 63*(3), 18–24.

Lehrer, R., & Kim, M. J., (2009). Structuring variability by negotiating its measure. *Mathematics Education Research Journal, 21*(2), 116–133.

Lehrer, R., Kim, M.-J., & Schauble, L. (2007). Supporting the development of conceptions of statistics by engaging students in measuring and modeling variability. *International Journal of Computers for Mathematical Learning, 12*(3), 195–216.

Lehrer, R., Kim, M.-J., Ayers, E., & Wilson, M. (2014). Toward establishing a learning progression to support the development of statistical reasoning. In A. P. Maloney, H. Confrey, & K. H. Nguyen (Eds.), *Learning over time: Learning trajectories in mathematics education* (pp. 31–59). Charlotte, NC: Information Age Publishing.

Lehrer, R., & Schauble, L. (2012). Seeding evolutionary thinking by engaging children in modeling its foundations. *Science Education, 96*(4), 701–724.

Leinhardt, G., & Steele, M. D. (2005). Seeing the complexity of standing to the side: Instructional dialogues. *Cognition and Instruction, 23*(1), 87–163.

Lemke, J. (1990). *Talking science: Language, learning and values.* Norwood, NJ: Ablex Publishing Corporation.

Levin, D. M., Hammer, D., & Coffey, J. E. (2009). Novice teachers' attention to student thinking. *Journal of Teacher Education, 60*(2), 142–154.

Levin, D. M., & Richards, J. (2010). Exploring how novice teachers learn to attend to students' thinking in analyzing case studies of classroom teaching and learning. In *Proceedings of the 9th International Conference of the Learning Sciences,* Volume 1 (pp. 41–48).

Levin, T., and Long, R., (1981). *Effective instruction.* Alexandria, VA: ASCD.

Lieberman, A. (1995). *The work of restructuring schools: Building from the ground up.* New York: Teachers College Press.

Linquanti, R. (2014). *Supporting formative assessment for deeper learning: A primer for policymakers.* Washington, DC: CCSSO. Retrieved from CCSSO website: http://www.ccsso.org/Documents/Supporting%20Formative%20Assessment%20for%20Deeper%20Learning.pdf

Lortie, D. (1975). *Schoolteacher: A sociologic study.* Chicago: University of Chicago Press.

Loucks-Horsley, S., Carlson, M. O., Brink, L. H., Horwitz, P., Marsh, D. D., Pratt, H., Roy, K. R., & Worth, K. (1989). *Developing and supporting teachers for elementary school science education.* Washington, DC: The National Center for Improving Science Education.

Lovell, J., Duckor, B., & Holmberg, C. (2015). Rewriting our teaching practices in our own voices. *English Journal, 104*(6), 55–60.

Marzano, R. J. (1991). Fostering thinking across the curriculum through knowledge restructuring. *Journal of Reading, 34*(7), 518–525.

Marzano, R. J., Pickering, D., & Pollock, J. E. (2001). *Classroom instruction that works: Research-based strategies for increasing student achievement.* Alexandria, VA: ASCD.

Masters, G. N., & Wilson, M. (1997). *Developmental assessment.* BEAR Research Report, University of California–Berkeley.

McClain, K., & Cobb, P. (2001). An analysis of development of sociomathematical norms in one first-grade classroom. *Journal for Research in Mathematics Education, 32*(3), 236–266.

McCloughlin, T. J., & Matthews, P. C. (2012). Repertory grid analysis and concept mapping: Problems and issues. *Problems of Education in the 21St Century, 48*(1), 91–106.

McConville-Rae, D. (2015) The effect of higher-order questioning on pupil understanding, as assessed using mind maps and the SOLO taxonomy. *The STEP Journal, 2*(2), 5–18.

McCroskey, J. (2015) *Quiet children in the classroom: On helping, not hurting.* Retrieved from http://www.jamescmccroskey.com/publications/92.htm

McManus, S. M. M., Formative Assessment for Students and Teachers (Program), & Council of Chief State School Officers. (2008). *Attributes of effective formative assessment.* Washington, DC: Council of Chief State School Officers. Retrieved from http://www.ccsso.org/Documents/2008/Attributes_of_Effective_2008.pdf

Mehan, H. (1979). *Learning lessons.* Cambridge, MA: Harvard University Press.

Meier, D. (1995). *The power of their ideas: Lessons for America from a small school in Harlem.* Boston: Beacon.

Meier, D., & Schwartz, P. (1995). Central Park East Secondary School: The hard part is making it happen. In M. Apple & J. Beane (Eds.), *Democratic schools: Lessons in powerful education* (pp. 26–40).

Mewborn, D. S., & Tyminski, A. M. (2006). Lortie's apprenticeship of observation revisited. *For the Learning of Mathematics, 26*(3), 23–32.

Miles, K. H., & Darling-Hammond, L. (1997). *Rethinking the allocation of teaching resources: Some lessons from high-performing schools.* Retrieved from Consortium for Policy Research in Education website: http://www.cpre.org/rethinking-allocation-teaching-resources-some-lessons-high-performing-schools

Minstrell, J. (1992). Facets of students' knowledge and relevant instruction. In R. Duit, F. Goldberg & H. Niedderer (Eds.), *Research in physics learning: Theoretical issues and empirical studies* (pp. 110–128). Kiel, Germany: Kiel University, Institute for Educational Measurement Education.

Minstrell, J. (2000). Student thinking and related assessment: Creating a facet-based learning environment. In N. S. Raju, J. W. Pellegrino, M. W. Bertenthal, K. J. Mitchell & L. R. Jones (Eds.), *Grading the nation's report card: Research from the evaluation of NAEP* (pp. 44–73). Washington, DC: National Academy Press.

Mok, J. (2011). A case study of students' perceptions of peer assessment in Hong Kong. *ELT Journal, 65*(3), 230–239.

Moyer, P. S., & Milewicz, E. (2002). Learning to question: Categories of questioning used by preservice teachers during diagnostic mathematics interviews. *Journal of Mathematics Teacher Education, 5*(4), 293–315.

Myhill, D. (2002). Bad boys and good girls? Patterns of interaction and response in whole class teaching. *British Educational Research Journal, 28*(3), 339–352.

Myhill, D. (2006). Talk, talk, talk: Teaching and learning in whole class discourse. *Research Papers in Education, 21*(1), 19–41.

National Council of Teachers of Mathematics (2000). *Principles and standards for school mathematics.* Reston, VA: Author.

National Research Council. (1999). *How people learn: Brain, mind, experience, and school.* Committee on Developments in the Science of Learning. J. D. Bransford, A. L. Brown, and R. R. Cocking (Eds.), *Commission on Behavioral and Social Sciences and Education.* Washington, DC: National Academy Press.

National Research Council. (2001). *Knowing what students know: The science and design of educational assessment.* Committee on the Foundations of Assessment, J. Pellegrino, N. Chudowsky, & R. Glaser (Eds.). Board on Testing and Assessment, Division of Behavioral and Social Sciences and Education. Washington, DC: National Academy Press.

Natriello, G. (1987). The impact of evaluation processes on students, *Educational Psychologist, 22*(2), 155–175.

Newmann, F. M. (1988). A test of higher-order thinking in social studies: Persuasive writing on constitutional issues using NAEP approach. *Social Education, 54*(4), 369–373.

Newmann, F. M. (1996). *Authentic achievement: Restructuring schools for intellectual quality.* San Francisco: Jossey-Bass.

Newmann, F. M., Bryk, A. S., & Nagaoka, J. (2001). *Authentic intellectual work and standardized tests: Conflict or coexistence.* Chicago: Consortium on Chicago School Research.

Noguera, P. (2008). *The trouble with Black boys and other reflections on race, equity, and the future of public education.* San Francisco: Jossey-Bass.

O'Connor, M. C., & Michaels, S. (1993). Aligning academic task and participation status through revoicing: Analysis of a classroom discourse strategy. *Anthropology and Education Quarterly*, *24*(4), 318–335.

Oliveira, A. (2010). Improving teacher questioning in science inquiry discussions through professional development. *Journal of Research in Science Teaching, 47*(4), 422–453.

Palinscar, A. S., & Brown, A. L. (1984). Reciprocal teaching of comprehension-fostering and comprehension-monitoring activities. *Cognition and Instruction, 1*(2), 117–175.

Paris, D. (2012). Culturally sustaining pedagogy: A needed change in stance, terminology, and practice. *Educational Researcher, 41*(3), 93–97.

Perrenoud, P. (1991). Towards a pragmatic approach to formative evaluation. In P. Weston (Ed.), *Assessment of pupil achievement: Motivation and school success* (pp. 79–101). Amsterdam: Swets & Zeitlinger.

Piaget, J. (1936/1953). *The Origins of Intelligence in the Child.* (Margaret Cook, Trans.) London: Routledge & Kegan Paul; New York: International Universities Press.

Pierson, J. (2008). *The relationship between patterns of classroom discourse and mathematics learning* (Unpublished doctoral dissertation). University of Texas at Austin.

Pimentel, D. S., & McNeill, K. L. (2013). Conducting talk in secondary science classrooms: investigating instructional moves and teachers' beliefs. *Science Education, 97*(3), 367–394.

Pjanić, K. (2014). The origins and products of Japanese lesson study. *Inovacije u Nastavi-časopis za Savremenu Nastavu, 27*(3), 83–93.

Plaut, S., & Sharkey, N. S. (Eds.). (2003). *Education policy and practice: bridging the divide* (No. 37). Cambridge, MA: Harvard Educational Publishing Group.

Pope, D. (2001). *"Doing School": How we are creating a generation of stressed out, materialistic and miseducated students.* New Haven, CT: Yale University Press.

Popelka, S. R. (2010). Now we're really clicking! *Mathematics Teacher, 104*(4), 290–295.

Popham, W. J. (1997). What's wrong—and what's right—with rubrics. *Educational Leadership*, *55*(2), 72.

Popham, W. J. (2008). Formative assessment: Seven stepping stones to success. *Principal Leadership, 9*(4), 16–20.

Powell, A. G., Farrar, E., & Cohen, D. K. (1985). *The shopping mall high school.* Boston: Houghton Mifflin Co.

Pulfrey, C., Buch, D., & Butera, F. (2011). Why grades engender performance avoidance goals. *Journal of Educational Psychology, 103*(3), 683–700.

Pulfrey, C., Buch, D., & Butera, F. (2011). Why grades engender performance avoidance goals. *Journal of Educational Psychology, 103*(3), 683–700.

Resnick, L. B. (1987). *Education and learning to think.* Washington, DC: National Academy Press.

Resnick, L. B., & Resnick, D. P. (1992). Assessing the thinking curriculum: New tools for educational reform. In B. R. Gifford & M. C. Connor (Eds.), *Changing assessments: Alternative views of aptitude, achievement, and instruction* (pp. 37–75). Boston: Kluwer Academic.

Richmond, S. S., DeFranco, J. F., & Jablokow, K. (2014). A set of guidelines for the consistent assessment of concept maps. *International Journal of Engineering Education, 30*(5), 1072–1082.

Roberts, L. (1997, March). *Using maps to produce meaningful evaluation measures: Evaluating middle school science teacher change in assessment, collegial and instructional practices.* Paper presented at the ninth International Objective Measurement Workshop, Chicago, IL.

Roberts, L. (1997, March). *Using maps to produce meaningful evaluation measures: Evaluating middle school science teacher change in assessment, collegial and instructional practices.* Paper presented at the ninth International Objective Measurement Workshop, March 21, Chicago, IL.

Roberts, L., and Sipusic, M. (director). (1999). *Moderation in all things: A class act* [Film]. Available from the Berkeley Evaluation and Assessment Center, Graduate School of Education, University of California–Berkeley.

Roberts, L., Sloane, K., & Wilson, M. (1996, April). *Local assessment moderation in SEPUP.* Paper presented at the Annual Meeting of the American Educational Research Association, New York.

Roberts, L., Wilson, M., & Draney, K. (1997). *The SEPUP assessment system: An overview.* (BEAR report series. SA-97-1). Berkeley, CA: University of California.

Roberts, L. (1996). *Methods of evaluation for a complex treatment and its effects on teacher professional development: A case study of the Science Education for Public Understanding Program* (Unpublished dissertation). University of California–Berkeley.

Rogoff, B. (1998). Cognition as a collaborative process. In W. Damon (Ed.), *Handbook of child psychology, Volume 2: Cognition, perception, and language* (pp. 679–744). Hoboken, NJ: Wiley.

Rowe, M. B. (1974a). Pausing phenomena: Influence on the quality of instruction. *Journal of Psycholinguistic Research, 3*(3), 203–224.

Rowe, M. B. (1974b). Reflections on wait-time: Some methodological questions. *Journal of Research in Science Teaching, 11*(3), 263–279.

Rowe, M. B. (1974c). Wait-time and rewards as instructional variables, their influence on language, logic, and fate control: Part one: Wait-time. *Journal of Research in Science Teaching, 11*(2), 81–94.

Rugg, H. O. (1918). Teachers' marks and the reconstruction of the marking system. *The Elementary School Journal, 18*(9), 701–719.

Ruiz-Primo, M. A., & Shavelson. R. J. (1996). Problems and issues in the use of concept maps in science assessment. *Journal of Science Teaching, 33*, 569–600.

Rye, J. A., & Rubba, P. A. (2002). Scoring concept maps: An expert map-based scheme weighted for relationships. *School Science & Mathematics, 102*(1), 33–44.

Sadler, D. R. (1989). Formative assessment and the design of instructional systems. *Instructional Science, 18*(2), 119–144.

Sahin, A., & Kulm, G. (2008). Sixth grade mathematics teachers' intentions and use of probing, guiding, and factual questions. *Journal of Mathematics Teacher Education, 11*(3), 221–241.

Schwarz, B. B., & Glassner, A. (2007). The role of floor control and of ontology in argumentative activities with discussion-based tools. *International Journal of Computer-Supported Collaborative Learning, 2*(4), 449–478.

Scriven, M. (1967). The methodology of evaluation. In R. W. Tyler, R. M. Gagne, & M. Scriven (Eds.) *Perspectives of curriculum evaluation,* (pp. 39–83). American Educational Research Association Monograph Series on Curriculum Evaluation, 1. Chicago: Rand McNally.

Shavelson, R. J., Moss, P., Wilson, M., Duckor, B., Baron, W., & Wilmot, D. (May, 2010). *The promise of teacher learning progressions: Challenges and opportunities for articulating growth in the profession.* Individual papers presented at the Teacher Learning Progressions symposium for Division D-Measurement and Research Methodology. Denver, CO: American Education Research Association.

Shavelson, R. J., Ruiz-Primo, M. A., & Wiley, E. W. (2005). Windows into the mind. *Higher Education, 49(4),* 413–430.

Shepard, L. A. (2000). The role of assessment in a learning culture. *Educational Researcher, 29*(7), 4–14.

Shepard, L. A. (2005). Linking formative assessment to scaffolding. *Educational Leadership, 63*(3), 66–70.

Shepard, L. A. (2009). Commentary: Evaluating the validity of formative and interim assessment. *Educational Measurement: Issues and Practice, 28*(3), 32–37.

Shulman, L. (1987). Knowledge and teaching: Foundations of the new reform. *Harvard Educational Review, 57*(1), 1–23.

Shulman, L. S. (1986). Those who understand: Knowledge growth in teaching. *Educational Researcher, 15*(2), 4–14.

Shute, V. J. (2008). Focus on formative feedback. *Review of educational research, 78*(1), 153–189.

Singer-Gabella, M., Cartier, J., Forman, E., Knapp, N., Kannan, P., Shahan, E., Barrick, N. (2009). *Contextualizing learning progressions for prospective elementary teachers of mathematics and science.* Paper presented at the Annual Meeting of the American Educational Research Association, San Diego.

Siskin, L. S., & Little, J. W. (Eds.). (1995). *The subjects in question: Departmental organization and the high school.* New York: Teachers College Press.

Sizer, T. R. (1984). *Horace's compromise: The dilemma of the American high school.* Boston: Houghton Mifflin.

Sizer, T. R. (1996). *Horace's hope: What works for the American high school.* Boston: Houghton Mifflin Co.

Sleep, L., & Boerst, T. A. (2012). Preparing beginning teachers to elicit and interpret students' mathematical thinking. *Teaching and Teacher Education, 28*(7), 1038–1048.

Smith, F., Hardman, F., & Higgins, S. (2006). The impact of interactive whiteboards on teacher–pupil interaction in the National Literacy and Numeracy Strategies. *British Educational Research Journal, 32*(3), 443–457.

Smith, J., diSessa, A., & Roschelle, J. (1993/1994). Misconceptions reconceived: A constructivist analysis of knowledge in transition. *The Journal of the Learning Sciences, 3*(2), 115–163.

Snyder, B. (1970). *The hidden curriculum.* New York: Knopf.

St. John, M. (1991). *Science education for the 1990's: Strategies for change.* Inverness, CA: Inverness Research Associates.

Stahl, R. J. (1990). *Using 'Think-Time' behaviors to promote students' information processing, learning, and on-task participation: An instructional module.* Tempe, AZ: Arizona State University.

Stake, R. E. (1976). *Evaluating educational programmes: The need and the response: A collection of resource materials.* Washington, DC: Organization for Economic Cooperation and Development.

Stiggins, R. J. (2002). Assessment crisis: The absence of assessment for learning. *Phi Delta Kappan, 83*(10), 758–765.

Stigler, J. W., & Hiebert, J. (1999). *The teaching gap: Best ideas from the world's teachers for improving education in the classroom.* New York: Free Press.

Sweedler-Brown, C. O. (1992). The effect of training on the appearance bias of holistic essay graders. *Journal of Research and Development in Education, 26*(1), 24–29.

Sweller, J. (1994). Cognitive load theory, learning difficulty, and instructional design. *Learning and Instruction, 4,* 295–312.

Takahashi, A. (2006). Characteristics of Japanese mathematics lessons. *Tsukuba Journal of Educational Study in Mathematics, 25.* Retrieved April 24, 2012 from http://www.criced. tsukuba. ac.jp/math/sympo_2006/takahashi.pdf.

Tharp, R. G., & Gallimore, R. (1991). *Rousing minds to life: Teaching, learning, and schooling in social context.* Cambridge: Cambridge University Press.

Tobin, K. (1986). Effects of teacher wait time on discourse characteristics in mathematics and language arts classes. *American Educational Research Journal, 23*(2), 191–200.

Tobin, K. (1987). The role of wait time in higher cognitive level learning. *Review of Educational Research, 57*(1), 69–95.

Tobin, K. G. (1980). The effect of an extended teacher wait-time on science achievement. *Journal of Research in Science Teaching, 17*(5), 469–475.

Topping, K. J. (2013). Peers as a source of formative and summative assessment. In J. McMillan (Ed.), *SAGE handbook of research of classroom assessment* (pp. 395–412). Thousand Oaks, CA: SAGE.

Tyack, D. B., & Cuban, L. (1995). *Tinkering toward utopia.* Cambridge, MA: Harvard University Press.

van Zee, E., & Minstrell, J. (1997). Using questioning to guide student thinking. *The Journal of the Learning Sciences, 6*(2), 227–269.

Vygotsky, L. S. (1978). *Mind in society: The development of higher mental process.* Cambridge, MA: Harvard University Press.

Walsh, J. A., & Sattes, B. D. (2015). *Questioning for classroom discussion: Purposeful speaking, engaged listening, deep thinking.* Alexandria, VA: ASCD.

Walsh, J. A., & Sattes, B. D. (2016). *Quality questioning: Research-based practice to engage every learner.* Thousand Oaks, CA: Corwin.

Warren, B., Ballenger, C., Ogonowski, M., Rosebery, A. S., & Hudicourt-Barnes, J. (2001). Rethinking diversity in learning science: The logic of everyday sense-making. *Journal of Research in Science Teaching, 38*(5), 529–552.

Warren, B., & Rosebery, A. S. (1995). *"This question is just too, too easy!" Perspectives from the classroom on accountability in science.* Santa Cruz, CA: National Center for Research on Cultural Diversity and Second Language Learning.

Wash, P. D. (2012). The power of a mouse! *SRATE Journal, 21*(2), 39–46.

Weil, M., & Murphy, J. (1982). Instructional processes. *Encyclopedia of Educational Research* (5th ed.). New York: Macmillan.

Wells, G. (1993). Reevaluating the IRF sequence: A proposal for the articulation of theories of activity and discourse for the analysis of teaching and learning in the classroom. *Linguistics and Education, 5*(1), 1–37.

Wiggins, G. (2012). Seven keys to effective feedback. *Educational Leadership*, *70*(1), 11–16.

Wiggins, G. P., & McTighe, J. (2005). *Understanding by design* (expanded 2nd ed.). Alexandria, VA: ASCD.

Wiliam, D. (2007). Keeping learning on track: Classroom assessment and the regulation of learning. In F. K. Lester (Ed.), *Second handbook of research on mathematics teaching and learning: A project of the National Council of Teachers of Mathematics* (pp. 1053–98). Charlotte, NC: Information Age Publishing.

Wiliam, D. (2007). Keeping learning on track: Classroom assessment and the regulation of learning. In F. K. Lester, Jr. (Ed.), *Second Handbook of Research on Mathematics Teaching and Learning: A project of the National Council of Teachers of Mathematics* (pp. 1053–98). Charlotte, NC: Information Age Publishing.

Wiliam, D. (2014). The right questions, the right way. *Educational Leadership*, *71*(6), 16–19.

Wiliam, D., & Black, P. (1996). Meanings and consequences: A basis for distinguishing formative and summative functions of assessment? *British Educational Research Journal*, *22*(5), 537–548.

Wiliam, D. & Thompson, M. (2007). Integrating assessment with instruction: What will it take to make it work? In C. A. Dwyer (Ed.), *The future of assessment: Shaping teaching and learning* (pp. 53–82). Mahwah, NJ: Erlbaum.

Wilson, M., & Sloane, K. (2000). From principles to practice: An embedded assessment system. *Applied Measurement in Education*, *13*(2), 181–208.

Wilson, P. H., Mojica, G. F., & Confrey, J. (2013). Learning trajectories in teacher education: Supporting teachers' understandings of students' mathematical thinking. *The Journal of Mathematical Behavior*, *32*(2), 103–121.

Windschitl, M., Thompson, J., & Braaten, M. (2011). Ambitious pedagogy by novice teachers? Who benefits from tool-supported collaborative inquiry into practice and why. *Teachers College Record*, *113*(7), 1311–1360.

Winger, T. (2005). Grading to communicate. *Educational Leadership*, *63*(3), 61–65.

Wollman-Bonilla, J. (1991). Shouting from the tops of buildings: Teachers as learners and change in schools. *Language Arts*, *68*(2), 114–120.

Wright, C. J., & Nuthall, G. (1970). Relationships between teacher behaviors and pupil achievement in three experimental elementary science lessons. *American Educational Research Journal*, *7*(4), 477–491.

Wulf, S. (1997, October 27). Teach our children well (It can be done). *Time*. Retrieved from http://www.cnn.com/ALLPOLITICS/1997/10/20/time/special.teaching.html

Wylie, C., Lyon, C., & Formative Assessment for Students and Teachers (FAST) State Collaborative on Assessment and Student Standards. (SCASS). (2013). *Using the formative assessment rubrics, reflection and observation tools to support professional reflection on practice*. Washington, DC: Council of Chief State School Officers.

Yin, Y., Tomita, M. K., & Shavelson, R. J. (2008). Diagnosing and dealing with student misconceptions: Floating and sinking. *Science Scope*, *31*(8), 34–39.

Yin, Y., Vanides, J., Ruiz-Primo, M. A., Ayala, C. C., & Shavelson, R. J. (2005). Comparison of two concept-mapping techniques: Implications for scoring, interpretation, and use. *Journal of Research in Science Teaching*, *42*(2), 166–184.

Yip, D. Y. (1999). Implications of students' questions for science teaching. *School Science Review*, *81*(294), 49–53.

Yurdabakan, I. (2011). The investigation of peer assessment in primary school cooperative learning groups with respect to gender. *Education 3–13, 39*(2), 153–169.

Zhang, W. (2008). Conceptions of lifelong learning in Confucian culture: Their impact on adult learners. *International Journal of Lifelong Education, 27*(5), 551–557. doi: 10.1080/02601370802051561

Zwiers, J. (2007a). Teacher practices and perspectives for developing academic language. *International Journal of Applied Linguistics, 17*(1), 93–116.

Zwiers, J. (2007b). *Building academic language: Essential practices for content classrooms.* San Francisco: Jossey-Bass.

Zwiers, J. (2013). *Building academic language: Essential practices for content classrooms, grades 5–12.* Hoboken, NJ: Wiley.

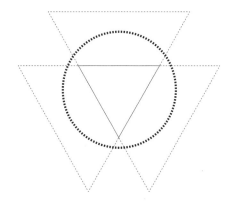

Index

Note: The letter *f* following a page number denotes a figure.

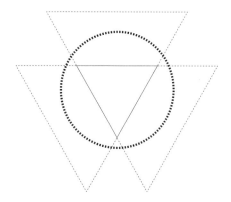

About the Authors

Brent Duckor, PhD, is an associate professor in the Department of Teacher Education at San José State University. He taught government, economics, and history at Central Park East Secondary School in New York City in the 1990s before returning to the University of California–Berkeley, to study educational measurement, testing, and assessment with the passage of No Child Left Behind. Brent's research on teachers' understanding and use of formative assessment in the K–12 classroom and validation of teacher licensure exams in state, national, and international contexts seeks to integrate a developmental perspective on teachers' growth in the profession. He has coedited several international journals including *Psychological Test and Assessment Modeling* and *Pensamiento Educativo*. Brent's most recent scholarship has appeared in *Teachers College Record, Journal of Teacher Education, Mathematics Teaching in the Middle School, The English Journal,* and *Phi Delta Kappan.* He can be reached at brent.duckor@sjsu.edu.

 **Carrie Holmberg** is a lecturer and preservice teacher educator at San José State University. She taught at a Title I comprehensive high school in Silicon Valley for nearly a decade and has extensive experience mentoring new teachers. A National Board Certified Teacher and Bay Area Writing Project teacher consultant, Carrie earned a Bachelor of Arts in English from Stanford University and a Master of Arts in education from the Stanford Teacher Education Program. In addition to supervising teacher candidates, coauthoring articles, and writing a book, she is pursuing her doctorate at San José State University in Educational Leadership. Carrie is committed to researching, developing, and celebrating educators' knowledge, skills, and professionalism. She is an enthusiastic ambassador for teachers, educational leaders, and the people and systems that support them. Carrie lives in Silicon Valley with her family. She can be reached at carrie.holmberg@sjsu.edu.

Related ASCD Resources: Formative Assessment

At the time of publication, the following ASCD resources were available (ASCD stock numbers in parentheses). For up-to-date information about ASCD resources, go to www.ascd.org. Search the complete archives of *Educational Leadership* at www.ascd.org/el.

ASCD EDge® Group

Exchange ideas and connect with other educators interested in formative assessment on the social networking site ASCD EDge® at http://ascdedge.ascd.org/

Print Products

Checking for Understanding: Formative Assessment Techniques for Your Classroom, 2nd Edition by Douglas Fisher and Nancy Frey (#115011)

The Formative Assessment Action Plan: Practical Steps to More Successful Teaching and Learning by Nancy Frey and Douglas Fisher (#111013)

Formative Assessment Strategies for Every Classroom: An ASCD Action Tool, 2nd Edition by Susan M. Brookhart (#111005)

Formative Classroom Walkthroughs: How Principals and Teachers Collaborate to Raise Student Achievement by Connie M. Moss and Susan M. Brookhart (#115003)

Grading and Group Work: How do I assess individual learning when students work together? (ASCD Arias) by Susan M. Brookhart (#SF113073)

On Formative Assessment: Readings from Educational Leadership (EL Essentials) edited by Marge Scherer (#116065E4)

Teaching Students to Self-Assess: How do I help students reflect and grow as learners? (ASCD Arias) by Starr Sackstein (#SF116025)

Test Better, Teach Better: The Instructional Role of Assessment by W. James Popham (#102088)

Transformative Assessment by W. James Popham (#108018)

Transformative Assessment in Action: An Inside Look at Applying the Process by W. James Popham (#111008)

For more information: send e-mail to member@ascd.org; call 1-800-933-2723 or 703-578-9600, press 2; send a fax to 703-575-5400; or write to Information Services, ASCD, 1703 N. Beauregard St., Alexandria, VA 22311-1714 USA.